KONGO POLITICAL CULTURE

KONGO POLITICAL CULTURE

THE CONCEPTUAL CHALLENGE OF THE PARTICULAR

Wyatt MacGaffey

Indiana University Press

Bloomington and Indianapolis

This book is a publication of

Indiana University Press
601 North Morton Street
Bloomington, IN 47404-3797 USA

http://www.indiana.edu/~iupress

Telephone orders   800-842-6796
Fax orders   812-855-7931
Orders by e-mail   iuporder@indiana.edu

© 2000 by Wyatt MacGaffey

The paper used in this publication meets the minimum requirements of American National Standard for Information Sciences—Permanence of Paper for Printed Library Materials, ANSI Z39.48-1984.

Manufactured in the United States of America

Library of Congress Cataloging-in-Publication Data

MacGaffey, Wyatt.
    Kongo political culture: the conceptual challenge of the particular / Wyatt MacGaffey.
        p.   cm.
    Includes bibliographical references and index.
    ISBN 0-253-33698-8 (cloth: alk. paper)
    1. Kongo (African people)—Rites and ceremonies. 2. Kongo (African people)—Politics and government. 3. Power (Social sciences)—Africa, Central. 4. Witchcraft—Africa, Central. 5. Esaya, Lutete. I. Title.
DT650.K66M33 2000
306.2'089'963931— dc21

                                                    99-43432

1   2   3   4   5   05   04   03   02   01   00

Widi Noé DIAWAKU DIANSEYILA,
nlongi, nkundi.
Masangu mayuma, vana mo kwa nkwambanzi.

CONTENTS

MAPS

PHOTOGRAPHS

PREFACE

The Cameroonian philosopher F. Eboussi Boulaga, in *Les Conférences nationales* (Paris: Karthala, 1993), is among the most recent of African intellectuals to attribute the contemporary political and social disorder of the continent to the colonial legacy of social pluralism, which he calls "heteronomy," and to appeal once again for cultural authenticity in public institutions. The colonial administrative apparatus, handed over to indigenous elites, has no authentic relationship, he says, to local values, institutions, and political processes; it has become a "fetishized" state, tricked out with the forms of government but lacking the substance, maintaining its control by lies and violence. Ideologically, this alien and alienating imposition justifies its demands by appealing to supposedly universal reasons and values which disguise their own historical and political context. Against this background, in the early 1990s, constitutional conventions, remarkable for their length and their cost, were held in several countries, Zaire among them. They were generally denounced as ineffectual, but Eboussi Boulaga argues that the criteria of material efficacy and market rationality which grounded these adverse judgments are part and parcel of the same supposedly universal but historically alien ideology, and that the conferences should instead be regarded as at least potentially a new beginning, the debut of an authentic political process. To understand what was going on, we should have recourse to anthropology and recognize that the proceedings were supported by a series of indigenous models, which he calls the festival, the game, the therapeutic séance, the palaver, and the rite of passage, all tending toward the creation of a political community by mobilizing cultural resources from deep in the unconscious.

The philosopher's argument is too complex and too passionate for me to pursue it further. I hope, however, to have suggested in this book, through the details of one particular example, an approach to that cultural "unconscious" which enables us to take it seriously as the product of an ancient and still vital tradition, or "civilization," as Eboussi Boulaga calls it. Increasing specialization in the social sciences has effectively fragmented the study of African cultures into alien categories, each studied by scholars asking different kinds of questions governed by unrelated sub-disciplinary paradigms and overly responsive to current Western ideological concerns. Paradoxically, this involution has progressively intensified the ethnocentrism of African studies, although at the same time we increasingly assert our obligation to respect African cultures in their own terms. This book, by contrast, reintegrates the perspectives of art history, political science, political economy, religion, and linguistics in a holistic anthropology of power. The focus of the study is a set of early-twentieth-century indigenous texts, collected by K. E. Laman, that portray political leadership and social control as mediated by rituals of chiefship and magical retribution. The material is, by its sheer volume, its rich language, and its intimate cultural reporting, unique in African studies.

Kongo political leadership was deeply implicated in the economics of the nineteenth-century Atlantic slave trade, but its style and theory transcend those historical and geographical boundaries. From remote times to the post-colonial present, the responses to political events of not only Congolese but Central Africans in general have been governed by a continuously developing cultural tradition. Understanding this tradition requires a fresh look at oral history, the structure and semantics of ritual, the organization of matrilineal descent, and the place in Kongo thought of philosophical considerations, sociological and cosmological models, and spectacular violence. Paying full and close attention to the poetics of indigenous cultural interpretation, I look beyond the terrain of Kongo society itself to explore central questions of anthropology: the effectiveness of words, the power of images, the sources of social power, the boundaries between persons and things, and the inevitable distortions of cultural translation.

This book continues explorations into basic themes in Kongo cosmology, social structure, and chiefship already developed in other publications by myself and others, but I have tried to complement rather than duplicate those other studies. One of the principal differences is the amount of space and consideration given to the writings of Kongo authors, with respect both to their content and their style. I emphasize the lacunae in these texts and the difficulties of interpreting them. For that reason, and because they are fascinating in their own right, I include in the book, in addition to translated selections, two chapters of KiKongo texts described verbatim, with my translations, as at least a sample of the data I have used, so that other scholars, especially Congolese, may study them directly. Since the book went to press two studies of related themes have been made available: Z. Volavka's *Crown and Ritual* (Toronto: University of Toronto, 1998), which deals with the Lusunzi shrine in Ngoyo, and J. N'soko Swa-Kabamba's *Le Panégyrique Mbiimbi* (Leiden: CNWS, 1997), which discusses the role of violence in praise-songs addressed to Yaka chiefs.

The original KiKongo manuscripts have been microfilmed and are available in that form from the National Archives, Stockholm. Laman's typed monograph is also available on microfilm from the Center for Research Libraries, 6050 Kenwood Avenue, Chicago, IL 60637. Texts related to *minkisi,* kept in the Ethnographic Museum, Stockholm, have been published in my *Art and Healing of the BaKongo* (1991), together with drawings of the objects and photographs of some of the authors of the manuscripts.

Sigbert Axelson first introduced me to K. E. Laman's KiKongo monograph; he said that he had been trying for years to interest somebody in it and was glad to give me the copy he had found on the floor in the mission at Mindouli. For occasional but crucial help with translations I am indebted to Gérard Buakasa, Kimpianga kia Mahaniah, and Matuka Yeno Mansoni. Pastor Jacques Bahelele, just before his death, was able to fill in, from his unique personal knowledge, many personal details concerning the evangelists and teachers who wrote the manuscripts Laman had solicited. To those who were so good as to read and comment on all or part of the book in draft I am most grateful, especially Karin Barber, John Comaroff, Johannes Fabian, Laurie

Kain Hart, Phyllis Martin, and Jan Vansina. Annette Barone, Diskin Clay, Susan Herlin, John M. Janzen, Alisa LaGamma, Zoë Strother, John K. Thornton, and Hein Van Hee helped in many different ways.

The translation of the KiKongo texts on which this work is based was supported in part by a grant from the National Endowment for the Humanities, an independent federal agency. Most of the book was written during my tenure as a Fellow of the John Guggenheim Memorial Foundation. Essential help was also given by the National Museum of African Art and, at Haverford College, by the Academic Computing Center and the James McGill Library, whose personnel were indefatigably responsive to my importunities. Parts of my text were originally incorporated in articles published by *Africa, The Journal of Southern Bantu Studies,* and *Etnofoor.*

Wyatt MacGaffey

ABBREVIATIONS

BMS:
Baptist Missionary Society

CMA:
Christian and Missionary Alliance

LKD:
Laman, *Dictionnaire Kikongo-français,* Brussels, 1936

LKG:
Laman, *Grammar of the Kikongo Language,* 1912

LKI–IV:
K. E. Laman, *The Kongo,* 4 vols., 1953–67

LKM:
"Laman's KiKongo monograph"

SEM:
Svenska Etnografiska Museet; the Ethnographic Museum,
Stockholm

SMF:
Svenska Missionsförbundet, Swedish Covenant Church

KONGO POLITICAL CULTURE

1. INTRODUCTION

For the concept of a society as a closed unit, a sort of thing
distinguishable from like things in the same way as one house is
distinguishable from another or one animal from another, we
must substitute the concept of society as a socio-geographic
region, the social elements of which are more closely knit
together among themselves than any of them are knit together
with social elements of the same kind outside that region.

—MEYER FORTES

This book is an extended commentary on the political culture of the BaKongo of Lower Congo, inhabitants of what is now the western province of the Democratic Republic of Congo, particularly but not exclusively at the beginning of the twentieth century. (From 1972 to 1997, under the dictatorship of Mobutu Sese Seko, the country was called Zaire.) Its chapters record my investigations and reflections as prompted largely by certain ethnographic texts in the Kongo language, KiKongo, written by young Kongo men between 1914 and 1916 at the instigation of a Swedish missionary, K. E. Laman. The nature of this archive and the story of its creation are described in Chapter 2. The principal texts to be considered were written by Lutete Esaya, a teacher at the Lolo and Vungu stations of the Christian and Missionary Alliance, who was the most prolific of the authors. In his writing Lutete (Loutété) devoted much of his attention to aspects of Kongo ritual and religious belief, including *minkisi* and the rituals for the installation of chiefs. The original text of what he had to say about chiefship is printed, with translation and notes, as Chapter 9.

"Political culture" means how BaKongo understood, and still understand, the experience of power in their lives; the reporting contained in the texts does not include political practice in the sense of case histories, although much can be inferred. The fundamental powers are those of life and death, which BaKongo felt they could influence, principally through the rituals associated with chiefs and *minkisi*. Although chiefs were human beings and *minkisi* were objects (explained below), they were very much alike in the way BaKongo thought of them and in the rituals that made them mediators of power. Since the writing of the texts, chiefs have disappeared, but the conceptions of power associated with chiefship and *minkisi* continue to dominate political thought. Such conceptions are by no means limited, however, to "the BaKongo," whose modern ethnic identity is in part a product of the same historical transition into the colonial period which the texts illuminate; on the contrary, they are general among the speakers of Western Bantu languages from Cameroon to Angola, and are central to the evolving politics of many African states.

Why Political Culture?

And why African, or Kongo, political culture? Members of any society have at least one theory of political life, just as they must also have an anthropology; that is, a set of more or less accepted ideas about their own society and how it differs from others. Such bodies of knowledge guide the interpretation of events and shape responses to them; a growing number of studies report the contemporary importance of indigenous knowledges in the national politics of Ghana, Nigeria, Cameroon, Kenya, and South Africa, for example. "Throughout the continent, discourses on sorcery or witchcraft are intertwined, often in quite surprising ways, with modern changes. Nowadays, modern techniques and commodities, often of Western provenance, are central in rumors on the occult" (Geschiere 1997, 2).

As political scientist Michael Schatzberg has written, "Most of the theoretical frameworks which Western social scientists have generated make certain culturally-based assumptions about causality and explanation, as well as about the nature of power itself. . . . [W]hen confronted with Congolese realities they have often seemed seriously incomplete" (Schatzberg 1997, 1). In Central Africa, at all social levels, the exercise of power in social relations is understood as *kindoki* (or a cognate term), conventionally but inadequately translated as "witchcraft" or *sorcellerie*. *Kindoki* is necessary to all effective leadership and is a component of all exceptional success, though it is also an instrument of evil. It is all too easy for Western social scientists to dismiss this "religious" factor as something distinct from the "political" and the "modern." We tend to recognize as "modern" institutions with which we are familiar, and to treat others as survivals from a primitive past; to mitigate the implication of primitivism, we may then charitably interpret witchcraft eradication movements, for example, perhaps as "resistance" to the modern, as an irrational attack on the effects and representatives of "progress." In fact, *kindoki is* modern, intrinsic to the modern world as BaKongo understand it, not a separate entity. But it is also an element in a Central African cultural tradition that has evolved over centuries.

The Folk and the Philosophers

To call *kindoki* or any other body of popular knowledge a "theory" invokes all of the same problems that have vexed the study of philosophy in Africa: Are quasi-articulate folk opinions to be placed on the same footing as the products of critical discourse among scholars? (Masolo 1994). Probably not, but the issue is not as one-sided as it might seem. The debates in philosophy are partly semantic: "A great deal of the controversy becomes pointless, once we agree to distinguish between philosophy, the Western discipline with full rights to its rules of exclusion and modalities, and the intellectual processes through which people apprehend their universe and negotiate their relationship with it" (Owomoyela 1997, 128). The debates are also partly driven by political considerations: the felt needs to legitimate African culture by crediting it with intellectual achievements comparable to those of the West, or to guide it along the path already followed by the West. In reply to the formal pretensions of philosophy, a number of African scholars have argued that it is not so much a distinctive property of

Western culture as it is the relatively isolated tradition of a few specialists, that its elevation to the status of universal truth is a form of intellectual imperialism, and that in any case the intellectual imperialist has no clothes—that is, the claims of philosophy are exaggerated (Owomoyela 1997, 138). Even in Europe, the idea that philosophers are uniquely competent to guard and explicate the foundations of knowledge is a relatively recent, post-Kantian development, itself an object of controversy.

Folk theories do not undergo testing by debate among specialists, but it is notorious that the work of specialists is carried on in isolation from the rest of the world, and moreover that their debates continue, largely unresolved. The more an academic discipline declares itself "scientific" and "rigorous," the greater the risk that it will lose touch with the rest of culture and with secular events (Rorty 1979, 5). Folk theories, on the other hand, are constantly argued by diviners, politicians, and public assemblies, and are tested by their correspondence with experience; one should not exaggerate romantically, but it is unrealistic to assume that what is misleadingly called "traditional" knowledge has existed ab initio, implicit, spontaneous, and collective (Jacques 1997, 55; Owomoyela 1997, 137). Like the society which sustains and is in turn shaped by it, witchcraft has evolved in changing times.[1]

Witchcraft as Political Theory

In Central Africa, people do not believe in "witchcraft"; they believe in, or as they say, they experience *kindoki, toro, iloki* or *evu,* and other similar concepts whose translation as "witchcraft" conceals both their differences and their internal complexity. The translation allocates the concepts to a domain, together with "magic," "religion," and "superstition," in which they are subject to analyses that question their rationality. Charitable interpretations of "witchcraft" evade outright condemnation by retranslating it as "mystical causation" or as a set of metaphors for relations supposedly better described in the vocabularies of sociology and psychology. In fact, *kindoki* (or rather, talk about it among BaKongo and their neighbors) belongs with other theories of the uses of power in society; as such it may be evaluated for its strengths and weaknesses. The "relative rationality" of such ideas (rational, that is to say, within a set of unquestioned prior assumptions) has been well understood since Evans-Pritchard's work on Zande belief (Evans-Pritchard 1937; Wilson 1970). Witchcraft is "a construction of the world no more and no less intellectual than its analogues in our own society—'race,' the 'value' of gold, the 'self' and its cognates," says Karen Fields. Such beliefs are "so enmeshed in routine social life that their reality is created and recreated by people acting in the light of them" (Fields 1982, 586).

The weaknesses of witchcraft as political theory are obvious; it includes erroneous ideas of cause and effect, specifically those that describe witches as engaged (for example) in a kind of real but invisible cannibalism or that attribute harmful effects to packets of animal, vegetable, and mineral elements concealed in an opponent's house. Its possible strengths may be suggested by comparing it with democracy, another view of how power is or should be distributed, which also has its strengths and weaknesses. I will not dwell on the strengths, which are asserted every day by the U.S. government; I agree with Winston Churchill that democracy is the worst system of government except for all the rest. In the 1990s, however, many Americans of differing political stripes felt uneasily that democracy, in its high school version at least—"the people choose their leaders through free and fair elections"—did not adequately describe their political experience or account for the current evolution of American society. From the District of Columbia to Montana, Colorado, and Texas more or less paranoid political movements arose which, if they had occurred in Africa, might well be classified as religious because of the apparent irrationality of their belief in occult forces (Pipes 1997). These various movements shared similar purposes and exhibited a common emotional tone, but they lacked a common theory, although the notion of a sinister "global elite" controlling all the world's banks, governments, educational institutions, military forces, the United Nations, the drug trade, and the AIDS epidemic came close. By this standard, *kindoki* is relatively coherent, if only because it is generally shared and supported by institutionalized processes. By the same token, *kindoki* does not travel well; its rationality is only apparent in relation to the society that supports it, and its ideologues lack the kind of position in world affairs which would enable them to assert its theoretical universality.

Democratic government is not as transparent as its advocates imply; power is said to come from the people, but how does that work? Numbers of Americans are unable to see the Supreme Court or the Bureau of Alcohol, Tobacco and Firearms as "representing the people." It is easier to understand power based on violence or patronage than power conferred by the ballot box; in South Africa after the overthrow of apartheid, a rise in witchcraft anxieties was associated with a popular sense that democracy was a front for something else (Comaroff and Comaroff 1997). In Ghana, as in South Africa, democracy and economic liberalization have opened up social competition expressed in consumerism, which in turn arouses jealousy and the quite justifiable suspicion that the success of some is due to hidden operations at the expense of the rest. Neither political power nor wealth manifested in the consumption of imported goods self-evidently explains their origins; both are popularly understood in modified versions of ancient and widespread assumptions. Presidents, like chiefs, are said to acquire their power by sacrificing some of their subjects to invisible brokers (Gruénais et al. 1995, 189); in much of sub-Saharan Africa, the dangerous source of wealth is the Mami Wata (or *la sirène*), a mermaid-like figure in which an image of Indian origin, modified under the influence of Western pornography, has been grafted onto the indigenous concept of the water-spirit (in KiKongo, *simbi*).[2] At the cost of one's soul, or the souls of relatives, Mami Wata makes offers of illicit sex and luxuries imported from across (or, supposedly, "beneath") the ocean. Campaigns to clean up corruption in high places or to eradicate witchcraft use different vocabularies to articulate similar understandings and goals.[3]

In interviews with the press during 1997, President Museveni of Uganda pointed out that democracy is not obviously to be recommended in Africa, because the structural preconditions for it are absent in most of the continent. The coalitions of real interests—drug companies, armament makers, pensioners, lawyers, banks, labor unions, and so on—that parties represent in a Euro-American democracy do not exist in effective, corporate form. Instead, in Congo/Zaire, for example, patrons and would-be patrons could do little but appeal to ethnic and regional constituencies with promises of governmental largesse. Each of the resulting "parties" readily segmented into factions supporting local leaders. "Democracy" does not mean the same to Congolese as it does to the State Department. In Zaire it meant in the first instance any form of government alternative to Mobutu, and more generally one that the speaker approved of; secondly, at times when the United States seemed inclined to take a benevolent interest in Africa, it meant a line of talk calculated to attract U.S. support. But Congolese set no great store by "free and fair elections" and have a low opinion of political parties, which they see (with reason) as self-serving factions. They hope to have a chief of state who will listen to the people, deal equitably with their problems, and distribute goodies; they do not much care how he gets the job. Mobutu, after all, was popular at first precisely because he suppressed "politics" and promised benevolent dictatorship. This is not to say that there are no Congolese with conceptions of democracy more in line with those of the State Department, and is certainly not to suggest that there are none who are dedicated to the best interests of their country. In the political culture of Congo/Zaire, however, an honest leader was unlikely to gain respect as such, since all leadership was publicly understood in terms of self-seeking traffic with the occult.

Regional Studies and the Disciplines

The challenge that African and other "area" studies present to the ethnocentrism of mainstream social sciences has been widely ignored by those same sciences. Developments in the way research is funded and evaluated in the United States have placed a premium on supposedly universal factors and criteria which lend themselves to formal and mathematical approaches and tend to deny the significance of culture; Africanists are said to hinder the advance of theory by focusing on unique local data, a charge which backhandedly emphasizes just what the challenge is (Harbeson 1997). "The rush to embrace a global framework ignores the profound need for locally grounded knowledge and understanding without which global analysis too often becomes an exercise in grafting imported theory onto incompletely understood local/ regional contexts" (Berger 1997, 6). Mainstream political science, which occasionally turns its attention to the possibility that local institutions and political cultures might have some bearing on political events, in so doing reveals its commitment to the "local data" of a single "area" defined by industrialization and bureaucracy, to a unilinear concept of progress defined in economic terms (the Gross Domestic Product), and to a narrowly ethnocentric view of institutional variation.

In African studies, political science necessarily (if only for methodological reasons) takes a very different direction, but has been handicapped by its preoccupation with "the state," an ill-defined and normatively loaded concept closely related to "modernization," the twentieth-century version of social evolution. In his Abiola Distinguished Lecture to the African Studies Association in 1996, T. Mkandawire listed some of the adjectives that have been attached to the state in Africa in attempts to rescue the original concept from its deficiencies: swollen state, soft state, predatory state, patron-clientalist state, rent-seeking state, overextended state, perverted capitalist state, etc. Usually these phrases, he remarked, mean nothing in particular; instead of corresponding to the exigencies of new discoveries, the accumulating epithets seem to be driven by "flippancy, disdain for the object of analysis, academic hubris that fuels the quest for originality if not in conceptualization at least in labeling" (Mkandawire 1997, 32). Political scientists are often well aware of the importance in Africa of indigenous political culture and of the political effects of unfamiliar institutions, but their disciplinary terms of reference scarcely allow room to discuss them; the welcome given for a while in the 1980s to the idea of civil society, vaguely defined in Africanist discourse as complementary to the state (although without reference to Hegel, Marx, or Gramsci), testified to this awareness. In practice, "civil society" tended to be limited to civic associations, nongovernmental organizations (NGOs), and other agencies staffed by elites that are readily intelligible in Western terms (Robinson 1994).

African states are post-colonial, which means that they inherited the plural institutional form of their colonial predecessors and the resulting lack, or at least serious weakness, of legitimacy. Individual leaders and regimes, such as Nkrumah's in 1960 or Mobutu's a decade later, have had popular support, but the institutions through which government operates are inconsistent with those of the various indigenous societies incorporated in the state, despite the extended efforts of several governments to forge alliances, compromises, and new, nationally homogeneous institutions (MacGaffey 1982). The most obvious example of the problem is that of incorporating "traditional" kingdoms or chiefships; in Zaire, Mobutu made the mistake of declaring all traditional rulers to be civil servants, whom he then ordered rotated to other domains! (The experiment was short-lived.)[4] The subject population experiences the "modern" through systems of wage labor, taxation, police, justice, and hospital medicine that apply alien and alienating procedures and act against their interests as they perceive them, even when corruption and incompetence are not at issue. Central to this alienation is the apparent failure of the government, colonial or post-colonial, elected or not, to deal with witchcraft, which it seems to encourage by ignoring it. In Northern Rhodesia (now Zambia), as Karen Fields has shown, "witchcraft practices" were so much part of the moral fabric of the community that British district officers were forced to rely on them as an alternative to less subtle forms of control (Fields 1982). When I spoke at the University of Lubumbashi in 1980 about the Zairian government's new policy of replacing local chiefs and elders with a national corps of plenipotentiary magistrates, a student in the audience declared that the scheme could not work because magistrates were not invested with traditional powers. "Only the other day, near here," he explained, "we had a man struck by lightning [presumably sent by witches or nature spirits]; only the traditional chiefs know how to deal with such matters!"

The challenge of area studies can also be met by denying it. According to Iris Berger, area studies are criticized by many who share "a post-structuralist view of a world in constant and breathless motion as multi-directional flows of people, capital, technology, culture and ideas render local, national and regional borders meaningless. In this post-modern global configuration, area studies [it is alleged] hark back nostalgically to an era of fixed boundaries and less complex identities" (Blier 1993, 157; Berger 1997, 5). In fact, it is quite some time since anybody seriously entertained, if anyone ever did, the much-caricatured image of a continent divided into innumerable, discrete, unchanging, and essentially unique "tribes" upon which an equally essentialized "modernity" impacted. Even now, globally distributed persons and products do not reach uniformly into all corners, and where they arrive they may be understood and used in local ways. "To diminish the importance of [locally grounded knowledge] risks becoming a new way of asserting the superiority of Western intellectual production" (Berger 1997, 7). Is it not perhaps that today's hybrid intellectual is no more comfortable with the manners and customs of natives than his or her nineteenth-century predecessor?

Where and what is the local? Africanists tend to be either lumpers or splitters. Lumpers offer generalizations about sub-Saharan Africa, presuming on a unity which they do not demonstrate. The implicit basis of this assumed unity is race, a concept whose incoherence discredits it even before we begin the critique of its reduction of culture to genetics. On the other hand, splitters insist on the uniqueness of each village on which they happen to have fieldnotes. Such uniqueness is tautologically true but unproductive; the fact, evident to common sense as strongly as it is to scholars, is that there are culturally distinct regions in Africa, despite the long-standing and various circulation of goods and ideas among them. Regional studies are, if nothing more, a better bet than either lumping or splitting. As Susan Vogel says about art, "The close studies of recent times lead us back to the conclusions of an earlier generation of scholars: there obviously are in Africa some broad regional characteristics, style areas, and concepts that span vast distances" (Vogel 1997, 77). In this book I rely on other work that has demonstrated the cultural unity of the area occupied approximately by speakers of the Western Bantu languages (MacGaffey 1972; Kuper 1979; Vansina 1991). It remains an unsettled question whether, as Herskovits and others suggested, the West African coastal forest zone should be included in this region.[5]

A regional tradition evolves in time as well as in space. In Central Africa, a distinguishable cultural tradition has evolved over a period of 2,500 years; "the Ba-Kongo," speakers of the KiKongo language in its various dialects, are one product among many of the continual changes and adaptations this evolution entailed. More recently, the BaKongo have been in contact, sometimes intense contact, not only with the rest of the region but with Europeans since the end of the fifteenth century; their language is full of buried Portuguese, French, and English terms, recording that history. Uniquely extensive documentation from European and sometimes from Kongo sources is available for the whole period, permitting at least some assessments of change. Scholars generally agree that a major political transformation, brought on by changes in the volume and organization of the Atlantic trade, occurred at the end of the seventeenth century. A second transformation took place at the end of the nineteenth century; this book is principally concerned with the structure of society and thought between those two periods of change.

The basic task of this book, and the challenge it presents, is the traditional anthropological task of cultural translation. Although relocating *kindoki* to proximity with other political theories may liberate it from critiques based on the a priori of its irrational or "religious" nature, it does not fit any more comfortably into the category "political theory" than it did in "religion." These categories are, as G. Bateson put it, points of view we take in our studies rather than separate realities existing in the world (Bateson 1972, 64). Regional studies should lead us to question the theoretical adequacy of disciplines focused on such reified abstractions, which barely emerge as discrete domains even in Western society. An "interdisciplinary approach" which retains the separate disciplinary vocabularies, problematics, and ideological commitments cannot provide a solution.

The Primary Materials

The extensive writings of Lutete and his colleagues, written in their own language at a time when the transformation of Kongo institutions effected by colonial rule was just beginning, provide in many respects a uniquely authentic ethnography, although that assessment needs qualification (see below). This unique resource has been largely suppressed by the circumstances of colonial rule in Belgian Congo and by general indifference to indigenous voices on the part of anthropologists and others. To reopen it now in a more favorable climate is to confront the problem of understanding the period to which the texts refer, the nineteenth century, and that of relating the texts to the context of their composition in the twentieth. What can we learn from these distant voices, and how do we learn it?

Already materials from the archive have transformed our understanding of Kongo art, one of the most distinguished in the traditional African canon (MacGaffey 1991). The present work focuses on political culture and history. The BaKongo are documented in greater historical depth than any other people in sub-Saharan Africa. From the sixteenth to the mid-nineteenth century they were among the principal suppliers of slaves to the Americas (Thornton 1983; Hilton 1985), with the result that Kongo culture generated one of the most prominent African traditions in the Americas. We can tell that in the eighteenth and nineteenth centuries the slave trade brought about profound changes in Kongo social organization, although by then European reports of Kongo were largely restricted to the coastal areas. At the end of the nineteenth century, after the end of the slave trade, the territory of the BaKongo, incorporated in European colonies, became the Atlantic threshold of the Central African interior, with the result that the people were both Europeanized, at least outwardly, and in many respects overlooked by reporters hastening to record exotica in the "Heart of Africa."[6] Under colonial rule BaKongo came to be one of the best-educated and eventually one of the most powerful groups in Belgian Congo, Angola, and the French colony of Moyen Congo. The texts collected by Laman document, from the indigenous perspective, the critical period in which this transition took place, from about 1840 to 1915.

Four principal concerns frame the presentation of the texts themselves: translating the experience of power from the institutional matrix that generated it to the one in which this book is written (the problem of translation); the historical context in which the manuscripts were written; the economic basis of power in Kongo society in the nineteenth century before Belgian rule abolished chiefship and repressed the use of *minkisi;* and what can be learned from the detailed study of these manuscripts about the evolution of the Central African cultural tradition. Whenever possible, I note connections between the early twentieth century and the seventeenth century or earlier, and between Kongo and other parts of Central Africa; the accumulation of such details makes historiography possible.

Kongo, by definition the area inhabited by KiKongo speakers, is neither internally homogeneous nor sharply distinguished from its neighbors. An essentially similar form of social organization and culture is found in a vast area of Central Africa in which, over the centuries, local communities have adapted a common tradition to local pressures and opportunities (Rey 1969; Dupré 1982; Vansina 1991). When it first became known to Europeans in 1483, Kongo was the domain of the kingdom whose capital was Mbanza Kongo, in what is now northern Angola. After the destruction of the old kingdom in 1665, the Atlantic trade was the principal force that shaped Kongo society.

In Angola, the nature of the landscape and particularities of relationships between KiKongo speakers and Europeans gave the Atlantic trade and the social formations related to it a somewhat different form from those of the forested northern regions. The greater openness of the savanna placed few barriers in the way of movement and made slave-raiding possible, giving rise to a long tradition of fortified towns, large armies, and pitched battles. In the north, and only in nineteenth-century Mayombe, there were fortified villages at most. The slave trade from the interior passed south through Angola and north through the Kouilou/Niari valley until about 1800, when Ngoyo and the Zaire estuary became the main export region. In Angola, the Kongo kingdom, though its fortunes rose and fell, was consistently supported by its relation to Portugal and the Catholic Church, which provided the legitimating symbols of the kingship itself and the closely related Order of Christ (reflected at lower levels in the brass crucifix/fetish for chiefs, *nkangi kiditu*). Through its Christian identity, the kingdom retained into the nineteenth century the privilege of invoking political as well as religious relations with Portugal; it remained both a source of ritual authority and a center of economic power. In the twentieth century, more or less forced labor on coffee plantations and the absence of any policy of "preserving" indigenous social structure through "indirect rule" (as in Belgian Congo) were relatively destructive of the social fabric. The ethnography of both Angolan Kongo and the Kongo of what became the French colony of Moyen Congo is relatively weak compared with that of Belgian Congo.

Between Kinshasa and the coast, a series of cataracts interrupt navigation on the Congo River; as the Atlantic trade developed, caravans of porters were needed to move goods between the depots in Kinshasa and the various European stations on the coast. Some traditions describe the BaKongo as expanding northward after the destruction of Mbanza Kongo in 1665, but I will argue that the nineteenth-century distribution of the BaKongo represents a degree of cultural homogenization rather than a migration, as both northern and southern communities adapted to the trade. The nodes of the transportation network generated the wealth and power on which chiefships were founded.

At first the trading ports were located along the coast, from Loango in the north down to Luanda in Angola. At the beginning of the nineteenth century European traders moved into the Congo estuary and Boma became the principal port for the trade as a whole. The traders—variously Portuguese, Dutch, English, and French—maintained depots called "factories," from which the terms of trade were arranged with local chiefs. After 1860, as the traffic in slaves was suppressed, other goods such as ivory, palm oil, and peanuts replaced slaves. Inland, however, slaves became increasingly important as agricultural producers. In 1884, representatives of the European powers met in Berlin to divide up the interior of Africa among themselves. In 1885 they awarded the Congo basin to Léopold II, King of the Belgians, as a personal estate, on condition that other nations be allowed free access to this vast territory's commercial possibilities. On this account the new colony was called, in English, The Congo Free

State (in French, l'Etat Indépendant du Congo). It included the central portion of Kongo; the Portuguese took the southern part, in Angola, and the French the northern part, as French Congo. "Congo" was derived from "Kongo"; "Zaire," likewise, comes from the KiKongo word *nzadi,* "large river," applied at first to the Zaire River, formerly "the Congo."

As the conquest proceeded, the agents of Léopold II penetrated the interior and diverted much of the labor formerly devoted to agriculture and commerce to transportation in aid of European commerce and of the apparatus of control. At the same time, from the 1880s onwards, Protestant missionaries also entered the hinterland, often in advance of the agents of the Free State. Converting and educating BaKongo, initially in small numbers but by the hundreds and thousands in the second decade of the twentieth century, the missionaries fostered an elite of teachers, evangelists, and potential political leaders. Newly literate, these men communicated among themselves by letters and through the Protestant mission bulletin, *Minsamu Miayenge.*

By 1908, the Free State had become not only a financial disaster but an international scandal on account of its brutalities; disorder, disease, and banditry combined to reduce the Kongo population by more than half. Belgium itself took over the colony as "Belgian Congo," and by 1912 bureaucratic order prevailed in Lower Congo, not only in local government but in the missions. The ravages of disease persisted, but murder and the burning of villages were no longer regular events; most men of working age, at least those within reach of the expanding educational system, worked for wages. At the same time, however, the political problems to be expected in a colony began to emerge.

In the new social order Africans were confined to their own institutional sphere as "natives" governed by "customary law" (largely a colonial invention) and were admitted to European institutions, including the missions, trade, and government service, only in relatively menial positions and on sufferance. Racial discrimination and segregation were increasingly evident. Already in 1908 and 1910, dissidents among the Protestant mission elite began to develop centers of unrest, using the language of the Bible to express their frustrations. The first generation of BaKongo to grow up under European rule massively expressed its discontent in the great religious movement of 1921 led by Simon Kimbangu (MacGaffey 1983).

Kimbangu, a Protestant reformer whose beliefs nonetheless reflected ancient and fundamental Kongo ideas concerning the organization of the universe and the operation of power in it, preached against both witchcraft and magic in the name of God and for the restoration of moral order. Although Kimbanguism did much to weaken indigenous religion in favor of Christianity, Catholic (and, to a lesser degree, Protestant) missionaries and the governments of the three colonies in which the BaKongo lived regarded Kimbanguism as a threat because they did not control it; they suppressed it, tightened their grip, closed the frontiers between their respective colonies to inhibit the movement of people and ideas, and imposed censorship, obliging publications addressed to Africans to limit themselves to "instructive and edifying" contents (Desroche and Raymaekers 1976; MacGaffey 1986b).

By 1922, most BaKongo were Protestants or Catholics, although their fundamental cosmological beliefs did not change. In 1960 Belgian Congo became independent as the Democratic Republic of Congo; in 1972 it changed its name to the Republic of Zaire. Lower Congo, the province of Belgian Congo occupied by BaKongo, became Lower Zaire. The French colony of Moyen Congo, its capital Brazzaville, also became independent in 1960 as the Republic of Congo. In May 1997, after the overthrow of the dictator Mobutu Sese Seko, Zaire became once again the Democratic Republic of Congo.

The ethnographic texts to be presented and commented on in the present work were written at a specific juncture in the history of Lower Congo, the time between the ending of disorder and the imposition of censorship. During this decade, the State abolished Kongo chiefship in favor of a new system of local government, created a completely new system of transportation, displaced many villages to new locations, re-deployed male labor in capitalist enterprises, and invented a model of "customary law" which concealed some of the effects of these changes. Chiefship as Lutete and others remembered it had taken shape during the preceding century, when commercial competition brought increasing violence into the lives of most BaKongo, and considerable wealth to a few.

Chapters 2, 3, and 4 deal with the origin and nature of the texts, the traditions of migration they report, and how the traditions can be read with regard to, on the one hand, the organization of trade in Lower Congo in the nineteenth century and, on the other, problems of cognition, ideology, and translation. The "answers" to the problems are necessarily personal and provisional; they are partial results of my own long-standing engagement with Kongo culture, less interpretation than dialogue. Among other conclusions I argue that, viewed in the perspective of political economy, the "matrilineal clans" of the BaKongo are best understood as a slave-holding oligarchy; that the traditions of the clans reflect not migrations but the routes of nineteenth-century trade; and that these routes were organized by rituals of predatory empowerment, including chiefship and *minkisi;* and that the traditions also incorporate the ideological models of the dominant class.

The rest of the book deals with the rituals of power as the texts report them. For most of the discussion I rely on translated extracts, but Chapters 7 and 9 are devoted to texts reprinted in extenso, in KiKongo with English translation; additional and alternative glosses on their contents are possible besides those that I present. The scale of events is small, the details concrete, the language subtle; though the horizon of comparison in this book is wide, extending beyond Kongo to the whole equatorial forest, we begin here with micro-history, telling of villages no longer on the map and of petty chiefs whose memorials in now-forgotten cemeteries once recalled wealth ill-gotten from the slave trade. The organizing focus of the whole is Lutete's home region, in the northeast corner of what is today the district called Mayombe, where we are able to examine in great detail a particular expression of a much more widespread cultural pattern.

What can we learn from these accounts of ritual? First, a great deal about Kongo chiefship, *minkisi,* and the relations between the two, showing the principles governing ritual action. The conventional idea of an African chief as a monarch on the European model, the head of an administrative and political hierarchy, is revealed as radically inappropriate to the Kongo political system, in which the chief is as much object as person, and as such often merely the representative or even the prisoner of an oligarchy. The texts offer an idealized picture, still entertained during the period of my own fieldwork in the 1960s as something that had once existed; they do not provide for individual villages the case histories that modern anthropology would like to have, but they do provide a rich account of political and economic processes in the region during the nineteenth century.

The level of detail the texts make available also has broader historical implications. Since 1960, the enthusiasm of historians for outlining the pre-colonial history of Africa in terms of alleged migrations has steadily diminished in favor of tracing religious, military, and commercial movements by which goods, dances, techniques, rituals, and insignia, rather than populations, were diffused across the continent; for this sort of work, cultural minutiae are essential. Both the "war" *nkisi* Simbu and the large cowrie shell prominent on the belly of *nkisi* Mangaaka, for example, clearly link Mayombe to Gabon in the north, just as the term *nganda* for "central place" (rather than *mbanza*) links it with the east.

Practices of Power

A few important Kongo terms and concepts are central to the concerns of the authors of the manuscripts. *Minkisi* were (and are) ritual complexes intended to bring about improvements in the well-being of individuals and groups, curing disease, identifying and punishing wrongdoers, averting misfortune, and favoring fertility and prosperity. In the narrow sense, *nkisi* (the singular) is the focal object in such a complex, often an elaborate composition with a wooden figure as its base. Some but not all types of such *minkisi* have come to be regarded as African art. They were composed and operated by an expert instructed in their use, the *nganga* (pl. *banganga*). The nature and functions of *nkisi* and *nganga* are examined in detail in Chapters 5 and 6; Chapter 7 presents three extended texts dealing with a particular *nkisi*, Mbola.

Chiefs (*mfumu*, singular and, usually, also plural) were, like *nganga*, ritually qualified figures through whom occult powers of benefit to the community of their followers were controlled. Although we would be inclined to think of chiefs as "political" (perhaps with "religious" functions or attributes) and of *minkisi* as "religious" or "magical," in Kongo thought they were very similar, to the point that the chief himself could be called both *nganga* and *nkisi*. The slave trade itself, the principal source of wealth in the nineteenth century, was (and is) thought of in terms of witchcraft, the export of souls to another world. Chapter 8 analyzes what the manuscripts say about chiefship; Chapter 9 consists of Lutete's text on the subject.

Wrongdoers were also thought to use, or misuse, occult power to steal, to cause disease and death, and to enrich themselves at the expense of others. Such people were called *bandoki* (*ndoki* in the singular), and the power they used was called *kindoki*, "witchcraft." But chiefs, *banganga,* and other defenders of the public good also had to be empowered by *kindoki,* which was therefore morally ambiguous. In use, too, it was ambiguous, in that one never knew for sure who were the defenders and who were the enemies of the public good. The distinction was established by ritual means such as initiation, divination, and various ordeals, behind which lay the secular realities of political power—the ability to mobilize wealth, violence, and oratorical support in local competition. In such competition the loser was proved to be a "witch," the winner was accepted as a "chief" or *nganga. Kindoki* is a language of conflict and negotiation, not consensus.

This complex of roles and the functions associated with them constituted "a moral matrix of legitimate governance" (Schatzberg 1993). The complex is not a descriptive list of observable people or objects but a contrasting set of morally and politically significant distinctions found among the BaKongo in the twentieth as in the seventeenth century and, with various changes of content, throughout the area of the western Bantu languages from southern Cameroon to southern Angola, and also in some parts of East and West Africa (MacGaffey 1972; MacGaffey 1977b). It presupposes a cosmology in which events that disrupt the even tenor of life are explained by reference to forces emanating from the land of the dead, to which possessors of *kindoki* have legitimate or illegitimate access. Here the focus must be not a few villages in Mayombe nor even "Kongo culture" but a cultural region. During the eighteenth and nineteenth centuries social structure between the interior of the Congo basin and the coast changed so that in areas closer to the trade routes and depots slave-holding matrilineal corporations emerged, stratification was more marked, and powerful chiefships were more likely to develop. Chiefship, divination, and rituals for the management of power adapted to these changes. In the part of Kongo on which this book focuses, specialized *minkisi* and ritual associations such as Lemba organized trade relations, whereas in Angolan Kongo the Order of Christ served this function.

Though Kongo chiefship was surrounded and defined by ritual, the concept of divine kingship as it has been elaborated by De Heusch, Girard, and others with reference primarily to East African societies does not suit it. The Kongo chief was not a rainmaker, and nowhere do the traditions indicate that his physical health affected the well-being of his country; his body was not, as it is among the Cewa of Malawi, a model for the land itself or for the body politic, and his rituals did not rejuvenate the cosmos or favor the harvest (Richards 1939, 248–50; Kaspin 1996). Physical deformities were not a disqualification, and he was not expected to be sexually potent; his relationship to communal prosperity was not metonymic. The contrast with chiefships in eastern and southern Africa is clear. BaKongo make use of the human body as metaphorical material for statements about power, social transitions, success, and failure, just as they also use figurines and calabashes. A village, for example, is like a body; for all to be well, its entrances and exits should not be "blocked" by noxious charms buried there. Individuals who are unsuccessful in their occupations are believed to have had their bodies "tied" or "blocked." A "chief" is an optional form of *nkisi,* realized only in particular circumstances (see Chapter 8).

The governing idea is that souls and bodies are built in modular fashion, so that an animating force can inhabit objects and animals as well as human beings and can be transferred from one to another. Bodies of power include those of *minkisi*, witches, chiefs, and healers. The Kongo chief's body, like an *nkisi,* was a container for power, thus placed under control and made useful; it contrasted with the bodies of innocent, powerless people (*banaana* or *bampamba,* "vain, empty"), and those of the victims of witchcraft, zombies (*nzambi*), whose vital souls had been wholly or partially removed and transferred to other bodies, other containers, to add strength to them. In local theory, these additions and subtractions constituted a zero-sum game. The myths of chiefship explained it as the source of order in society, establishing right eating, right marriage, and right government; its rituals, by dramatically representing power in objective form, enabled the public (all those whose own bodies were "empty" and vulnerable) to identify with it, the dynamic equivalent of monuments and works of art. The rituals carried out the kind of "conversation of gestures" which for G. H. Mead is constitutive of both thought and selfhood, in which, as Mead notes, inanimate objects may form parts of the generalized other with whom individuals "converse" (Mead 1934). The ambiguities of the body and the routines imposed upon it by cult obligations incorporated the transformative ambiguity of metaphor itself, linking superficial appearance to deeper meaning, accident to structure, and the diurnal to the eternal. The chief's ritual transformation at death into a stone constitutes an icon of the stability and permanence lacking amid the turmoil of real life.

Ritual performance is thus a kind of theoretical practice, of thinking by doing and being. Lévi-Strauss writes that one is tempted by the content of initiation rituals, in which passages are represented as "births" and "deaths," to think that "at this stage" thought is wholly embedded in praxis. But that would be to see things backward, for it is on the contrary scientific praxis which "among ourselves" has reduced the notions of birth and death to simple physiological processes, leaving them unfit to carry other significations. In societies which have initiation rites, birth and death provide the material for a rich and varied conceptualization that transcends the distinction between the real and the imaginary: a full meaning, of which, says Lévi-Strauss, we scarcely know how to evoke the ghost, on the reduced stage of figurative language. "What looks to us like being embedded in *praxis* is the mark of thought which takes the words it uses seriously, whereas in comparable circumstances we only 'play' with words" (Lévi-Strauss 1962, 264–65). For us they are metaphors, metonyms, figures of speech (Chapter 10).

Practical thinking meant in this instance both that human beings were manipulated objectively and that objects were credited with subjectivity. Chiefs, although they were human beings, present all the ontological problems traditionally associated with "fetishes." In historical fact, some chiefs were powerful, others failed; but in ritual the chief is presented to us as both a supreme ruler ("a lion, a leopard") and as an *nkisi* whose animate quality is no more marked than that of an *nkisi* of wood, both of them deemed capable of agency which, to the skeptical eye, is no more than imaginary. The "agency" attributed to *minkisi* is easily dismissed as superstition or the product of chicanery, but it should perhaps provoke the more interesting question of the nature of agency in human beings, which we tend to think of as simply a personal endowment. The chief (*mfumu*), whatever his personal character and achievement, was a product and representative of an oligarchy of the free (*zimfumu*), the *bamayaala* or governors who installed him, sometimes even against his will. Instead of asking why BaKongo and other Africans violate the Cartesian distinction between persons and objects, we might note that among ourselves (in the capitalist West) the distinction between real rights and personal rights, between things and persons, is not given in nature but in law, as "the essential condition for a part of our system of property, transfer, and exchange" (Mauss 1990, 47). To begin to translate and understand Kongo rituals, in all their apparent otherness and irrelevance, is to recognize how deeply our own thought is embedded in praxis, and to begin to see how difficult it is to know the world in any other categories than those naturalized for us by our own institutional habits.

Politics in Zaire

The KiKongo texts open to us a political system which is both real and imagined; more generally, they offer us a window onto Central African thought about the political. The present work provides a setting for some of the texts, or extracts from them. Besides their ethnographic value, they often have a rich literary quality, conveying a sort of poetry of the experience of power. Though the rituals of Kongo chiefship have faded to a memory, the political consciousness or imagination that I attempt to describe remains the medium through which BaKongo (and, more broadly, Congolese) interpret and respond to their daily experience, as they have in the past (Bockie 1993). For this reason, despite my best efforts, readers will notice that the dominant tense in the story sometimes shifts uncertainly between past and present; a cultural tradition is the present and the future even more than it is the past. My main focus is on documents dating from the beginning of the twentieth century, but though ritual practices have changed since then, as have the material conditions of the people (for the better, and then once again for the worse), the political values of the BaKongo remain much the same. As Mbembe observes for West Africa in general, "From the era of the slave trade, the sufferings of black people pose the question, Why? The old categories still claim to provide answers to this question. . . . Tensions, conflicts, anxiety, secret fears and natural disasters are understood by reference to the invisible" (Mbembe 1988, 63–64).

In the 1990s the Zaire of President Mobutu Sese Seko returned to something like the state of barbarism that characterized the country when it was the Free State, 1885–1908. Once again the death rate rose, although there are no statistics; a major cause was, as before, sleeping sickness, to which was added AIDS. Populations rural and urban fled from marauding soldiers, who looted and killed at will. In more remote districts life was safer than in Kinshasa, the capital, but none of the advantages of modernity was generally available any longer: medical care, education, industrial products. The old skills (ironworking, for example) are gone. The state has been privatized; no national economic institution exists in more than name: banks, taxes, customs, price regulation, even currency (there was, in the 1990s, a black market not only in dollars but in *counterfeit* dollars). Islands of predatory exploitation were controlled by Zairois in league with international carpetbaggers who channeled to world markets the country's wealth in gold, diamonds, coffee, and cobalt.

It may not be appropriate to speak of the "collapse" of Zaire, since one of its most baffling characteristics was the persistence of its peculiar system of organized theft and decay, despite an endless sense of imminent crisis; in 1997, after the departure of Mobutu, the curiously functional "collapse" continued. The usual vocabulary of public life, referring to banks, currency, balance of payments, legitimacy, legislation, law, order, and the state no longer fits. On the other hand, indigenous institutions (healing, divination, tests for witchcraft, kinship, hereditary chiefship) have been forced to take on new functions. The corresponding indigenous vocabularies and conceptual schemes are used by Congolese themselves to comprehend and guide their lives: "The popular collective imagination views the politicians in powerful images of witchcraft and cannibalism" (De Boeck 1996, 102). Contemporary politics can only be understood by referring to beliefs in the occult. The political elite has organized itself since 1960 in terms of membership in secret societies which, although their rituals and symbols were often obtained by mail order from the international market in the supernatural, are thought of by the members as mediators of effective power. In Mobutu's Zaire, the leading *banganga* in Kinshasa constituted a parallel political network to that of the politicians, their clients; appointments to and falls from high office were attributed to magical machinations. At the National Constitutional Assembly a former minister of justice, a MuKongo, who in 1980 had suggested admitting diviners as expert witnesses, recommended that all judges be initiated in *kinganga* so that they would be able to evaluate evidence of witchcraft themselves; his recommendation matched the pragmatic solution that British administrators adopted in colonial Zambia (see above). Some medical doctors went through "initiations" to improve the chances of the success of their clinical treatments, thus combining two functions formerly carried out in parallel by Africans and Europeans.

De Boeck, in a vivid account of contemporary Zaire, argues (with Mbembe) that both the crisis of the times and responses to it were "to some extent rooted in a moral, social and symbolic matrix that reaches beyond the fractures inflicted by the postcolonial world and the myth of modernity, and that also draws from precolonial sources" (De Boeck 1996, 100). He also asserts that political relations in Zaire were not satisfactorily described by any simple model of oppressors and oppressed; instead we should think of a continuous, collective process of negotiation and compromise popularly known as *l'arrangement* (idem, p. 99; see also MacGaffey 1990). This process is mediated not only by indigenous conceptions of power (*kindoki*) but also by the rituals of chiefship, kinship, and tributary payment, in much the same ways that Laman's collaborators describe.

The final chapter reflects on the ambiguous relationship between the real and the imagined in the texts we have been considering. I argue that stories about chiefs and their journeys to and from the land of the dead include "theoretical" models of Kongo society by which it is rendered intelligible to its members. They are components of the ideology of a society whose structure owed much to the Atlantic trade, as it developed in the eighteenth and nineteenth centuries. The structural results of the trade are evident particularly in the societies of the southern edge of the rain forest, variously and inaccurately characterized by anthropologists as "matrilineal" or "bilineal." The ideology itself, however, is much older and more widespread than the effects of the slave trade. Its fundamental or cosmological components are common to the whole area inhabited by speakers of Western Bantu languages and date back thousands of years, but its local expressions include ritual themes and practices invented and diffused at later dates from different centers. Among the strongest of the ancient values are those that tend to identify social order with the exercise of legitimate violence; this theme is incorporated in rituals of chiefly investiture in varied and ambiguous ways that raise questions not only about the relation between the "real" and the "imaginary" but about the history of cultural innovation, particularly in southern Congo. I conclude with comments on the role of real and imagined violence in the politics of contemporary Africa.

Perhaps the greatest challenge that Lutete and his colleagues present to the reader is to *listen* to them. Though the texts are not poems, the kind of attention they deserve is like that of poetry, a "poetry of the experience of power," as I have already suggested, rich in provocative images. The temptation—more than a temptation, a professional imperative—is to interrogate them, to sort their statements into the "religious" and the "political"; to demand that they produce grist for our mill, to tell us about demography, about women, about the lives of slaves, about "what happened" in Lower Congo in the nineteenth century. The silences we identify, the inconsistencies and gaps in the stories, begin to seem like imperfections, failures to address the issues of current interest to the academy. There is, or should be, nothing shameful about our agendas, but we should be willing to suspend them from time to time, and to recognize the *irreducibility* of these testimonies to life in another world and to imagine in our turn a reality based on very different assumptions about personhood, agency, life and death, and the nature of power. "That academic envelope serves only to protect everything the story says and does not say, an inner afflatus always on the verge of being dispersed at contact with the air, the echo of a vanished knowledge revealed in the penumbra and its tacit allusions" (Italo Calvino, *If on a Winter's Night a Traveler*).

2. TEXTS AND CONTEXTS

This chapter sketches the origin and historical contexts of a remarkable ethnographic project undertaken principally north of the Congo River, in the modern districts of Manianga and western Mayombe, in the second decade of the twentieth century; it provides a frame for a number of the indigenous texts that the project produced. Selections from these texts that deal with the powers of chiefs and *minkisi* are to be examined in subsequent chapters, but to do so we should first understand what was happening at the time they were written, within two or three years of 1915. At this time, the institutions the authors of the texts describe were being actively repressed by the newly created government of Belgian Congo. This context of rapid change may seem to explain why the authors usually write about chiefship "in the old days," but I will suggest in later chapters that the concept of "the old days" was built into the concept of chiefship itself, that chiefship as a practice was a perpetually unsuccessful effort to recover a past that never existed. On the other hand, the existence and the character of the texts as ethnography are directly related to the changing times of their production.

Chiefship of the kind described in the manuscripts, and also a number of the *minkisi* (how many one cannot be sure) emerged in the seventeenth and eighteenth centuries in response to the Atlantic trade; as trade changed in content and political organization, the rituals of power also changed. The nature of the change, and the nature of power, were understood in very different terms by Africans and Europeans, as to a considerable extent they still are.

The Atlantic Trade

Permanent European trading stations, known as "factories," began to be established in the Congo estuary after 1840, creating a demand for foodstuffs to feed both the traders, their house slaves, and slaves awaiting shipment.[1] When the slave trade effectively ended, in 1863, trade in ivory, peanuts, gum copal, rubber, and other products replaced slaves in the export trade; the ivory trade was the most profitable, for those who could afford to enter it. The new cultivations increased the local value of slaves, for which there was an inland market until the 1920s.

In the 1840s, the kings of Boma, through their commercial agents, the "linguisters" (*madingizi*), entered into contracts with the factories (English, French, Portuguese, and eventually Dutch) and also imposed taxes on goods arriving from the interior. Alexander Delcommune, who had been in charge of the French factory at Boma, estimated that in the mid-1870s, when purchases ran to 100,000 kilos on good days, each of the nine kings had an annual income of 8,000 to 15,000 francs, while some linguisters often made much more. In 1863, one of them was reportedly worth 100,000 francs in imported goods.

The chiefs at Boma, titled and commercial, spent their enormous wealth on imported goods such as crockery, silver, enamelware, furniture, and extravagant clothing, which they showed off in European-style houses. Inland, chiefs and their families competed to have the most expensive funerals; huge amounts of trade goods such as blankets, guns, tusks, crockery, and even slaves were buried in the graves or displayed on them. At least two artistic traditions developed to supply the need for items of conspicuous consumption: soapstone sculptures and funerary urns. Soapstone figures (usually but perhaps erroneously called *mintadi*) portrayed chiefs in arrogant poses and copied imported items such as guns and sewing machines; large, ornate terra-cotta urns (*mabondo, nkudu*) were made uniquely as grave furniture (Thompson and Cornet 1981; Schrag 1985, 251). During the late 1870s, however, severe droughts in the interior reduced the supply of goods to a trickle; the well-to-do at Boma never recovered their former prosperity (Delcommune 1922, 45).

It is not clear that inland chiefs ever had wealth on anything like this scale, but they followed the pattern as best they could. Lutete's stories of the great chiefs mention urns and soapstone figures imported from the coast; even in a relatively marginal area such as Mbanza Manteke graves carried guns, umbrellas, rows of gin bottles, *mintadi*-sculptures, and Toby jugs, still visible in the 1960s. Important corpses were wrapped in hundreds of imported blankets, and families impoverished themselves to give their dead honorable funerals.

Chiefs could make money from commerce, financed ultimately by the sale of dependents as slaves, or, if they controlled fords, bridges, and other passages, by taxing passing caravans:

> Traders would go to markets three or four days away. Preparing in their villages, they got together a great quantity of goods, including the gifts they would have to leave at the villages they passed through, since they would not be allowed to pass for nothing (Kavuna, Cahier 54).

Local chiefs controlled the markets through which foodstuffs and other goods were channeled. Markets were not found everywhere, however; Mvubu Thomas, from Maduda in northern Mayombe, mentioned in *Minsamu Miayenge* his surprise at seeing a market on a trip to Kibunzi in 1916, "because in our country we have no markets." In a given district, a small market would be held in a different place on each of the four days of the Kongo week (Nsona, Konzo, Nkenge, Nkandu), after which the markets were named (Janzen 1982, 29); larger markets, attracting many hundreds of people, were held every eight days.

> We hear that there were large markets in our country [between Vungu and Boma]. Nsona Kungu was very large indeed; it was owned by the late Kungu Nkazu, an important, wealthy and powerful chief. There were also the Nkandu of Na Mwanda and the Nkenge of Lunga at Mumba. Beyond Kungu's market there were Nkenge of Nzanzi, Nkandu of Ngombe and others, but Kungu's Nsona was the one that attracted most people. This market rivaled the Nsona at Mboma in fame (Kavuna, Cahier 54).

The market called Manyanga, located at a point where the principal routes to the coast from the Malebo Pool divided to run north and south of the river to various points on the coast, was described by H. Johnston in 1884:

> Manyanga is a great food center. I have already hinted at its abundantly supplied markets, where eighty or ninety fowls, fifty goats, troops of sheep, and hundreds of eggs may be purchased at a single time. The favorite medium of exchange here is blue glass beads, and handkerchiefs and stuffs will scarcely be taken at any sacrifice. Indeed it is quite a false idea to entertain that you can go anywhere in Africa with any sort of bead or any kind of cloth. Each district has its peculiar tastes and fancies to consult, and you might starve in one place with bales of goods that would purchase kingdoms in another. . . . Between Vivi and Isangila you will find red handkerchiefs, striped cloth, brass "tacks," gin and wire useful. At Manyanga blue beads rule the market; at Stanley Pool brass rods (Johnston 1884, 131).

The blue beads were European hexagonal glass prisms, dark blue, 4 millimeters long, called by the name of the old Kongo shell currency, *nzimbu.* Ten necklaces of 100 beads each were called a *kulazi,* and ten of those were worth one franc. A specialized kind of trader went around the markets collecting defective necklaces to make up full-value necklaces. By 1892, raffia cloths, another old Kongo currency, had disappeared from the trade routes, replaced by another import, the brass rod (*ntaku*), 2.5 × 52 centimeters, which cost about eight-hundredths of a franc in Europe. Another unit, a bundle of 12 white cotton handkerchiefs worth 4 shillings 6 pence in Europe (called *malenswa* in KiKongo, from the Portuguese *lenço*), was used to pay wages and to buy local foodstuffs. Many other kinds of cloth were used as currency, but they varied in value according to supply and demand; new designs or colors depreciated old ones.[2] Cloth, increasingly in use for other purposes, was eventually replaced as currency by Belgian francs.

Women and men traded separately, each category selling its own products in different sections of the market. They kept tally by means of knotted cords or notched sticks. Women made baskets, thread, pots, and brooms; they also sold corn, peas, beans, peanuts, bananas, greens, manioc, and cooked foods to passersby and caravan porters. As they are today, beans and the like were set out in small piles on a mat, each pile worth two, three, four, or ten necklaces. Women measured the piles with the small end of a gourd, varying in size from one trader to another; leaves of corn were stuffed in the bottom or removed, according to the current demand for the product in question. Men made pipes, traps of all kinds, and mats; they sold palm wine, chickens, goats, sheep, dried and smoked fish, pork and goat meat, and meat from game animals, including elephant, antelope, and buffalo, all of which were still abundant at the time. They also sold European products such as cloth, gunpowder, salt, and rum. Cloth was measured by the width of extended arms (*vwata*).[3]

According to the Free State's first annual handbook, published in 1903, imported goods included hats, sheathed machetes, knives, guns, gunpowder, salt, umbrellas, matches, tobacco and smokers' supplies, and many different kinds of cloth, some of them identified by Kongo names. Some of these goods, items of prestige such as guns and umbrellas, are still to be seen on old Kongo graves. Others are preserved as components of *minkisi.*

Creating a Colony

As Chapter 1 explained, the Cahiers were written at a particular juncture in the history of Lower Congo as the Free State became Belgian Congo. No comprehensive account has yet been written of what happened on the ground in this area between 1880 and 1921. In the first stage of the European occupation, the principal concern of the invaders was the reorganization of labor, effected mostly by force. "The general policy of the Powers who have divided up this part of Africa is to say as little about it as possible to the natives, letting them believe in their own independence, but making prisoners or burning down villages from time to time in a most unintelligible and arbitrary manner" (Phillips 1887, 165).[4]

Léopold's agents became internationally notorious for the brutality they used in compelling Africans to collect quotas of wild rubber. Africans were also obliged to provide food and transport for traveling officials and their troops. Protests were put down by burning the villages of recalcitrants and by brutal flogging, which both missionaries and military officers believed to be the only way to extract obedience from Africans. The nicknames given to Europeans often identified violent characteristics; one such was Kikwanga, from *kwanga,* "to beat or knock down."[5] Initially, until the BaKongo became accustomed to the new order, labor was imported from West Africa. "There are crowds of imported workmen [in Boma], who complain bitterly of their treatment by their employers. 'No good here for Sierra Leone man; plenty sick, too much flog'" (Lapsley 1893, 58).

Simon Kavuna, writing some years after the government of Belgian Congo had abolished the worst excesses, understood the Free State's recruitment of labor for work in the new port of Matadi as a continuation of slaving:

> They were taken to a cave called Nsafu a Mumbala. There their heads were completely shaved and they were given to a middleman (*dingizi*) who passed them on to the European. After three or four days they were sold for two measures of gunpowder, two machetes, two measures of salt and one or two measures (four yards each) of the cloth called *mbembe.* When they had been sold they were put in a prison, men and women, all naked. They sang the song, *Bomba, ntangu wele, ntangu una lambila bana wele* [= *bwabu diambu dimeni*], "Be calm, the sun has gone, the sun is setting [it's over]." Then they were all flogged and put in a house, never to be seen again. (Kiananwa, 66)[6]

Caravans

To transport goods to and from the interior, porters were needed because cataracts on the Congo between Matadi and Mpumbu (Kinshasa) rendered the river unusable. Porters carried their loads for the equivalent of two cents a week (in the dollars of 1900), and those who brought ivory from the interior might be paid only in rum, gunpowder, and salt.[7] At first, the porters were from Loango on the coast, or they were "Zanzibaris"; the BaKongo were said to be above such work. In fact, they were busy with trade of their own, which the Europeans were to take over. For centuries the BaKongo had been the middlemen between the coastal factories and Kinshasa, where the River Congo became navigable; Bobangui and other canoemen carried goods to and from Kinshasa into the distant interior. L. Van de Velde wrote, *"La rage pour le négoce atteint son paroxysme dans ce pays"* (The frenzy for commerce reaches its height in this country).

Kongo porters in what became Belgian Congo first worked for Europeans in 1881, when they began to carry 30-kilogram loads from Vivi to Isangila, on the route to Kinshasa, along an unimproved track through mountainous country. The supply of porters, though good, was inadequate to the increasing demand. From 1883 to 1887, the number of loads carried to Kinshasa grew from 12,000 to 50,000. "In the history of human labor, this is a remarkable and inspiring example of prompt adaptation to labor of barbarian peoples" (*Le Congo Illustré* 4 [1895], 4).

Lt. Frederik van de Velde described the personnel of an expedition he assembled in Boma in 1889 for an expedition to Kwango (east of Kongo). They included an interpreter called Luizo, who spoke Portuguese, English, and several local dialects and retained his belief in fetishes despite long association with white people; forty Dahomeyan soldiers, tall, very dark, "d'une nature très sauvage," and prodigiously resistant to fatigue, who were commanded by Corporal John, a Yoruba who spoke English and some Dahomeyan dialects; forty "Zanzibaris," who in fact came from various parts of East Africa, and whose commander, Mohamed, also spoke English. ("Toute cette troupe avait l'allure la plus martiale.") In addition, it included a competent cook from Sierra Leone who had been taught by Protestant missionaries, five young domestic servants, and an unspecified number of Kongo porters.

The soldiers were paid one franc per day and their supplies. The porters earned a little less, paid in cloth and brass rods; since they were the slaves of the chief who provided them their pay went to him, but they were also given a tip (*matabich*) which they were entitled to keep for themselves. The route was mountainous, the porters carried little food, and the roadside was littered with the husks of kola nuts they chewed to keep themselves going.[8] Eventually, there were "thousands of skeletons" to be seen along this route (Samarin 1985, 277).[9]

Nor was the suffering limited to the porters. Van de Velde remarks with apparent naïveté that the vicinity of the caravan route was deserted because those who formerly lived there "could not get used to the disturbance caused by the traffic." Phillips, describing the north bank route to the Pool, saw it differently: "So many villages had been attacked, men killed, women ravished and then murdered, that a strip of country which [Stanley] left flourishing and well populated had been abandoned by the natives" (Phillips 1887). After the completion of the railroad from Matadi to Kinshasa in 1898, porters were no longer required in such numbers. The railroad itself facilitated the movement of newly educated Christian men into wage labor.

Belgian Congo

The Free State never consisted of more than a heterogeneous collection of separate enterprises that were partly in competition with each other. They included European plantations that produced coffee and palm oil; trading companies; Catholic and Protestant missions, each group autonomous in its own territory and supported by different parent organizations in Europe or the United States; and the agents of the state, many of them adventurers, such as Conrad's Kurtz, badly paid, isolated in and predatory upon some arbitrarily designated part of the country.[10]

In 1908, in the face of mounting protest abroad and mounting debt at home, Léopold ceded his private empire to the Belgian State as Belgian Congo. By 1910, the Belgians had begun to bring the vast area of their new colony under administrative control (Jewsiewicki 1983). They created a hierarchy of districts and district officers, replaced arbitrary exactions with regular taxation, and initiated public health measures. The bureaucrat replaced the freebooter. A combination of taxation and recruitment to wage labor nearly destroyed the indigenous market networks; villagers were called upon to supply food to the expanding towns but were prevented from rivaling European production. A policy of indirect rule implemented from 1918 onward instituted the fiction of "customary law" in rural areas to guarantee that Africans were excluded from the legal protections and economic opportunities of the "modern," but it also conferred a limited degree of autonomy on them. In this zone, the language of witchcraft and the practices of divination (sometimes conducted in Christian and biblical forms) regulated interpersonal relations and the ongoing politics of "slavery."

Mission Stations: Vungu and Lolo

Before the military occupation of Lower Congo began, Protestant missionaries had moved into the interior. After a disastrous initial attempt in 1885, the year in which the Congo Free State was created in the territory that became the Democratic Republic of Congo, the Christian and Missionary Alliance, a U.S. Protestant organization, succeeded in founding a string of stations among the BaKongo. The stations extended roughly northward from the mission's base at the port of Boma, capital of the Free State (see Map 1). By 1899 there were seven stations, including Vungu, Lolo, Kinkonzi, and Maduda, with 27 native evangelists and a total attendance at public worship of 405 persons.[11] These stations happened to fall in the area of conjunction or intermingling of the Nsundi (Manianga) and Mayombe chiefship complexes (see Chapter 8).

The station at Lolo was always something of a problem. In 1889 it had garnered a number of converts, notably Ngoma Petolo and Lwamba Josefi, but the missionaries found the area too difficult and left. In February 1903, when the Alliance re-founded the station, Lwamba was one of the principal evangelists. As the Alliance's bulletin had noted in 1901, "The most encouraging feature of our Congo mission is the way God has raised up and used native workers in this mission." The cost of a native worker was a mere fifty dollars a year; some of the teachers in charge of village schools were no more than fifteen years old. In 1904, Lwamba was joined at Lolo by Lutete Esaya, who had been born nearby and had attended the original school; after its demise, and after much heart-searching on his part, he had decided to continue his education at Vungu, where he was baptized in 1899.

Vungu itself is a place whose name has a special resonance in Kongo history.[12] According to a tradition reported in 1624, the alleged founder of the Kongo kingdom at Mbanza Kongo in modern Angola was the youngest son of the king of Vungu, an ambitious young man who killed his aunt and crossed the river in canoes with his many followers, among whom he divided the new territory at a place called "the Hill of Partition," Mongo Kayila. The tradition says that the adventurer's name was Motino-Bene, which may redundantly combine *ntinu,* "king," with *(m)wene,* "chief." A more probable reading, however, is "a certain king." A later report gives this man the name Lukeni, a name implying violence.[13] The Vungu kingdom was destroyed by brigands in 1627.

Those who were baptized made their decision in a time of extreme violence, from which the missions offered a degree of protection. Between 1885 and 1920, thousands died from sleeping sickness attributable to the relocation of villages into refuge areas infested with tsetse flies. Every death provoked others, as relatives and neighbors suspected of causing it by witchcraft were subjected to poison ordeals and the possibility of execution. Missionary travelers frequently reported seeing the remains of convicted witches whose bodies had been dismembered and burned so that they could not return to trouble the living any further. A missionary who had known Lolo in 1892 noted with shock, nine years later, that villages that formerly had forty or fifty houses were reduced to eight or ten. Lutete Esaya, revisiting his own home village in 1905, found that many others had died out altogether. In one, he found only two survivors, one of them a man who had awarded himself the praise-name Fwakatinwa, "Death fled from him."

The Alliance had troubles of its own. Missionaries succumbed to disease at an appalling rate, some of them after only a few weeks in the country. Converts were few at first, and it was difficult to be sure they understood what they were converting to. The annual report for 1910 noted, "The native mind does not easily grasp spiritual truth, it is usually filled with palavers about pigs and women." Even the teachers and evangelists were often causes of concern. From time to time it was reported that one or more of them had "backslid," and some of them seriously misused their position as representatives of foreign power. At Maduda in 1903 missionaries discovered that "bogus schools had been set up in the most populous sections of the district where we had hoped to place true light-bearers. It was comparatively easy for them at first to blind the eyes of their own countrymen, and for a season the school flourished and unlimited success seemed before them." In time, however, "the real object of the schools" was laid bare: "gathering wealth by oppressing people and by infamous trading, while by courting the readily given friendship of the neighboring Belgian state officials, their doings have the appearance of legality with the easily terrified natives, whose fear of the state soldiers renders them submissive" (Sixth Annual Report [1903], 102).

By 1911 the work at Lolo was going well, with eleven native helpers and seventeen schools in neighboring villages. The local people, formerly indifferent, had become very enthusiastic, although the report expresses uneasiness about the depth of true faith in the converts and stresses the constant need for white missionary supervision—native evangelists were not enough. By this time, the mission's reports were less and less likely to name any natives at all, so we do not know who was doing good at Lolo. A history written by a leading Kongo pastor in 1984, however, mentions with respect Lutete Esaya, long since dead (Kuvuna ku Konde Mwela 1984, 87).

Catholic missionaries from Belgium arrived later than the Protestants, who complained bitterly that "Romanism, with its attendant evils, is given every possible advantage at Boma." In 1910, the Alliance complained "one of our best and oldest teachers was badly beaten by the Romanists. . . . The priests attempt to subvert our teachers, drawing them into their missions to learn French, with the promise of big salaries later. They seize children by force" (Annual Report [1910]).[14] In this fierce competition,

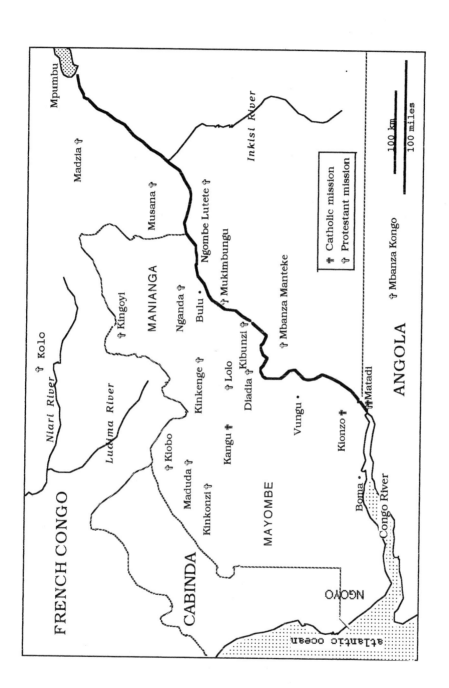

Map 1. Mission Stations

Catholics complained to the minister of colonies in 1909 not only that the Protestant missions used their wealth to attract natives by paying them outrageously, but that the State's own agents were often anticlerical and hostile (Kratz 1970, 166, 366; Mudimbe 1994, 115). On the other hand, they admitted that their permissiveness with respect to palm wine counted heavily in their favor. Both sides agreed on the deplorable quality of local customs and the unfortunate tendency of catechists to backslide.[15]

In spite of such problems, by 1914 the Alliance, which had sent missionaries all over the world, regarded Congo as its most successful field. Missionaries were no longer dying within a few weeks of their arrival. The following year, readers of *The Alliance Weekly* learned that at Lolo, "two old women have been saved and lately baptized. It is almost impossible to reach Congo old women, but God has done the impossible at Lolo." Missionaries increasingly withdrew from direct evangelical contact, which was left to indigenous pastors and teachers, and devoted themselves to managing a large and rapidly growing organization whose bureaucratic form paralleled that of local government. The Alliance's Foreign Department reported in 1920 that there were 278 outstations in the area; that 5,203 pupils attended the 266 day schools; and that total membership of the churches was 3,587. Offerings had increased by 50 percent over the past year. In several stations the problem was not to attract applications for baptism, but to sift them.

The same report mentioned remarkable instances of God's speaking to the people through dreams and visions. Since the Alliance's theology predicted the second coming of Christ, the missionaries welcomed what they saw as "signs of the near coming of our King. Congo has not escaped the spirit of unrest, and other signs are appearing which cause us to lift up our heads for our redemption draweth nigh." These signs were not quite what they appeared at first to be.[16] For some years the BaKongo had been responding to the stresses of colonial rule by preparing a movement of their own for which, in 1921, the prophet Simon Kimbangu provided the necessary catalyst. Kimbangu had been baptized by the British Baptist Missionary Society in Ngombe Lutete. A later Kimbanguist manuscript described what happened:

> In Nkamba [Kimbangu's birthplace] a man appeared who had never studied at a mission station, but he was a believer and had learned to read and write a little from a village teacher. His name was Simon Kimbangu. He raised the dead, caused the paralyzed to stand upright, gave sight to the blind, cleansed lepers, and healed all the sick in the name of the Lord Jesus. But he chased away those who practiced witchcraft. . . . When the prophet was revealed, the dead in stretchers and the sick of all kinds were brought to the Prophet of God. . . . Since the coming of the missionaries it had never happened that the dead arose, the lame walked, and the blind saw; or that the people of their own free will threw away their fetishes, or wanted to pray to God. And only then did we the people of Kongo know that God and Jesus remembered us. The grief and suffering of our fathers were heard by God the Father, and the tears of us the black people were wiped away in Kongo. (quoted in MacGaffey 1969)

The apparently syncretistic ambiguities of this story with respect to healing, witchcraft, and divine inspiration, which are those of the Kimbanguist movement itself, have been debated by missionaries, district officers, and scholars from 1921 to the present. Kimbanguism, initially repressed by the government at the instance of Catholic figures who regarded it as a product of Protestant free thinking and as a threat to colonial rule, went on to become, after Congo independence in 1960, a nationally and internationally recognized church, the Church of Jesus Christ on the Earth by the Prophet Simon Kimbangu (Desroche and Raymaekers 1976; MacGaffey 1983). Its beliefs appear to be the result of a specifically Kongo cultural reading of the Bible and of mission teaching.

As we have seen, this ambiguity was already insidiously present in the Alliance's own congregations, where the missionaries constantly worried whether their converts were "truly saved" and where what they saw as "backsliding" was a frequent occurrence. Backsliding had two dimensions, moral and cultural, that were difficult to distinguish. Conversion and adherence to the missions meant abstaining, at least in public, from participation in rituals regarded as pagan, which the missions and the government were beginning to suppress when the manuscripts were written. Until about 1920, conversion was a social as much as a religious shift; the missions created communities of a new kind, with schools, dispensaries, housing, and new occupations. After 1920, shifts in both mission and administrative policy defined a plural society in which Africans were clearly excluded from the European sphere, except in subordinate roles, and were legally expected to lead their lives principally within the framework of indigenous institutions, seriously modified though they were by the imposition of colonial rule. This framework preserved to a considerable extent the indigenous cosmology, through whose categories the people understood their experiences (MacGaffey 1983).

The View from the Other Shore

The Kongo understanding of what sort of people the Europeans were and what their arrival meant was very different from what the Europeans themselves thought. In Kongo thought to this day, the universe is divided into the two worlds of the living and the dead, separated by water. Africans who die travel to the land of the dead, where they change their skins and become white. Except in the case of the very old, such transfers (deaths) are believed to be caused by witches, who profit by selling the souls of their victims or are able to put them to work and profit by their labor. The slave trade is understood in this way, and modern industrial accidents, as when a worker is killed by a crane in the port of Matadi, are believed to be the visible results of contracts between Europeans and individual BaKongo who seek to better themselves by becoming white (MacGaffey 1968; MacGaffey 1986a, 62).

The land of the dead (*nsi a bafwa*) is variously underground, in the forest, in the cemetery, across the river, across the Atlantic, and under the water. It is called Mpemba, which is the same word as *mpemba,* chalk or white kaolin clay. White, besides being the color of the dead, is also the color of innocence, purity, and enlightenment. The color of movement between the worlds is red, like sunrise and sunset, or like blood. Accordingly, corpses and the bodies of those who returned from initiation were painted red. The following paraphrase of Babutidi's description of the land of the dead is typical, although some of its details are contradicted in other accounts.

> The soul does not remain long in the grave, but emerges and goes to become a ghost in the land of the dead. He first climbs a hill and then descends into Mpemba. On arrival, he asks for his relatives, those of his clan who died before him. They will interrogate him as to name and origins; if his answers are not satisfactory he will be treated as a slave. Once admitted, he is painted with red camwood so that his body becomes parti-colored; a party is held for him. The dead marry and have children; they are more prolific than we, and disease is unknown. They visit the white people to trade with them. There are rich chiefs among them, but poor people also. They can eat pepper without dying again. A *nganga* can see the dead on the strength of his *kundu* [internal witchcraft gland]. The dead may help themselves to your belongings, but you can call *nganga* Mpodi, who will go to Mpemba and ask for an explanation. If the dead have good reasons, he will come back and tell you so; if not, they will return your things to you. (Cahier 6)

Specially qualified individuals can go to the land of the dead in their sleep; some are able to go and come back by dying and rising again from the dead. The special powers of chiefs, diviners, and *banganga* were acquired in rituals of initiation during which they were believed to make such journeys. "There is not the remotest notion that death can be a cessation of being" (Bentley 1889, 64). As the quoted text shows, dealings with the otherworld were modeled on those that obtained between villages among the living.

Mpemba contrasts with the world of the living in time as well as in space; it is also the world of night and of sleep, although to the dead themselves what we call "night" is daytime.

> To see the dead, apply to your own eyes the ocular secretions (*bihota*) of a dog. When going to the forest to get medicines for acquiring wealth, tell nobody; the best time to go is at noon, or just after, for at that time the dead will be fast asleep. If you go at the wrong time and they are still awake and see you, they will laugh at you and you will fall seriously ill. (Matunta, 314)

In the forest, which is their village, the dead repeat the activities and social forms of their descendants. "We say they are in the forest, but they say it is we who live in the forest, they who are in the village" (Diafwila, in MacGaffey 1986, 49). Wild animals are the livestock of the dead; their chief is the leopard, who, like his counterpart among the living, kills both by day and by night, in the village and in the forest.

Cosmological assumptions explain why Kongo reports of the European invasion and its violence convey an impression of the soldiers and missionaries markedly different from the ones they gave of themselves. In French Congo, Matunta was told that the first white people came from up river, traveling by water; these strangers must have been H. M. Stanley's party in 1877. They were not taken for living people, but as blacks who had already died, been "skinned" (*bunuka*), and come back here to the land of the living (*nseke a mpanga*). It was supposed that the great chief Na Bidi, recently deceased, had returned to his village on the bank of the Congo. Stanley's porters were taken for the chief's dead servants. "Oh look, his servants, their bodies have been rebuilt, but they no longer remember their language and have become foreigners (*bantsangani*), skin-changers from deep in the earth! (*bamatalu ma londo*)." So people came from far and near to see Na Bidi risen from the dead. Others fled, fearing that a malevolent *nganga* had created this spectacle. "Others said, we all die; to this day, many think that Europeans are black people, we die, we change our skins in the country of the deep (*nsi na vinda*)" (Matunta, 296). Stanley wrote, "They have a curious idea in their heads that I must have come from some place south of the Bakongo country and floated down some great body of water" (Stanley 1879, v. 2:414).

Loko, writing from the Manyanga market area, reported what may have been an earlier incident on the same expedition. The local people took the travelers for the following of chief Niakunu, clan Mazinga, who had died that same day and, as they supposed, become white. The white man appealed to the people to help him cross the river in the boat (*nzaza*) he had built. When they tried it turned out not to be strong enough, because it was made with poor planks that split. So they went to get a very large canoe in which they crossed, though at that place the traverse was very difficult (Loko, 153). It would be nice to think that this was the incident that Stanley recorded on July 13, 1877: "Three chiefs, after we had camped, advanced and offered their services, which were at once engaged, and the next morning 409 natives conveyed the canoes and boat below the fall in admirable style, though one small canoe was wrecked. . . . The Ntombo Mataka people I regarded as the politest people I had encountered in Africa, and they certainly distinguished themselves by a nobility of character as rare as it was agreeable" (Stanley 1879, v. 2:428). A little further on, however, he met others of whom he said, "The Basundi are a most wretched, suspicious and degraded race, quarrelsome and intensely disposed to be affronted" (434).

Much further from the Congo, at Kiobo in Mayombe, Mvubu reported that the first white people he knew of were missionaries; later it was said that government agents were coming to oppress the people and to do terrible things, but nothing of the sort happened. The elders, however, thought that when children went to school they would have to hand over [the souls of] their fathers and mothers as the price of their initiation. White people were believed to be witches who bought people and ate them; their canned meat was human flesh.[17] They were said to have come from the water and to be *minkisi,* not human beings, because of their white skin, their eyes, and their incomprehensible speech. Their excrement was taken to use in composing *minkisi* (Mvubu, 343–44). "Their white skin is a kind of shirt; they change, as we black people do when we are sold in Europe by witches. We think that a body pale like that has no strength" (Kiananwa, 70).

Such accounts describe interpreted events, experiences to which explanatory comment was intrinsic; they are not simply reports of "what happened." The outsider may want to say, "This was the event, this the interpretation that followed," but in fact the event and its interpretation simultaneously constituted the experience. Nor is the account simply wrong. The Kongo explanation for the strange habits of Europeans— their aversion to pepper, for example, their tendency to take naps at noon, and their enthusiasm for sea-bathing—by the "fact" that they were natural inhabitants of the otherworld is parsimonious and in that sense eminently scientific. As an anthropology of cultural difference it compares not unfavorably with some European anthropologies.[18]

The needs of the invaders for labor and for foodstuffs to support their enterprises, particularly the transport from Matadi to Kinshasa, prompted them to establish inland posts:

> The coming of the white people of the government (*mindele mia Bula Matadi*) was a matter of amazement and fear, because the government made war on the people and captured them. The whites came to build at Bulu, which was their first station on our bank of the river. Bula Matadi came at speed, they saw his boat being rushed down the river. He asked for permission to build, but the chief, whose name was Mantadi, refused. The white man accepted this rebuff, but he said to them [in crude vehicular KiKongo], "Just you wait, I'll come and burn your village." He returned across the river to Mbanza Ngungu, from whence he came. But the people argued with the chief, and they agreed that the white man could build, so they called to him to return. He came back, and had his soldiers (*zimbulu-mbulu*) clear a place. At that time the missionary (*mundele wanganga Nzambi*) came to the village and built a place. After they had built, they began to appoint chiefs and headmen (*zimfumu zampalata ye bikapita*). (Loko, 153)

> The first headman was Mavwemba, the first warrant chief was Mantadi. The work of the headman was to arrange the transport of loads; that of the chief, to govern and to provide the required porters to the soldiers. The white man created the districts of Nganda and Nsende. The name of the first white man at Bulu was Bivumu, "Big Belly"; when he had set up in Bulu, he turned his attention to another site, called Kinsungu. There a fight broke out [in November 1883] in which the white man called Mapeka ["the traveler"; Henri Plancq, a Belgian officer] was killed; another [Baltus], called Lema-Lema ["the brusque"], fled, badly wounded, to the missionaries at Nganda. The fight broke out because he wanted to take the place and the houses of the people by force. Another European came with more troops; his name was Masiampa. He built in another place which had not participated in the fight. The people were oppressed, obliged to provide food and labor. (Loko, 153)[19]

Ndibu Kapita Joseph reported that at first he fled from white people from fear that if he saw one he would die, but a brother of his persuaded him to speak to a missionary who was visiting the local market. About this time, Bindele Biakwanga was appointed chief by the government; he went around the villages obliging the inhabitants to send in chickens and bananas. Ndibu persuaded them to comply, for their own safety, and was appointed headman (*kapita*) on account of his name (Cahier 348). In 1911 Bindele was assassinated while collecting market taxes at Manyanga (MacGaffey 1986b, 266).

Religious Commissions

The cosmology outlined above and its persistence to the present time explains why Kongo (and, more broadly, Congolese) interaction with Europeans has often resembled a dialogue of the deaf, each party hearing only its own voice but assuming that it has been understood. Cosmological givens at the most general level govern secondary assumptions and practices, which in turn generate many of the problems of translation to be considered in the next chapter. Certain terms and values are central both to ritual practice and to the task of interpreting Kongo political thought in a foreign language.

Politics is about power and its uses; all Kongo cults are regarded as means by which initiates can acquire power from the land of the dead, for which they must exchange the souls of some of their own relatives. Such a transaction is only reprehensible if, on balance, the public good is judged to have suffered; in that case, the agents will be accused of *kindoki,* although legitimate power holders must also have *kindoki.* At the end of the nineteenth century missionaries were thought of as priests of a particularly powerful cult whose members could "eat people," *dia bantu,* that is, cause their deaths in order to sell their souls abroad. The baptized were supposed to be acquiring *kindoki,* in exchange for which members of the clan of the baptized would die—the missionaries would eat them (Loko, 153).[20]

The several uses to which occult power can be put define a set of roles, or commissions. Commissions differ from offices in that there is no fixed number of them as elements of the social structure and at the death of the incumbent there need be no replacement. The principal roles of concern to us are those of chief, defined by use of the power to kill in the interests of the community, and *ngang'a nkisi,* defined by the use of remedial powers directed to particular ends. In addition, the BaKongo recognize priests of spirits called *bisimbi,* generally benevolent but also capricious, whose powers affect local communities; they are intensely preoccupied by the presumed activities of witches (*bandoki*), who are their own malevolent neighbors using the power to kill for personal ends. This set of commissions, with their associated functions, is common to the speakers of Western Bantu languages, although it has varied considerably in its content over time and space, in Kongo as elsewhere. In modern times the idea of chiefship persists although there are no longer any traditionally invested Kongo chiefs.[21]

Even where there were no specially consecrated chiefs, to be effective at all in their responsibility to protect their dependents, lineage elders disposed of a power of death called "witchcraft for looking after the clan" (*kindoki kya ndundila kanda*). Although this power was believed to help the elders to defeat witches in nocturnal struggles, sometimes they were obliged to hand over the souls of one or more of their own dependents as the price of security for the majority. The ability to kill other human beings is something that ordinary people do not have; it is obtained from the land of the dead in the course of some kind of initiation. Though its effects are perceived in this world, it is obtained and exercised in occult fashion, in the land of the dead, at night.

An invested chief was supposed to have acquired not only the power to kill but the power of life obtained in the rites of installation from the tutelary *simbi* spirit of his domain. As Lutete reports, such a ritual declared "The chief is *simbi,* the chief is leopard" (Lutete, 235). In the most general sense such a chief, whatever his particular title, · was *mfumu a nsi,* "local chief." Invested chiefs combined the powers appropriate to the government both of lineages, whose members were dispersed, and of lineally heterogeneous local communities (women married out of their clans and men commonly lived in the villages of their fathers or grandfathers). The word *nsi,* meaning "country," but also "below," did not imply a bounded domain but a center of power that was physically represented by the cemetery of the chiefs, the cave in which candidates for chiefship were tested by the spirits, or a grove in the forest where the *nkisi nsi* (the *nkisi* of the domain) was buried. Local communities turned to *bisimbi* for favorable harvests, freedom from epidemics, and a high birthrate.

In economically marginal areas, a chief might be invested, on the recommendation of a diviner, only in the case of an individual or epidemic illness. Toward the coast, during the time of the slave trade, there may have been chiefs whose administrative responsibilities were continuous and required a perpetual office; even in such cases, as far as the evidence goes, it was likely that the death of a chief was followed by a prolonged interregnum while the successor accumulated enough wealth for the rites of installation or rival contenders competed for support. In principle, where the wealth generated by the trade sufficed, there might be hierarchies of titles, but rank order was not well defined. Chiefly titles that were acquired competitively consecrated individual accumulations of wealth and power. "Investiture is about getting money. A man is likely to think about being invested if he has a great deal of money. . . . [If] a chief had many followers and much wealth but his following and his wives died off, and his powers were not as they had been, his authority faded away and people no longer respected him" (Kinkela, 94).

The power of death, acquired by a chief or headman from his or her matrilineal ancestors, seems to be related to the real-life function of lineage heads in regulating lineage membership by distinguishing free-born members from slaves and by trading in the latter.[22] It is notable that the word for "chief," *mfumu,* also means a free-born member of the a clan, as opposed to a slave.[23] Supposedly, true members of the lineage could trace their pedigree in the female line to a founding ancestor; those whose forebears had been assimilated as purchased slaves or as refugees occupied an inferior status. In practice, the legitimacy or otherwise of one's pedigree was a political matter, governed ultimately by force. Slaves were not entitled to become chiefs or headmen (though some of them eventually did), could not be responsible for their own civil affairs (such as marriage and lawsuits), and were at more risk than free persons of being sold or of being sacrificed in rituals that celebrated the power and wealth of chiefs. One of the soothing fictions that accompany accounts of the slave trade is that those who were sold were "criminals"; in fact, they were political losers who might or might not have committed some crime.

Initiation to a magico-political title required political support and relative wealth, as we shall see. "Chiefs" in this sense emerged only at nodes in the commercial network where wealth could be accumulated. Elsewhere, governmental functions and public rituals were assured by lineage headmen and the owners of *minkisi. Minkisi* (in the singular, *nkisi*) are ritual complexes exhibiting all the ambiguity of *kindoki,* "witchcraft," the kind of occult power which anybody of social importance should have, although one can never be sure that those who have it are using it for good. The primary moral connotation of *nkisi,* like that of *kindoki,* is that it is anti-social, the supposed user being open to the accusation that in benefiting himself he necessarily did harm to . others. In theory, chiefs, who uphold the public good, are opposed to *minkisi,* and indeed Kongo history from the fourteenth to the twentieth centuries reports campaigns against these devices. We read that in the east no *nkisi* could be placed in the hut containing the basket of ancestral relics. "Formerly, the chief, priest of the cult of the ancestors, could not keep one even in another hut. This spatial separation marked the distinction of domains" (Van Wing 1959, 346). Nevertheless, chiefs not only included *minkisi* among their ritual equipment but, as we shall see, were themselves literally *minkisi.*[24]

Whereas chiefly titles were specific to particular clans and the communities they dominated, but benefited the public generally, *minkisi* usually controlled particular diseases or other afflictions of concern to individuals. The oldest and most powerful *minkisi,* however, had many functions and were usually owned by particular clans, whose chiefly titles incorporated the name of their *nkisi.* In practice, therefore, the distinction between personal and public concerns was thoroughly obscure, as it usually is in politics the world over.

The owner and operator of *minkisi* was *nganga,* or *ngang'a nkisi,* the initiated expert who deployed the power of life for the benefit of individual clients in exchange for payment.[25] Ideal Kongo society is not libertarian; BaKongo do not believe that the pursuit of self-interest is conducive to the greatest good of the greatest number. Personal profit is always supposed to be achieved at the expense of others; competition gives rise to jealousy, *kimpala,* which is the source of witchcraft. The *nganga* defends individuals against the witchcraft of others, and against the ill will of spirits; though his activity as *nganga* does not open him or her to accusation, he is under suspicion of also using his powers illegitimately, of being in fact a witch. The difference between innocent and anti-social activity lies not in the activity itself but in the moral judgment rendered about it, supported by political power. The chiefs themselves, in real life if not in the abstract, were also *nganga* and therefore open, like anyone else, to the accusation of being witches. In short, these values and labels are not descriptions of what anyone in fact did; they are the currency of political dispute.

To "be" a witch (*ndoki*) was simply to be the object of a successful accusation, carried through in an institutionalized manner. One who believed himself, on account of disease or misfortune, to be the victim of witchcraft, consulted a diviner such as *nganga* Ntadi, the operator of *nkisi* Ntadi (from *tala,* to look at); the person accused by the diviner might have to undergo testing by an ordeal such as Nkasa or Mbundu (MacGaffey 1991, 10–32).[26]

At first sight, the witch is a figure very different from the chief, but in fact to "be" a chief was to have undergone, like the witch, a qualifying ritual. Both figures had to dispose of the ambivalent power called *kindoki* by which they caused death, and both were credited with such activities as flying about at night and doing combat with other possessors of occult power while ordinary people lay decently asleep. Even *minkisi* behaved similarly; one of the components of *nkisi* Lunkanka was a piece of tortoise shell, "because the tortoise goes about in the bush looking for things that it eats, but when it sees a human being it immediately draws its head inside, so as not to be seen. So likewise Lunkanka can hide herself as the tortoise does and not be seen by witches and other *bakisi.* If there are other *bakisi* about, they might fight the whole night long" (MacGaffey 1991, 140).

An important difference between witches and chiefs lay in the fact that chiefs represented hierarchy and redistributive order; witches on the other hand formed egalitarian associations called *kitemo,* based on the principle of fair shares. This latter kind of organization was and is also the means for petty capital accumulation, each participant paying his dues and drawing in turn on the resulting fund. Here is part of the negotiation in such a group, as imagined by Konda Jean:

> So one says to the other, "Give me your mother." But he says, "Oh, my mother, no. I don't think so." "Well, your brother then." "Oh, my brother, no, I couldn't." And so on,

until the witch agrees to hand over someone. Then he closes off the victim's voice, or removes his arm or leg. Later the arm or leg that has been handed over will develop a sore because the witch has taken its essence (Cahier 120; Janzen and MacGaffey 1974, 46).

The sinister *kitemo* of the night symmetrically inverts the daylight *kitemo* of ordinary traders, who contribute a small amount of money each week so that each may in turn be allowed to use the accumulated fund; witches, in contrast, share out each week the body of the relative that each is obliged, sooner or later, to contribute. Anybody seen to do well can fall under suspicion of witchcraft, simply because doing better than your neighbor is what witchcraft is all about—they are the same thing.[27]

> Although witches recognize one another, no witch can ever admit to himself that he is one. Non-witches just use their eyes. If they see a woman who always seems to have money, they know she operates a money *kundu*. If they see a hunter who always hits his quarry they know he has composed a gluttony *kundu*. Who eats people eats game in the forest. (Lunungu, 170)[28]

That is not all: Wealthy people are admired for their ability to consume, to "eat" (*dia*), but witches are supposed literally to consume the substance of others, to "eat people" (*dia bantu*); although they do this "at night," in a mysterious fashion, the evidence may be visible in the morning in the form of bones lying around the base of the silk-cotton tree in which the *kitemo* convened. Yet the silk-cotton tree, *mfuma*, the tallest tree in the forest, is proverbially analogous to the chief, *mfumu*![29] Chiefs (and in Zaire the President of the Republic and his associates) were believed to increase their power by acquiring the vital force of their victims.

These terms—*mfumu, nganga, kindoki, nkisi*—constitute a set whose significance is simultaneously moral, political, and even economic. In English translation, these functions attract discrete vocabularies, just as the marked and unmarked senses of the words, related to contextual judgments, call for different glosses which inevitably and misleadingly resolve their intrinsic ambiguities. Even to call the associated concepts "religious" on the ground that they refer to "spiritual beings" may mean merely that they are not part of our experience.

Ethnography and the Closing of the Frontier[30]

Missionaries and the military agents of Léopold II's Free State spent the early years of their occupation of Lower Congo penetrating difficult terrain inhabited by autonomous, largely unknown, and frequently hostile communities. In a relationship of direct confrontation the leaders of these communities, as individuals known by name, had to be induced to agree to "treaties" allocating land or political rights to the invaders. To help them in this task the invaders, like the explorers before them, needed African assistants, many of whom made a career of this work. For Protestant missionaries the next task after establishing a base was to learn the language and customs of the people; the turn of the century was therefore a period rich in ethnography and in anecdotal description of frontier life. R. Thornton has described how the "discovery" of Africa was a "discovery for paper," a production of texts that fell into two genres destined for two different audiences:

> [In] reports that appeared in the evangelical and mission society bulletins, the narrator addressed the reader directly, in the first person; and, while not self-reflective, nevertheless revealed the European observer in the context and process of observation. . . . In the ethnographic monograph, however, patterned after "objective" scientific genres, the reader lost sight of the narrator, the observer himself, and was presented only with a kind of disembodied narrative. (Thornton 1983, 507)

As the foreigners consolidated their control the relationship between them and the natives became hierarchical and the names of individual Africans tended to be replaced in documentary records by the numbers of healthy adult males or of persons baptized, of revenues collected and schools opened. The invading organizations no longer reported news of the frontier when there was no frontier; ethnography disappeared with the relationship of confrontation. The image of Self replaced the image of the Other.

In Lower Congo many missionaries wrote in both genres; a sharp contrast appears between their comments in mission context on the "darkness" of indigenous culture and their dispassionate ethnographic reporting of it. The most dedicated of them was the Swede K. E. Laman (Söderberg 1985). The Swedish Covenant Church (Svenska Missionsförbundet, SMF) acquired Mukimbungu from the American Baptists in 1886 and subsequently built stations as follows, in the area north of the Congo that came to be known as Manianga: Kibunzi, 1888; Diadia, 1888 (reduced to an outstation in 1906); Nganda, 1890; Londe (Matadi), 1892; Kingoyi, 1900; Madzia (in French Congo), 1909; Musana (also in French Congo), 1910; Kolo (in French Congo, but to the north), 1916. These dates show the Swedes pioneering a colonial advance northward into essentially unconquered territory between the principal Belgian route and bases just south of the Congo and the corresponding French government apparatus in the Niari valley between the coast and Brazzaville.

On his arrival in Matadi in 1891 Laman (1867–1944) was given responsibility for the Protestant bulletin, *Minsamu Miayenge,* which began to appear monthly in 1892. Newly literate converts eagerly subscribed. Laman made the mastery of KiKongo his major work, developing an unrivaled expertise. An autodidact, he corresponded with the German linguist C. Meinhof and published an exhaustive grammar of the language (Laman 1912) and a dictionary which long remained the greatest achievement in Bantu linguistics (Laman 1936). He also made special studies of fish and of traps used in fishing and hunting, among other subjects.

The Cahiers

To ascertain the manners and customs of the natives during the period of initial penetration and conquest, many territorial agents and missionaries made use of questionnaires or invited literate converts to write essays for them. By far the most thoroughgoing of these ethnographic endeavors was Laman's. I have been unable to find an exact model for his questionnaire; perhaps he composed it himself. His basic categories were:

1. history
2. geography
3. appearance of the people
4. food and drink
5. care of the body
6. houses
7. food production
8. division of labor
9. markets

10. pregnancy
11. sex, marriage
12. diseases, death, and burial
13. ownership, loans, services
14. authority, social control
15. rules, adjudication
16. villages
17. government
18. arts and crafts

A second and highly productive series of questions, which I have not been able to reconstruct fully, dealt with beliefs and rituals.

20. songs, games, and stories
23. sleep and dreams
24. the dead
26. *bisimbi* and mountains
27. father's clan
28. powers of *minkisi*
29. *minkisi*

30. *minkisi*
31. composition of *minkisi*
32. sickness and treatment
33. other uses of *minkisi*
34. the poison ordeal
37. cursing and blessing
38. taboos

This questionnaire is far better adapted to local realities than others in use in Belgian Congo at the time and is unique in that it is addressed not to Europeans but to Africans. "The object of the mission," Laman wrote, in English, in a circular to missionaries, "should be to try to get such a copious native literature that the missionaries might be able to find the people's own manner of speaking and reasoning. This literature ought to be printed and translated, because it will be of the highest value for the coming missionaries in the study of the language and of the people and then for science and the coming generations of the people" (Söderberg 1985, 161). As the manuscripts came in, Laman added detailed supplementary questions grounded in his already considerable knowledge of Kongo culture. The product amounted, in Laman's estimate, to 10,000 manuscript pages, written in KiKongo in 429 school notebooks (cahiers) that dealt with every aspect of Kongo culture. This archive is unique in African studies.

Among the sixty-seven respondents, at least forty-nine belonged to the SMF; at least six belonged to the CMA. The others belonged to the British or American Baptist missions, or were of unidentifiable affiliation. The ethnographic coverage includes all of Manianga, with additional material from, to the north and east, French Congo; to the west, the eastern edge of Mayombe; to the south (across the Congo), Mukimbungu and little else. Individual responses differed greatly in length and detail; only the shorter and less interesting notebooks go through the questionnaire systematically. Some of the replies were perfunctory. Mbaku Simon wrote briefly and with some hostility: "Why are you asking all these questions?" (Mbaku, 325). Only one notebook was written by a woman, Nsakala Elisa.

The most productive writers were Laman's own closest associates at the mission stations of Kinkenge, Kingoyi, Nganda, Mukimbungu, Diadia, Lolo, and Musana, converts and teachers who participated in his enterprise out of a sense of their national interests and wrote long essays about what interested them (MacGaffey 1991, vii; Map 1). To them Laman addressed supplementary questions at what is often an astonishing level of detail. When Kavuna went north to Kolo and began research there, Laman gave him the following list of questions: How do their clan names compare with ours? What are the oldest clans? If they have praise-names, or stories of origin, write them down. What was the first clan to arrive? Who were the greatest chiefs and what were their deeds? Government and laws? (Kavuna, 62). The most voluminous single contribution is that of Lutete of Lolo, who by Laman's count wrote 1,200 out of the total of 10,000 pages.[31]

The Authors

The names of a few of Laman's collaborators, particularly those who assisted him in his translation of the Bible, are recorded in mission literature, but biographical details are scarce.[32] Most of them were born during the early years of European intrusion; they joined the missions as boys and became their pioneer catechists and teachers. They were attracted by the frightening power and strangeness of the European camps and by the possibility of employment as servants, by which one could earn knives, cloth, and other special goods. Kilola Esai described his own conversion:

> I was living in the village when I heard that a missionary had come to Nsweka and was killing many elephants. The people accepted him on account of the meat. Then, after building a house, he began to take in boys to teach them to read and write, paying each one a knife. So I was happy in my heart to hear this and wanted to go to the mission to read, so that I could have my knife, but my uncle forbade me, saying, "Which one of your relatives will you hand over at the mission [by witchcraft, as payment for magical knowledge]? Go there, and it will cost you an arm and a leg!" (*Minsamu Miayenge* 1903, no. 2)

Eventually Kilola earned a little money by acting as porter for a Kongo teacher, who advised him to work for the missionaries when he was a little older. He made his way to Nganda, where he learned to read and write and was baptized, at the age of about seventeen, in 1895. Other converts were escaping from a variety of pressures in their own communities, including forced labor, witchcraft accusations, and the lack of other economic opportunities. Kavuna Simon recalled his pleasure when, after waiting on mission tables in Nganda for two years, he came to Mukimbungu for schooling and found himself living in a brick house that kept out the cold. Kiananwa Abeli, the first Kongo contributor to *Minsamu Miayenge* (in 1892), declared, "God sent the white man to teach us better things; we wear good clothes, have good houses and can travel wherever we like without fear of *nkasa* [poison ordeal] or kidnapping."

Teachers and other converts were not, however, admitted to the new order on equal terms with white people; as they developed into a distinct group in colonial society, the record shows the development of a political consciousness among them. In 1908, at one of the annual meetings of black teachers, called for purposes of religious instructions, Kiananwa indicated the existence of some degree of tension by asking whether they could meet by themselves, without the presence of white people. Two years later, when the government, as part of its reform of local administration, imposed taxation from which Catholic teachers were excused, the teachers sent a delegation including Babokidi, Matunta, Lumbu, and Demvo to protest. The political intentions of the teachers were also directed against some practices of the missions themselves. In 1912, many teachers, apparently feeling that their grievances were not being met, boycotted the meeting. Those who attended demanded an explanation of the budget: "How is the money collected in the churches here used to further the work of God?" (Mindoki). "What is the policy for paying teachers?" (Matunta). "Could not married teachers be paid a little more?" (Ntungu). "Why are we not paid while on sick leave?" (Lutete). The missions decided that a teacher on leave for a whole month could receive half pay.

Besides their concern for their personal economic interests, the teachers were aware of themselves as leaders of a new kind of community, that on which colonial usage conferred the label "tribe." In 1910, Kavuna Simon published an article about respect for the KiKongo language which anticipated by forty years the program of the Kongo political party, the Alliance des Bakongo. "What is KiKongo?" he first asked, and explained that it was the language of the BaKongo, those who lived in Lower Congo. All three of these entities (language, tribe, province) were new. Missionary work in translating the Bible, teaching literacy, and standardizing vocabulary was creating a KiKongo which was in many ways a European language (see Chapter 3). The geographical and ethnic identity conferred on Lower Congo by colonial administrative practice defined it as a unit in contrast to, and in latent competition with, other "tribes." We BaKongo, wrote Kavuna, must respect our language, speak it at all times, and not allow it to be corrupted. In the years immediately before independence, the political implications of this message rapidly became apparent.

Exercising conspicuous leadership among their fellow teachers and conscious of themselves as members of an emerging elite, Laman's collaborators were engaged in defining their culture and its values in contradistinction to those of others, African as well as European, and creating for the future a record of a vanishing past. They knew they were participating in a collective endeavor; they reported on their field trips (Babutidi went from Kinkenge to Mayombe by way of Matadi in 1916 and again in 1917) and sometimes compared notes on their findings. After a series of articles in KiKongo in *Minsamu Miayenge* in which Laman first published the results of his researches into the history of the BaKongo, Lunungu Moise at Nganda wrote to congratulate him:

> We should not be hostile to someone who writes up our history in a book, for who knows whether the generations to come will know how to preserve tradition. Already it is difficult to inquire from the elders about the rules they used to observe. It is good that our country should change, but we should examine the skills and customs of other countries to see whether they are good for the soul and the body. (*Minsamu Miayenge* 1916, no. 10)

Their incorporation in the new colonial society made it possible for the teachers to be ethnographers. Above all, they approached Kongo institutions as strangers, even though they continued to participate in some of them (Janzen 1985, 235).[33] As strangers they were obliged to conduct field research (for which Laman paid them). Scraps of information in *Minsamu Miayenge* and in the notebooks hint at the character of a massive ethnographic undertaking. Kiananwa Abeli, visiting Kisiasia, a village near the northern frontier, wrote:

> There are not many people. They plant trees all round their houses, and carve wooden plates and mugs. They do not wear much clothing, just a raffia square before and behind. They smear their bodies with red and black cosmetics and make their hair very long with the same materials. They smell terrible. They keep close to their village for fear of kidnapping, and there is much fighting. If a village chief dies, his wives smoke his body for five or six months. At the burial there is a big feast and they carry his body around the neighboring villages. (Kiananwa in *Minsamu Miayenge* 1904, no. 4)

Babutidi Timotio described a return trip he made from Kinkenge to Mayombe by way of Mukimbungu to make further inquiries on certain topics. From Matadi he went north to Kionzo and Vungu where, he reported, they kept up the old customs, installing chiefs and initiating boys to Nkimba. Kavuna Simon, who was from the south, worked for Laman among the BaBembe in Kolo on the Niari River in 1916. "It is a fine village," he wrote, "but the people are as we used to be, naked, in darkness, and their customs evil. Any man on a journey carries five weapons with him. When they sit down they fail to tuck in their clothes properly no matter who is present, sister, mother-in-law, or white man." Their language was difficult to understand, full of r's, but he was making progress in it and had begun to preach. Kavuna became one of Laman's principal informants on the BaBembe, and on the whole his reporting is good. "Rumors," he remarks, "are not reliable, but I will try to say what I have heard from the elders" (Cahier 54). Malumba Benyamin found that the elders were not always cooperative: "It is quite difficult to understand everything, because the elders are very suspicious when we start to talk about traditional matters. They think that when we write down their names in a notebook we will eat them by witchcraft. So I was not able to do more than write down the names of the clans without interpreting them" (Cahier 270). When Matunta, one of the most industrious contributors, came to the last of Laman's questions, "Are there any other kinds of *bisimbi*?" he wrote in evident fatigue, "Oh goodness, I don't know, maybe the elders would know; I'm just a child, I know very little!"

The teachers learned the art of discursive prose for the benefit of foreigners and future, literate generations. They showed their awareness of the properties of the new medium by including in their texts parenthetical glosses and interpretations, sometimes tabulating their information, or advising the reader with a remark such as, "For conjurations, see *nkisi* Mukwanga Yulu, and for curses, Mwe Kongo" (Nsemi, 390). Occasionally they added notes on the names of their informants, what they paid them, or the difficulties of research. In October 1916, Lunungu noted two days' fieldwork and 80 cents in informants' fees. At the end of Cahier 409 we read, "Ntwalani is the writer, Na Nsongi the informant" (*nkambi a mambu*). The schedule of questions, despite its relative sympathy with Kongo culture, represented an ethnographic perspective foreign to the writers; concluding his account of Lulendo, a chiefly title, Wamba Enoki wrote:

> It is difficult for us of the young generation to write all that concerns the elders of former times, for our fathers did not have the skill of writing, but some things we can attempt. It is difficult to interpret all of Tata Laman's questions. (Cahier 424)

Asked to describe the physical appearance of his people, David Mato wrote, "Some are tall, some are short; tall is preferred. We hear with our ears and see with our eyes" (Cahier 279).

To some extent the Kongo writers shared the sense of European writers of two different audiences for which distinct rhetorical forms were appropriate. At this point in the imperial penetration of Africa, ethnography was established as a well-defined genre, marked by static and impersonal descriptions under conventional topic headings (Vansina 1987). In 1912, Matunta described the killing of a leopard near Musana. Greatly rejoicing, the villagers fetched a new cloth worth 20 francs in which to vest the royal victim, and carried it home; they seated their chief, honorably dressed, on the leopard and carried him about the village in a procession with his wives, flags waving before and behind, with dancing and singing. "See," wrote Matunta in the mission bulletin, "how in this country the people know how to respect an animal, but not the Maker of all animals and of man, too." His remark summarizes the devaluation of traditional chiefly titles in the new order and the distance from traditional institutions of which mission teachers like himself were conscious. Later he described the same event again in his role as ethnographer (Cahier 303), adding a few details but omitting all moral judgment.[34]

The Cahiers also show subtle differences from the ethnographic genre. They tend to describe particular chiefships rather than "Kongo chiefship" in general, including in the account stories (real or legendary) of the deeds of named individuals. Their accounts of *minkisi* and of witchcraft are often vividly imaginative or personal in tone. They are alert to differences between what they observe on their travels and the customs "back home." They tend to describe custom "as the elders remember it," but (as I will argue later) this preference for an ideal past is not simply the result of European prodding. As a function of personal interests and values, they vary considerably in the amount of space they devote to different sections of Laman's questionnaire (religion, agriculture, marriage practices), but they do not select their material for what Europeans might consider its exotic appeal. The principal limitation of the texts as ethnography is that with few exceptions they describe abstract, conventional practice, with no accompanying case studies of real individuals maneuvering in real situations.

The Kongo authors (all young men, with the exception of a couple of older men and one woman) varied in the extent of their alienation from indigenous culture. Kiananwa Abeli was perhaps born in 1880; in 1890 an American missionary newly arrived at the coast wrote home: "We are very much interested in two little Fiote boys who are here in charge of a Swedish missionary from upcountry. They sing gospel hymns very sweetly in their native Ki-Fiote. One of them, Kiananua, had his teeth filed sharp like a saw for fighting, before he knew Christ. Now he is in training to preach Jesus among his own people" (Lapsley 1893, 55).[35] In 1892, Kiananwa was the first Kongo contributor to *Minsamu Miayenge,* and he wrote for it often in later years. Five of his hymns are included in *Nkunga mia Kintwadi,* the Protestant hymnbook. He held responsible positions, first at Diadia, later at Kibunzi, often traveled to other mission stations to preach, and was well known for his opposition to alcohol, dancing, jewelry, and nudity. In 1897 he helped found the station at Kinkenge, and in 1903 he accompanied Laman on an ethnographic expedition to the north. In one of his articles in *Min-*

samu Miayenge, "Wherein lies the force of *minkisi*?" Kiananwa adopted a rationalistic approach to these complex rituals, arguing that the powers attributed to them were not derived from spirits, as the heathen supposed, but from healthful herbs created by God, who does not make anything in vain. It is not surprising that his ethnographic contributions dealt with *minkisi* only in generalities. On the other hand, Lutete Esaya's preferred topics were *minkisi, simbi* spirits, and the rituals and traditions of chiefship.

The notebooks do not provide a comprehensive picture of developments in Lower Congo at the time of writing. By virtue of their conversion to Christianity and their professional commitments as teachers and preachers, Laman's collaborators were absorbed into the small, exclusive world of the mission stations, which protected them from much of what was going on around them, including the effects and opportunities introduced by wage labor, the railroad from Matadi to Kinshasa that opened in 1898, and new forms of distraction and temptation. More than other converts, as the surviving photographs show, their dress and domestic life conformed to the European model (Axelson 1970, 283–88). Mayoka Yakobi was the only contributor to join the emergent bourgeoisie of small traders who brought cloth, tools, and other manufactured goods to the new, wage-earning rural population of plantation workers, mission employees, and cash crop farmers (see Appendix). Only incidentally do the texts document anything of the massive change in local administration effected by the new Belgian administration after 1908.

Since about a dozen of the most prolific contributors met at least annually at teachers' assemblies, even when they came from different stations, and felt themselves to be collaborating in a common project, it would be unrealistic to assume that their texts are entirely independent. To some unknown extent they were probably each other's informants and critics.

Because the product included an enormous mass of material compiled by many hands, arbitrary limitations had to be imposed in this study. The longest and richest of the political texts was written by Lutete Esaya in the mission station of Lolo (a substation of Vungu) in 1916. Accordingly, the principal geographic focus of this study is on eastern Mayombe, for which we have a considerable amount of material from the missionary ethnographer Bittremieux, a modern ethnographic report (Doutreloux 1967), and Norm Schrag's economic history (Schrag 1985).

The Monograph

As the notebooks came in, Laman read and annotated them in a mixture of Ki-Kongo and Swedish; often, it seems, he was able to interrogate the authors for clarification. He collected the Cahiers in alphabetical order by author and numbered them; internal evidence suggests that some notebooks were lost along the way. From his study of these materials Laman derived a number of articles published in Swedish in the 1920s; his *Dictionary* (1936) was largely based on the notebooks, although he also used published dictionaries and vocabularies. He retired from the mission in 1932.

Laman's major work was originally intended to be a collaborative undertaking. From the notebooks he selected the best passages on any given topic, arranged the topics more or less in the order of his original questionnaire, and had them typed verbatim, each extract followed by the name of the author. Among them he included contributions of his own, in KiKongo, identified by his initials; sometimes these passages report his own observations, sometimes they evidently summarize what informants told him. The whole runs to perhaps 2,500 pages.

This remarkable work, for which I have found no title, I call "Laman's KiKongo monograph" (LKM).[36] Although in his introduction to the *Grammar* (1912) he describes the people of Kongo as "sunk in sin and darkness," Laman's attitude toward Kongo practices was remarkably tolerant. He did, however, remove not only uninformative passages, including the entire contributions of some authors, but also many little indications of the process by which the information was gathered. For example, he crossed out as irrelevant the part of the following passage by Lunungu that I have enclosed in square brackets:

> [The matter of *kindakazi* is not well understood by our elders, but when I was in Mukimbungu talking to Kutanda, he said that] *kindakazi* was the same as *nkinda kiyazi.* On our side of the river *nkinda kiyazi* would be *nkinda bweno.* Such *nkinda* are safeguarded by creatures such as snakes, game animals or some other thing accepted as a *kinkonko,* a familiar. (Cahier 171)

Laman also deleted numerous pious Christian comments from Mindoki's accounts of the powers of *minkisi,* for example. As a result of such elisions, the monograph (hereafter referred to as LKM) tends to conform more closely to the ethnographic genre than do some of the original texts.

By the 1920s, when Europeans had generally relegated African cultures to history's trash can, the monograph had become an anachronism. Who would publish a set of volumes in KiKongo? By the time of his death in 1944, Laman had been persuaded to begin a reduced version in a Swedish translation, described in Chapter 3. Swedish colleagues finished the work, had it translated into English, and published it in Uppsala in four volumes called *The Kongo* (Laman 1953–68, vols 1–4 [LKI–IV]). The tendency toward ethnographic homogenization is still more marked in the English version than in LKM.

In dealing with this enormous volume of rich material over a period of years I have attempted to impose a degree of discipline by studying *all* of the texts in a given category, no matter how arbitrarily that category may have been defined. In *Art and Healing* (1991), I assembled all the texts that could be specifically associated with *nkisi* objects located in the Ethnographic Museum, Stockholm. Subsequently I translated all the texts that dealt with the *nkondi* category of *minkisi.* In this book I draw principally upon the *nkondi* texts and on all those that relate to chiefship.

3. TRANSLATION, EXOTICISM, BANALITY

*At every point and turn new surprises were met with, as the
richness, flexibility, exactness, subtlety of idea, and nicety of
expression of the language revealed themselves.*

—W. HOLMAN BENTLEY

*I am treating the act of communication as something very
extraordinary, so that the next step would be to lose faith in it
altogether.*

—WILLIAM EMPSON

Minkisi and chiefship comprise the principal forms of legitimate power as the Ba-Kongo understood it in 1900 and, in modified forms, as they still do. They form a continuum, from *minkisi* dedicated to purely individual concerns and, as such, regarded with suspicion as potentially illegitimate, to chiefship as the principal guarantor of social order, itself regarded nevertheless with some ambivalence. In between, chiefs relied heavily on major *minkisi,* objects which were themselves "chiefs." In turn, chiefs were also *minkisi,* treated at times as though they were objects.

To translate such concepts in an effort to understand them is to engage not simply in a philological or cognitive exercise but in what is and has been itself, ultimately, a political process: one more extension of the confrontation between European and Kongo political cultures. Laman's contributors, like the villagers of Mbanza Manteke in 1965, wrestled with the differences between what they thought of as a "chief," endowed with *kindoki,* and the European concept of the chief as a secular leader and administrator, the *chef médaillé* (MacGaffey 1970, ch. 11). Colonial administrators, like post- or neo-colonial commentators and statesmen trying to understand and perhaps manipulate the politics of Congo, Rwanda, or Cameroon, faced a similar problem from the opposite point of view; their temptation was to dissolve the problem by dismissing African political cultures.

The problems of translating KiKongo begin with orthography. The language has been written and printed since the sixteenth century, but general literacy only began to be introduced by Protestant missionaries in the 1880s. W. Holman Bentley, of the Baptist Missionary Society (BMS, British), published his *Dictionary* in 1887 and directed the first translation of the New Testament into KiKongo in 1893. The orthography used in these early works established the forms that are still used today, although

Congolese academics have begun to use fancier conventions. Because they began their work in Mbanza Kongo itself (São Salvador), the BMS used the dialect of that region as their model and carried it with them when they moved north into what became Zaire; on this model Laman commented that its extensive use of the apostrophe and of so-called articles, as well as the new meanings given to many words, made it very difficult for natives of other districts to read (Laman 1912, 11). The work of the SMF gave wider acceptance to a standardized version of the Central or "Mazinga" dialect; the independent work of the Belgian Scheut Fathers in Mayombe did much to set off modern KiYombe as a distinct dialect.

Ordinary written KiKongo makes no allowances for vowel length, semantically significant tone, or phonemes not recognized in English; it does not distinguish, for example, between a labio-dental and a bilabial voiced fricative, both of which appear as "v". Nor does it distinguish between what Laman later called "light" and "heavy" nasals (see below). This is the style used in Laman's own early work: the translation of the Bible (1905), *Masonukwa Manlongo;* the Protestant mission bulletin, *Minsamu Miayenge,* directed by him (1892–); and his *Grammar of the Kongo Language* (1912). This is also the way KiKongo is written by all the authors of his ethnographic note-books.

When Laman published his *Dictionary* (1936), he adopted the conventions sponsored at the time by the International African Institute. Among other less important innovations, he introduced indications of vowel length and tone, together with a new letter to show the difference between the two different /v/, and a contrast between vowels and semi-vowels (Laman 1936, x–xi). *Sala* (short vowel), to work, contrasts with *saala,* to remain; *kànga* (low tone), to bind, and *kánga* (high tone), to roast. He explains in the introduction that the principal vowel of a radical "is long when it is preceded by a semi-vowel or followed by a nasal group," such as /-mb/ or /-ng/. Readers of the *Dictionary* must understand that Kongo, for example, is to be pronounced *koongo,* Mbumba as *mbuumba;* an unexpected short vowel which is semantically significant is indicated by doubling the subsequent nasal, as *kánnga,* a kind of bird. In ordinary KiKongo, one writes *diata,* to walk, but the *Dictionary* writes *dyata,* which is read as *dyaata.* Laman also distinguished /n'/, /m'/, which he called heavy nasals (corresponding to /mu-/), from the "light nasals" /n/, /m/: thus, *n'kaaka* (pronounced with a glottal stop), squirrel, but *nkaaka* (pronounced *nkhaaka*), grandparent; *mbu,* mosquitoes, but *m'bu,* ocean; *wan'sidila salu,* "he promised him work," but *wansidila salu,* "he promised me work."[1]

Laman also had clear ideas about the morphology of KiKongo, that is, how the syllables should be grouped into words, but his collaborators did not follow these rules in their several manuscripts.

There are more complexities to the Laman system, but these examples are sufficient. He continues his introduction with a long and idiosyncratic account of "musical tone" which is virtually unusable because it confounds semantically significant tone with melodic intonation. In my experience, tone is much less significant in modern KiKongo than Laman indicates, but that is only one of a number of systematic impoverishments that have occurred during the twentieth century. By 1980, the younger generation in the towns no longer spoke KiKongo but Lingala, the national lingua franca.

Transcriptions

At some early point, Laman had the first eighty-one Cahiers typed verbatim, in the orthography of the manuscripts. Later the project was restarted, using conventions that showed vowel length, the two different nasals, and the difference between bilabial and labiodental /v/. This version, which I call the Monograph (LKM, see below), included only selections from the manuscripts but amounted to about 2,500 pages. His typist was Anna Nyvall, a Swedish missionary (1867–1938) whose long stays in Kongo gave her the knowledge of the language necessary to transcribe manuscripts that were often barely legible. Marginal typing instructions and annotations by Laman indicate that this work was done in 1920–1921. Numbers added to the manuscripts themselves indicate where selected passages are to be found in the typescript. This set of extracts offers linguistic information not available in the manuscripts and it is also, unlike many of them, highly legible; its disadvantage is that it omits many passages of interest and censors others. My transcriptions inconsistently use either the original orthography of the manuscripts or the improved version of the Monograph.

After the publication of the *Dictionary,* and given that his idea of publishing an enormous book in KiKongo was unlikely to find any support in an age when imperialists congratulated themselves on having replaced indigenous cultures with civilization, Laman began to reduce his Monograph in size and scope. The four volumes, eventually published as *The Kongo* (1953–1968), comprise a marvelously rich but at the same time enigmatic contribution to African ethnography (Janzen 1972). Although it is convenient to say, "According to Laman . . ." with reference to these volumes, it is often difficult to know what, in fact, was his contribution to the text without referring to the original manuscripts. The original idea of listing passages identified by author under ethnographic headings was abandoned. Many passages are reproduced as they were written by the Kongo authors, but the English text does not indicate who wrote what, nor when one extract ends and another, by a different author, begins. As a result, anthropologists using the volumes have been led astray.[2]

It is possible to annotate the English text (and sometimes also the *Dictionary*) to show the sources of the information. The introductory chapters of the first volume, even in the KiKongo version, turn out to be a hodgepodge of traditions of origin from which Laman was vainly trying to produce orderly history. On the other hand, the account of hunting techniques in the chapter on "Means of subsistence and occupations" is by Matunta (Cahiers 289–300), though the material on traps and nets is by Laman himself, who made a special study of the subject. Elsewhere, many individual paragraphs turn out to be the work of several hands, not always exclusively those of either Laman or his Kongo collaborators; a statement presented as a generalization may be derived from a single text referring to a local practice. The editor of the Swedish text, the anthropologist Sture Lagercrantz, facing the considerable problems generated by the length and cultural density of the materials, found it necessary to introduce explanatory comments from time to time and to eliminate what he regarded as repetitions. Passages that declare what "the natives" do are evidently not by native hands. It is also evident that in making translations Lagercrantz referred to the *Dictionary,* not always choosing the right entry.

KiKongo Written and Spoken

Protestant missions, in Kongo as elsewhere, taught converts to read so that they could study the Bible for themselves. Writing offered them the exciting possibility of communicating at a distance and created a new community of the literate. The Protestant monthly bulletin *Minsamu Miayenge* attracted 400 subscribers in its first year of publication, 1892; in five years the number had doubled. Contributors to *Minsamu Miayenge* clearly enjoyed reading news of events at other stations than their own. The first 1,000 copies of Laman's translation of the Bible (1904) sold out in two months at a price equivalent to a month's wages for an unskilled worker.

Writing not only represents language but transforms it: The speaker's relationship to the audience is "hot"; the writer's is relatively "cold." Effective speech has redundancy built into it because the audience has no opportunity to re-read an obscure passage. The speaker is able to "play" the audience by provoking reactions which can constitute a kind of dialogue; in Central Africa in particular, the form of public discourse is that of "call and response," dialogical rather than linear. Moreover, the speaker can probably count on a great deal of local knowledge shared with the audience, such as proverbs, songs, and references to current or historical events and personages. Public speeches are more likely to be politically intended, in that the occasion brings together speaker and audience for some specific purpose. Even the most perfunctory "speech act," in which the purpose is no more than to meet the ritual requirement that there be a speech, presupposes an immediate and particular relationship among the speaker, the occasion, and the audience which need not occur in the case of a library book, for example.

By the seventeenth century, written KiKongo was already a Europeanized language; as Bentley put it, describing the language of the Catechism of 1624 (the first surviving document in a Bantu language), it is "white man's KiKongo." The grammar and vocabulary may, in a formal sense, be authentic, but the linearity and economy of this and subsequent written forms of KiKongo eliminate both the redundancy and the interplay with the hearer or audience that give the spoken word its almost uninscribable form.[3] Semantic changes accompanied the formal ones induced by writing. Written forms of KiKongo were developed in specific contexts related to Christian evangelization. Protestant missionaries wanted their converts to be able to read the Bible for themselves and to sing Protestant hymns. Like the musical tunes, the translated hymns often followed their English originals word for word, but they have now become the standard accompaniment to Kongo funerals, Catholic as well as Protestant. There is thus a rough correspondence between "written KiKongo" and "Christian KiKongo."[4]

Problems

It would seem that with Laman's *Dictionary* in hand one would not find it difficult to translate documents on which the dictionary itself is based. Moreover, the published volumes of ethnography (LKI–IV) consist largely of translations of identifiable passages in these same documents. Translation would frequently be completely impossible without these aids, but many problems remain.[5]

Laman was not personally familiar with all the words in his 1,183-page dictionary, some of which he took from published sources. Many others were known to him only through their occurrence in particular manuscripts, from which he deduced their meaning. (For example, in Babokidi, Cahier 5, we read as the reply to a question about geophagy, a topic deemed important by ethnologists at the time, "Yes, red earth from termite hills is eaten, as is *mfundi* earth, but only by children." In the *Dictionary*: "*mfundi,* an earth eaten only by children.") It follows that in some instances the indications of tone and vowel length may not be reliable. Occasionally, of course, the original handwriting offers the possibility of more than one reading, and there are errors of transcription in subsequent versions—as, no doubt, there are in my own.

The *Dictionary*'s gloss on a given term may well be simply Laman's best guess as to what the word signifies in a passage from a particular manuscript. Sometimes in my translations in this book I have preferred a different interpretation, or one derived from multiple occurrences of the word. Such glosses are always compromises. It is rarely the case that no suitable equivalent can be found for a given word in context, but the chosen equivalent fails to evoke the same range of associated significances as the KiKongo term. The verb *koma* provides an example. In everyday modern use, *koma* means "to hammer," as in *koma nsonso,* "to hammer nails." In connection with the wooden figures (*nkondi*) into which nails were driven to provoke the spirit associated with them to take violent action, *koma nsonso* was not used; instead, a common expression was *koma nloko,* "to hammer a curse." This second expression could also be used to refer to provocations addressed, without nails or hammering, to other kinds of *minkisi* and also to chiefs. In such a case, "to arouse, provoke" would be a better gloss (see Chapter 6). The composition of an *nkisi* (*mpandulu*) was effected, in some accounts, by "stuffing" (*koma*) medicines into it. Nkisi Lemba might "arouse itself" by appearing in a dream to someone who was thereby summoned to compose the *nkisi* (Janzen 1982, 234).[6] To take the poison ordeal was *koma nkasa,* to provoke the poison. Lastly, still in the context of *nkisi* rituals, *koma* could mean "to hammer, to arouse" in a sexual sense.

One of the most elementary problems is that of gender. Pronouns and noun classes in Bantu languages are not gender specific, but this apparently inclusive language does not correspond to gender equality in social life; even though some women were and are more influential than most men, women in general take second place, as the Cahiers regularly reveal. In translation I have used the masculine pronoun and the generic "man" except where the text refers to, or is probably referring to, a woman. For example, a person drawing water is presumably female, since that is a woman's task.

In the Bantu languages, nouns are classified into classes, singular and plural, roughly comparable to gender classes in a language such as German, in that the members of each class tend to have semantic features in common. Each class is identified by a prefix with which qualifiers of the noun must agree. So *mu-/ba-* are the singular and plural prefixes for the personal class, whereas *ki-/bi-* is the class for cultural objects; a given stem may change its meaning when a different prefix is applied to it: *banganga,* ritual experts; *kinganga,* what *banganga* do or say; *bunganga,* the art or skill of the *banganga*. Noun classes, however, are grammatical categories, not defined by ontological realities; the semantic content of an expression must always be evaluated in context. The BaKongo (both the authors of the Cahiers and today's villagers) may put the same word in two different classes in the same sentence. So, *minkisi* and *bakisi, banganga* and *zinganga, minkondi* and *zinkondi, bisimbi* and *basimbi*. BaKongo do not distinguish as sharply as do Europeans between persons and objects; in a particular expression, there may be only a nuanced difference between *bakisi* (relatively personalized), for example, and *minkisi* (relatively objectified), or between *bankuyu* (ghosts) and *minkuyu* (the same spirits incorporated in fabricated objects). The meanings of both prefixes and stems vary somewhat from one dialect to another, as Laman's *Dictionary* shows; *minkisi* sometimes becomes *zinkisi*.

As there are no articles, definite or indefinite, one must often guess which English form to use. In the language as spoken, tone can take care of this problem, particularly in relative clauses.

Individual texts include more than one discursive genre. The narrative form which the authors learned from their missionary mentors frames songs (*nkunga*), proverbs (*ngana*), and quotations from the indigenous genres of *kinkulu, kinzonzi,* and *kinganga,* the verbal arts of, respectively, the headman, the debater or lawyer, and the ritual expert.[7] Discourse in these genres was deliberately intended to be obscure and exclusive, to impress the uninitiated with a sense of mysterious knowledge and to limit effective communication to a socially qualified elite. Buakasa, an anthropologist and native speaker of KiKongo who carried out extensive research on ritual and belief in the 1960s, remarks on the difficulty of interpreting ritual formulae, which may not be fully understood by the speakers themselves. Even for the ritual expert, the incomprehensibility of the formula confirms its mysterious character (Buakasa 1973, 259).[8] In theory, the meanings communicated in these genres were specific, for those in the know; in practice, the expressions were like poetry, in that they were capable, within conventional limits, of supporting a variety of interpretations (MacGaffey 1986a, 13–15, 27). To have one's interpretation accepted was to establish one's social authority in a particular context.

Insisting on the need to work within the categories of the language, Buakasa says that he has been led to make translations not very faithful to the spirit of French but, using French words, faithful to the spirit of KiKongo (Buakasa 1973, 7). What even a native speaker offers as "the" spirit of KiKongo is necessarily an interpretation beside which others could be placed, but I also have often found the "spirit" a better guide than the "letter."

In semantically extreme cases, certain expressions were simply what was traditionally said at a given juncture and had no other meaning. An example, which also testifies to the continuities of Kongo ritual life, is the exclamation *Madiomina?* which elicits the reply *Kaa!* This formulaic call and response occurs in Olfert Dapper's description in 1668 of the priest of the *nkisi* Boesi-Batta (Fondation Dapper 1989, 262) and also in Demvo's account 250 years later of *nkisi* Mbundu (MacGaffey 1991, 18); in both instances, it "means" that spirit possession is present, and no translation is necessary.[9] After another transcription of ritual formulae, the writer, Mampuya, though a native speaker working in his own area, admits that he does not understand what he has written down and says that those who want to know the meaning will have to ask!

(Mampuya, 276). In the Christian context, converts learned to use new words, or new uses of old words, without necessarily reflecting on their "meanings."

Problems of translation arise at a higher level than that of the word or sentence. The English-speaking reader expects information to be delivered in a linear sequence with some logic to it. Although the Kongo authors made use of the linear conventions (for example, "see above"), their knowledge was not, or could not, always be reduced to this form. Diafwila's account of Na Menta, for example, and Lutete's descriptions of chiefships follow circuitous paths. Despite my preference to respect the integrity of the texts, I have found it necessary to reorder the sequence of paragraphs (see Chapters 7 and 9); "it may be argued that anything which makes sense of something is reduction-ist . . . even if it makes sense by showing complexity" (Morphy 1994, 142n. 10).

The texts deal with institutions that no longer exist, except in attenuated form. No one knows any more what this or that gesture looked like, what this plant was or what it signified. It is virtually impossible to discover what was the resonance of ritual ges-tures such as those one feebly translates as "to bless, consecrate, fortify"; in addition to the intrinsic difficulty, the corresponding gestures varied in different areas, and some of them have been taken over and converted to Christian usage. Even when the institution or idea is still current, there may well have been no corresponding practice or idea in Europe and in European languages (Malinowski 1923).

When European or Asian texts deal with forgotten institutions, the translator or interpreter has the advantage of participating in a long scholarly tradition in which critical instruments have been developed (Steiner 1975, 24, 416). As I have already indicated, Laman's *Dictionary* does not stand apart from the texts as an independent authority, and modern KiKongo has been molded by the French, Portuguese, and En-glish into which one might seek to translate it. There is no *Oxford English Dictionary* at hand to show the evolution of language and the range of associations of any given word (though Laman's first step is extraordinary).

In making my translations, I have been fortunate to have the help of a number of Kongo intellectuals, men who hold doctorates and speak French, English, and other languages besides KiKongo. Usually, their first reaction to difficult passages from the Cahiers has been to call for the *Dictionary*! This response is due not only to the archaic form of many expressions, to obsolete vocabulary and forgotten institutions, but to their own linguistic experience. Intellectuals usually use French, or in some instances English, in their private and public lives. They commonly compartmentalize their lan-guages, thinking in one or the other according to context and thus avoiding the problem of translation. Even in KiKongo, their language has been heavily influenced by Euro-pean thought and syntax. The late Noé Diawaku, my teacher, was a Kongo nationalist who translated parts of Vansina's *Kingdoms of the Savanna* (Vansina 1965) into Ki-Kongo; he also wrote a book of folktales to encourage children not to lose their Ki-Kongo, but their narrative style is purely European and several of them turn out to be not African but European in origin.[10] None of them can be read aloud in a style faithful to that of oral folktales.

The inadequacies of orthography and the variations of dialect often create mul-tiple possibilities, but in addition most intellectuals are unaccustomed to reading any but the simplest texts in KiKongo—letters from their home village, for example. I have seen my friends poring over texts with one finger, word by word, and have been asked on occasion to read the text aloud—although of course such a reading presupposes that one understands it and has solved the puzzles. The greatest help I have received has been from readers who, without necessarily understanding a passage in detail, have been able to tell me about its mood or feel (humor or irony, for example), which often led to a resolution of ambiguities.

Besides the question of "literal" translation there is that of style. Individuals differ in style, written or spoken. Some of the Cahiers do no more than plod; others are alive with real and imagined experiences—the difficulty here is to recreate some sense of this vivid reality without committing the translation to an inappropriate genre of the English language. The translator's own style, literary education, and resources affect how he reads and translates a text. This aspect of translation is the most subjective; I can only say that this is how these texts read to me. My reading is informed by thirty years of study of Kongo culture punctuated by periods of living among KiKongo speakers and guided by my present sense of what my likely audience expects. As I struggle with translations, my sense of the context from which they emerged is enriched.

Much of the vividness of the most challenging texts is due to the relationship between the words used and the nature of the experience they report. *Nkisi,* for example, refers simultaneously to an object, the animate force it embodies, the ritual in which it is addressed (with music, dance, alcohol), and the effect it has on the lives of individuals and groups. The object, as apprehended by its name, leads the mind away from the wooden thing itself both toward a cosmological domain of spirits and toward the physiological experience of disease. The reference of the term is thus to at least four analytically distinct domains, in each of which it contrasts with other terms: 1) the set of spirit classes, including ancestors and *bisimbi,* among which a diviner chooses; 2) the set of *minkisi,* each with its particular features, such as drum rhythms, food taboos, myths, and procedures; 3) the social relations of the afflicted individual or group, with their tensions and alliances; and 4) the catalogue of diseases, according to Kongo nosology. To see, recognize, and name the elements of an *nkisi* (see Chapter 5) is to rehearse a theory, in the broadest sense, of experience.

The multidimensionality of key terms enriches the language and by the same effect renders it untranslatable. "The good ethnographer must . . . use categories and labels in an ambiguous manner, or use some that have a degree of ambiguity already in his own language, and hope that by applying enough of them, he will enable the reader to create from their elements new combinations that will be closer to the 'native experience' being recorded. I call this the method of language-shadows" (Ardener 1989, 94). In addition to following Ardener's advice, I include two chapters of texts in KiKongo (with English translation), even though most readers will not be familiar with the language. As Johannes Fabian says in similar context, translations (like the original texts) are documents of a process, and should be regarded as rehearsals and contingent performances, not as definitive products (Fabian 1990, 99).

Three annotated examples illustrate some of the compromises at work, including the non-translation of *nkisi* and *nganga,* and also briefly exemplify an *nkisi* "of the above," one "of the below" (water), and a distinct type of quasi-*nkisi,* the *muzidi.* All three texts are in the dialect called Northern by Laman (/h/ is an allophone of the bilabial /v/). The distinction between "above" and "below" is explained in Chapter 5.

Translation Exercises

1. Causing the People to Shout

Here is a transcription of part of a speech, as written down by Kiananwa, in which the speaker elicits responses (*nkumbusulu a bantu,* causing the people to shout) by means of a series of conventional, often elliptical, phrases. Similar rhythms may be employed even in very small and informal gatherings. The genre is that of *kinzonzi,* public debate, although this example is not much more, by Kongo standards, than rhetorical boilerplate.

Tu zimfumu ye mfumu?	*Tu nganga ye nganga!*
We are all freemen and?	Banganga!
[opening expression roughly equivalent to "Ladies and gentlemen!" except that at a public meeting in Kongo women participate only marginally, if at all.]	
Vo watambula lekwa yabongo kiau,	
If you have accepted the matter I brought up,	
yabonga—tambula?	*Yatambula!*
I brought up, accept?	I accepted!
Vo katambula kio ko, mono mu tambula esiki?	*mpiaa!*
If he does not accept it, my acceptance is?	Finished!
Vo diambu ka diena nkanu ko	
If it is not matter for a trial	
vo mfundusu ko, buna diambu kongo?	*kindele!*
or for accusation, then it can?	rest!
Vo lekwa kamona kio ko,	
If no one sees a problem,	
mono [mu] mona kio tu?	*niamba!*
what do I see?	Nothing!
Vo wamona kio, mono bu yamwena [kio] ku nsi?	*bwau!*
If you saw it, what did I see underneath?	Zero!
Ku nsi?	*bwau!*
Underneath?	Zero!
Vo una tonta vuna, buna ngiangia, ngia?	*ngiangia!*
If one should try to lie he's a cheat, a?	a cheat!
E nsilu ka ya ko?	*yayoyo!*
And the end, is it not?	Right there!
Vo zolele toma vova kedika nadede,	
One who really wants to tell the truth	
buna wata ye butu?	*tenduka!*
then speaks out freely.	Speak out!
Kani vo muntu zolele dia vo baba kiani	
If anyone wants to deceive,	
buna wamana kio dia beto yaku mfutu budimbu?	*nama!*
when he has done so the fine, like resin?	sticks to him!

> *Vo bole bavanga lekwa nkila a siasia?*   *ngangula yimosi!*
> If two make the spring of the gun, there is?   only one smith![11]

To transcribe such speeches into a readily intelligible written form requires that the new text incorporate explanatory footnotes or the equivalent (see below).

2. Nkondi Mukwanga (Kibangu, 74)

The text begins with straightforward narrative. *Nkisi* Mukwanga, we are told, "is not for healing but only for cursing." The procedure described is excessive for a mere dream, which however would doubtless be only one symptom among others of a threat from witches. As with all ethnographic texts, even a "literal" transcription fails to record or describe the personal and emotional factors which would energize invocations such as this.

Muntu bu kena yela ye una loto ndozi yambi
A person when he is ill and has a bad dream
[*loto* is a passive: "he is dreamed a bad dream"; the "illness" is the dream. Dreams give evidence, obscurely enough, of the activity of occult forces.]
ntumbu landa nga nkondi vo mukwanga.
he seeks out Nkondi or Mukwanga
[*ntumbu,* "straightway," is simply a conjunction indicating sequence; Nkondi and Mukwanga are two names for the same *nkisi*]
Nga nganga bu kakwiza sema,
When the *nganga* arrives to conduct the ritual,
[*sema* was a verb common but obscure even in Laman's day; in general it seems to mean to conduct a ritual which removes a person from the effects of dangerous contact with occult forces (in this case, witchcraft; MacGaffey 1991, 54).]
bakedekedi mbau au yibayotila.
(his assistants) bang together irons from the forge.
[*Kedekedi* is onomatopoetic; the rest of the sentence literally says, "their hot iron at which they warm themselves." This gesture of cursing or exorcism is reported from the seventeenth century.]
Mbo nganga bu nianguna nkondi
Then when the *nganga* has unwrapped Nkondi
bongidi yo ye tebedi lusakusaku lu kamusakumunina.
picked it up and scraped *lusakusaku* with which to bless it.
[Plant's name puns on *sakumuna,* "to bless, consecrate." *Teba* is a technical term for preparation of medicines by crushing or scraping a few fragments.]
Bu kamana lo sa mu munwa didi kikankatu
When he has done this (and) eaten (a certain) mushroom,
bongidi mbezi, sengodi ngo Nkondi ya yulu kanda diaminkento
he picks up a knife, raises Nkondi in his left hand.
[*Sengodi,* prob. from *sengula,* to place; *ngo,* honorific prefix; "left," lit. "of women," the prefix *mi-* indicating an abstract category.]

The author now reproduces the *nganga's* invocation or curse, in the kind of language (*kinganga*) appropriate to rituals. This genre differs from *kinzonzi* in being much less open to public comprehension; the diction was formulaic and also archaic, even in 1915. The varieties of violence are highly nuanced, but it is clear that Nkondi is being urged to appear in the form of a tropical storm of the kind that in those days could literally blow away an entire village.

Mbo kobwa kumusakumuna ti fu 1 fu 2 fu 3 fu 4 fu 5

He drives in (the blade) to arouse the *nkisi*, striking it five times. [Passive form of *koba*, to go in deep. *Sakumuna* (usu.= "to bless") here = to galvanize. Given the mushroom in his mouth, one would expect the *nganga* to "bless" the *nkisi* by spitting on it.]

tane kento wa tane bakala

(He says,) "Seize women, seize men;

vukula-vukula nkundu zabuko bwaku za munzadi aku zaziwadile kasabwanga. A baya-ya ngwa, bula butotokedi Nsondi.

grab the pubic hair of your mother-in-law, your sister-in-law!

the village has become a laughingstock (?).

[In-laws practice avoidance; the obscenity insults and therefore arouses Nkondi. *Vuku-la-vukula* obtains part of its effect by the vigor of its sound. Obscenities present the same problems to the translator as do religious terms; the resonance counts for more than the "literal" meaning.]

Bangulu bahuta, bambwa balola, kitembo, kimbongila.

The pigs complain, the dogs bark, the storm, the whirlwind. [These animals portend the coming of Nkondi as a storm. *Ba-* prefix indicates categories of animals, not that they are persons.]

Kumongo bazaka ku banda bazaka ha nkati nsi hakwebuta mulodi

They strike on the hill, they strike in the valley, on the ground where the dog barks [and]

fundu-fundu diatobula bala bansusu meso.

the dust puts out the eyes of the chickens.

We found it impossible to create an equivalent in English for the rest of this invocation. Part of the effect of the original is obtained by the sheer sound of the words, as in this description of how *bisimbi* can frighten people by stirring up storms: *Biena lulendo mu daba biela biabantu ye kitula bio nahongolo, nazebezebe, nazelangani, natididi, naholangani, nayukuyuku ye bwisa bantu kimomo ye bwisa kenda ngayi mpe,* "They have the power to break people's courage and render it feeble, weak, limp, petrified, hollow and fevered, stunned and groveling in terror" (Kavuna, 57).

3. Ndundu (Babutidi, 15)

Nkisi Ndundu is not for cursing but healing, and its reference is to terrestrial water. A man whose whole body has become very skinny, though his belly is swollen, thinks *nkisi* Ndundu has got him (*umbeki*). *Ndundu* means "albino"; the predominant color of the medicine bag of the *nkisi* is white. Albinos, like twins, are thought to retain special links with the *bisimbi* (water spirits) in the otherworld under the water, where the people are white in color. The cure includes feeding the patient every day a pinch of the medicines in the *nkisi* (MacGaffey 1991, 83). Ndundu, like many *minkisi*, is a cult of affliction, in which the illness is an invitation to become a *nganga* and so to heal oneself and become a minister of healing to others. Thus the following account describes the training and investiture of a *nganga* in "the land of the dead," a ritual enclosure.

Kansi vo yandi kibeni nganga una baka bela buna si kenda
But if the nganga himself falls ill, he goes

ye bukulu ku nlangu. Ku nsi a zinga kiokio kia ndundu kwena nkulu
to be treated in the water. In that Ndundu pool [a pool believed to be the abode of *bisimbi*] there is the old one

yavanda nkisi wowo ukumbukanga. Bu kalweki,
who (first) composed the *nkisi* which treats him. Having arrived, [this "old person" is not a lineal ancestor but the founder of the line of *banganga* who have operated this *nkisi*]

buna i ntumbu dibuka kaka ye nsanda ye mpidi andi
he plunges in with his loincloth, his cargo basket
[*nsanda* is made of the bark of the fig-tree, *n'sanda;* the fig tree, which is in effect a cultivated species, is associated with the fertility and prosperity of the community. The *mpidi* is to carry the *nkisi*]

ye nti andi va koko va zinga kiokio. Beno bankaka lulenda banza
and his staff in his hand, into the pool. You may think

vo mu nlangu kadibukidi
he has jumped into the water,

kansi kiongo nlangu wowo i nzila a bwala kwandi
but really the water is the road to the village [of the dead].

Nganga bu kadibukidi va zinga kiokio, buna ndiona nkulu
When the *nganga* has plunged into the water, then the elder

yatekila koko i ntumbu kwiza kunkika ye kunsonga nzila
who preceded him there comes to welcome him and show him the way

a nzo andi. Bu kalweki mu vata dina,
to his house. When he has arrived in that village

i ntumbu kunlambila madia ye kunnwikina bonso bufweni.
(they) cook food for him and give him drink as is fitting.

Mboki nganga yetikila koko si katoma kumbuka
Then the first *nganga* will treat him thoroughly [*buka* is "to treat" but not necessarily "to heal," *nieka*]

mu nkisi wowo wandundu. Mbuta lenda ko tenta bilumbu biole
with *nkisi* Ndundu. He may continue for two

vo bitatu bonso bukazolele.
or three days as he wishes.

Bu keka mu vutuka ku vata,
When he is ready to return to the village,
[*keka,* from *ka,* an auxiliary verb; rare]

balenda toma kunzaka nsuki ye kunsindika
they may trim his head in a special way and send him off

mu madia ye vana minlele bonso bubazolele.
with food and giving him cloths as they please.
[cloth imported from Europe, a coveted sign of wealth, was believed to be made by the *bisimbi* under the ocean; it contrasts with his fig-bark rag]

Bu kavutukidi ku bwala, buna bisi vata bana yitukwa beni
When he returns to the village the villagers are astonished
mu kummona mu diambu dia bameni kunkusa mpemba
to see him, because (the spirits) have smeared him with white
ye tukula ye toma kunzaka nsuki. Bu kalweki,
and red and clipped his hair short. Upon his arrival
buna bameni kuntanda mpe nsala zankusu ye zamalemba
they present him with feathers of the parrot and the *malemba,*
[*tanda* is not the ordinary verb for "to give" but has the sense of a prestation. Red parrot feathers are a sign of the ability to speak of hidden things;[12] LKD says unconvincingly that *malemba* may be a pelican.]
ye bu bamweni nsuki zatebo, buna yitukwa beni.
and when they see his clipped head they marvel [at the bizarre haircut].

4. Muzidi (Kavuna, 65)

The fourth text is a brief extract from a twenty-page essay in which Kavuna vividly captures the popular experience of *mizidi,* the spindly, cloth-wrapped ancestral "dolls" of the BaBembe in north Kongo (Kavuna 1995). A *muzidi* is like an *nkisi* in that it is a fabricated container for a protective force. It is different in that the force is that of a particular deceased man, an ancestor of the lineage that commissions it, not a particular affliction. When the *muzidi* is composed the spirit (*nkuyu*) is tempted to come within reach by the sight of a good meal; the *nganga* catches it dramatically and puts it in the *muzidi.*

Bwe tuzeyi vo kotele mu kiteki vo mu muzidi?
How do we know that it has entered the figurine or *muzidi?*
[the pronoun could be he, she, or it.]
I mu madia makadidi ye wuyolukanga
From the food it has eaten and the way it chatters
mu ngongo a lukaya yibakumbakilanga,
in the packet of leaves in which they catch it,
kadi bu bavikitinanga ngongo ye zibikanga yo,
because when they pounce on the packet and open it
buna bawanga mpila lekwa kikwalakasanga
they hear something rustling.
[both *vikita* and *kwalakasa* are very evocative verbs]
Mbatu hana mu zitu kiakiteki vo muzidi bazabilanga.
Also they can tell by the weight of the figurine or *muzidi,*
Kadi bu babongele muzidi ye sinsa ye vo bamweni
because when they pick it up and heft it and find
vo muzidi weka walema [zitu] buna bazeyi vo kotele ye wena momo.
that it has become heavy they know that the ghost has gone inside.
[things and people that are "heavy" deserve "respect," *luzitu*]
Ka bobo kaka ko, kansi bakunyuvulanga mpe.
And that's not all, because they also interrogate it.
Babonganga muzidi ye bakumvwetilanga ha kemvo mu moko mole
They take the *muzidi* and bend over it, holding it in both hands

ye bakunyuvulanga bonso bwabu: Bwa kedika ti nkati angeye kibeni
and question it like this: Is it true that you have really
kotele mu muzidi wau wu wabedi tombang'e? Buna vo wena momo
entered into the figure as you were asked to do? If it is in there
buna bavutuka mona muzidi wahangazala [colorful verb!]
they will in return see the *muzidi* moving about authoritatively
ha moko ma mfumu andi.
in the hands of its master.
Sika-sika, wuyinama, uvumbuka, uyinama wuvumbuka.
"*Sika-sika* (it says), at your service, all in place . . ."

Epistemology

Discussing the problem of translating philosophical concepts into the languages of Ghana, Wiredu says that many Akan-speaking Christians educated in English use a convenient Akan term while annexing to it a significance associated with an English word, thus "thinking partially in English while ostensibly speaking (or writing) in Akan" (Wiredu 1992, 310). The illusory "success" of such a mode of translation will vary in proportion to the thinker's familiarity with not only the English language but the philosophical traditions embedded in it (Hallen and Sodipo 1986).

Whereas Protestant practice in Kongo at the turn of the century was to find "equivalent" KiKongo expressions for foreign terms, often with highly ambiguous results, Catholic practice domesticated such terms as *ukaristia* and *penitensia*, thus emphasizing rather than concealing the difference between indigenous and Christian philosophies (Janzen 1985, 15–17; Wiredu 1992, 316).

In translations from African languages in such fields as religion (or insults) the converse problem arises. One may try "equivalents" such as "charm" or "priest," or insist on the use of KiKongo terms such as *nkisi* and *nganga;* the result of the second maneuver may be that the words are no more than English concepts in drag unless the reader learns something of the cosmology taken for granted by KiKongo speakers, and what the differential value of the terms is.[13] *Nganga* in the proper exercise of his profession cannot be accused of being *nganga*, but if he is believed to have misused his knowledge he may be taken for *ndoki*, a witch and virtually a criminal ("Sometimes there is not much difference" [Demvo, 32]). It is the business of the chief to combat witchcraft (*kindoki*) but to be effective he must himself have *kindoki*. These values do not and cannot emerge from the translation of the terms individually into another language. Within "witchcraft" itself more subtle distinctions are found. For example, since chief and *nganga* are *ndoki*, the designation is not necessarily derogatory, but *nloki* (a variation on the same stem) refers exclusively to a wicked person who destroys others by cursing (*loka*). This action contrasts, within *kindoki*, with *yungula*, an attack intended to steal the soul of the victim in order to sell it or imprison it in an *nkisi*. Individuals, however, vary in their understanding of such distinctions; there is no orthodoxy.

It is not even clear that a "religious" vocabulary is the appropriate one in which to look for equivalents. Beliefs in all kinds of "spiritual," "mystical" and "supernatural" entities and powers have been attributed to Africans (Wiredu 1992, 324), whose entire mentality has often been described as religious. But such categories do not exist in Akan (or Kongo) thought, in which there is no conceptual cleavage between the natural and the supernatural, the physical and the spiritual. The non-human beings in whom these peoples believe "are an integral part of this world" (Wiredu 1992, 325). The most remote and powerful of Kongo spirits are not metaphysical entities but rocks; there are no good answers to the question whether the rocks "represent" or "contain" the spirits. The "otherworld" of Kongo thought, the land of the dead (*nsi a bafwa*), is as it were in the next room, around the corner, or even right here, for those who have eyes to see.

The Exotic and the Banal

That the dead are mundane raises the problem of exoticism in translation (Olivier de Sardan 1992). *Nganga* can be re-situated in different domains, open to different criteria of evaluation, by alternative translations such as witch doctor, expert, doctor, savant, or herbalist. When I once hesitated on being asked whether there was witchcraft (*kindoki*) in the United States, the next question and its answer were, "Are there thieves, adulterers, and people who quarrel in the village at night? Well then, you have *kindoki*." Yet what is banal in an African culture is not what is banal in the West, so an exchange of banalities does not give true translation. We have "thieves, adulterers," but it is not part of our American view of such people that they meet weekly in the top of a silk-cotton tree to feast on one of their neighbors. The problem is to preserve the strangeness of the data without committing it to our own categories of the exotic, with sensationalist results. Nor is there anything about banality that excuses it from an interrogation that might reveal it as strange after all.

A temptation as strong as that of exoticism is its opposite. In African studies, both historians and political scientists have shown marked selectivity in what they regard as data, discarding what is by European standards irrational or at best "symbolic." Part of this selectivity is a function of a charitable, liberal unwillingness to suggest that African thought falls short of what Europeans consider to be their own best standards of rationality. Another part of it is derived from a kind of rationalism, built into social science, which also distorts studies of early European history. In this connection, Fuglestad argues that modern historians, whether they are Marxists or not, have generally regarded materialist factors, but not ideology and religion, as the prime movers in the historical process (Fuglestad 1992, 317). The result, he says, is a type of history from which the cultural and, in part, mental dimension has been obliterated, so that in a given study it is no longer clear that one is in fact dealing with Africa (or, Fuglestad says, pre-Christian Scandinavia), except in a purely geographical sense. The behavior of culturally nondescript actors is presented as universally intelligible, and problems of translation, motivation, and cosmology disappear. Social science can thus be as cosmographic (or world-defining) as the African discourses it studies. Conversely, much of what we take to be "religion," "myth," and even "history" in African (specifically Kongo) culture includes elements of "social science," defining, in its own terms, the nature of the European and the "modern"; one should not assume that "folklore" consists of unreasoned, uncritical raw data passively awaiting professional analysis (Hallen 1995, 69).

What Fuglestad says about history applies also to political science, whose practitioners may well be aware of the extent to which the assumed reality of occult powers plays a part in the politics of African states but are unable to integrate them in their studies without incurring charges of exoticism or worse.[14] Similar censorship by squeamishness often occurs in the strangely hybrid world of African art, where the awesome powers of a Yoruba king or Kongo chief are rendered safe by sentimentalizing them in the pastel shades of "mystical leadership."

Instead of trying to decide where on a continuum from the exotic to the banal our translation should be located, it is more rewarding to probe the nature of the exotic by juxtaposing it to the banal, and likewise to probe the banal by trying it against the exotic (MacGaffey 1978); are the moral and empirical ambiguities of *kindoki* very different in kind from many aspects of the "international communist conspiracy" in the 1950s United States? This is the method of "language shadows." Fred Myers, drawing on Bakhtin, has recently insisted that the filtering processes whereby we domesticate the accounts of others of their own culture are as challenging to the ethnographer as anything he may bring back from Aboriginal Australia (Myers 1995). In the process of translation, it will be necessary to suspend the kind of cognitive and moral commitments that deny serious weight to African institutions and values of which outsiders may be inclined to disapprove for their own good, ethnocentric reasons, and also to recognize as strange our own intellectual agendas.

Institutional Incompatibility

In African studies generally, the models traditionally used are ethnocentric composites of heuristic and normative elements; as Fuglestad suggests, aspects of African culture that are neither readily intelligible nor morally acceptable, according to the models, are ignored, marginalized or, as Owomoyela puts it, "pathologized" (Owomoyela 1994). "Translation" should involve not just matching up our terms with theirs (more or less loosely) but also a radical questioning of assumptions. In a long series of provocative essays, Robin Horton has insisted that it is not simply a question of hunting in the English dictionary for the equivalent words, but of self-consciously scrutinizing the categories of Western thought and the cognitive commitments of the translator. This process, he believes, will necessitate the re-amalgamation of areas of discourse which have become separated in the course of Western history and will probably require that Western concepts themselves be modified to accommodate African concepts (Horton 1993, 9, 303).

The principal separation that Horton has in mind is that between religion and science, which has established itself as a totemic metaphor for the difference between primitive and modern, between Them and Us. For us, religion is a matter of belief, faith, conversion, and similar terms which already exoticize it. Other divisions are generated by the history of modern institutions. When we deal with the substance of Kongo culture, and no doubt other cultures as well, we have to re-synthesize our concepts of not only religion and science but politics and economics as well. In the United States in particular, it is taken for granted that these domains are independent, governed by their own values expressed in incompatible vocabularies; politicians and editorial writers proclaim that the Church should not interfere in Government, and that Government should stay clear of the Market. Since the beginning of social science in the 1840s, theorists have addressed the same concerns in more pretentious language, arguing inconclusively about whether material (economic) or ideal (cultural) factors are "determinant" in history and social relations and situating political structures ambiguously between the two (Sahlins 1976; MacGaffey 1981, 228–23). Rarely in this discussion has the list of categories itself been questioned; why these three? why not four or six? The answer is that they are functional categories of our ("modern") social organization, masquerading as logical necessities.

In the confrontation of one institutional structure with another, we will come to regard the inevitable use of multiple glosses in translation ("language-shadows") as a regrettable compromise only if we have assumed that there is one right and single meaning for which, ideally, we ought to find a just equivalent. In fact, the ill-defined range of "meanings" convened by any powerful term, such as *kindoki,* is precisely what makes it powerful. It implicates several levels of experience and escapes from each of the institutional categories (economy, politics, religion) in which we would like to put it. The different meanings reaching into different niches of Kongo culture reveal to the foreigner its inner relationships (Overing 1987). Glosses are only necessary when our understanding of that culture is to be expressed in English, and in a relatively short space. They should therefore be accompanied, as they are here, by extended passages in which their inadequacy becomes apparent and by frequent reference to the original expressions.

Several anthropologists, like Horton, have adopted what we might call an optimistic approach to the impossibility of translation, seeing it not as a failure of old knowledge but as a source of new knowledge. Malcolm Crick urges us to transcend oppositions between not only religion and science but also thought and emotion, expression and action, literal and metaphorical, and says we should respond to the lack of finality in semantic investigations by regarding translation as a form of commentary (Crick 1976, 165). Joanna Overing argues that the vocabulary of "magic," "religion," "shamanism" and the like, loaded with nineteenth-century concepts of human nature and human progress, keeps us from attaining more interesting insights into other ontologies and epistemologies than our own (Overing 1987, 82–84). Like Crick, she favors the use of formal, abstract categories that are as little baggage-laden and as content-specific as possible; she regards translation as a creative process.

One of the results of this sort of process, with respect to *minkisi* in particular, will be to continue and perhaps consciously to hasten the progressive modification of Western concepts to accommodate Kongo (and more generally, African) realities. This process has been going on since the sixteenth century, when traders and travelers were forced to abandon their initial categories of "idolatry" and "mohamedanism" and to adapt instead an ill-defined Portuguese term into what became not only the word "fetish" but also a whole theory of African culture (Pietz 1987). "Fetish" as a concept did not exist ready made; it evolved over 200 years as a result of European experience, not of "Africa" but of institutionalized relations with Africans in what Pietz calls the intercultural space of the West African coast. The theory developed subsequently by European philosophers served to define "civilization" itself in opposition to "fetishism"; later, in the hands of Marx and Freud, "fetish" became an instrument for ironic critiques of civilization. In recent times it has itself been subject to critique and revision.

As a minor sign of this revision, *minkisi* in museum collections became "power objects"; it is to be hoped that before long they will be known by their proper name.[15] This sort of process works in the opposite direction, too, as Africans engaged in translation from European languages transform the meanings of indigenous terms (Matory 1994, 221).

The goal of such efforts at revision should not be to find grounds for approving or disapproving of African cultures, but to acknowledge their historical weight and stability. By way of analogy, consider the weight in U.S. history of the belief in (and institutionalization of) the idea that the human species is divided into a short list of genetically discrete races. Most Americans are surprised to hear that race, so far from being given in nature, is a relatively recent invention whose content has changed markedly during its 150 years or so of existence. In the nineteenth century race was a matter of bones and head shape, and anthropologists were concerned largely with the "races" of Europe; race was indexed by color only in the twentieth century, when it came to be primarily a question of allegedly essential differences between "white" people and others. Americans are highly resistant to repeated demonstrations that race is a cultural artifact, because it is institutionalized to such an extent that its seeming truth is confirmed in daily experience and therefore appears to be a fact of nature. They can also point to a library full of books old and new, written by credentialed scholars, which take this "fact" for granted and argue about how to evaluate the genetic properties of races and their phenotypical manifestations. An anthropologist from some other civilization would be confronted with the traditional and vexing problem of the rationality or otherwise of the natives, whose ideas make no sense to him but are clearly fundamental to their way of life and must therefore be taken seriously. The constituents of Kongo political imagination, "true" or not, have that kind of weight (see Chapter 10).

4. TRADITION AND TRADE

Among the native tribes of the Congo basin there exists no form of history. There is no written language; no tradition of the past; and no indication of an attempt, on the part of the natives, to perpetuate any epoch of their lives by means of monumental erections.

—HERBERT WARD (1895)

Until the publication of Vansina's *De la tradition orale* in 1961, pre-colonial Africa was supposed by scholars not to have any recoverable history; oral traditions of the past could not substitute for written archives (Vansina 1961). Since 1961, Vansina's assertion that oral traditions could be treated as texts has been both influential and highly problematic. Many of the problems are reviewed by Vansina himself in another book on the same subject (Vansina 1985). Although it is now clear that traditions can rarely be taken literally as history, in the sense of "what happened," discussion continues about the kinds of historical information that it may be possible to extract from them. One of the key ideas is that of genre, which implies a particular audience for the stories. Audiences are manipulable by storytellers, but also impose certain kinds of control on what is said and how it may be said. Sociological contexts may permit the historian to reinterpret a tradition and its competing variants in such a way as to deduce historical "facts." There can be no general rule, however, about how to deduce them, because "oral tradition" is not rendered homogeneous by the mere fact of its orality.

Kongo traditions (*kinkulu,* "history") belong to a distinct genre of recitation appropriate to occasions when the authority of a chief or the rights in land of a descent group need to be reasserted. Traditions are similar in form but differ in content; there are no general stories in circulation today of the origin of the world, the people, or the Kongo kingdom. In indigenous theory, tradition is taught to the chief's or headman's chosen successor or revealed to him later in a dream. In the nature of *kinkulu,* according to this theory, it cannot be correctly known to a usurper or upstart. To recite it is an exercise of power, to write it down is to corrupt it—although, in modern times, tradition is usually written down in court records and in private papers, some of which are copied from European authors. Moreover, although supposedly quasi-secret, tradition is and always was generally known to the public by virtue of the fact that it is recited. It is the business of a clan's Children and Grandchildren, members of other clans, to know, guard, and authenticate its tradition and the sacred relics associated with it. The idea of its secrecy legitimates innovation through the authoritative "revelation" of versions not heard before, and permits the continuous adaptation of history to political contingencies (MacGaffey 1970, ch. 2).

The Laman manuscripts are not *kinkulu* in the sense indicated above. They belong to the hybrid and transient genre of "essays written by natives" that is virtually restricted to the era of European conquest. They cannot therefore be dismissed as inauthentic representations made up simply in response to European demands. It is clear from the manuscripts themselves and other writings by the authors that their intended audience was people like themselves, as well as Laman and other missionaries. If there is a problem with their reports, it is that the authors, mostly young men, were not privy to many of the "secrets" of either tradition or ritual. That criticism itself accepts the misleading assertion that there were in fact hidden truths known only to ritually qualified persons (MacGaffey 1986a, 15). Although the manuscripts are obviously "texts," they are perhaps better regarded as "performances," improvisations in response to a particular, unique situation (Fabian 1990, 7–15). As such, their authenticity is not only that of the cultural knowledge of the authors (acquired by participation and by more or less deliberate observation) but also that of their personal productive effort, with its inevitable complement of idiosyncrasies, from loose ends to imaginative transformations to deliberate syntheses. "Ethnographers, although some of them can say what they have to say more clearly and succinctly than others, are destined to tell baroque and tortuous tales" (Fabian 1990, 15). Beneath the "surface" of the text is an ongoing process in the life of an author such as Lutete, of which we only catch glimpses but which includes his position in his village, his status as a Christian evangelist, and his growing knowledge as a literate ethnographer.

Anatomy of Tradition

The reading of Kongo history from *kinkulu* has been bedeviled by essentialist assumptions about the identity of clans and ethnic groups, with the result that it is usually addressed in the wrong terms. It makes no sense to evaluate as the history of a given group a narrative about its origin in the distant past if that group is recent and transitory. Tradition includes two principal kinds of stories—those that serve as models through which chiefship was imagined (in relation to social order, marriage, and prosperity), and those that reflect the political organization of trade in the eighteenth and nineteenth centuries. Chapter 10 will present additional conclusions relative to the history of inland areas.

A MuKongo (pl. BaKongo, but this is a modern term and concept; in KiKongo one says *mwisi Kongo,* pl. *bisi Kongo*) should be able to claim membership in a local section of a matrilineal clan (*kanda*) by descent in the female line. Those whose pedigree includes a female ancestor allegedly transferred in some way from another clan are "slaves" (*basumbwa, bamvika*). The question of who is or is not a slave is essential to the nature and structure of matrilineal descent in Kongo; it is also the basic issue in village politics (MacGaffey 1970). Clans are nominal categories without corporate organization; although nominally matrilineal, they arose as aggregates of groups who shared a common *mvila,* "praise-name," as a sign of participation in the same politico-magical configuration (LKII, 48). The local section of a clan is (but only as a first approximation) an exogamous, land-owning matrilineal descent group, with its own headman, divided into "houses," which are in turn divided into "lineages."

Any self-respecting clan-section (*kanda*) asserts that it owns a tract of land; its leaders recite a tradition of migration (*kinkulu,* history) to legitimate that claim (Mac-Gaffey 1970). Several generations of scholars have struggled to make historical sense of local ensembles of such traditions, but with little success, since the stories are forensic instruments in unending disputes about sovereignty.[1] In the 1950s, some of these disputes began to relate to the economic value of land, but the principal issue, as in the past, was a matter of situating the clan-section in a local hierarchy of political authority and ritual empowerment (Doutreloux 1967, 50, 153).

Traditions of origin describe events on two different historical scales. On the smaller scale, the traditions, presupposing an already constituted society, describe petty migrations of small groups between named villages, usually not far apart. These stories, supported by ritual practices such as that of transporting the body of a deceased chief back to the village of origin for burial in the cemetery associated with this particular line of chiefs, probably have some historical value, but no matter how fervently their narrators believe in them they are all contested by other narratives and all reflect merely the pullulating formation and reformation of communities numbering a few hundred inhabitants at most.

In small-scale traditions the migrating unit is a clan-section or a segment thereof, a matrilineage, together with its extralineal associates, including in-marrying wives, children of men of the lineage, and slaves.[2] Narratives on the grand scale describe a migration from an original center across a great river to an unoccupied land in which a community began to take shape. They use a relatively limited number of motifs to express the themes of disorder, transition, division of the people into clans, and the institution of chiefship on this side of the river, the scene of the narration. The themes of order and disorder are elements of the conceptual aspect of political culture. Alleged affiliations to an original clan enable individuals to assert links of distant kinship with any other individual when it is convenient to do so, but otherwise they have no effective existence (MacGaffey 1970, 17).

Lunungu and Fieldwork

In 1965, I experienced great difficulty in trying to reduce traditions of origin to some sort of historical order. Like others, I was tempted to attribute the confusion of the material to disruptions brought about by colonial rule, but I eventually concluded that the "confusion" is essential to the political system and that though order does exist, it is found at the level of form, not narrative content (MacGaffey 1970, 35).

In 1915, when the institutions to which the traditions purportedly relate should have been relatively fresh in collective memory, Lunungu Moise, collecting traditions for Laman in Manianga, had a similar experience:

> When I asked [my own elders] where did we the people come from? They said: "The elders used to tell us that we crossed the river called Yambi." And the elders recited the names of the villages from which their forebears came. The elders around Kinzambi and Nsundi Mamba say they came from Mutala, but they do not know which Mutala. Some say it is in the direction of Makungu, others that Mutala is toward Kinkenda, and others know only the name, Mutala. This is all very confusing. (Cahier 172)

Eventually Lunungu stumbled on the ethnographer's dream, a rewarding informant: Ya Ngoma of Kisiasia, clan KiMbanga, could recite tradition properly. Lunungu transcribes his conversations with Ya Ngoma, the questions and the answers. "Ya Ngoma and many other elders say that there was one original clan which divided so that there could be intermarriage, but they are not clear what was the name of the original clan."

> Then I found a way to ask him, "Say, if the KiMbanga clan came first, where did they come from?" He did not avoid replying, because he thought it was just curiosity. He said that the ancestors used to say we came from where the sun rises. I said, "What name did they call the place?" He said, "Mpumbu."[3]
> By inquiries of this kind with other elders I succeeded in everything.

In the village of Makungu, Lunungu met an elder called Me Kikita, a free member of the KiNdamba clan and a child of KiMumba (that is, his father belonged to Ki-Mumba; *mfumu Kindamba, mwana bisi Kimumba*), thus a person qualified as a witness to the traditions of KiMumba.

> The first question I asked was this: "Which clan was senior in Mutala?"
> Me Kikita replied, "KiMumba."
> I asked, "Why was it thought to be the first clan?"
> Me Kikita: "KiMumba was the first to invest a man as chief. So all the [other] clans are Children of Mumba."
> "How is their praise-name recited?"

The reply to the last question is incomprehensibly arcane, but Me Kikita's reasoning is transparent: *Because* the chiefs are KiMumba, that clan had historical priority. Mutala, the supposed "origin of the clans," is the name of the chiefly cemetery and investiture site; "Muntala looked at (*watala*) all the clans." It is located in the modern village of Muntala, southwest of Nsundi Mamba in the modern administrative division of Kimumba, where Lunungu was asking his questions. Names such as Mumba, Mwembe, and Bidi, all indicating cemetery investiture sites, pervade Manianga traditions (Cahier 160).

Lutete in Lolo provides one example, out of tens of them in his texts, of tradition on the small scale: Na Ngoma Lubota led his people from Ngoma after quarrels broke out there. Na Ngoma was invested as chief in Lutala [between Vungu and Lolo], together with Na Ngoma Niati.[4] They ruled Mazinga [near Lolo], and Na Ngoma Lubota is buried there. He was succeeded by Na Kayi Ngoma, but Niati went to Kungu [near Vungu, site of an important market]. Under Na Kayi Ngoma the clan flourished. When he died his body was taken to the cemetery of the chiefs, in Kintudi, near Isangila, to be buried with others of his line (Cahier 216). In this kind of tradition, river crossings do not require magical powers, the narratives do not include sociological models, and the events are mundane: petty quarrels rather than famines, and travel over short distance between known villages. Even so, there is no evidence that such traditions ever amounted to coherent local history. Immediate political need inspired the shaping of narratives out of the many fragments available.

The boundary between the modern districts of Mayombe and Manianga corresponds approximately to that between clans who claim to have migrated from the south and those who trace their origin to the east. Kinkela Ngoma of Vungu (Cahier 84; LKI, 26) provides a classic example of tradition on the grand scale, in a southern version.[5] It includes a typical "Tower of Babel" story, explaining the origin of discrete clans, and a model of an orderly society based on right government, right marriage, and right eating.

Kinkela in Vungu

Everybody in our area came from Kongo dia Ntotila on the other bank [the south bank of the Congo]. The reason why our forebears left is this: One day a woman gave birth to a child with its placenta, and they ate them—for in those days they were all cannibals. When those people had taken the child and the placenta and eaten them, the owners of the woman were angry and began a war in the midst of that group. The struggle was intense, on account of the gluttony of those who ate the child together with the placenta.

In those days they had nothing else to fight with but *nkanda,* which they found underground.[6] This they did, to throw them: they made a point for it and then bent another [piece of iron?] and a little thing like a nail which they put on the head of the *lunkanda* which they had parted, and forged it to the part they had bent. It would then go wherever they aimed it. In this fashion they fought until the other side lost.

A certain chief fled with a large following and came to a country called Bangala ba Nanga, where there were no other people and chief Nanga was the first to settle.[7] Once again some of the ancestors killed young people to eat them. Then the chief said, "No, it is not good to continue in this country; if we go to a faraway land we will cease to eat one another." So they left that country in search of one far away, and came to the place called Nsenzebele ["flat stone"], where there was nothing but sand.

There they saw the other shore, where we are now, and they thought it would be good to cross over, for there were no people, and perhaps it would be a good place to settle. With their throwing knives they felled a silk-cotton tree, trimmed it, and hollowed a canoe. When they had hollowed it they sat in it; the canoe was too small, but nobody wanted to remain behind. Some sat on the shoulders of others, and some stood. They tried to set forth, but the vessel was small and it filled with water. One of them said, "This is no good, trying to cross all together. This is how we will cross: we will divide into groups, one to a boat." The chief and the whole group approved.

They began to cross. When the canoe arrived at the other side, they grouped together those who crossed in it, and so they knew how many could get in one load. So they came to this bank. Chief Nanga Na Kongo[8] spoke up and said: "You performed a service when we were all trying to cross together; you said we should return to shore to divide into groups, and so we crossed over safely. But now we are in a land without other people, only animals and birds. So divide up the group into parties, and choose a headman for each one, every man his own group and his own place, that we may spread out in this land without people."

In those days there were no clans (*mvila*), but only a kin-group that reproduced itself. Then a certain man stood up and began to choose the headmen: Mbenza Na Kongo and the people who were to go with him; Mpudi a Nzinga, Manianga, Numbu a [N]zinga, Mankuku, Ngimbi, Mamboma.[9] But they all called Nanga their chief. Then they founded their villages by the Nzadi, but the chief went to what is now called Vivi.[10]

Nanga said, "You who are so good at dividing us should be called Makaba." He too chose his followers.[11]

When the people began to multiply they did not wish to start eating one another again, because every headman wanted his village to be at peace. Two of them, however, agreed to make war on their chief, Nanga; their names were Makaba and Numbu.[12] This, the first war on this shore, was hard-fought; Chief Nanga had holes dug in the ground to hide in. They went on fighting until he lost and fled to Nkondo a Nanga, which is now called Ngangila.[13] When Nanga had fled and left the country he formerly ruled, now called Vivi, Numbu succeeded him. Their quarrel was over, and they were on good terms again.

The villages grew and began to spread out, but they were mostly set near the Nzadi because it was very difficult to break a road through to where we are now [in the Vungu forest]. We were told that when the Nanga people multiplied, eagles came and began to eat children, so some fled from that country and returned to Nsunga, on the other shore, while others fled to Isangila.[14] Some began to find a way to where we are now, a place called Yila. Thus it was that people moved close to the places where we are now. People came to be familiar with the territory by hunting game. Hunters might travel all day to kill animals and smoke the meat, and they might see a fine country to dwell in. Returning to the village they would tell what they had seen, and some would decide to go there to build.

My fathers[15] formerly lived in Mboma, but they left there for this reason: a brother and a sister fought because his pigs had despoiled her crops, whereupon she insulted him by exposing her sexual parts.[16] He was not there at the time, but on his return his children told him of his sister's insult. He was angry, they argued and fought, each calling to others for help. They fought long and hard. This war was fought near where Boma is now; it was called Bengenene ["exceedingly red"] because it was so bloody and caused so many to flee. As it continued, the brother and many others fled to a place called Nsafu, where he drove an awl into his navel and died. His following dispersed.

So it was that our country was filled with people. Some sought a dwelling place in anger. They had no common chief; Chief Nanga Na Kongo himself distributed chiefship to others. In our area they did not fight other nations, but only among themselves.

Commentary

Kongo dia Ntotila is, or refers to, Mbanza Kongo, the ancient capital of the Kongo Kingdom in northern Angola (the word *kongo* seems to mean an organized space, related to *nkongolo*, "circle"; *ntotila* from *tota*, to gather). The first two incidents, describing "cannibalism," establish a condition of social disorder from which the ancestors escape by "crossing Nzadi" ("large river," from which the name Zaire is derived). "Eating people" means witchcraft, the epitome of social disorder. The "empty land" into which the people cross is the prerequisite for the creation of a sovereign chiefship in direct communion with the spirits of the land (Doutreloux 1967, 47). Social organization under the authority of the new chief begins with the division of the people into the nine clans corresponding to the canoe loads. The only element of specifically historical interest in the story so far is the throwing knife, a weapon that probably disappeared from use in the eighteenth century. Throwing knives, a weapon of great antiquity in Central Africa, remained in use elsewhere than in Lower Congo; they were often highly ornate, intended for ceremony and display rather than warfare.

In Kongo tradition, the founding heroes are not represented, as they are elsewhere in Central Africa, as uncivilized strangers. The land into which they lead their followers is vacant, except perhaps for a few "little people" who are more likely to be *bisimbi* ("nature spirits") than Pygmies (MacGaffey 1986a, 193–94).[17] It is not said, as it so often is said elsewhere, that the invaders took over political control but left ritual responsibilities for the land in the hands of the autochthons. These functions are shared by the invaders, between the chief and the *nganga* who invests the chief. Lunungu explains:

> The chiefship of Nkumba Kongo is like that of Na Mumba, to oppress and kill and make war upon other clans. When Nkumba became a chief, Nanga and Nsundi were "wives of the chalk," who were also invested.[18] That is, from the Nanga clan came a woman who sat with him when he was invested. Nsundi provided another. These were the women he married at his investiture, therefore they are called "wives of the chalk [of investiture]." (Cahier 160)

The model for this relationship of paired clans is that of two brothers who agree to separate so that they may intermarry "in order to multiply children." Intermarriage could take the form of patrilateral cross-cousin marriage, which has egalitarian implications for the groups concerned, or matrilateral cross-cousin marriage, which implies and maintains a hierarchy between the groups. The model of patrilateral cross-cousin marriage allows chiefship to circulate between two or more clans and at the same time to descend from a father to one of his sons. Matrilateral cross-cousin marriage links groups in asymmetrical relationships between patrons and clients (MacGaffey 1986a, 33). In either event, intermarriage is explicitly contrasted in Kongo thought with enmity and "cannibalism."

The river once crossed, the story begins to bring in real place-names and the kind of petty war that was endemic in Kongo from the eighteenth century onward. New incidents in the narrative, however, repeat the theme of division and dispersal to escape disorder represented as improper eating: the eagles and the quarrel of brother and sister. The sister's insult is a denial of matrilineal solidarity, as is the brother's suicide by stabbing the Navel of Origin (*Nkummba a Wungudi*), a common element in Mayombe traditions. Both events are said to have caused the disintegration and dispersal of an original unity. In short, tradition on the grand scale consists largely of narrative statements of social norms and models, in the form of dramatic, magically loaded incidents.

Babutidi on Nsundi

Kinkela wrote about the Vungu area from the point of view of a native, a descendant of clans that traced their origin to the south, from Vivi and Boma. Timothy Babutidi, who belonged to the SMF at Kinkenge, made at least three extended research trips in northeastern Mayombe in 1916–1917. Babutidi was an unusual man; among the pioneer evangelists and teachers who spread the Christian gospel he was one of the few to learn French, if only because he was in charge of a school district, administered from Kinkenge, which lay in French Congo, where at an early date the French required that all instruction be carried on in the French language. It is also clear that he took the responsibility of conducting research for Laman's project very seriously, traveling widely, noting down what he had heard in different parts of the country, and endeavoring to make sense of it.

Babutidi gives us tradition as viewed by clans who claimed to have come from the east and identified themselves as Nsundi (BaSundi). Their original capital, according to these traditions, is not Mbanza Kongo but Mwembe Nsundi.[19] There was a Nsundi chiefdom in western Manianga, just west of Kibunzi, in the eighteenth century (Janzen 1982, 67), but many places carry the same name.

Babutidi's view of Kongo history is that the Kinkenge people came from the "up country," crossing a great river called *mvwe-mvwe-mvwe*. Originally they all belonged to one clan, Nsundi. Whereas, for Kinkela, the cause of the original migration was "cannibalism" (an excess of eating), for Babutidi it is insufficient eating: "They came here principally on account of a famine; everything had dried up because the rains had failed. So Na Noki stood up and with his four children came to this country.[20] That they might intermarry, he divided them, each to his own clan, and consecrated them. The first to be blessed was Mazinga Na Tona, 'who sees to the affairs of the country'" (Cahier 13).[21] This happy arrangement is implicitly linked to "right eating," which has a double significance: The chief is expected to arrange that his followers eat, that is, consume adequately, and also to prevent witchcraft, that is, "eating" of one's substance by evil neighbors.

Babutidi goes on to say that once arrived in Mayombe the Nsundi group encountered other clans which had crossed to the north bank from Mbanza Kongo to escape the oppressive rule of the king there. As subordinates of Kongo, they carried the suffix "Na Kongo," as in Nanga Na Kongo. Babutidi then describes the encounter between the eastern and southern clans, near Maduda. His statement of the original relationship between the two follows:[22]

> Mbangala is the name of the elder who gave rise to the Nsundi clan, for when people began to multiply Mbangala made an agreement with Ma Lwangu: Let me, Mbangala, father the free members of Nsundi (*zimfumu zansundi*) and you, Ma Lwangu, father those of Lwangu, that we may intermarry. They also set a rule that you, Ma Lwangu, may not marry the women of your clan but must marry them to me, and I also may not marry my nephews and nieces but must marry them to you, that we may aid one another in reproduction. So Ma Nsundi married the sisters of Ma Lwangu and Ma Lwangu those of Ma Nsundi.

> But Ma Nsundi fathered many more nephews and nieces for Ma Lwangu than Ma Lwangu fathered for Ma Nsundi. The following of Ma Lwangu being much more numerous, Ma Lwangu took the chiefship and ruled over Ma Nsundi. Later, however, the dependents of Ma Lwangu showed much greater respect for their father Ma Nsundi than for Ma Lwangu, so their uncle became angry and said, "Since you do not respect me, I no longer wish to leave you my chiefship when I die; let Ma Nsundi rule over you when I am dead." (Cahier 13)

The story represents the Mbangala chiefs of the Nsundi clan (or group) as equals of the Ma Lwangu, allied by exchange marriage [*kimpiisa*], and recognizes the upsetting effects of demography and politics on such treaties. In short, the text is a narrative version of a sociological model or diagram. It also says that Ma Lwangu was superior at first, until Ma Nsundi overthrew him, but we can have little confidence in the historical value of this report as either an event or a class of events.[23]

Later in his text (Cahier 18) Babutidi asserts that after further political divisions and migrations resulting from Nsundi pressure, the people from Lwangu (the subdistrict south of Tshela) migrated to the coast to create the Loango kingdom. Any historical movement must surely have been in the opposite direction; the eastern Yombe communities were situated at the limit of the political, ritual, and commercial influence of the coastal kingdom. In his account of chiefly rituals, Babutidi describes in some detail the ritual of Kindunga, a body of masked retainers active after the death of a chief or his wife. Although Babutidi attributes this ritual to the Nsundi chiefs, it was and is well known on the coast (Mulinda 1995).

Far from being a naive account of "tradition," Babutidi's text incorporates interpretations at three levels at least: the syntheses developed by politically active and knowledgeable informants (like Lunungu's Me Kikita); sociological models in the form of stories (such as that of Ma Lwangu and Ma Nsundi) which Babutidi heard; and his own attempted (and ragged) synthesis. He concludes his work with this testimony to the difficulties of research carried on in addition to his professional responsibilities:

> I have heard of many other aspects of the rule of Ma Nsundi, how he governed and judged the people. I have arranged what I intend to write, but on account of other work that burdens me I have not had the time to tell you of them; and I do not know whether I will have time in the future. These things I have written, do not suppose that I myself preserve all this tradition—on the contrary! For I am only 26 years old. But because I travel to many places to write down tradition for Tata Laman, I have written them as I have been told, and pass them on to you, my friends who read *Minsamu Miayenge,* since I think that you also may be eager to hear them.

Trade Routes and Origins of Chiefship

The interpreter of oral histories should not, without corroborative data, pick and choose the bits to be regarded as truly historical; skepticism should reign uniformly. It is possible that important numbers of people or of "aristocrats" migrated across the Congo from Mbanza Kongo in the seventeenth century and that other groups dispersed toward the west from the original Nsundi center near the Manyanga market, but other evidence is needed besides the traditions that say so, because so much else that they say is not credible. For example, the traditions usually assert that the migrants occupied a land that was empty before they arrived—an assertion that cannot possibly be true. It is worth exploring the hypothesis that whatever local movements took place, the "dispersal" of Nsundi and other chiefship complexes records not migrations but political alignments that made regional trade possible in the eighteenth and nineteenth centuries. The "clans" and "ethnic groups" supposed to have migrated were integral to the trading system, but they were products rather than preconditions of it.

Ethnic Groups

The BaKongo are commonly regarded by scholars as divided into "tribes" or "subtribes." The most extreme recent exponent of this point of view, basing himself on a considerable antecedent literature, is R. Lehuard, the leading expert on Kongo art (Lehuard 1989). At the beginning of a two-volume study he speaks of the collective term "Kongo" as a source of confusion and deplores those who classify a given piece of sculpture as Kongo when, in his view, it should be recognized as belonging to one of no less than fourteen types, one of which he divides into thirty-two subtypes (Lehuard 1989, 40). This taxonomic excess takes for granted the static essentialism of nineteenth-century anthropology and ignores the known fact that successful Kongo sculptors established ateliers in which their individual styles were copied by apprentices.

Lehuard attempts to compare the physical types shown in Kongo sculptures with those of the "ethnic groups" who produced them, ignoring the fact that the ethnic labels were generated by administrative needs at the beginning of the twentieth century (Janzen 1982, 38–45; Dupré 1985, 26–28). He assesses physical type in the nineteenth-century manner, identifying cranio-facial measurements as the important features. He quotes a 1959 memoir by a French physician, Chabeuf, who provides nasal indices and classifications of chin form, eye form, and the like for groups called Vili, Yombe, Bembe, Lari, Sundi, and Kunyi, together with figures for the average stature of these groups and comments on which ones have thinner lips. Physical anthropology of this sort was already old-fashioned in 1959, and long before 1989 was recognized as absurd. The "classification" is the tautological result of the premises of the research.

The exhaustive survey of "ethnic" labels by O. Boone (Boone 1973), a compilation of everything written on the subject, reveals generations of struggle on the part of ethnographers and district officers to classify the BaKongo.[24] Although Boone herself frequently complains of the absence of good data and notes that most of the names are either recent, regional, or both, she persists in drawing maps of ethnic distributions and boundaries. Here is some of what her own evidence shows. Mayombe is the name of a region, not an ethnic group; formerly it meant "savages in the interior." BaYombe is the name of those who live there, but the BaYombe do not call themselves by this name, using instead the name of their district or clan (Boone 1973, 90–103). Bwende is the name of a region, not an ethnic group, and may be a nickname for the BaLari (Boone 1973, 104–108). The people around Luozi call themselves Kongo, but are called Manianga by others; originally the name of the famous market, later of the region to which this market gave access, Manianga is not an ethnic label (Boone 1973, 109–113). Ndibu, which came into use at the beginning of the century, refers to a speech mannerism allegedly characteristic of the inhabitants of a region. Nsundi (Sundi, BaSundi, etc.) cannot be assigned a territory because it is often considered a clan name (Boone 1973, 129; Schrag 1985, 22–28). The category "Nsundi" exists, but it is not an "ethnic group," an original community demarcated by physical or cultural characteristics.[25]

The cultural unity of KiKongo speakers, including the BaVili, BaKunyi, and BaBembe in French Congo, was recognized by Laman in 1916, after extensive journeys investigating language and history.[26] In recent decades, the principal groups recognized by the BaKongo in the Democratic Republic of Congo, all regional and all of twentieth-century origin, are (from west to east) BaYombe, BaManianga, BaNdibu, and BaNtandu (the last meaning "people up-river") (Monnier 1971, 370).

Clans

In principle all BaKongo belong by matrilineal descent to one of either nine or twelve original clans. In practice, it is impossible to sort the innumerable corporate matrilineal groups into the nominal categories of which they are supposedly sections; there is every reason to suppose that "nine" and "twelve" are products of the pervasive Kongo tendency to find multiples of three and four aesthetically satisfying.[27] Each group has a name, which may be some form of one of the "original" names, or may be quite different, and also has, or should have, a tradition which traces its origin to one of the original clans.

In practice, as we have seen, such traditions are always fragmentary and disputed. Babutidi, trying to clear up a messy situation, mentions that the clans also have auxiliary names: Nanga Na Kongo is also "KiNtamba," for example. In fact, any group was given a name corresponding to the political, local, or ritual affiliation that the speaker wanted to attribute to it, in a given context of political possibilities (MacGaffey 1970, ch. 3). Lutete says, of the chiefship of Yema di Yanga, "This clan is [called] Mwembe Nsundi, but they are not BaSundi. They lived in Kintete, in Nsundi country, but the chief, Me Yanga, did not want to go on living there but to have his own domain, that he might be chief" (Cahier 234). In other words, for Lutete, when this group abandoned its Nsundi patron it ceased to be Nsundi except in name. Elsewhere he says that a Nanga group ("Nanga" being one of the famous clan names) were Kimbenza when they arrived but because they wanted to build on "higher" (*nangama*) ground they changed their name! (Cahier 216, 70).

Local clans (clan-sections) are also internally heterogeneous. They are divided into "houses" and these in turn into "lineages." Three carved stone bracelets in the collection of the National Museums of Congo represent such a structure. One shows a head representing the founder of the clan Nanga Ne Kongo; another with two heads shows his two "daughters" (houses of the clan), Ndombe ya Nkanga ["black"] and Tukula dia Nkanga ["red"]; and a third with three heads shows the three "daughters" (lineages) of Ndombe: Nkenge a Nsungu, Tumbu a Nsongi [*sic*] and Nsula a Nsungu (Cornet 1975, 37). In each house at least one lineage will be regarded by the others as of slave origin (though the "slaves" will reject this status if they can and claim that they are the free members and the others are the slaves, strangers from elsewhere). Much the same happens at the level of the houses within a clan and ultimately of the clan itself which, in competition with the other clans in the vicinity, will assert that it is the original occupant of the area and thus the owner of the only authentic political title. A clan may admit one or more others as its partner, with which it intermarries reciprocally, but will assert that the rest are its clients, being the descendants of refugees, war captives, or purchased slaves. The traditions that purport to substantiate such rival claims are usually latent until they are mobilized in the context of some active dispute over land or witchcraft accusations; supposedly they are secrets known only to the elders of the free houses or lineages, but in fact they are pieced together out of frag-ments of fact and fiction as the need arises. Successful politicians include orators who know how to declaim impressive traditions according to the conventions of the genre.

The lines of matrilineal descent are thus always contested. Power, in the form of oratory (*kinzonzi*), wealth, force, magical claims, and ordeals decides the outcome of contests. Accepted pedigrees and traditions mark temporary phases of political equi-librium. "Descent," as linkage between lineages, houses, local clans, and clan config-urations grouped around particular titles—themselves unstable consecrations of pow-er—is and was mostly a matter of voluntary or involuntary clientage. As Doutreloux says, the idea of clan, which in principle should bring some order to Yombe society, "in reality only serves to justify the present situation of each group, especially its superi-ority to every other" (Doutreloux 1967, 197). There is no reason to suppose that the Nsundi category and its component local groups were any exception to this picture.

To understand chiefship we need to supplement the traditional anthropological focus on descent groups with two other concepts, alliance and class. "Class" in Kongo, an essentially contested relationship, subordinated "slaves" to the "free." To maintain slaves in subjection, the free formed alliances by marriage with neighboring clans strong enough to call themselves also free, constituting an oligarchy. Individual free men could choose to live with their own clan, with their Fathers (father's clan), or with their Grandfathers (father's father's or mother's father's clan). The preferred form of marriage, with a woman from father's clan, cemented a reciprocal alliance between the groups and also meant, from the point of view of the offspring of such a marriage, that they were not only members of their own clan but also numbered among its Grandchil-dren. Slaves, by definition, had the freedom neither to arrange their own marital alli-ances nor to choose their place of residence. The population of a given village included the clan believed to be the founders (many of whose members lived elsewhere), resi-dent Children and Grandchildren, in-marrying women, slaves, and other clients. The (male) Children and Grandchildren occupied managerial roles with respect to the af-fairs of the founding clan (including a chiefship if there was one) so powerful that the founders often seemed to be their subordinates, and the chief merely a manipulated symbol of the oligarchy of the free. The power of chiefs apparently varied, from this extreme of impotence to "big man" status of considerable weight, as a function of proximity to the trade routes and sources of imported goods, but in any case it surely remained as unstable in practice as it is ambiguous in historical retrospect.

Commercial Relations and Ritual Clientage

The "migrations" of the clans in the Vungu area correspond to the three traditional sources of chiefly titles: Nsundi (Manianga) in the east, Mbanza Kongo to the south (via Noki), and Loango in the northwest.[28] These are also, from a Vungu point of view, the principal directions of trade.

In the eighteenth and nineteenth centuries, the principal routes to the coast from Malebo Pool, where canoe transportation on the upper river was replaced by porters, ran either south of the Congo, through Mbanza Kongo, or north of it (Martin 1970; Vansina 1973, 260–65; Vansina 1991, 222 and Map 7.4). The northern route diverged from the other at a point on the left bank of the Congo River, near the original Mbanza

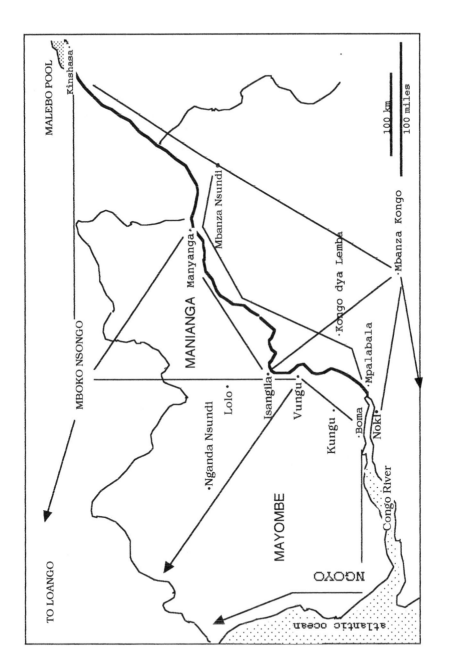

Map 2. Trade Routes

Nsundi and opposite the Manyanga market. From Manyanga, one branch went north to the Niari River and another west to about six miles north of Isangila, where it in turn divided into one that went north to the Ludima valley and the copper mines at Mboko Nsongo and another that went south to Boma (Johnston 1884, 116). The distribution of the Nsundi chiefships corresponds roughly to these routes (Janzen 1982, 62–67).

South of the Congo the principal trade route from the Pool ran to Mbanza Kongo and was at least partly controlled, even in the nineteenth century, by the Kongo king. Southern clans commonly add the suffix "Na Kongo" to their names to indicate their patron. On the south bank west of Mbanza Nsundi a lesser route, which grew in importance as agricultural goods replaced slaves in the Atlantic trade, became the one that the Europeans developed as their way to the Pool. The eastern stretch of this route was dominated by Nsundi clans which, despite being on the south side of the Congo, did not add the suffix "Na Kongo." At its western end one branch ran through the ford at Isangila to Vungu. Another connected with Kongo dya Lemba and Noki. Boma, although it was on the north bank, was most closely linked with Solongo chiefs and traders on the south side and only became important in its own right in the third decade of the nineteenth century. The branch of the southern network that ran from Boma to Vungu is the route of the "migrations" of the southern or "Kongo" clans, as described by Kinkela, Lutete, and Babutidi in Vungu.

The two scales of migration reported in the traditions, together with the differences in their content, correspond roughly to the difference between long-distance and short-distance trade. Magic, wealth, trade, and warfare were closely related; there was no public security, or any guarantee that enterprise would receive its reward. "If anyone crossed a barrier or entered a village where he was not known, they would capture him and put him in a slave-shackle, or even sell him if his people did not redeem him. He had to know his clan, his father's and grandfathers' clans" (Kavuna, 54); these affiliations would enable the captive to find local relatives as protectors. An *nkisi* called Mayodi, whose composition included an exchange of body hair between the dead and the *nganga,* was modeled on real-life treaties; it enabled the *nganga* to visit the village of the dead with impunity to negotiate the return of moribund persons whose souls were supposed to be held prisoner there (Lutete, 223). Commerce relied on ritually sanctioned alliances, which included *minkisi,* marriage, and chiefly titles. Comparing lists of *minkisi* from the seventeenth century to the 1870s, Janzen concludes that, along with adjudication, aggression, and fertility medicine, the category of *minkisi* that expanded most was that relating to trade and entrepreneurial undertakings (Janzen 1982, 56).

In Manianga and northern Mayombe an institution parallel to and probably of more importance than chiefship was Lemba, an *nkisi* whose initiates formed a prestigious association. Janzen in his definitive study describes Lemba as the transcendent institution of northern Kongo from the seventeenth to the twentieth centuries. A cult of affliction which recruited the wealthy, Lemba is remembered, according to Janzen, as a medicine (*nkisi*) of the village, fertility medicine, sacred medicine of governing, the government of multiplication and reproduction, and a sacred medicine integrating people, villages, and markets (Janzen 1982, 4).

Markets, which constituted the nodes of the trade network, were heavily protected by ritualized violence. Sales on credit were guaranteed by a respected *nkisi* (Kavuna,

54). The traditional punishment for those who broke market rules was to be buried alive in a highly ritualized fashion. In the area of modern Luozi, a form of chiefship (or, a market *nkisi*) called Lulendo was developed during the 1880s to control markets and protect trade from European encroachments (MacGaffey 1987).

Trade between markets could be protected by contracts with relatively powerful chiefs who provided ritual insignia as laissez-passer. Associations of initiates to *minkisi* such as Lemba offered similar security. Strict rules governed the manner in which a caravan passed a village so that it should not be mistaken for a war party. On the other hand, villages could try to trick members of a caravan into "stealing" food, or violating a real or pretended *nkisi,* for which offense they would perhaps demand a slave as compensation. The porters themselves had often been sold without their knowledge; small wonder that they carried out rituals to return their souls (*vutula nsala*) when they arrived safely back from the coast. In addition to the "real" dangers, the journey to the coast was thought of, as it still is, as an excursion toward the land of the dead.

To acquire an important *nkisi* was not just a matter of a talisman but of an alliance with a superior, the *ngudi a nganga* or the chief who provided it and who supervised its ritual maintenance. Fragments of this system have been documented. In 1870, the Kongo king could block trade by burning *minkisi* and forbidding their use (Jeannest 1883, 63); at this time he owed part of his wealth to his practice of selling titles to people who paid appropriately. Groups changed their patrons, and ambitious individuals acquired new titles of their own, which cost more than inherited ones.

Chiefs in turn requested investiture with ritual powers from others on whom they depended for goods. According to tradition, Na Mbinda of Boma, for example, went to the chief Nkulu lwa Mpanga on the Solongo [Angolan] side of the Congo and said, "Come to rule, you who come whence appear salt and useful things!" So Nkulu came to Boma to confer the title (Kinkela, 84).[29] Neamlau, one of the principal traders and pirates on the north shore, was invested with his title and provided with his ritual wife on the south side, where he had to be buried in the cemetery of the Solongo princes. In 1887, when Neamlau died, his people secretly ferried his body across the river in defiance of the European authorities, who wanted to provide a grand funeral in Boma (Dennett 1906, 16).

Similarly, the Nsundi chief at Nganda Mbuku in Mayombe was subordinate to the Ma Nsundi who remained in Mwembe Nsundi. If this chief died in Mayombe the BaSundi there were not allowed to choose a successor; they had to take the story back east to Mwembe Nsundi where a new king would be chosen. When he arrived he was authorized to take over the inheritance and the wives left by his predecessor (Babutidi, 13).

It is likely that the linkages between western and eastern Nsundi "clans" were those of economic and political dependency, not migration. This did not mean that there was one great Nsundi paramount, nor that all traffic from Manyanga market to the coast followed a single track. Since at least the sixteenth century there had been a number of routes through the mountains from Manyanga (Mbanza Nsundi) toward Mboko Nsongo, the copper mining district, and on to Loango on the coast. Each Nsundi chief referred his title to an earlier one farther east, but probably had a choice of patrons. The overall legitimation of the series was provided by traditions "on the grand scale," which were made up of cosmological and sociological elements, a theory of the system rather than an account of an organized reality. The largest unit was the group of clans recognizing the dominance of one of them and the paramountcy of its invested chief; in theory, all of them shared the same praise-name (*mvila*); their links with the paramount were not necessarily, or even probably, matrilineal.[30] The subordinate clans were clients, ruled by ordinary chiefs, their members more likely to be sold as slaves than those of the dominant clan (LKII, 48).

Dupré, describing the BaBembe of northern Kongo, argues that such patronage networks were transitory arrangements that were constantly disrupted and rearranged by warfare. Well-established villages, occupying ground favorable to agriculture, trade, and defense, could produce the resources (prestige goods, weapons, and manpower) necessary to mount trading expeditions or to make war on their neighbors. To participate in trade, weaker villages would have to hand over slaves to the stronger villages in exchange for the necessary goods (cloth, guns, salt, liquor—all imported from the coast) as they would also have to do when defeated in war. The expanding population of the stronger villages would eventually outgrow its subsistence base, segment, and found a new village whose origin was recorded in "small-scale" tradition (Dupré 1985, 83).

Conclusion, and a Further Problem

Historians have tended to take literally the stories of the migrations of the clans "from Mbanza Kongo" (presumably after the transformation of the kingdom at the end of the seventeenth century), although there is apparently no other evidence for them than the traditions themselves. BaKongo may identify the mythical Nzadi of tradition with the geographical one (the Congo), encouraging us to believe that narratives of crossing are historical, but the weight of the evidence indicates that it is in fact a cosmological boundary. Similar stories of crossing Nzadi (the name given to any large river) are told by people who live south of the Congo and east of the Inkisi (MacGaffey 1970, 21).[31] The significant elements in the stories are precisely the miraculous events that often attend the river crossing rather than the river itself; these events, which the rationalist social scientist is inclined to discard, warn us that this is no ordinary river.[32]

Because Nzadi the geographical feature was also Nzadi the cosmological boundary, chiefs, who embodied the power of life on behalf of their communities (see Chapter 8), were forbidden to see the Congo River and some other streams because to do so meant dangerous contact with the land of the dead on the other side of the water. In the 1970s, sailors out of the port of Matadi, accustomed to visiting Belgium, the United States, and Japan, were open to serious charges of witchcraft because they had the ready opportunity to sell the souls of relatives across the Atlantic, another version of the cosmological boundary. Individuals among them believed in the reality of witchcraft no less than did their stay-at-home neighbors.

This identification of what is, from my point of view, a real with an imaginary space is not uniquely Kongo, but has been reported several times from elsewhere in Congo and in West Africa. For the BaYanzi, in the Lower Kwilu region east of Kongo, the village of the dead may be in Kinshasa, the capital, as well as in Europe (De Plaen

197, 259). On the Igbo-Idoma borderland in Nigeria, "the ancestral masks are seen as coming from a home of the dead which mirrors, on another plane of existence, the home of the living." This home is identified with actual towns at some distance. The Agila masquerade Ogbodo Aba is the name of a real town, Ogbodo Aba, to which no Agila person would willingly go (Kasfir 1984).[33]

Traditions of migration "on the small scale" are reflexes of the politics of trade though they may also record migrations of small groups over short distances. Traditions on the grand scale, with their mythological references to the beginning of things and the origin of institutions, consist largely, I have argued, of social norms and models in the narrative form of dramatic, magically loaded incidents. Reporting the tradition of the Bweno title in Nganda, Lunungu writes (Cahier 172): "The name of the woman from whom the *nkisi* (Bweno, or Mpu) came was, I think, Musau. That's what Me Kikita said; I'm not sure, but Musau will do. Musau ["who crosses over"] gave birth to the *nkisi,* in the following way. She being pregnant, when the time of birth came she brought forth four things: a human being, a leopard, a snake called Muziki and a stock of chalk."[34] Later in the same manuscript we find that these elements constitute a succinct model of a particular ritual for the Bweno investiture. To be invested, the chief must enter the forest to be "licked by the leopard." Subsequently he is marked with the sacred white clay that the clan brought with it from Mbanza Kongo. Other members of his clan, however, who wander into the sacred grove will find their exit blocked by a python, from which they can escape only by paying the fine of a pig. The forest is the land of the dead, separated from the village of the living by the skin-changing snake, and the investiture combines the power of death, represented by the leopard, with that of permanent life, represented by the chalk. In short, the "incredibility" of the story is a clue to its meaning.

What then are we to make of Mbanza Kongo in the southern versions of these stories? On the north bank, the names of the places of origin—Mumba, Mutala, Mwembe, Bidi, and others, which recur over and over—are the names given to the cemeteries from which, literally, chiefs derived their titles. In the southern traditions, Mbanza Kongo seems to be the same sort of place, a land of the dead, renowned for its cemeteries containing the tombs of the kings and numerous aristocratic graves; in the eighteenth century, the bodies of southern chiefs were taken there for burial. In 1994 the founder of a Kongo church made the connection explicit when in his spiritual biography he wrote, "When I died in 1969 and went to the Kongo shore (*ku simu Kongo*), the land of the dead, I was designated Teacher of Kongo by the ancestors and instructed to rid the country of lies and disorder." Why the BaKongo "need" a land of the dead at all is a question to be addressed in Chapter 10.

The texts of the Cahiers are particularly difficult to interpret historically because of the "genre" to which they belong, peculiar as it is to the colonial context. They are neither archives nor oral tradition but a sort of hybrid, addressed both to BaKongo (in familiar language but a strange form) and to Europeans (in a familiar form but strange language). Having no natural home, they wait in a no-man's-land at the frontier, offering us polyvalent reflections of the liminal.

5. COMPLEXITY, ASTONISHMENT, AND POWER: THE PERSONHOOD OF OBJECTS

Nkisi is a thing to help people who are sick and to tell them things that other people do not know.

—Lutete Esaya

We live in societies that draw a strict distinction (the contrast is now criticized by the jurists themselves) between real rights and personal rights, things and persons. Such a separation is basic: it constitutes the essential condition for a part of our system of property, transfer, and exchange. Now, this is foreign to the system of law we have been studying.

—M. Mauss

Power comes from the land of the dead and, in pre-colonial times, was present and available for use in two principal forms, *minkisi* and chiefs, who were themselves *minkisi* of a sort. In the moral matrix of Kongo governance, chiefs are supposed to stand for power used in the public interest, whereas *minkisi* are concerned with particulars and therefore potentially under suspicion as anti-social. Nevertheless, chiefs were supported by important *minkisi,* especially of the kind called *nkondi* or *nkosi* (see Chapter 6). Lutete writes that the first *nkisi* was Mbundu (which is an ordeal to test suspected witches), followed by Mabyala Mandembe, an *nkisi nkosi* which was made in Ngoyo before Mayombe people acquired it. *Minkisi,* he says, are a class of *simbi* (*kanda dia bisimbi,* local tutelary spirits) that exist to help people who are sick.

Minkisi are fabricated things, yet they can be invoked to produce desired effects and they may willfully command the behavior of human beings. They cannot speak or visibly move of their own accord, but they are believed to be superior in other respects to ordinary people, able by mysterious means to produce effects at a distance. People depend on *minkisi* to do things for them in many conjunctures of everyday life, even to make life itself possible. An adequate account of *minkisi* must be as complex as the phenomena it addresses, including both the rituals and the objects now residing mutely in the vitrines and storage cabinets of our museums.[1]

BaKongo think of every human being as a vessel for an empowering soul or spirit. A given spirit may be replaced by another and transferred to a different container. If the animating factor is removed entirely the vessel is dead, or "empty." *Minkisi* are constituted in the same way, although the containers are not human bodies but figurines, clay pots, gourds, or bundles, among others. The empowering spirits of *minkisi* come from the land of the dead (Mpemba, *nsi a bafwa*), where the four classes of the dead include ancestors (*bakulu*), local spirits (*bisimbi, bankita*), ghosts (*minkuyu*), and those that are incorporated in *nkisi* objects, voluntarily or otherwise. Containing objects for ancestral spirits include graves, baskets of relics, and the bodies of living chiefs or headmen. In northern areas certain figurines and composites (*muzidi*) served as portable containers or feretories for ancestors (Kavuna 1995 [1915]).

The descriptions of *minkisi* provided by Laman's collaborators are often enormously detailed and profoundly authentic as records of indigenous understanding, but they must be read as interpretive documents of a specific character rather than as unmediated reflections of the original nature of *minkisi*. Kwamba, Demvo, Nsemi, and their colleagues were not profoundly experienced in the specialized knowledges of their culture, and as Christians they were usually spectators, rather than initiated practitioners, of the ritual practices they described. Furthermore, a text, no matter how detailed, is a reduction and transformation of a multi-dimensional experience; these texts in particular are not scripts for performances.

Since the texts were written, the use of *minkisi,* though still widespread at every level of Congolese society, has been camouflaged in response to repressive action by secular and religious authorities. Modern *minkisi* tend to lack the spectacular and dramatic qualities preserved in both the objects and the texts collected by Laman; they include charms made up in correction-fluid bottles to help schoolboys pass examinations, the magic that enables soccer teams to win or politicians to obtain ministerial posts, and sunglasses to preserve taxi drivers from accidents. In the minds of their users, such sunglasses are transformed by the fact that they have been ritually treated by a qualified *nganga.* Members of the elite search the world (Europe, Asia) for potent preparations and formulae to help in the political and economic competition among them.

General Description of *Minkisi*[2]

The Kongo term *nkisi* relates etymologically to other Central African words often translated as "spirit." Such a translation captures the important fact that *minkisi* are local habitations and embodiments of personalities from the land of the dead, through which the powers of such spirits are made available to the living. Ultimately, all of the dead can be contacted through the earth; consequently, *minkisi* normally include clays, stones, or grave dirt, incorporating the dead by the principle of metonymy (contiguity). Important *minkisi,* tutelary spirits of localities, were approached at fixed places or shrines in the earth, but most of them were in some degree portable. Whole communities depended on the most important ones for justice, healing, and prosperity. Lesser *minkisi* served particular needs for protection, wealth, or healing. The least of them sound almost familiar: Mungani (meaning "Someone else's"), to help young men attract women ("it comes from the jackal, who is always hungry"); and, conversely, Kibwa Ntombe ("It happened at night") to inflict impotence upon anyone who should try to sleep with your wife.

What is an *nkisi*? As we find it in these texts, in different aspects it is: a presumed original object, such as a calabash, "brought up" from the otherworld by the founder of this *nkisi;* a particular, focal object (the successor of the original calabash) supposed to have been derived directly or indirectly from the original; a collection of related objects, including costumes, musical instruments, cosmetics, and perhaps a special enclosure, constituting the material apparatus for the ritual activation of the focal object; and possibly, amulets or special-purpose derivatives of the focal object. These material manifestations of the *nkisi* correspond to a hierarchy of persons: a force from the land of the dead, embodied in the original object; the founding *nganga;* the present principal *nganga* (*ngudi a nganga*); the junior *nganga* or novice; and the patient or eventual beneficiary of treatment. In its most inclusive sense, "*nkisi* such and such" refers to all of these elements, present or implied in the ritual process of composition or activation.

The whole series of objects, paralleled by the persons to whom they are intimately related, constitutes a chain, a metonymically linked hierarchy of potent mediation extending from the invisible spirit to the client. (In many *minkisi* this hierarchy was reduced, and in a few there was no visible object at all besides the medicated body of the client.) Ultimately, the *nkisi* is an invisible personality, with a certain specific identity, which has chosen, or been induced, to invest itself in these objects and persons, through whom the powers attributed to it become effective. "The *nkisi*-object is a mechanism and a manner of domesticating, imprisoning, capturing *simbi* spirits in a material object which both represents and re-doubles them" (Buakasa 1973, 295). The complete *nkisi* is best understood, however, as including not just its material infrastructure but the entire complex of procedures, rules, persons, songs, and recitations with which the objects were necessarily associated.

In economic terms, the metonymic chain is the successive gifting of an inalienable object, the *nkisi*-package, including the knowledge of how to compose the charm, what songs to sing, and what rules to observe. The original giver, in the case of Mbola, for example, is the benevolent ghost who wants to make himself useful to the living (see Chapter 7). The first *nganga* of the *nkisi* passes on the gift to his successor for a fee; the *nkisi* object (a figurine, for example) partakes of the human personality of the donor and therefore demands respect in the form of gifts and obeisances. Each successive *nganga* provides the benefits of the *nkisi* to a client in return for a fee and the observance of rules. The *nkisi*-package remains the property of the original giver, who revokes it (that is, the benefits are no longer in effect) when the subservience expressed in the observance of rules is denied by ignoring them; the *nkisi* is then profaned (*sumuka*) and reverts to the status of an ordinary object. The mystification involved is that whereas the benefits are imaginary the fees are real.

Above and Below

All *minkisi* were classified by their cosmological domain of operation, which corresponded to their function, broadly defined. The principal functions were those of death-dealing and affliction and those of life-giving and healing. The domains were those of the above (*ku zulu*), meaning the sky and celestial waters, and of the below (*ku nsi*), the earth and terrestrial waters (Hagenbucher-Sacripanti 1973, 105; Dupré 1975).

These differences related to others, between political concerns (crime, punishment, treaties, transfers of persons between lineages) and those of health and fertility; between masculine and feminine, sky and earth, upper and lower parts of the body.[3] Masculine and political concerns were characteristically violent; the *minkisi* that answered to them were associated with storms, birds of prey, and diseases of the upper part of the body; such *minkisi* (of which the most important were called *nkondi* and *nkosi*) were likely to be the ones owned by chiefs to supplement their authority. *Minkisi* with predominantly masculine functions could be profaned by contact with women. *Minkisi* of the below were not so powerful and were generally restricted to healing; the texts often specify that a given *nkisi* can be used only for healing or only for cursing. *Minkisi* of the below related to sex, stomach ills, swellings, childbearing, and other functions of the lower part of the body. They are often identifiable by white clay covering them or shells attached to them; those of the above may wear feathers.[4] Others were specialized as *minkisi* for neither cursing nor healing but divination; Mbenza, Nkita Nsumbu, Mambuku Mongo, Na Maza, Ma Nsundi Mbumba, and Mfumu Kongo (for madness) are divinatory water *minkisi,* "which may give replies but cannot deal with witches" (Lutete, 216).[5]

This classification, explicit in a number of the Cahiers, is neither consistent nor exhaustive; many of the most powerful *minkisi* had multiple functions and were said to operate both above and below.[6]

> Nkondi is an *nkisi* of the above, that feeds both above and below, and so has four forms: Nkondi of the Water, Nkondi a Mungundu [the "sawing-bird," whose call resembles wheezing], Nkondi a Mantuku [causes difficult breathing] and Nkondi of the Sudden Curse. They are made up in statuettes with packets in which their medicines are kept. Some are used in the same kind of treatment, for others the treatment differs, as does the disease they inflict. The Water Nkondi eats in the water; if it is to strike someone, it meets him in the water and kills him there. If people find him half dead they seek out the *nganga* of Nkondi, to have him operate his *nkisi* and put medicines on his body so that he gets better. (Konda, 119; Lunungu, 173)

Since the human body is treated as a microcosm, the domain of origin of an *nkisi* corresponded to the part of the body that it was most likely to affect. *Minkisi* of the above characteristically afflicted the head and torso, causing headaches, bad dreams, insanity, and especially chest pains, pneumonia, and the like. These *minkisi* might also cause one to fall from a palm tree. *Minkisi* of the below controlled sexual and reproductive functions and diseases of the abdomen.

All *minkisi* were animated by *basimbi,* but violent ones required the incorporation of additional, malevolent forces.[7] The force chosen to animate violent *minkisi* was the ghost of a man known as violent and successful in his lifetime, not an ancestor (the clients of an *nkisi* did not constitute a descent group); or else it was the soul of someone, selected by his neighbors and mysteriously killed by the *nganga* for the purpose, which would take out its fury at being thus imprisoned on the *nganga*'s targets (Kiananwa, 73). In the case of Mbola (Chapter 7), the story of origin mentions a *simbi,* a remote and anonymous person from the land of the dead, who appears, apparently by chance, to one of the living at the water's edge, which is the appropriate place for such encounters.

Nkisi as Container

An *nkisi* in the ordinary or restricted sense, that is, some kind of portable shrine or feretory, was basically a container for the forces represented in it. This is consistent with Kongo notions to the effect that all personalities are those of human beings, alive or dead, and that they consist of a soul or spirit, capable of action, contained in a shell or housing from which it can be transferred by various occult means into other shells or bodies. The recipes for *minkisi* all specify what kind of thing the container (*nitu,* body) was to be; often it was a raffia bag, a snail shell, a clay pot, a gourd, or a wooden figure. This container was usually kept in a basket lodged in its own shrine-house or in a specified place in the owner's dwelling. The basic container might itself contain other bundles, shells, pots, or figurines.

Two kinds of exchange took place in the production of an *nkisi* whose basic container was a sculpture. (If it was not a sculpture, no special craft was called upon; in modern times, wooden figures are rarely used.) The carver who made the figurine did so for a price; this was an exchange in the subsistence sphere, from which no social relationship emerged; nor was there any sense that the figurine was anything but an object of utility, like a climbing loop or a mat. It became an *nkisi* only when it was filled with medicines, in the approved fashion and by a qualified expert, on behalf of a novice who was charged a fee and who entered into a relationship of permanent clientage to the principal *nganga.* The new *nkisi* was regarded as potent, rather than merely useful; its potency was guaranteed by the social hierarchy linking its new owner to the master, through him to the original *nganga* of this *nkisi,* and beyond him to a personality in the land of the dead.

None of the containers was an image of the spirit contained in it; a figurine that was part of a given *nkisi* complex was not an "idol." The container, as a whole and in detail, was a metaphorical expression of the action to be expected of the spirit, itself invisible and formless until it had been fixed (*kumwa*) in a particular body. Metaphorical and metonymic relations were not fully discrete; an element might be present in a complex for metaphorical as well as metonymic reasons. White porcelain clay (*mpemba,* kaolin), an almost universal ingredient of *minkisi,* is a good example of this multivocality. It is found in streambeds, thought of as the land of the dead; by its contact with them it assures their presence in the charm, but its whiteness may also metaphorically represent clairvoyance conferred upon the *nganga.*

The visual impression of containedness is itself a basic metaphor, a physical representation of the idea that the powers in question have been captured and remain under control; also, that their action in turn is to capture and control hostile forces.[8] The verb that best expresses this idea is *kanga,* "to tie, to bind," which can refer both to the evil action of a witch in preventing his victim from leading a good life and to magic protective against such a fate. Shrine-houses were made with knots (*makolo*) in the branches covering them, and many *minkisi* have knots added to them as an auxiliary expression of the concept of control. In the 1960s, screw-capped jars conveyed the same impression, with knots added to emphasize it.

An *nkisi* called by a given name did not always take the same form; Konda explains:

Malwangu is composed in many ways and takes many forms, some in gourds, also Malwangu the Mongoose and others. There is a Malwangu in a net with its sculptures, thus there are many different forms. Malwangu has a large bag and a *kunda* bell for pronouncing curses; tokens are buried for them in the villages. It is made up with colors of red ochre and kaolin, which are also ground into a powder. The powder is tied in a raffia cloth and firmly tied to the head of Malwangu. Those that have this kind of powder have no statue, just the bag and the bell for cursing. (Konda, 116)

When the *nkisi* was a wooden figure the most common form of subsidiary container of medicines was a pack sealed with resin, called the heart (*ntima*) of the *nkisi.* Round, imported tobacco tins made a useful pack. Such packs on the belly or chest of the piece were often symbolically "anchored" with one or more special nails and faced with a mirror, said to be the eyes of the *nkisi.* Many such mirrors are divided into quadrants, or marked in some way with a cross to indicate the directions from which danger may come (MacGaffey and Harris 1993, 65). Before mirrors were imported, any shiny material would do to frighten evil spirits by its glitter; a water-filled pit provided diviners with a reflecting surface.[9] A cowry shell appears on some well-known statues, and on one figure I found a large molar in the same position; these items may have a similar function to mirrors, but no explanation of them is available. Was the tooth chosen for its whiteness or its aggressive implication?[10] The power figure of an *nkisi* in the Museum of African Art, Seattle, is a European territorial agent seated to collect taxes; he has packs with mirrors on his chest, his back, and both shoulders, so that his "eyes" face in all directions. An *nkondi* in the National Museum of African Art, Washington, D.C., has a total of twelve mirrors, four of them facing in the four directions and the rest attached to various medicine containers hung all over the figure. It did not matter, for seeing witches, that the mirrors were often covered with the residue of sacrifices and other materials.

A pack may be placed to medicate the head, seat of intelligence; Makundu says that such packs serve to keep open the fontanelle, by which inspiration may enter (Cahier 258). Diviners in the 1970s protected their heads similarly, and for the same reason, with special hair treatments and caps. Packs are also found between the legs, attached to the ears (so that the *nkisi* may hear better) and attached in tightly wrapped bundles, gourd ends, and grass stalks (*maduda,* "guns" for shooting witches).

The Medicines Contained in the Nkisi

The container itself was a mere object, said to be empty or worthless (*mpamba*) until medicines were put in it. An animating force or forces from the land of the dead were included in the form of clays, such as kaolin or grave dirt. The priest or agent (*nganga*) of the *nkisi,* including both the founder and his successors, was identified with it by relics (hair, nails) included in it and by procedures of initiation, rules of avoidance, and items of dress. In use, *minkisi* were incorporated by means of medicines in the bodies of the individuals over whom their power was directly exercised, including the *nganga* and his client. Elements associated with the client or victim were put into the *nkisi* in the form of tokens, and elements of the *nkisi* were put into the client, too, in the form of a potion that he drank and of materials that were rubbed on his body or attached to it. The hierarchical sequence, from spirit to villager, was constituted metonymically, by a succession of contiguities.

Bilongo, "medicines," whose significance was given metaphorically, directed the power of the dead toward particular needs of the living. Medicines included animal, vegetable, and mineral materials, but these categories themselves were not recognized in the composition of *minkisi.* The word *bilongo* is related to *nlongo,* "taboo, sacred," and might better be translated as "sacra," although it is applied nowadays to aspirin and prescription glasses. Early ethnographers, including Laman, painstakingly collected the seeds and leaves commonly found in *minkisi* on the assumption that they constituted a Kongo pharmacopoeia whose chemical properties might explain their use.[11] Though some Kongo "medicines" have the properties of drugs, mostly purges and tranquilizers, most of them function as material metaphors that describe the powers attributed to the particular spirit. An *nkisi,* as De Heusch puts it (writing about the cognate Luba concept of *bwanga*), consists of "spirits of the dead metonymically caught in a metaphorical trap" (De Heusch 1971, 182). The metonymic chain linked the present use of the *nkisi* in ritual to its mythical foundation in the past and to the spirit that empowered it; the metaphorical components expressed social relations in the present, mediated by the *nkisi,* and the kind of effect that it was expected to produce.[12]

In his inventory of an *nkisi* Mbumba in his collection, the longest such list available for study, Laman identifies more than ninety medicines. For Ntadi, he gives nearly forty different kinds of medicine, each listed with its place and function in the assemblage, whether included in or attached to the bag (*teba vo tuula, komba va salu mu keba*), to be painted on the *nganga* (*mu kila*), to fortify him for the composition or invocation (*mu vanda*) of the *nkisi,* or for divination (*mu fiela*) (MacGaffey 1991, 26, 65).

The central elements are the grave dirt, kaolin, or sometimes a bone or other relic of a deceased former priest of the charm. The second and more numerous kind of material is that which states metaphorically the powers attributed to this personality, the charm, and its priest. A given element earned its place in the assemblage on one or perhaps both of two principles, verbal and visual. The first is a sort of punning principle by which the name of the element is made to evoke a particular concept. The ingredients put in the *nkisi,* Nsemi tells us, were named like the diseases in the body in order to help the *nkisi* in its work. "If an *nkisi* lacks medicinal ingredients it cannot accomplish a thing. So the *nkisi* takes medicines which become its being, its hands and feet, its eyes; medicines are all these. For this reason, an *nkisi* that lacks medicine is dead and has no life" (Nsemi, 391). The ingredients of particular *minkisi* include: *lusaku-saku* (a perfumed plant, *Cyperus articulatus* Linn.), "may I be blessed"[13] (*saku-munwa*); *kala zima* (charcoal) "that it may extinguish (*zima*)" witchcraft; *mpezomo* (copal resin) that it may flash (*vezima*) like lightning and blind the witches; *nguba nsamba* (a leaf) to represent the *malavu ma nsamba* (palm wine) that the *nganga* would undoubtedly receive as part of his fee. On the whole, the "verbal" metaphors serve to describe the capacities of the *nkisi* and its *nganga*: vigor, swiftness, and perception, for example. Some six or eight of the items that evoke these qualities recur so often in *minkisi* that Laman lumps them together as "the usual medicines."[14]

The second compositional principle is that of representation by metaphors that are visual rather than verbal. These metaphors state the conditions of which the *nkisi* is the master, those that it is supposed to be able both to inflict and to relieve. These elements, unlike the verbal ones, are relatively specific to the kind of function the *nkisi* performs. An *nkisi* such as Mutadi, for divination, consisted preponderantly of "verbal" statements about the *nganga's* generalized powers as a diviner, but an *nkisi* that inflicted damage, cured, or procured good things included visual "descriptions" of the condition in prospect.

The container of the *nkisi* itself usually embodied one or more such metaphors. The snail shell *kodya,* for example, by its name evokes the verb *kola,* to be strong; its spiral shape, *kizinga,* evokes *dizinga,* long life. Such shells are therefore appropriate containers for *minkisi* intended to favor childbirth and other situations in which the human body as a container is to be strengthened. An example is *nkisi* Nzyodi, whose function is succinctly described by Demvo:

> This *nkisi* Nzyodi is used to treat people suffering from stomach pains and those who pass watery feces and blood. With respect to blood, the *nkisi* is most used to safeguard women; if a husband is jealous he may guard his wife by this *nkisi.* If the husband has a pain in his rectum he may be treated with Nzyodi. (Demvo, 28)

Color is one important though somewhat limited source of significances. Many *minkisi* show the natural color of the container, probably darkened by smoke from being stored in the roof of a house or by the blood of sacrifices. Often, however, the *nkisi* in its entirety is colored in one of the standard colors of red and white, more rarely black, or a combination of these. One level of signification in these colors may be cosmological: white (*mpemba,* kaolin) signifies the land of the dead in general, red indicates mediation between the worlds, and black connotes both witchcraft and sexuality. But color significances may also be specific to the kind of power contained in a particular *nkisi.* For example, Nkondi Me Mamba was made up in a gourd bearing a sort of necklace of intricate knots and unreadable oddments; the whole thing was colored red with a paste of clay. Lutete says: "This *nkosi* is invoked when someone has the sickness of vomiting blood, or if others have epilepsy or die very suddenly. Then whoever is most in touch with this *nkosi* invokes it and a pig is killed for it" (Lutete, 224). The Nzyodi just described consists of two snail shells, one filled with red and the other with white material; usually, and specifically in this instance, such a pairing connotes male and female elements, respectively. *Nkondi* figures show no consistent color scheme; some are all black, some all red, some red with white spots, black with red stripes or red and white spots, etc.; *minkisi* concerned with water and fertility are likely to be all white. In connection with *minkisi* of the above, dark cloths could induce rain; blond or albino hair (*mfumbu*), which was for sale in markets, kept the skies clear; its whiteness (*kimpembe*) was believed to avert rain (Diafwila, 47).

An *nkisi* for blindness in the Musée de l'Homme, Paris (92.52.4) offers a fascinating variation on the usual forms. It consists of a canoe, to go to and fro across the water between the worlds. It carries medicine packs amidships, one with a mirror; one end of the vessel is colored white, the other red; these are the colors of mediation between the seen and the unseen, between life and death (see below). An *nkisi* from Ngoyo, in the National Ethnographic Museum, Lisbon, may draw upon the slave trade for its dominant metaphor, though its function is unknown; showing a couple confined in the bottom of a blood-red boat, it had the reputation of being extremely dangerous (Bastin 1994, 76).

Besides colors, animal, vegetable, and mineral elements carry relatively specific connotations. For example, the head of a *kintombo* bird, whose cry foretells the future, might be included in an *nkisi* for divination (Mutadi), the head of a viper in one that attacked wrongdoers, round stones in one that cured tumors (Mbumba from Kingoyi). A stone may also be present, however, because its name, *tadi,* invokes the verb *tala,* "to look," and the function of divination. The *kinkanda* monkey is very strong in resisting death; the *nsengi* monkey steals food with exceptional malice (*kimfunya*) and finds out secrets by spying on people's dreams. The *nzuzi* wildcat, like the mongoose, looks after the clan, but is superior to the other animal in that, like the leopard, it can leap a great distance, so that if trouble breaks out it can escape; it also takes revenge for you by eating other people's chickens (Kwamba, 147). The appropriate animals for any given *nkisi* were revealed in dreams.

Because "spiritual" forces are associated with birds and other flying creatures, *minkisi* were sometimes equipped with feathers, especially those of raptors, to form a kind of headdress such as the *nganga* himself might also wear. The "feathers," however, may be made out of raffia, as in the case of Ngovo; this charm is contained in a buffalo horn, to which cut strips of raffia, bound at the ends, have been tied as though they were feathers.[15] For practical reasons, the actual material in an *nkisi* is synecdochic; that is, a part stands for the whole: the beak for the bird, the leaf for the tree, and so on; much of the work of the *nganga* in preparing medicines consists of scraping off (*teba*) small portions to be included in a bundle or medicine pack. When such medicines are attached to the wooden figure, beneath a ball of resin, they are not, of course, literally visible. Many *minkisi* advertise their inner secrets by the outer flamboyance of bells, rattles, supplementary *minkisi,* and strips of animal skin, among other things.

Matunta, describing Lunkanka, illustrates the role of visual metaphors:

> The little packet that is in Lunkanka contains medicines, including the teeth of vipers and of all snakes that bite with especial viciousness. Also the claws of mongoose and jackal, so that the *nkisi* should be as active in seizing wrongdoers as the mongoose is eager to snatch chickens and the jackal to dig up corpses. (Matunta, 307)[16]

Besides elements whose presence is explained by a specific metaphor, some were included merely because they were remarkable to look at and occasioned astonishment. This is particularly but not exclusively the case for *minkisi* such as Funza that were strongly associated with creative, life-giving powers, represented by strange, twisted roots and oddly shaped stones. Pieces of quartz and fossilized resin might likewise be put in partly because they are visually interesting. Among the contents of Mutadi are a bead (*lubwela*) and a knot, both said to be included for appearance only (*mu dyambu dya ntoko kaka*).[17] In the cult of Mbenza in Mayombe astonishing objects (*mangitukulu*) were supposed to be revealed to the finder in trance as evidence of contact with the Mbenza spirit (see Chapter 9). A common element of *minkisi,* enclosed in the container or hung outside it, is the cocoon of the lictor bagworm, which serves no other function than to enhance by its remarkable character the apparent sacredness of the *nkisi;* in form it is itself a miniature *nkisi* (MacGaffey 1988, 196).

The protective or healing powers of an *nkisi* were made effective by having the patient lick some of the medicines, or by giving him or her an amulet, a "child" of the *nkisi,* thus completing the metonymic chain from the original power source to its specific beneficiary. Hair from the heads of participants in the ritual might be included in the *nkisi* to show that it, the *nganga,* and the client were in close fellowship (*nkisi, nganga ye ndiona vendi wo bana kalasana nki ntwadi nadede*); this hair is their life or essence (*lunzi;* Lutete, 216).[18] In the case of an aggressive *nkisi,* tokens of the crime, called "dogs" (remnants of something stolen, for example), were attached to the *nkisi* itself to make the precise connection (see Chapter 6).

Nsemi asserts that the construction of an *nkisi*—the ingredients and the songs—must follow the original model. "If you put the ingredients together helter-skelter you injure the *nkisi* and it will become angry over your failure to arrange the ingredients in the proper order. An *nkisi's* strength is rooted in how it was discovered originally; the ingredients are put in as they must be, else it loses its strength and gets confused" (Nsemi, 391). This theory, however, is simply an ex post facto legitimation for an *nkisi* that commands respect because it is believed to be effective. One that does not work, as Nsemi goes on to explain, is presumptively one that the owner designed himself; he will be ridiculed accordingly. In practice both the items and the significances attributed to them vary considerably even within the same region. The visual vocabulary is never so precise that we might construct for it a dictionary of meanings or a recipe book; the looseness of the relationship between *nkisi* elements and the significance attributed to them is necessary to the sense of mystery they convey and not simply the result of lack of precision on the part of either the ethnographer or his informants. Although anybody can form an approximate idea of the reasons for the presence of given elements, the theory of them asserts that only persons who have been properly initiated can know exactly what they mean. This theory is, literally, a mystification.

We could continue to examine *minkisi* and the explanations of them offered by indigenous writers, but the principles are clear. In sum, there are five categories of elements in *minkisi:* two that are metonymic, linking the powers of the spirit first with the *nkisi* itself and then with the persons affected by them, including the *nganga;* two that are metaphorical, whether verbal or visual; and one that adds to the "astonishment." The verbal associations, built out of folk etymologies, link the names of *nkisi* components to the general powers with which the agents of such a spirit are credited. The specific functions of the particular *nkisi* are signified visually. As in other uses of metaphor and metonymy, the two elements are often compounded in complex ways that make up an intellectual game from which many BaKongo derive pleasure and satisfaction.

It is noticeable that the field of metaphorical items is much more diverse and at the same time much less structured than that of the metonymic elements with which we began. This finding is consistent with De Saussure's observation that in a syntagmatic chain "a term [such as kaolin] acquires its value only because it stands in opposition to everything that precedes or follows it. . . . Whereas a syntagm immediately suggests an order of succession and a fixed number of elements, terms in an associative family occur neither in fixed numbers nor in a definite order" (De Saussure 1966, 123, 126). The metonymic hierarchy of mediators between the original spirit and an amulet worn by the victim of some personal affliction is literally a story line, set out in the myth of origin of the particular *nkisi* and the history of its successive priests. Around each link in the chain, heterogeneous metaphorical elements that give it specific character cluster like so many iron filings.

Auxiliary Objects

The focal object (pot, shell, statue) which in a restricted sense is the *nkisi* is only a part of its material infrastructure. Prescriptions for the composition and use of important *minkisi* include mention of the musical instruments (drums, rattles) to be used; some *nkisi* rituals even had distinctive rhythms—the rhythm for Mbola is *ndebekete mbidimbiti* (according to Nsemi, 390; but Konda, 116, says *bukwimvi, bukwimvi, bukwimvi*). Musical instruments were (and are) believed to call down spiritual forces which manifested themselves in a sense of exaltation among the participants, often in trance behaviors. As voices of the dead, musical instruments, or models of them, became *minkisi* in their own right when medicine packs were added to them.

Several instruments formed part of the metaphorical resources deployed in *minkisi*. The small double-ended wooden bell was perhaps the most important; by its shape it suggested mediation between worlds—a significance underlined by the use of double clappers—and its name, *kunda*, carries the sense "to pay homage."[19] The dog-bell, *ndibu*, was appropriate to *minkisi* that hunted witches. *Minkisi* of the *nkondi* type, which shared functions with chiefs, wore miniature *ngongi* bells, characteristic items of chiefly regalia associated with official announcements.

The appearance of the *nganga* sometimes matched that of his *nkisi* in being equally spectacular and repeating some of the same features. He wore feathers in his cap, bells on his ankles or in the cloth around his waist, and ornaments which were part *nkisi,* part jewelry (MacGaffey and Harris 1993). Particularly if he were a diviner he might carry a whisk, made like a broom, which helped to identify the sources of evil; it shook when he was "getting close." Such a whisk (*mpiya*) was itself medicated, an *nkisi* in its own right. To compose it, the *nganga* "captured" the ghost of a rich and belligerent man by taking earth from his grave (Kavuna, 65; MacGaffey 1991, 24).

Costumes usually included lines (*makila*) drawn on the body to outline the limbs, that the body might thereby be protected (*kidukwa*). The first step in the ritual of composition was to outline the eyes with white lines called *mamoni* (from *mona,* to see), to indicate powers of occult vision. While he applied these lines the priest of Mbenza sang, "Oh, lines around the eyes, the eyes of understanding!" (Lutangu, 211; MacGaffey and Harris 1993, 52).[20] Lines might also be drawn on the *nkisi.*

Besides the requirements of performance at the time of composition or invocation, each *nkisi* impressed itself on the consciousness of its owner and on the beneficiaries of its action by imposing taboos on them, in effect making use of their bodies as part of its material apparatus. These obligatory behaviors constantly recalled properties of the *nkisi* and aspects of its relation to the cosmos and to ritual practice. Commonly, *nganga* Nkondi was forbidden to eat anything roasted, lest his contact with fire become excessive, or to eat certain foods, especially a cock, in company with the uninitiated. Nkondi could not be composed when storms threatened, nor might it be transported in such weather. Persons related to a water *nkisi* might have to make special obeisances before crossing a stream; Ta Kayi Mbele, *nganga* of Bambimi, who relieved a village of the murderous assault of his *nkondi* by having the people bathe in the river, was himself obliged to bathe only in his house, lest his contact with water become dangerously excessive (Kimbembe, 80). The owner of crops that had been protected by Yoba (*yoba,* to bathe) might not eat of them without first showing them to *nganga* Yoba; a woman treated by this *nkisi* was obliged thereafter to throw water plants on the fire before cooking anything (Kibangu, 74). Kimpanzu, which cured "the disease of the ribs," *lubanzi,* contained a slat or "rib" from the wall of a house, the house itself being analogous to the human body; the *nganga* of Kimpanzu was forbidden to break off such a slat, to draw a knife across the ribs of a house, or to play the *diti* ("marimba"), whose keys were made from ribs of palm leaf (MacGaffey 1991, 36). One limitation on the number of *minkisi* one might acquire, besides that of expense, was the number of restrictions they imposed.

If the container is a simple bag (*salu*) made by gathering the corners of a raffia square, the *nkisi* only assumes a spectacular quality when it is undone to be put to use by the *nganga* (Hagenbucher-Sacripanti 1973: pl. 25). Very often, however, spectacular complexity begins on the outside of the container with the profusion of objects attached to it to suggest the powers within. External complexity of surface is usually evident in the case of *minkisi* intended to be carried or worn, as are amulets and those that are made up in a shoulder bag (*nkutu*). The bag of Mutadi is hung about with monkey skins and the bells and rattles the *nganga* would use for divination. Items are often attached to the exterior of a container by painstaking labor; Nkoko Bondo is a bag dressed in a whole macramé of knotted strips of colored cloth and pieces of raffia, with more knots inside the inner bag of the *nkisi* (MacGaffey 1991, 115). Nkubulu, for smallpox, is a complex of small, carefully made bags of varying sizes, colors, and textures, each in its tightly knotted net (MacGaffey and Harris 1993, 53). Such highly detailed appearances helped to convey the message that the *nkisi* was a remarkable and presumptively potent object.[21]

Anthropomorphic figures were dressed like the *nganga,* similarly painted and hung about with amulets. Often, the *nganga* caused the *nkisi* to shake as though it, too, were possessed. Na Maza is contained in a calabash colored red with a camwood paste; the contents, now missing, were also colored red. An attachment, linked by several strings, consists of a pack of medicines built on a small antelope horn (*mbambi*) that wears a kind of skirt made of strips of two kinds of cloth. These cloths were once covered with pigmented pastes in such a way that the outside was black while the inside was red. The pack of medicines was red, too, so that when the object was waved about it would flash its red underskirt and the medicines it partly concealed (MacGaffey 1991, 82).

In some *minkisi* the names of the *nganga* and his or her assistants, like the medicines, bore the names of properties attributed to the ritual; the *nganga* of *nkisi* Mpodi, a water *nkisi* for "sucking out" (*vola*) irritating creatures from under the patient's skin, had four assistants with such names as Mabeeta (*beeta,* to snatch, tear off) and Mayungi (*yungula,* to steal by magic). The *nkisi* itself included a series of small female sculptures with the same names, which were washed as though they were people. The principal statue was said to require the soul of the *nganga's* mother. Twenty or thirty women at once might be initiated to this *nkisi;* "the year in which Mpodi is composed is nothing but one party after another" (Konda, 119).

Procedures

There were many minor, special-purpose *minkisi,* such as Kinswiti, for treating the oversexed, and Matalatala ("Look at me!") for having a good time at dances, but the usual role of an *nkisi* was to control a disease or misfortune, both inflicting and curing it. A disease or misfortune might indicate that the victim was being punished for some crime he had committed, or it might mean that the *nkisi* was demanding that he or she be initiated to its mysteries and become its *nganga.* The source of the problem would be indicated by the *nganga* of an *nkisi* for divination, which answered questions but did not treat anything. A candidate *nganga* might also be summoned in a dream, or as he walked by water he might see an object bobbing in it; the sight would cause him to fall into ecstasy (*tuntuka*). The composition of an *nkisi,* which included the initiation of its *nganga,* might also be called by this verb. The ability to tremble, *mayembo,* manifested in the shoulders, was a requirement of many *minkisi;* one who lacked it might pay an *nganga* for a treatment to develop it, for example by composing *nkisi* Suku. Suku was "a small *nkisi* in a bag; it can be composed in only ten minutes" (Kionga, 96).

Initiation

The stories of the call to become *nganga* are uniformly conventional, though the details may be updated. The story of an unexpected encounter with a marvelous object at a watercourse, followed by spirit possession, is found from Sierra Leone to Zambia. Modern versions employ modern media. In an interview, a *nganga,* born in 1941, told how he suffered from recurrent illness, until his sister, recently deceased, appeared in the dream of an old woman in the village to tell him to become *nganga.* His immediate success in this occupation aroused the jealousy of the local nurse-clinician and obliged him to obtain authorization from the government (any official-looking paper would do). Thereafter his fame attracted journalists and a TV crew from Kinshasa (Dimomfu 1984, 9).

The initiation of a new *nganga* included the composition of his *nkisi.* Necessary personnel included the candidate (*mwan'a nganga*), sometimes his wife, and a team of performers whom he paid: the instructing *nganga* (*ngudi a nganga*), musicians, and dancers. The complex choreography of initiation to an important *nkisi* contrasted public séances, more or less theatrical, with private phases, equally impressive by their mysterious exclusiveness (Janzen 1982, 133). As Christians, Laman's young collaborators cannot tell us what went on in the initiation enclosure.

> One who acquires knowledge (*kinganga*) of a water *nkisi* may first be ill for a month with the disease of the *nkisi.* Then he begins to shake, and runs to the water, entering into it to the place where the *minkisi* are. He may stay there for three or four days learning about the liminal *nkisi* he wants to compose (*nkisi wowo wazimpambu ukazolele vanda*). On the fifth day he will enter into trance and emerge [from his initiation enclosure] trembling (*ku nsi a mayembo*), with his *nkisi* on his chest. He runs to his house, where eventually he is brought out in view of the public by the *nganga* in charge. (Makundu, 250)

In a version of Na Kongo from Bulu, near the modern town of Luozi, the candidate being initiated to the *nkisi* was secluded for several weeks and said to be sojourning in the land of the dead under the water. Excitement in anticipation of his return was kept up by his wife, initiated with him as his assistant, who appeared spectacularly "from under the water" into the view of the assembled singers and musicians, "with her *mpidi* basket and the wand of Na Kongo in her hand." Eventually the *nganga* himself appeared, in even more impressive fashion, to take his seat upon a mat in full panoply of paint and charms.[22] The *nganga* was himself part of the composition of the *nkisi;* his appearance was often made to resemble the charm (or vice versa), its functioning depended upon his observance of its rules, and he was to some extent himself part of the material apparatus: "When they wanted it to rain they put their *nkiduku* charms in the water and stood statues out of doors, or put them too in the water. No rain. Then the *banganga* would be hazed and pissed upon and beaten with sticks to make it rain. Still no rain. Then they would give up and say, 'It is God who made man, and he is preventing the rain'" (Kunzi, 134).

During the composition of an *nkisi,* a song described each item and its function as it was prepared and inserted. Although the words were performative utterances specifying the function of the item, none of the texts indicates that they were "spells" essential to the efficacy of the composition. Other songs likewise described what was going on; the training of the novice consisted in part of learning all the songs, which thus directed the stages and components of the ritual.

> When they are composing the *nkisi,* the instructing *nganga* teaches the invocations for the *nkisi* to the one for whom he is composing it, and sings as he adds the medicines together, preparing two, three, four or five of them for the people who are composing it. For each medicine there is a song, beginning with responses, like this: *"Ri-ri-ri-ri ndundu mba?"* [Reply:] *"Mbaka!"* *"Ndombila santu, mama ziezie, Mahungu?"*— *"Yoya!"* (Ecstasy!) Then he chants, "Where the python slept, the *simbi* arose." [A riddle:] "Your mother! Don't you hear the drum?"—[Answer:] "Palm wine." When he has been given palm wine they drink, then prepare another medicine and sing another song.

> The one for whom the *nkisi* is being composed follows his instructor: *"Ri-ri-ri-ri, ndundu mba?—mbaka! Ndombila santu, mama ziezie, Mahungu? Yoya!* Continue the work, I have palm wine. At the approach of the storm, the [weak] *nsafu* tree fell. These things may not be spoken. *Ri-ri-ri-ri ndundu mba? mbaka! Ndombila santu, mama ziezie, Mahungu? Yoya!* Palm wine to invoke magic, to invoke priesthood. *Ri-ri-ri-ri, ndundu mba? mbaka! Ndombila santu, mama ziezie, Mahungu? Yoya!* Continue the work, I have palm wine. The partridge in the grassfields, the partridge, the crest of the beautiful one who loves traveling. *Ri-ri-ri-ri, ndundu mba? mbaka! Ndombila santu, mama ziezie, Mahungu? Yoya! Malavu. Ri-ri-ri-ri, ndundu mba? mbaka! Ndombila santu, mama ziezie, Mahungu? Yoya!* Continue the work, I have palm wine and a chicken. I asked for palm wine, lest I contradict my teacher. *Ri-ri-ri-ri, ndundu mba? mbaka! Ndombila santu, mama ziezie, Mahungu? Yoya!* Palm wine to invoke magic, to invoke priesthood. *Ri-ri-ri-ri, ndundu mba? mbaka! Ndombila santu, mama ziezie, Mahungu? Yoya!* Continue the work, here is palm wine. Oh, oh, in the palm trees a matter

befell, the judgment of Na Kongo [the *nkisi*] will settle it, roaring is heard in the waters." (Kavuna, 58)

The formula, *Ndombila santu,* is a request for palm wine; the answer, *mama ziezie,* "Here it is!" *Ndundu mbaka,* equally formulaic, refers to *simbi* spirits (Matunta, 299). The python "asleep" is the *simbi* in otherworldly phase. The "roaring in the waters" is the voice of *bisimbi* as heard at the waterfalls where they live. The complex of meanings conveyed in initiation constituted an exclusive body of knowledge which was a source of authority, a space for creative thought, and a convincing experience of a reality no less real for its artificiality, as we also find in complex computer games and the highly literary mysteries of some Western intellectuals (Barth 1975, 79; Luhrmann 1986, 317).

An obvious feature of Kongo songs is their repetitiveness; a song usually consists of one line repeated over and over, with minor variations, forcing the group to focus intensively on a single idea until it tires. The function of songs, whether in judicial contexts or in the composition of *minkisi,* is not simply to announce what is happening, or to comment on it, but to make it happen. Songs and music of all kinds are thought of as instruments that make spirits present, rather than as accompaniments to the action. In modern prophetic churches, which have partly replaced the *banganga,* songs are tested for their effect and rejected, like *minkisi,* if they do not "work."

Invocation

The *nkisi* once composed could be invoked by the procedures *lokila, ntangumunu,* and *nsibulu.* Though Kiananwa contrasts them (Cahier 73), the difference is not always apparent. *Lokila nloko,* or *koma nloko,* is an appeal to a spiritual entity, perhaps to *bisimbi* to request healing, but in this instance to a violent *nkisi* to have it hunt down a thief:

"Lord Nsansi, come search for my chicken that has gone astray; I do not know who stole it, but do you look for it. Prick your ears, a man, a woman, who may be dead, or from far away. Who ate it, follow them, two or three, don't you hear? Strike them with fire, with the knife, with the gun, destroy in the sky. Plunder and strike, whether he is drinking water or smoking, seize him with fire. If he takes up his knife, bind him; if he lifts his gun, bind him! Whoever stole my hen, from whatever group, find him! If they make medicines, cancel them. Search, sweep, Lord Nsansi, prick your ears. Be strong! Don't you see them in their village? If it was just an animal that took it, *po kya nkondi kyatuuka,* do no harm, but if a witch, a sorcerer, deal with him!" Then he sings this song:

Eh, cut down the silk-cotton tree, *wolo e e e!*

There he was summoned, *wolo!*

Female witch, male witch, he did not pay the debt at all, he did not sell it, they ate him. There they ate him, two of them, three, maybe five. Seize them both, throw them down, restore the village.

Eh, there where he was sent, eh, *wolo,* cutting down the silk-cotton, eh, *wolo.* There where they conspired, there were two of them, aah! three of them, aah! many indeed they were. Are not you a dog with four eyes? Seek him for me, I do not know him.[23]

The adjuration is a string of phrases and references, both elliptical and conventional, which were available to anyone. Some speakers built more symmetries into their prayers than this one did. *Wolo* is the sound of the rattle that accompanies the song. The branches of the silk-cotton tree (*mfuma*) are the usual place for the village witches to congregate, there to consume any who has not acquitted himself of his debt to them. Dogs, domestic animals that mediate between the village and the forest, are hunters and have eyes for both the visible and the invisible. It all sounds rather excessive for a mere chicken. The supplicant allows that perhaps an animal took it, in which case Nsansi should relent. *Po* conventionally represents the sound of a dash of water coming from the *nkisi* (*kya nkondi kyatuuka*) as a blessing or release.

Kiananwa goes on to give an example of *nsibulu,* a curse pronounced while banging the *nkisi* on the head with the blade of a knife: "If he tries to urinate, seize him; he wants to defecate, grab him! Make him hot for the wives of other men. He can neither stand nor sit. If he goes to war, may he be killed by birdshot!"[24] *Ntangumunu,* a recitation, is a declaration of innocence by the *nganga* on behalf of a patient who has unwittingly broken a food taboo.

Minkisi of the above, known in eastern Kongo as "blood *nkisi,*" often received sacrifices of at least palm wine or a chicken; expensive ones required a goat or a pig.[25] The act of immolation mimed the violence the *nkisi* was to inflict on its target; the blood poured over it, which it "drank," was to invigorate it. The meat provided a feast for the neighborhood, or at least for the *nganga* and his assistants.

Minkisis *in One Neighborhood*

In principle, since *minkisi* deal with problems of all sorts, a list of those in use in any given area might constitute an inventory of local concerns. At one point Lutete lists forty *minkisi* that deal with various diseases; at another, sixty-five assorted *minkisi* are named without comment. At the end of the second list he writes, "These are the powers of *minkisi* [according to] an *nganga* named Lubamba Mwanda," presumably an informant who was asked to name all the *minkisi* he could (Cahier 225). Eliminating some redundancies from Lutete's lists and adding some he does not mention which occur in the inventory of the Ethnographic Museum, Stockholm, or which are described by Lwamba Joseph, also of Lolo, we have a list of a little more than one hundred *minkisi* known in Lolo in 1915.[26] Of thirty of them nothing is known but the name. For another forty-five we have minimal information, including perhaps an object and a brief description of its function. For thirty-four *minkisi* we have descriptions varying in length from a paragraph to several pages; of these texts, fifteen have been translated and published (MacGaffey 1991). They include Bau, the hot iron ordeal to test witches; Lau, for good hunting; Mayanda, to correct weight loss; Mbenza, a begetters' cult; Mbongo, for divination; Mbumba, for warfare and to control rain; Nkengele, for war and hunting; Nkita Nsumbu, for prosperity; Nkoko Bondo, for masculine concerns including good hunting and the treatment of scrotal hernia; Nkondi Me Mamba, for vomiting blood; Nkondi ya Nsanda, which controls skin disease; Nkubulu, for smallpox; and Nsungu, to inflict lightning strikes.

Some of the *minkisi* listed separately are evidently parts, such as amulets, drawn from larger ensembles to serve some distinct function among those that characterized the *nkisi.* The given name of an *nkisi* often begins or ends with the name of its external form, such as *mbumba* (medicine bag), *nsilu* (amulet), or *kinzu* (pot). Some of those merely mentioned are described in detail in reports from other mission stations, showing that they were known over a wide area; some of the names also appear in seventeenth-century documents, so important *minkisi* appear to have been influential over broad expanses of space and time. We have no real assurance, however, that anything more has persisted than the name, which may well have drifted from one context to another, as did the names of descent groups and the praise-names of chiefs.

Lutete is silent about eight *minkisi,* well known from elsewhere, that are merely mentioned but not described in the texts from Lolo; they include Bunzi, Funza, Lemba, Londa, Ma Mbuku Mongo, Mbumba Lwangu, Na Kongo, and Ndungu. Bunzi, as found in Ngoyo, was one of the great shrines of the coastal area, though Lutete mentions it only as a cure for bellyache. Lemba was, from the seventeenth century until 1921, the most important *nkisi* in northern Kongo, probably more important as a factor in social organization than chiefship (Janzen 1982). Funza is described in some texts as a demiurge next in importance to Nzambi (God); he represented the essence of creative force, manifested especially in twin births and in strange, twisted sticks. Londa, in various forms, was an *nkisi* for women and childbirth. Mbumba Lwangu is a retributive *nkisi* of *nkondi* type, and also the name of the rainbow serpent mentioned by Bittremieux. Na Kongo, in various forms, is one of the most widely distributed and, if we can judge by the name, one of the oldest of all *minkisi.*[27]

Lutete mentions, but does not describe in detail, seven *minkisi* called *zinkosi* because they have the power to kill people suddenly; all are wooden figures: Nkondi, Kunia, Nkaya, Makonda, Mbenza Me Nsanga, Mpindi, and Me Tamba. If any of them falls over, everyone must lie prostrate until the *nganga* receives a male goat which he sacrifices, so that the statue may drink blood. The only *minkisi* of *nkondi* or *nkosi* type described in detail by either Lutete or Lwamba are Mungundu, Nkondi ya Nsanda, and Nkondi a Mamba. At least one (nameless) *nkondi* from Lolo is known to exist still (Lehuard 1980, fig.10); it belongs stylistically with some others that are apparently products of the same workshop in northeastern Mayombe. Other *minkisi* deal with a sadly banal range of medical complaints—fever, toothache, barrenness in women, the repeated deaths of children. Lutete describes Mbenza as a begetters' cult, for blessing the fathers of children; in Vungu, it was also an *nkisi* of chiefship, giving its name to purportedly the most important political complex in eastern Mayombe (Doutreloux 1967).

The thirty-five or so documented *minkisi* from the one region of Lolo, most of them described by Lutete himself, reveal a remarkable range of creative possibilities within the general compositional principles discussed above. Space does not permit a full account of this diversity, but here are some of its forms. Mwivi ("Thief") and Nsonde Ngovo were highly competitive *minkisi,* controlling success and disaster; afflictions treated by them included poverty and falling from a palm tree. They enabled their owners to be successful in hunting both game and married women and also to cause others to fall from trees, become poor, or lose their wives. Panzu, Mbongo, and Dipombo were said to be composed (*vanda*) by the dead, not by the living, who merely took the necessary components (raffia cloths [*mbongo*], a figurine, and a mirror) to the cemetery. "When the *ndungu* drum sounds in the village, the dead come to take the cloths and the figurine and go to compose the *nkisi.* After two days, when the drum sounds in the village of the dead, the assistants go to get the figurine, already composed [with medicines], and the bag, already prepared and tied up with the leaves of *matunga nyundu*" (Lutete, Cahier 223, in MacGaffey 1991, 14). As in the example of *nkisi* Mayodi (Chapter 4), the model for this acquisition of special power is that of relations between villages; in this instance, between a patron and a client in search of a ritual link. Nsungu and Mbambi za Luwanda were composed with lightning, that is, with copal resin, *mpezomo.* When lightning, *mpezomo,* is seen in the dry season, it is known that the *nganga* of such an *nkisi* has died; "[I]t is his inner envelope (*pupu kiena mu ngudi*) that goes to the sky."

Conclusion

Minkisi registered in a form both concrete and dynamic the characteristic experiences of Kongo life; some of them related to such lasting features as the climate, the problems of fertility, or the stresses of social competition, others to new diseases or new political pressures. This registration was not passive, since the rituals related to *minkisi* mediated the same stresses and pressures; indeed, the life process was outlined and guided by them. Their manifest functions of pursuing criminals or helping women to give birth were illusory, but the forces believed to activate them were real, in the sense that they were derived from the social tensions everyone experienced.

The invocation and activation of an *nkisi* inscribes the experience of disease, theft, adultery, or other problem in a standardized cultural register, so that it ceases to be idiosyncratic and unmanageable. The cultural prototype usually takes the form of a myth of origin for the particular *nkisi;* some such myths are common to the whole Western Bantu area and beyond, but others are traceable to historical episodes (MacGaffey 1987). The central figure in such a myth may be named, but the name itself may be simply a part of the symbolic apparatus of the *nkisi* rather than a personal one. At his or her initiation the *nganga* commonly took a name which obliquely coded part of its occult properties; this name might be recalled in the songs of the *nkisi* as the name of its founder.

By its "plot" such a myth appears to lodge the origin and significance of the *nkisi* securely in an ancestral past, but the successive events of the narrative correspond to the stages of the initiation ritual (*mpandulu*) by which the apprentice *nganga* composes the *nkisi.* The story, for example, of how Na Kunka came to possess the original Na Kongo by journeying to the land of the dead under the water is simultaneously an account, slightly transposed, of the ritual of initiation, that is, of the apprentice *nganga's* seclusion and eventual reappearance in his new capacity (MacGaffey 1991, 77–80). Myth and object thus specify important details of the performance of the ritual which itself is the *nkisi* in the broadest sense, embodying the sequence "institution, succession, performance" characteristic of the administration of power in all religions (Tambiah 1968).

Experienced as processes in which objects were metaphorically composed and deployed in a context of music, dance, costume, and operations performed upon the body, *minkisi* included a kind of theoretical analysis (not necessarily a very good one) of the problem at hand and conveyed a sense of participation in a manifold but still only partly structured, thus still mysterious, experience. In the terms suggested by McLeod, they are "process art" rather than "statement images." Statement images express what is formal, fixed, and timeless, as in ancestor figures or the portraits of kings. Process images depend on a range of linked codes (verbal and other) for their significance and may therefore vary more readily in form than statement images can. They do not stand independent of the rituals in which they are used and may, as *nkondi* do, take form over time as the signs of use multiply upon them. They provide complex metaphorical structures suitable to situations of readjustment, personal or social (McLeod 1976). Extracted from its context of use, because its medicines were lost, its rules were not observed, or its *nganga* died, an *nkisi* reverted to the status of mere object—in the case of wooden figures, to that of *ndubi,* an image.

Considered as art, as many *minkisi* are, they should be regarded neither as unitary works nor as collages but in a sense as texts, in which the relation between word and image is intrinsic and therefore much more intimate than that between picture and label, or between a sculpture and critical commentary upon it. W. J. T. Mitchell summarizes Nelson Goodman's comparison of pictures and texts in a way that illuminates *minkisi* (Mitchell 1986, 67–68). Writing, according to Goodman, is a "disjunct" system, depending on a set of discrete symbols, such as the letters of the alphabet, which contrast in precise ways. A painting, on the other hand, is semantically "dense," meaning that no mark may be isolated as a unique, distinctive sign; the meaning of a mark (a spot of paint) depends on its relations with all other marks in a dense, continuous field. The component "medicines" and other materials of an *nkisi,* though not quite "letters" or even "words," are disjunct, and readable separately.

6. NKONDI: MINKISI TO KILL PEOPLE SWIFTLY

In the Towne of Mani Mayombe is a Fetisso, called Maramba: and it standeth in a high basket made like an Hive, and over it a great house. . . . By this Maramba are all thefts and murders tried: for in this Countrie they use sometimes to bewitch one another to death. When any dieth, their neighbours are brought before Maramba: and if it be a great man that dieth, the whole Towne cometh to sweare. The order is, when they come before Maramba, to kneele and claspe Maramba in their armes, and to say; Emeno, eyge bembet Maramba: that is, I come to be tried, O Maramba. And if any of them that sweare be guilty, they fall down starke dead for ever.

—ANDREW BATTELL (1558)

Understanding the principles upon which *minkisi* in general are composed, we are equipped to consider the most spectacular and, at the same time, the most distinctively Kongo type, *nkondi,* which are wooden figures stuck full of nails and other hardware, now prized in museums as "nail fetishes." The name means hunter (from *konda,* to hunt alone and at night, rather than in a game drive), and the chief function of Nkondi is to pursue evildoers.[1] Most of the classic museum examples of Nkondi, such as Mangaaka, Kozo, Mabyala, and Pfula Nkombe, come from coastal areas; for coastal *minkisi* the descriptions left by collectors, missionaries, and travelers are sketchy and generally unreliable. Laman's documentation, derived from Swedish mission stations in the interior, is excellent, although his description of *nkondi* (LKIII, 8–91), which includes no more than brief and unidentified extracts from the texts, is superficial. This chapter, though it offers only selections and summaries, is based on translations of every text in the manuscripts that can be considered related to Nkondi (some hundreds of pages) and on visual inspection of *minkisi* in museums in Europe and the United States. Chapter 7 gives three different accounts of *nkondi* Mbola as samples of the original texts.

Before 1921, when the combined influence of missionaries and the Kongo prophet Simon Kimbangu suppressed their spectacular rituals, *nkondi* were regarded by Ba-Kongo as the most important and distinct type of *nkisi.* In practice, the *nkondi* type is identified at best by a cluster of features which overlap and merge with other clusters. In the coastal regions the term *nkondi* is not known, and there seems to be no substitute, although there were objects of similar description and function, some of which are among the most admired of African sculptures. It is often difficult, therefore, to tell whether an object in a museum is *nkondi,* unless by some near-miracle the indigenous

NKISI MABYALA

Congo. Le grand Fétish Mabialla
Mandembe.
(Congo. The large fetish Mabialla
Mandembe.)
Nkisi Mabyaala Ma Ndembe
Loango, French Congo (now Republic of
the Congo)
Photograph by Robert Visser, 1882–94
Publisher unknown, published ca. 1910
Postcard Collection
Eliot Elisofon Photographic Archives
National Museum of African Art

term is recorded in association with the piece. In fact, the word itself, though convenient, is not essential to any study of retributive *minkisi*.[2]

Form and Distribution

The distribution of approximately thirty named *minkisi* which one can describe
with some confidence as *nkondi* corresponds closely to dialect areas, as identified by
Laman.[3] There were undoubtedly many more *nkondi* than these (Lehuard 1980). The
Cahiers deal with *nkondi* under generally descriptive names such as *nkondi, nkondi a
nkoma* (nailing nkondi), *nkondi a mfyedila* (*nkondi* for divination) and *nkondi a ntilumuka* (flying nkondi). Other *minkisi* which were invoked to pursue witches and the
like, in much the same way as *nkondi,* were not called by that name, and some *minkisi*
named after famous but distant *nkondi* types exercised milder functions altogether.
Mabyaala in Lolo, for example, though it bore the name of one of the best known and
fiercest *nkondi* on the coast, was an undistinguished *nkisi* for divination (MacGaffey
1991, 11). The farther from its place of origin, the less elaborate an *nkisi* became.

Nkondi are one of the few features characteristic of Kongo culture in its widest
regional extension, a roughly triangular area extending from northern Angola and
southern Gabon, on the coast, to Kinshasa inland. This distribution provokes some

questions. It has been suggested by more than one author that the practice of driving nails into anthropomorphic wooden figures is derived from a seventeenth-century mis-interpretation of Christian crucifixes (MacGaffey 1986a, 266). It is true that devices of this type are found nowhere else, and that no other area of sub-Saharan Africa was as intensively exposed to Christian influence before the nineteenth century, so the idea has some plausibility.[4] On the other hand, as we shall see, this interpretation requires that the tail wag the dog. "Nailing" is part of an enormously complex set of ideas and practices which are overlooked when nails alone are seized upon as the distinctive feature.

Very little information on the characteristics of *minkisi* dates from before the sev-enteenth century. The missionary Luca da Caltanisetta, though he mentions no nailing, describes a priestess of thunder and lightning (*nganga nzazi*) whom he saw in 1698 banging together two idols she carried in her hands, in order to curse a suspected witch (Bontinck 1970, 121). The reference to lightning and the cursing function are both characteristic of *nkondi*. In two other instances he observed an *nganga* banging two anvils together for a like purpose. This banging would be *nkomono,* "hammering" the *nkisi* to "arouse" it (see Chapter 3). It would seem, therefore, that nailing replaced an earlier kind of hammering; it was only about this time that BaKongo began to make nails.[5] In modern times, the *nganga* of Nkondi Mukwanga is recorded as banging together two anvils to announce his arrival (Kibangu, 74).

More recently, in the early 1950s, the Munkukusa movement to cleanse villages of witchcraft used a procedure which included many features of *nkondi;* the continuity is striking. The Children of the owning clan of the village brought back mud from the cemetery to place on the altar of the local church, subsequently dumping it into a cruciform trench, the "cross of Jesus," dug outside the building. A person declaring his innocence of witchcraft knelt before a second cross made of wood, swore an oath, and drove a nail into the cross: *"Engwa yamana vutukila kindoki, e, lusonso koma!* If I have returned to witchcraft, may the nail strike!" (Janzen and MacGaffey 1974, no. 26).

Western	Northern	Central	Northeastern
Kozo*	Mafula	Makwende	Bambimi
Mabyala*	Maniangu	Na Mpindi	Mubwongo
Makongo Mbongo	Mayimbi	Mayimbi	
Mangaaka*	Mboko	Lunkanka	
Mavungu*	Mbola	Mbola	
Nkondi Mamba	Mukwanga	Musansi	
Nkondi Nsanda	Mungundu	Na Kongo	
Pfula Nkombe*	Nsambu Mpindi	Ngobila	Ngobila
Mbumba Cindongo	Mb.Cindongo	Nkondi za Mafula	
Mwalele (Me Mpembo)	Mabimba		
Malwangu[6]	Mwe Kongo		

Nkondi is at least partly interchangeable with *nkosi,* a term which presents some problems. It seems to be derived from *kosa* (to crush, smash), an action associated with the leopard. "All *minkisi* or statues that are nailed are called *nkosi,* because they strike people in the chest and can destroy a village in short order."[7] "*Minkisi* of *nkosi* type: if people in the community are dying of the disease of vomiting blood, or trembling with fear. Their power is to kill people swiftly."[8] The buffalo is said to have *lendo kiankosi* (*nkosi* strength) to kill people (Kwamba, 147). *Nkosi* ordinarily means "lion," and in that sense it is mentioned as inferior to "leopard" in a praise formula addressed to a chief; this specific association of the word with the animal occurs in one of Lutete's texts from Vungu but in no other. In other texts, *nkosi* appears to be cognate with the southeastern Bantu term *nkosi,* meaning "lord": "Nkosi is an *nkisi* for which they have extreme respect, almost like God" (Lutangu, 209). In none of these statements is there any explicit reference to lions, nor do lions appear in the lists of fauna provided in several Cahiers; in forested areas including Vungu there were no lions, though they were found in the savanna near Mbanza Kongo. In modern Kongo, however, *nkosi* (lion) and *ngo* (leopard) are regularly paired as examples of force.[9]

Although the indications are not fully consistent on this point, it appears that Nkondi held entire groups, probably villages or village sections, responsible for a crime, even though it was the work of a single individual. If any member (not thought of necessarily as the criminal) fell ill with the appropriate affliction, the group would have to reassert its own internal discipline, besides paying the *nganga* of Nkondi to call off the pursuit. Unlike other *minkisi,* which concerned individuals, Nkondi, like (and perhaps in conjunction with) the chief, maintained public order.

Containers: Figures and Pots

Wooden figures into which nails and blades have been driven are now the best-known form of *nkondi,* but not all such figures were called *nkondi* by their users, nor were all *nkondi* nailed. Nailing is merely one way by which an *nkisi* might be aroused; some examples of *nkondi* were made up in clay pots, into which, obviously, no nails could be driven. Though Nkondi a Mungundu, in well-known and documented examples, was a nailed wooden figure, one *nkisi* of this name has as its base not a wooden figure but a wine bottle (MacGaffey and Harris 1993, 76–77).

In a number of examples, the material apparatus for the ritual included both a pot and one or more figures, but some texts specify that there was no *teki* (statue); in others, the author may simply have forgotten to mention the pot or the figure. Babutidi says simply that Nkondi is in a pot or a calabash, in which there is the pit of an *nsafu* fruit (Cahier 6); the *nganga* bathes the patient afflicted by Nkondi in water from the pot and then has him lick the *nsafu.* A powerful metaphor for magical preparation is that of "cooking," and what is perhaps the best-known of all traditional sayings refers to *makukwa matatu malambidi Kongo,* the three hearthstones on which Na Kongo cooked (his medicines).

Since pots lacked the visual appeal of sculptures, collectors ignored them and few are now available for inspection in museums. In Cuba, however, where the Kongo tradition is strong, the use of pots rather than statues survives in the Afro-Cuban cult of Palo Mayombe. In the nineteenth century the ex-slave Montejo decribed a typical

Kongo procedure for "imprisoning" an opponent, who would thereafter fall ill or suffer misfortune:

> Drumming was part of the *mayombe*. A *nganga,* or large pot, was placed in the center of the patio. The powers were inside the pot: the saints. People started drumming and singing. They took offerings to the pot and asked health for themselves and their brothers and peace among themselves. They also made *enkangues* [*nkangi*], which were charms of earth from the cemetery; the earth was made into little heaps in four corners, representing the points of the universe. Inside the pot they put a plant called star-shake, together with corn straw to protect the men. When a master punished a slave, the others would collect a little earth and put it in the pot. With the help of this earth they could make the master fall sick or bring some harm upon his family, for so long as the earth was inside the pot the master was imprisoned there and the Devil himself couldn't get him out. That was how the Congolese revenged themselves upon their master. (Montejo 1968, 21)

Dapper describes an *nkisi* in use in Loango in the seventeenth century which could well be a pot-*nkondi:* a large pot heaped with red and white clays, marked on the sides with white lines and colored above with various colors, with a number of hooks, nails, and iron points stuck in it, to which were attached shells and bits of cloth (Fondation Dapper 1989, 259).

When Nkondi was a wooden figure, its form corresponded metaphorically to its function. "They are made with defects to show that these are what the *nkisi* inflicts. If someone has twisted arms or legs, everybody knows that Na Kongo did it. If nose or lips are missing, they know it is Mbola" (Kiananwa, 73). Nkondi ya Nsanda is not a nailed statue but a bag with twenty-two figures in it, two "parents" and their twenty children, all of which are missing arms, legs, or other parts (MacGaffey 1991, 150).[10]

The figure is often that of a human being, signifying aggressive intent by its uplifted spear, hands on hips, or bared teeth.[10] Many *minkisi* resembled warriors, who in the eighteenth century painted themselves red to make themselves invulnerable and who wore feathers "to protect their heads" and *panaches* to frighten the enemy (Proyart 1776). A very large figure (four to five feet high) was particularly threatening: "When the witches see that an *nkisi* as big as that has been mobilized against them they let go of the invalid" (Konda, 120). Staring or "naked" eyes were thought to be very threatening, and a protruding tongue was *lobalala* (an aggressive gesture). Such details should be read conservatively, however, because as Kiananwa warns us it may be that what you see is just made for show; the sculptor wants to demonstrate his skill (Cahier 73). A sculptor told Laman that it was easier to carve a figure with hands on hips because the arms were less likely to break off.

Despite the generally virile character of *nkondi* and their functions, wooden figures were sometimes female, or sometimes a couple (because a man should have a wife): "Nkondi is an *nkisi* in two sculptures, back to back. The powers of the male are more vigorous, but the female softens them. If they were two males, many houses would be burned by the storm" (Makundu, 258). Nsemi confirms the indication that female figures were meant to indicate a less aggressive mode of action than male ones: "If the *nkisi* cannot be persuaded to relent and let go of its victim, then it is male. But the female *nkisi* is different; it is less persistent and will let go, for it is of a more docile nature" (Cahier 391). The distinction is, however, relative at best. A female Nkondi carrying her child on her back is described as follows:

> The name of the *nkondi* is Lungwedi, "Talk," and of her child Manswela, "Tears." When the mother catches something she gives it to Manswela so that the child may eat and drink blood. If she doesn't get anything, Manswela bites her mother's back to demand food. (Demvo, 27)

In conformity with the hunting metaphor, tokens called *mbwa* (dog) were fixed in *nkondi*. Some *minkisi,* notably Kozo, take the form of a one- or two-headed dog covered with nails; the figure is not a picture of a dog as such but a statement about hunting wrongdoers and about movement to and fro between the worlds of the seen and the unseen. Hunting nets entangle the legs of some *nkondi,* and *madibu* (dog-bells) are among their common attributes.[12] When the *nkondi* included a pot it might be medicated and placed on a fire to boil, as a divination device; such a pot was supported, not on three stones as usual, but on sticks of *luvete* wood, a physical pun on the verb *veta* (to hunt).

Figures of *minkisi* that did or did not travel might be carved appropriately:

> Mabimba is a very large statue, but in the shape of a horse (*kavalu*), not a man. It also has a pot that is stood [on the fire] and tokens are tied to it. . . . Its wife is not shaped like the male but in the form of a person, though the image is without arms or legs because it always stays in the house and does not travel like the male. If you are carrying Mabimba on a trip, do not look behind you. Mabimba's own neck is not built to look sideways or gaze about, so don't you do so either. If you look back, Mabimba will twist your neck for you. So the one who carries Mabimba always looks straight ahead. And if anyone should come from behind you he is not allowed to look but must make a detour. (Konda, 116)

"Twisting the neck," *zeka nsingu,* was one of the typical injuries Nkondi was called upon to inflict. The reference to a horse dates this *nkisi.* Horses, mules, and donkeys were briefly and unsuccessfully introduced in the 1880s to provide transportation; they were regarded by the BaKongo as very frightening and as able to pursue witches at night. Unfortunately, no *nkisi* of this type has survived.

Nkondi a ntilumuka (flying *nkondi*) could travel on its own; an example of this type was Mukwanga Yulu, also called Mayima, replete with references to "the above":[13]

> This *nkisi* is called Mukwanga, "rattle," because it is carried in a palm wine tapper's calabash or little gourd [such as rattles are made from]. It is called Yulu because it is always "up in the air"; it has a medicine pack as base, but no base to stand on. Besides, it is thought to travel only up high. It is called Mayima, "hawk," because it circles about in the sky, watching wherever it has been sent. Mayima is like a man whose legs never rest but who goes about all the time to see whatever his master sent him for. (Nsemi, 388)

Elsewhere in the text we read of the wine-tapper's climbing loop, the *nkisi's* attack on the dreamer's head, the storm it brings on, and the rule that Mukwanga be stored in the roof of the house (see below).

Diseases, Lightning, and Vultures

Nkondi belonged to the category of *"minkisi* of the above," which were associated with rain, thunder and lightning, fire, and birds of prey, and which both cured and imposed afflictions of the upper part of the body. These afflictions included nightmares, headaches, skin diseases, stiff neck, and the disease called *lubanzi* (ribs), which probably included pneumonia and other prevalent chest infections. Kimpanzu cured *lubanzi* and Nsungu sent destructive thunderstorms, but neither was *nkondi*. Other afflictions "of the above" included falling from trees and dizziness.

The associations of *nkondi* with storms, fire, and the above are explicit. Nkondi was said to travel in the whirlwind; to dream of fire, or of roasting something, was to know you had offended Nkondi, whose *nganga* was forbidden to eat anything roasted (Lunungu, 154). To be dizzy and fall in the water, to fall in the fire, or to fall from a palm tree was to be seized by an *nkisi a nkosi* (Lutangu, 212). Lightning that fell in the bush was just lightning, but "if a person or an animal was struck by lightning they would consult the diviners (*nganga za Ntadi*), who would say, 'A dog has been buried in an *nkisi nkondi*'" (Mindoki, 334).[14]

The attack of *minkisi* of the above was likened to that of birds of prey, such as the vulturine fishing eagle, *mbemba* (*Gypohierax angolensis*), or the hawks, *mayimbi*. To dream of palm nuts being eaten was an omen of death. Kwamba shows with what extraordinary vividness the belief was realized:

> To look at, all *nkondi* have feet on which to go about when they wish to wreck a village, but Mukwanga flies to the attack. It has tied around it the feathers of hawks and owls, to show that these birds are the servants of Mukwanga, who fly off whenever it wishes to seize someone to shed his blood.

> People seek out the *nganga* of Nkondi to have him drive iron into his *nkisi*. When he has driven in spikes on account of the bad dreams the sick person is having, he tells the ghost [that animates the *nkisi*] about those who are pleased to carry troubles to that house. The ghost then activates an owl to go eat palm nuts on the roof of the witch's house, that he may stop eating the one who is seeing bad dreams at night.

> If the witch does not want to desist from his hostility towards others at night, the ghost enters into his servant the hawk to go and be seen in the villain's dreams. The hawk will perch on the head of the person, pluck out some of its feathers, drop them on him, and sink its claws into his leg to carry him off. Then [the witch] will cry out in his dream when he sees those terrible claws ready to drag him off.

> Another time he will see in his dream his house on fire and himself trapped in a palm wine tapper's climbing loop. There will be a raging storm, and people fighting. That will make him think the dreams have come to set him on fire, his mouth will be dry: "Nkondi Mukwanga has pursued me here, surely I will die in the same fashion." Not long afterward he will feel a burden on his back, a pain in the blood, blood will gush from his nose, and he will die of this affliction. People will say, "Nkondi Mukwanga came to take him, because of conflicts in the night, but now it is over." (Cahier 149)

The restlessness of pigs as a storm approached, or the scurrying of chickens when a hawk was about, were both warnings of impending attack by an *nkondi*.

Thunder is owned by the *bakisi* of the above, such as Nkondi. Someone who is the victim of theft invokes Nkondi: "Nkondi, your mother! Strike the village in which you find my things! Thunder, your thundering! Owls, your owls! Your *ntoyo* bird!" Thereafter, if the accusation is true, lightning will strike the village. The inhabitants will then send for *nganga* Nkondi lest lightning strike again. It is thought that lightning and Nkondi have existed from the beginning. Nkondi fell down from on high when the thunder rolled. Therefore lightning (*nzazi*) is contained in Nkondi. Lightning that falls just anywhere comes from the sky, but that which strikes a village is directed by an *nkisi.* (Lunungu, 173)[15]

These beliefs are ancient, and the dangers to which they correspond were real. Flimsy houses in exposed locations could be totally destroyed by storms; people and animals could be killed by lightning. In modern times, a fall from a palm tree is still regarded as the work of some particularly sinister force. In the seventeenth century, according to Girolamo da Montesarchio (1976, 193n9) unseasonable thunder was believed to be caused by *nganga nzazi* (lightning expert). In Nsundi, Girolamo found many "superstitious objects" used by *nganga nzazi* (he does not tell us what they looked like), which he burned, causing sorrow and hostility among the locals, who said the rain would not fall. "However, Our Lord caused it to rain heavily the following day."

Procedures

The basic procedure for motivating a retributive *nkisi* to pursue the unknown author of some misfortune was to drive nails or blades into the wood of the figure housing its powers.[16] The "hammering" procedure was called *koma nloko* or simply *nkomono.* In the simplest gloss, *koma* means "to hammer," and *nloko* means "a curse" (from *loka,* "to curse, bewitch"; from which also *ndoki,* "witch"). Guilt was revealed when, a few days after the cursing, some neighbor fell ill.

> Putting in a nail (*mpuya*) is like this: if a man has had something stolen and he asks in the village who took it, but nobody owns up, he goes to *nganga* Mwalele and asks permission to nail his *nkisi* on account of the thing that was stolen. The *nganga* says, "Very well." So he takes a wooden knife [?] such as Africans make and drives it into the statue as the knife of nailing (*mbeele ya mpuya*), "Ko! ko! ko!—Lord Me Mpembo [praise-name of Mwalele], bite his chest, bite his ribs; you are an *nkisi* of the storm, strike on high. If he stole this and that, go for him!" If the thief falls ill he will go to the *nganga,* who will calm his *nkisi* with [the juice of] *munkwisa* and then collect his pig [the fee for calling off the *nkisi*]. (Babutidi, 15)

The association between "the above," as of storms, and afflictions of the upper part of the body is particularly clear in this invocation. Tokens or "dogs" (*mfunya, mbwa*) could be attached to the nail, or to the figure in some other way, to remind the *nkisi* of the particular task confided to it. The *mfunya* is installed in the *nkisi* as a "dog" by being "nailed" (*komwa*) into it (*kimfunya,* malice). The tokens could be pieces of the manioc stolen by the thief, or bits of the hair or clothing of the plaintiff, and the like. Kavuna describes the setting of "dogs" in connection with *nkisi* Na Kongo:

Putting a "dog" in the *nkisi*. When any one has lost peanuts to an unknown thief, he takes two or three raw peanuts, bores holes in them, threads them on a string and goes to hang them on the *nkisi*. If one has lost plantains, he takes a little scrap and puts it in the *nkisi* as a sign. If he does not know whether his wife has committed adultery but suspects her, he cuts a few hairs from her head at night while she sleeps and puts them in the *nkisi*. One who has lost a chicken and does not know whether to blame an animal or a thief, puts two or three feathers in the *nkisi*. If someone's manioc has been eaten by a thief or a pig, and the owner of the pig will not pay, he takes all the stumps and gives them to the *nkisi*. (Cahier 58)

"Nailing" may be literal, or it may be effected in other ways, especially if the *nkisi* does not include a wooden figure. An alternative term is *ziika,* "to bury," in expressions such as *ziika maloki,* "to bury curses" in the *nkisi; ziika mfunya,* or *ziika mbwa,* literally "to bury the dog," that is, to insert the token of the matter at hand; clients of *nkondi* seeking the return of money were said to "bury it in *nkondi*." Symbols of *nkondi's* vicious attack might be buried in strategic places, such as the entrance to the village; the *nganga* of Nga Bambimi, investigating a death, killed a dog and a goat at the grave of the deceased, buried the heads of these animals and of two kinds of poisonous snakes in the grave, and then buried teeth of the dog and of the snakes around the village and at the principal bathing place before accepting a fee and going home. Some three weeks after his departure, when it became known that many people were dying, the *nganga* would be summoned to purge the village of the curse (Kimbembe, 80). A witch, however, supposedly might do the same thing for his own evil purposes. Signs are buried in the *nkisi* itself, in parallel with the noxious medicines buried at the edge of the village to protect it, or in this case to attack the evildoers within. In *minkisi* of Nkondi type, the affliction they impose often took the form of a feeling of pressure on the chest, as in pneumonia; the verb here is also *koma,* "to impose a burden." It was also possible to provoke the anger of an *nkisi* by striking the earth or by driving pieces of wood into it (Mulinda 1985, 213). These usages recall the affinity between *minkisi* and the graves of the dead.

Nailing also has an erotic significance; *koma nsonso,* to hammer in nails, is a euphemism for sexual intercourse. During the initiation of the *nganga* of Mwe Kongo, he and his wife retired to their house. While the other *banganga* surrounded it and sang, "*Koma tata, komakani koma,* Hammer it, Papa, go for it!" the couple had sexual intercourse three times, blowing the hunting whistle *mbambi* each time. When they reappeared, the apprentices fired shots to announce that Mwe Kongo had arrived (Nsemi, 387). The song that aroused Nkondi Nsanda to action is a riddle about sexual intercourse; it too was followed by the sound of a hunting whistle (MacGaffey 1991, 152). The *nkisi* Nzondo stood on one leg, an explicitly virile pose.[17] Some texts say that the *nganga* of Nkondi was always a man, though he might have a female assistant; in fact, women were sometimes principals.

Nails driven into a figure aroused Nkondi to action, and also represented the injury to be inflicted; characteristically, pains in the head, neck, and chest. "Nails and knife blades were put into large statues so that they might be hammered into the chests of people; they are called spears. When someone has pains in his chest he has been struck by the spears of the *nkisi*" (Kiananwa, 73). The chicken sacrifice which was often part of the ritual of invocation was said to feed and energize the *nkisi*, but also represented the violence that the *nkisi* itself would inflict on its victim (MacGaffey 1986b, 142). The feathered headdress, painted face, and upraised, threatening arm of many retributive *minkisi* in Mayombe clearly recalled the appearance and mission of warriors in the last, turbulent decades of the nineteenth century (Van de Velde 1886, 376). The violence embodied in retributive *minkisi* thus reflected the violence of the times, but was not limited to it.

Some *minkisi* were struck with sticks or thorny branches (Weeks 1914, 218, 235). In the seventeenth century, a magician reportedly bit his "idol," presumably for the same purpose (Bontinck 1970, 119). Nkondi could be aroused by exploding gunpowder next to it or by insulting it; insults ranged from the outrageous to milder forms: "'In some places they jeer at you, saying that you are nothing but an *nsafu*-thing and no *nkisi*.' So saying, the *nganga* pounds on his *nkisi*, mbu-mbu-mbu! to awaken it, that it should arise and go" (Babutidi, 7).[18] Outrageous insults drew upon the usual Kongo obscenities, referring, for example, to the genitals of the *nkisi's* mother-in-law.

> When he has offered *lusakusaku* to the *nkisi* he eats a certain mushroom and takes up an iron blade, arranges Nkondi on his left hand. He spits five times to bless the *nkisi* [and recites], "Strike females, strike males, seize your mother-in-law by the pussy, your sister-in-law. . . . The pigs complain, the dogs bark [at witches, spirits], the storm, the whirlwind, the *nkisi* has destroyed the village. Seize them in the valley, seize them on the hill and in between, where [the dogs] bark [?]. Dust [from a whirlwind] puts out the eyes of the chickens. Find out the wicked who are building a village of the dead [?]. Strike once, Nkondi, a second time to finish.[19]

Spitting could also be intended to insult *nkisi:*

> Spitting on the *nkisi* is done in order to transfer medicines (*miswa*) to the *nkisi*. This practice is intended to make the *nkisi* angry and send it after someone, and find out who did whatever it was. As with *nkondi* and *mabunzi* [type of *nkisi* that causes swellings], take off your cloth [an aggressive gesture], take a *kunda* bell in hand, swear an oath and spit on the *nkisi*. In the case of *nkondi*, spit in its eyes so that it may open wide its eyes and ears, and to strengthen it so that it shall be fierce and agile. But on another occasion spitting is intended to calm the rage of the *nkisi*: first blow on it, and then spit on its chest, as it were to calm its fury. (Demvo, 30)[20]

When the container was a wooden statue, much of the *nkisi* consisted of external attachments; when these were added in the course of use, as in the case of all *minkisi* provoked to pursue enemies by hammering in nails, the cumulative record of presumably successful cursing could be awesome indeed. The texts sometimes specify that the nails are removed when the problem is resolved; this practice explains why a number of statues are eaten away to the point of ruin (Musée de l'Homme 34.173.1). A description of Nkondi ya Mfyedila, "Nkondi for divination," says it is "a tall statue eaten away by blades driven into its belly; it has its little child with it and a hat made of the feathers of birds and chickens. It lies day and night in a *ntete* basket inside the house, hung up away from the heat" (Kwamba, 143).[21] It is a matter of controversy among art historians whether nails inserted in *nkondi* were removed when the case was over, but practice evidently varied from one region to another.

Often the most conspicuous features of these *minkisi* are the elements that linked the power of the *nkisi* to its clients or victims, thus metonymic rather than metaphorical. Identifying relics or exuviae (*mfunya*), often strips from clothing or, in the case of a thief, the remains of stolen items, were attached to the figure by means of the nails in three typical situations: when Nkondi was asked to pursue a suspected or unknown wrongdoer, when an individual sought protection for himself, or when parties were entering into a contract.

> If a man has been ailing for some time, with bad dreams, but does not know who is responsible, he attaches hairs from his head, or finger nails, or a little piece from his loincloth, wraps them in a rag and has the *nganga* attach them to Lunkanka, saying, "Look upon me, for I have come to put this relic in your body; it is my entire self I have come to put in safekeeping." (Matunta, 307)

> If they wish to enter into brotherhood with a stranger to the clan they fetch *nkondi,* which are large and awesome *minkisi* (*mibafweti vumina*). They lick the spikes and drive them into Nkondi, one for each side. Then they sacrifice two chickens and pour the blood on the spikes to strengthen them, so that whosoever should attack his fellow by witchcraft will be killed with his whole clan by the furious *nkisi,* which drives them mad and burns them with fire. (Lwamba, 240)

The pot component of an *nkondi* was usually used for divination, though some pots were tightly sealed containers of medicines (Musée de l'Homme, 92.52.34.1). Like the oriented mirrors also used for divination, the boiling over of the medicated water in the pot indicated the direction from which the danger came or the category of persons among whom the witch would be found. There were many different divination techniques; some progressed by successive eliminations: "Is the thief from the forest [that is, a spirit] or here in this world, *nseke a mpanga*? Male or female? Elder or junior?" Modern prophets follow a procedure that is similar but Christianized (Mac-Gaffey 1983, 164–66).

This is the divination procedure for Nsambu a Mpindi, a very large statue into which spikes were driven. The pot was set up at the entrance to the village:

> When its pot has been set up, the whole village must assemble. They collect *madyadya* fuel, and put four sticks around the pot [to hold it].[22] They wind *mambuzu* vine around the pot, and mark it inside with two lines, one in kaolin and one in red clay. In the bottom of the pot they mark a cross and two lines, one in kaolin and one in red clay. The lines have different meanings. The white one is for those who are not guilty of theft, witchcraft, adultery or the like. The red line is for those found guilty of theft or witchcraft, so that they may desist from this habit of harming people at night.

> Then the *nganga* recites his piece into the pot like this: "Lord Nsambu, strike and destroy! Whether there are two or three in his house, strike and destroy. A female witch, a male witch, arouse the dog, that he chase the rats. If witches have seized him, then kill women and men, but if he has not been seized by witches, then desist. If he has been seized by a female or a male witch, arouse the dog, pursue the rats." Then he draws a line on either side, one for women and one for men; on whichever side the pot spills over, that is where the witches are. When it has spilled he immediately takes it off the fire and repeats his declaration. Then he treats the patient with Nsambu, calming him on the sign

of the cross, so that he is cured. If after treatment he does not get better, then the divination by Nsambu must be completed with the *nkasa* poison ordeal. (Konda, 117)[23]

It is difficult to exaggerate the violence of the images comprised in invocations to Nkondi; presumably they expressed not only the violence of storms and birds of prey but the anger and grief of clients who felt themselves to be under attack:

> Have you not heard, Mwene Mutinu, that something has gone missing here? It is a difficult matter, we have asked everybody in the village. Their denial is, that they did not do it, that we should look for the culprit and punish him only. Therefore Mutinu, lick your mother! Strike, destroy, do you not see the village? Slash and sweep. Afflict them with boils, with sores that never heal; spread skin diseases throughout the village, give them all headaches, twist their arms and legs, Lord Mutinu. Infect all the children with coughs and colds. Spread confusion and misery among them. Whenever they seem to get better, strike them down again. Enfeeble them until they seek out the diviner who will identify you, Mwene Mutinu. Friends, see what a curse I have pronounced! (Kavuna, 58)

Invocations such as this explain the personhood attributed to *minkisi,* the animate character that has troubled anthropologists and missionaries for generations. They exemplify the "conversation of gestures" which for G. H. Mead is constitutive of both thought and selfhood. The basic principle of social organization, as he put it, is that of "communication involving participation in the other," requiring "the appearance of the other in the self, the reaching of self-consciousness through the other." The person so communicating "assumes the attitude of the other individual as well as calling it out in the other. He himself is in the role of the other person whom he is so exciting and influencing." Mead notes that inanimate objects may form parts of the generalized other with whom individuals "converse," insofar as the individual responds to such objects socially (Mead 1934, 154n, 253–54). In the West, a corresponding projection creates the illusion that a work of art "speaks" to you and is felt as having "presence."

Nkondi and Childbirth

Nkondi predominated among the *minkisi* of the above, but were often so powerful that they were believed to operate in more than one domain; they might kill "in the water" as well as in the air. As *minkisi* of the above they were generally masculine and violent in character and inflicted diseases upon the upper parts of the body, but as *minkisi* of the below, associated with the earth and with terrestrial waters rather than with the sky and thunderstorms, they often played an important part in rituals of childbirth. Some of this apparently feminine function can be attributed to the Kongo idea that the male is the principal contributor to the child's substance; as modern BaKongo put it, mother is merely "an envelope" in which father puts "a letter." Childbirth is also difficult and risky business, threatened by the witchcraft of jealous neighbors and the gripes of unsatisfied grandparents; on the advice of a diviner a pregnant woman might formerly have sought the protection of a retributive *nkisi* such as Na Kongo.

The power of Na Kongo, we are told, is in three parts: "The first is like that of Nkondi, because it can strike someone as Nkondi does, and it is nailed with tokens and oaths. . . . The second power it has is to kill game in the bush"; and the third, "If anyone gives birth, the child must be blessed with the baton of Na Kongo, that he may grow up strong."[24] The ritual for bringing out a child under the protection of Na Kongo is explicitly similar to the installation of a chief. In the first stage, the house was protected against witches. Then the mother's cargo basket (*mpidi*) was blessed by painting it inside and out with red and white "signs of abundance," and medicines were spat into it so that in effect it itself became an *nkisi,* with the invocation: "May she carry it in peace, may she carry it in tranquillity." Thereafter, the *banganga* went into the house to bless the child and its mother, whom they led out by her little finger, singing, "*Nsongi, nsongi nzila!* The guide, who shows the way!" They marked the infant with leopard spots of white clay and yellow ochre, as a chief is marked, and then took it to the water for more invocations before bringing it back to the house to sit it upon a raffia cloth for a final blessing. The text says, "They think of this cloth as a skin of investiture, *nkanda a luyadulu,* that the child may be strengthened in his body." The song sung at this stage, celebrating "The smith at the forge, who has trodden upon the royal mat, has been blessed," is the same as that sung for an actual chief, and the title Ne Nswami, "the Hidden One," given to a chief who has been consecrated (*byekwa*) but not invested (*yaala*) is also given to a child before it is named and brought out by an *nganga.*[25]

Political Functions of Nkondi

Nkondi was used to control relations between neighborhoods, each dominated by a localized clan (clan-section), with whom resided patrifilial Children, Grandchildren, wives, clients, and slaves (Dupré 1985, 90). A legend traces the origin of Nkondi za Mafula (Nkondi of the entrances to the village) to the need to put an end to the primordial war of all against all:

> The people were numerous in the country, and anyone who went to a village where he had no affines nor members of his own clan would be attacked and put in stocks until ransom was paid. Thus they made it known that this was a strong clan. But the elders said, if we carry on like this what will happen to us when we travel to other regions? Ah, it is not good to imprison someone with no fault to his charge; therefore it would be a good thing to set up Nkondi in the midst of the clans. But within the clan you may not invoke Nkondi. (Kwamba, 139)

This description accurately reflects conditions prevailing in most of Kongo during the period of the slave trade, from the mid-seventeenth century onward, when large tracts between settlements were unpopulated and unregulated. Traders depended on cultic associations and treaties to guarantee them safe passage and a kindly reception; often it was considered advisable to carry protective *minkisi* and to perform special rituals before and after an expedition. Where no chief had arisen to control a given area, treaties between clans forbidding war and permitting marriage were commonly sanctioned by Nkondi; the parties to the agreement invited the *nkisi* to attack anyone who broke it. "If two villages belonged to the same clan they could not take oath on Nkondi, because those of the same clan do not nail Nkondi" (Nsemi, 396). According to an English trader,

> These fetishes play a most important part in regulating the conduct of individuals or families—nay, intertribal feuds are settled by the same means, decisions enforced, dis-

turbances quelled. A large number of cases which, in the absence of fetishes, would be matter for governmental repression, are thus dealt with in a simple, private, inexpensive manner, never coming to the cognizance of [the European government's appointed] native chiefs at all. (Phillips 1887, 161)

Some such treaties incorporated small groups of refugees into a clan, including persons running away from oppressive chiefs; their appeal to the protection of the *nkisi* (in this case, Lunkanka) might be worded as follows:

Now Lunkanka, great one! Open your ears, be alert. Now me, I have been bought by Mr. X. In the village where I fell into debt I was given away as a pawn, but now I think I should transfer myself by day and by night [that is, permanently], for when the money Mr. X gave is used up I suppose that he might sell me and not settle me in his village, and I would be miserable and afraid. So in this great distress I am fleeing away. Do not you, Lunkanka turn a deaf ear; by night I complain, by day I fled, you see it. I speak [sincerely] on top of the tongue, not underneath it. (MacGaffey 1991, 129)

Where there was a chief to whom the refugee might turn, he would "insult" the chief in a standardized way to demand his protection; he would "tread on the chief's forehead" (*dyata va mbulu*), thus earning the penalty of enslavement. His original owner, wanting him back, would have to pay a heavy fine. This procedure was *koma nloko,* a phrase which also applies to arousing by nailing and reveals a parallel between chief and *nkondi.* One of the agents of Léopold II tells how once, when he was having lunch, a man who was being hotly pursued by a mob who believed him guilty of poisoning their chief burst in upon him and demanded his protection by smashing one of his plates (Van de Velde 1886, 391). Similar conventions are reported from Cameroon to Mozambique. When someone fired upon a canoe in which the intrepid Mary Kingsley was traveling, she jumped ashore and caught the aggressor, discovering in conversation with him that he was appealing for help against those who had seduced his wife; by local custom, the offended crew of the canoe would be obliged to help him pursue the original wrongdoers (Vincent 1990, 75).

Mobile Government

Minkisi at the turn of the century were characteristically portable; over and over, the texts say that in need one "sends for" the *nganga,* the man or woman who owns and operates the appropriate device.[26] The rules relating to a given *nkondi* often included instructions for carrying it:

The name of the *nkondi* of Ta Kayi Mbele is Ya Bambimi. When someone has died they fetch Ta Kayi Mbele, who will bring Nga Bambimi with him. The one who goes to fetch him takes a chicken and a length of cloth; the chicken is for Nga Bambimi, the cloth for the *nganga* himself. When he has sacrificed the chicken at the door of the [*nkisi*] house and saluted three times, he brings out the *nkisi.*

The one who agrees to carry the *nkisi* must throw a token when he comes to a fork in the path; if not, the statue becomes exceedingly heavy, so the porter knows that he did not throw a token. When he crosses a stream, too, he must throw a token in the water. (Mayoka, 323)

Water and partings of the ways are both places of contact between this world and the otherworld; the prescribed gestures dramatize the occult, otherworldly character and power of the *nkisi* itself, and its mission.

At the coast, where relatively important and stable regimes controlled the trading chiefdoms, regulatory *minkisi* tended to take the form of localized shrines rather than portable objects, though inland, too, statues were sometimes too large to carry about. Among the BaMboma of the northern shore of the Congo estuary, in the nineteenth century, *nkondi* of various names—Mabyala Mandembe and Mangaaka were among the most famous —were carried about from market to market, so that the public might witness the threats called down upon the bodies of wrongdoers (Schrag 1985, 244). A similar proceeding is reported from the end of the sixteenth century, incidentally illustrating the arbitrary oppressiveness characteristic of chiefs:

> A vassal of the Mani Mbangu lost some slaves; having acquired certain information about them, he went to the market with instruments of magic in order to curse those who held his slaves, but while dancing before his idol he happened to tread on the skirt of one of the Ngobila's concubines, who was passing by. Considering himself dishonored, the Ngobila seized the man to have him seriously beaten. (Bontinck 1970, 121)

When it seemed that a crime had been committed, *nkondi* was sent for. When it arrived, carried in the prescribed manner, at the scene of the crime, its mode of operation was as follows, from an account of *nkisi* Maniangu:

> This *nkisi* was put in a *mpeto* basket.[27] If someone has had manioc or plantains stolen and is unable to discover what person or thief stole them, then he cuts pieces of the manioc left by the thief and presents them to the Nganga Maniangu that he may put them in the *nkisi*. This is called putting *mfunya* in the *nkisi*.

> When these tokens have been placed in the *nkisi,* the *nkisi* will afflict the one who stole the manioc with the disease of the ribs (*lubanzi*) or with bloody stools. Then those who are responsible for the sick person will seek the help of a diviner. When the diviner comes, he will say: "They have fixed tokens in Maniangu, and therefore the *nkisi* has seized him." So then the owner of the sick man will go to the *nganga* of Maniangu and tell him all that the diviner said he had seen in the spirit. Nganga Maniangu will remove the *mfunya* from his *nkisi*. After taking them out, he treats the patient.

The author of the account then indicates another aspect of the matter:

> When he has been treated like this, the patient may get better, but paying the *nganga's* fee will cause him a lot of pain. The cost of this *nkisi* is a pig and cloths worth 20 francs, or even much more if the *nganga* is fetched from far. At that price people generally think it is much too expensive. (Babutidi, 15)

Minkisi in general, particularly the retributive and regulatory ones, were devices whereby the relatively rich and powerful contrived to extract a continuous flow of goods from the relatively unfortunate. Presumably, rituals did something to relieve the anxieties of people faced with disease, theft, or other problems. Belief in the possibility of being nailed by Maniangu and other retributive *minkisi* no doubt discouraged crime. It may well have been that the man who fell ill was indeed the thief, who intimated his fault to his family and indirectly to the diviner, but there can be no assurance of this connection and therefore we can have no confidence in functionalist explanations. There was theft, there were diseases, but the mere assumption or excuse of a connection among theft, disease, and a particular individual as wrongdoer ensured a flow of wealth from the vulnerable to those who had been able to invest in punitive devices. The most powerful *minkisi* were the most expensive, not only in initial outlay but in the periodic care and feeding they required; as investments, they were capable of generating impressive revenues (Schrag 1985, 246).

The regulatory function of Nkondi was often indirect; an English trader reported that a nail could be driven into a fetish for a shilling or so: probably thirty or forty would be asked for its withdrawal. A certain man dismissed his wife for being a scolding jade and took up with a younger woman. The wife had a fetish nailed so that her rival should not marry her ex-husband, but the elders decided she was in the wrong and obliged her to pay to have the nail withdrawn. "This cost her ten pounds, at a moderate computation, as the fetish-man could ask his own terms in the matter" (Phillips 1887, 159).

The political economy of *minkisi* is generalized by Kunzi:

> A magician wants things to be sacred so that his charm may be violated and he himself may receive money from the one who has broken the taboo. Such a person will fall ill, go to the magician, and pay the fine. If there were no taboo there would be no way to get money. The prohibitions of the chiefs are the same, but worse, since the violator can be accused and killed or fined by force, whereas one who breaks a magician's rules need do nothing unless he falls ill. (Cahier 137)

The predatory function of ritual in support of wealth and power is expressed in the composition of *minkisi* themselves: "When they compose an *nkisi,* they incorporate in it the spirit of some man who in his lifetime killed much game, owned much livestock and many slaves, one who was wily, wealthy, virile and successful in fighting other clans" (Kavuna, 65, describing *nkisi* Mbola).

Chiefship consecrated the power of wealthy men, and some women, who had accumulated exceptional wealth in followers, descendants, and slaves. In areas where no such accumulation was possible because of relative remoteness from the trade routes, powerful *minkisi* assisted or even replaced the chiefs in the regulation of public order between villages. *Nkondi* recapitulated much of the violence characteristic of chiefs. Their political role was sufficiently effective that, according to English traders in Loango at the time, by 1898 the Portuguese and French governments were confiscating *nkondi* statues because they prevented foreign interests from taking over trade.[28] *Nkondi* can be thought of as located between chief and *nkisi: nkondi's* action affected groups rather than individuals; whereas most *minkisi* were functionally specialized, *nkondi* was likely to control a range of diseases and other problems; like other *nkisi,* *nkondi* was mobile, whereas the chief and his *nkisi nsi* were attached to a particular domain (*nsi*) and were immobile or at least limited in movement.

A sort of bridge between chief and *nkisi* as specially endowed figure is represented by Lulendo, "Power," a short-lived complex that arose near Mukimbungu in the 1880s. It was called *nkisi,* and its master was *nganga,* but its limited function of regulating markets was one that usually fell in the purview of district chiefs. The master was accompanied at his initiation by a group of assistants (*bamayaala*) who took new names referring to aspects of Lulendo: Na Nkondo (law), Na Mayala (its enforce-ment), Na Mbele (the knife of execution), Na Mbangala (the rigor of the law), and Na Nkambakani (its announcement). The titles, and the persons who carried them, are thus strictly analogous to the material ingredients found in the bag or basket of an ordinary *nkisi*—a container of medicines apparently lacking in Lulendo. Lulendo en-abled the execution of market offenders; they were buried alive before a stake was driven through them by the *bamayaala* (MacGaffey 1987).

Minkisi as Memory Schemes

The dramatic quality and relative elaboration of *nkondi,* compared to other *min-kisi,* reveal the essential nature of these objects, particularly the anthropomorphic fig-ures. Chapter 5 explained how, as compendia of medicines, *minkisi* could be read as texts describing their own qualities. We now see that they are not images of an other-wise invisible force or spirit as much as a statement of the relationship between that force and the person or persons to be affected by it. They are memoranda, in material form, of their own operations, checklists of their own ritual requirements. Lastly, in the case of nailed figures, each nail or token could be a reminder of current business.

The tokens nailed or otherwise attached to Nkondi reminded it of the task at hand; supposedly, the *nganga* remembered each such task, and removed the right token to lift the curse. Van de Velde, denying that the BaKongo had any "idols" or "fetishes," de-scribed "ancestral" statues, used to discover wrongdoers, into which marks of several kinds were placed to record significant events; an elder was appointed to interpret these marks for the younger generation. "Rather than an idol, this is a history book or communal archive" (Van de Velde 1886, 392).

As we have seen, a token was something attached to the nail rather than the nail itself; in some instances, the necessary metonymic connection with the plaintiff or oath-taker was established by having him lick the nail. Some *nkondi* are covered with reminders of all kinds, especially pieces of cloth; others show only nails, which may have been licked but carry no visible means of identification. Yet others carry tokens but are not nailed.[29]

The initiation procedure, during which the novice was taught the medicines and the rules of the *nkisi,* coded in allusive songs and images, is to some extent replicated in the *nkisi* itself. *Minkisi* may wear the *mamoni* lines that the *nganga* will paint around his own eyes for occult vision. Their faces may be painted with *mansanga* (vertical stripes), the "tears" of their victims; they carry the appropriate musical instruments in miniature, and wear the fiber *nsunga* bracelet that protects against witchcraft. A hunt-ing net around the feet of the figure shows how the *nkisi* will trap its victim. The absence of feet in the figure of "the wife of Nga Bambimi" would remind us, if we could see it, that she does not travel; when the *nganga* is summoned, he takes with him only the male part of his *nkisi.* The aggressive, protruding tongue of many *nkondi* reminds us of the licking of nails and medicines.

In the most detailed checklist of *nkisi* attributes available, Matunta describes, paragraph by paragraph, the little-known *nkisi* Lunkanka, which he evidently had in front of him as he wrote (Cahier 307).[30] The face of the figure is that of a monkey, possibly *nsengi,* to recall *senga,* "to spy." In spite of the maximal violence attributed to it, the figure is female. A long cord is attached as a tumpline to carry it by, and to suggest that just as women carry burdens in a basket on their backs with the aid of such a cord, so will Lunkanka carry off her victims; also, "just as the tumpline is twisted, so will she twist her victims' necks." A thick, medicated collar around its neck reminds us of both the *nkisi's* neck-twisting violence and the protective amulet that a prospective victim might wear. A fragment of *nkasa* poison bark is attached (and marked "*nkasa*," in pencil) to remind Lunkanka to punish those who do not pay up after losing in the poison ordeal.

Matunta says that raffia cloths are both tokens of money that some client hoped to recover and reminders that no one may see the private parts of the *nkisi*. If it should happen that the figure falls over, all those present at the ritual must fall on their faces until the *nganga* begs Lunkanka's pardon.[31] A miniature knife recalls the procedure for swearing that you did not do something of which you are accused. Lunkanka holds her hands to her head in the classic gesture of grief for the anguish she will cause, as a mother does when her child has died. Miniature powder flasks represent the explosions that will fire up the heart of the *nkisi*. The kneeling posture of the *nkisi* recalls one of its taboos: Should the person carrying it drop it, he must kneel to beg its forgiveness; nor may he look about, lest Lunkanka twist his neck. A piece of tortoise shell signifies that Lunkanka can draw in her head so as not to be seen when there are dangerous spirits about. A whistle, carved like Lunkanka itself in the image of a grieving woman, is not only an analogical reference to the cry of the *ntoyo* bird, foretelling dire events; it is itself heard in the village at night as the *nganga* goes about on God knows what ungodly errand. "Lunkanka, you are mighty; hover as the vulture hovers!"

Although *minkisi* can be shown to incorporate records of the past at several levels, their function as memory devices should not be fetishized. All rituals state a connection in time between present powers and their origin, from an instituting event through a legitimating history down to today's practical application (MacGaffey 1986a, 12–13). More generally, all social interaction presupposes some reference to the past, by which, as in the case of pedigree or descent, the status of the actors is specified in advance of the interaction itself. Memory is thus intrinsic to ongoing social experience. Particular social processes relative to the distribution of power in the society in question may isolate some of this knowledge in memory devices, such as archives, souvenirs, genealogies, or monuments. To privilege any of such devices may be to endorse not only a particular kind of memory but also the distribution of power that produced them (Mudimbe, 1993).

In the moral economy of the BaKongo, *minkisi* in general are synonymous with self-seeking; the *nganga* is suspected of being a witch. Since the fifteenth century— and surely before that—chiefs have reasserted their authority by campaigns against them. In practice, this moral and political contrast is not clear; chiefs also used *minkisi* to strengthen their claims to represent the public good. In this connection, *nkondi* once again bridge the categories. As we have seen, they regulated relations between groups rather than within them (at least in principle!) and in so doing served the functions of chiefs, if they were not in fact aides to "real" chiefs. The term *koma nloko,* applied to the action of insulting a chief in order to seek his protection, even suggests the reverse priority, that chiefs served the functions of *nkondi*.

7. COMPOSITION AND POWERS OF AN NKONDI CALLED MBOLA

The texts in this chapter, besides describing the individual character of *nkisi* Mbola, provide examples of basic ideas and techniques which can be found combined and recombined in many *minkisi,* especially *minkondi.* They include the myth of origin, the empowering forces, the description and aetiology of disease, the medicinal ingredients, the processes of composition and invocation, the rules, the persons who unite in the performance of the *nkisi,* and the relationship between healing and punishment. The texts show clearly the relationship between Mbola and the collective affairs of villages and other groups; they also show why he is called "a great chief." Like other *nkondi,* Mbola dealt with the concerns of groups rather than of individuals. The chapter leads toward a consideration of chiefship itself, as presented to us in the Cahiers.

Kimfuzi of Kibunzi, in Cahier 83 (the only one of his in Laman's collection), and Nsemi of Kingoyi both describe Mbola. Their texts are unusually long and detailed, permitting comparison of two accounts of a single *nkisi* from different locations. Konda of Kinkenge also wrote briefly about Mbola, which was evidently important throughout a wide area. Laman's description of Mbola (LKIII, 103–104) combines and abbreviates parts of these three texts, and a fragment of another by Makundu of Mukimbungu. Some errors of translation in Laman's English text result from faulty transcription of the manuscripts.[1]

The three authors describe different aspects of Mbola. Nsemi is the only one who gives a myth of origin; his list of medicines is different from Kimfuzi's. The three texts agree that Mbola is the property of a residential group, a lineage, and its adherents, all of whom must observe its taboos, and that it collectively afflicts the clan or village of the wrongdoers it is set to attack. Konda denies that there is any wooden figure in the large basket characteristic of the *nkisi,* although Nsemi specifically details ritual treatment of such a figure. I have not found in any museum a figure labeled Mbola.[2]

Cahier 83, Kimfuzi in Kibunzi

Bo(m)vi, Wanyaka, and Venga are said to belong to the same group (*kanda dimosi*). They are not separate *minkisi* but aspects of Mbola; *bomvi* is a syphilitic ulcer and *venga* refers to skin disease. Wanyaka, an *nkisi* in a snail shell, is a variant of Mbola, addressed as "Mbola"; Kimfuzi describes its composition at some length. Wanyaka is also described by Makundu of Mukimbungu (Cahier 255), but the two descriptions only partly coincide. Makundu says that the *nganga,* when he composes the *nkisi,* sticks bits of cotton on his body to represent sores and to make himself ridiculous, "but nobody may laugh." This Wanyaka cures sores, but the only indication of an *nkondi* function is that it may be used to protect property from theft.

The order of Kimfuzi's paragraphs has been rearranged for the sake of narrative clarity.

1. This is the explanation of Bovi: sores that destroy the nose and the mouth and eyes, or the leg or the arm or the whole body, and do not get better until death, are called the sickness of Bovi, for they are the diseases it gives. The name of the *nkisi* is Mbola. Kimbovi, Wanyaka, and Venza are in the same group. It is invoked for this reason: A man has this kind of sore; the case is examined by a diviner, who says "Go find *nganga* Mbola, because Mbola has seized him. A curse has been pronounced against you, you may have been a thief, cantankerous, or quarrelsome; you may have been afflicted in this way because you cheated or failed to pay your debts. Invoke the *nkisi* and assuage this curse." When they hear this they take palm wine and seek out the *nganga* who owns the *nkisi.* When he arrives with his *nkisi,* and the food and drink have been consumed, the curse is lifted.

1. Mbangudulu a Bovi i yayi: Mputa zimananga mbombo ye nwa ye meeso vo za nitu ya mvimba zilembananga nyaka te ye mfwilu, ye vo ya kulu ye vo ya koko yilembane niaka. I zozo zibikwanga mbevo za nkisi a Bovi, kadi i yela koko mivananga. Nkumbu a nkisi Mbola. Wena kanda dimosi ye Kibomvi, ye Waniaka [nkisi] ye Venza. Tuku kia vandulwanga i kiaki: Vo bamweni vo muntu wena mputa za mpila yoyo ye fiedisa kwa nganga za Ntadi. Yandi bu kabikidi vo lutomba nganga Mbola, kadi Mbola wambeki, kadi nloko lwakomwa, evo mwivi wakala vo evo ntimbudi a mambu evo nkangi a nkole evo ndie bia nkita [nkwa bumbabu] vo bia nkumbi lwakomunwa nloko wowo, kansi vanda luvanda wo ye lulembisa nloko wowo. Bu bawilu wo, i nata malavu mu landa nganga yoyo yivwidi wo. Bu kizidi ye nkisi malavu ye madia bibilamene, nloko si kalemba [katula].

Composition

Like many important *minkisi,* Mbola was composed in the seclusion of a temporary shelter. The composition of a new version is a form of activation of the *nkisi* which leads directly to the purification of the village, relieving it of the affliction imposed by Mbola.

4. This is how Mbola is composed. The enclosure of the "great chief" Mbola is much respected; in it the medicines are prepared.[3] A bystander, a profane, uninitiated person, may not know about it. The enclosure is made of palm branches, and those who compose the *nkisi* are consecrated with white clay which they mark on their ears before they enter. To scrape the medicines they go under a cloth.

4. Bwabu i mpandulu a Mbola. Ngudi a nkama a Mbola ya mbalu, ngudi a nkama ya nzitusu kadi ku lumbu lolo lu ntebolo. Ka kulendi kwenda mumpisa ko, i nsemi walembwa semuka. Lumbu lolo i nsambu a ndala. Bavandanga wobabiekwanga mpemba bakuswanga mu matu, mboki bakotanga koko. Mu teba longo, buna bakotanga ku nsi a vunga.

5. They take a flat stone to scrape the medicines on. They stick leaves all over their bodies to resemble the sores [Mbola] inflicts. Each of those who go under the cloth to compose it [pays?] two chickens. They sing the song of consecration: "The girl I met on Nkandu fell asleep on the bed of palm leaves."[4] They begin to prepare the medicines on the stone under the cloth, banging their knives on the stone, which is surrounded by piles of gunpowder that they ignite with a firebrand of *mwindu* wood. Coming out from the cloth, they go to the crossroads and sing this song: "Go fight in the gullies [where spirits are], whither you were sent; go, yaya Mbola!"

2. (In a palm-rib tube shaped like a fish basket) they prepare as medicines skin and claws of leopard, skin of crocodile, and scrapings of its teeth, to be drunk with palm wine. One who is outside [the enclosure] may not drink them. [The medicines include] *mpekwa* that resembles a fruit bat; *ndingi* resin, pepper, *lwengi* and *booka* fish, *bimbambi* beans, skin of *nsesi* antelope, *nkandikila, tondi* mushroom, *nkiduku, lusaku-saku,* charcoal from the forge, *nkusu* [parrot?] and skin of *sidi* frog. These are put in with *lemba-lemba* leaves, *ntunga* insects, palmgrubs, *nzanzabala* and *dimbuzu* creepers, and basil, mixed with water and given to the whole village to drink; more of the mixture is sprinkled on the village, the animal pens, the houses and gardens. When they prepare the

5. Babongele tadi dia nsensebele ditebulwanga longo. Banamikini makaya mu nitu ya mvimba mu songa kifwani kia mputa zika-vananga. Bavandanga wo, mu kota ku vunga, muna muntu 1 nsusu za2 za2. I mwe yimbila nkunga wa mbiekolo vo mwana a ndumba u yabwana vana nkandu [dagen] va ntanda a ndala kaleka. I mwe toni teba longo, tula va tadi diodio diena yau ku nsi a vunga ye beti bembita mbele va tadi diodio dizungulu ku nsi a bikunku bia tia twa mputu tweti vubulwa mu sisi kia mwindu. Bu bavaikidi ku vunga, bele mu zimpambu ye bayimbila nkunga eu vo wenda tulumuna mabenge yaya Mbol'e. Muna wasindukwa i wende yaya Mbola.

2. [Mu ladi kia nsiensie kifwanane ye dudubudi kia nsiensie kina-tunwanga mbizi za Nzadi] tebele nkanda a ngo ye nzala ye nkanda a ngandu ye vempa meeno mandi ye malavu mana nwinwa koko. Wena ku mbazi kalendi mo nwa ko. Teba mpekwa yifwanane ye ngembo ye teba ndingi ye nungu za nsamba ye lwengi ye maboka ye bimbambi ye nkanda a nsesi ye nkandikila ye tondi ye nkiduku ye nsaku-nsaku ye kala zima dia luvu ye nkusu ye sidi biena kanda dia kimbiti. Bina tulwa va lemba-lemba ye ntunga ye nsombe ye nzanzabala ye dimbuzu, mansusu bunda nlangu ye nwika babo bena va vata ye mwanga mu zimpaka za bulu ye zinzo ye vata ye mazumbu. Bu bateba longo biobio bakotele ku nsi a vunga ye nsambu a ndala ye nsusu ya mbakala. Banganga bavwanga yo, kansi kabalendi yo keba ko

medicines they go under [the shelter of the] blanket with palm branches and a cock. The *banganga* make it, and those who do not enter the enclosure may not own the *nkisi,* only the initiated. It may not be touched by a profane person.

bakotanga ko, i basemuka kaka. Ka ulendi simba nsemi ko, kansi wasemuka kaka.

7. Over the basket they place a raffia cloth, and inside it the medicines I have listed, with white clay. It is tied on top with a cord. Then they put a carrying band to hang it up or to carry it by, because it is carried like a satchel. The palm and the *n'safu* become sacred and may not be eaten by the profane, only by the *nganga.* The name given to those who compose the *nkisi* is Nacieka-cieka dia mwana busi.

7. Va ntandu a ladi batulanga nlele wa mavonde [mbadi]. Mu ngudi a ladi i longo biobio bi nsonekene ye mpemba. I mwe kangi nsinga ku ntu. Mboki batulanga nsinga a mponda vo nsandi [nsadi] mu manikina wo ye mu natina wo. Kadi wanatunwa nkievo nkutu evo bumbikila. Batumbidi vo bieka ba ye nsafu. Biobio kabilendi dia mimpisa ko, kansi banganga kaka. I mwe vani nkumbu za bavendi wo i zazi: Nacieka-cieka dia mwana busi.

8. Then they make a fly whisk and an adze to go with the *nkisi.* The fly whisk shows that anyone who breaks the rules will get sores which he will have to brush with a whisk [and the adze stands for the way the *nkisi* carves flesh].

8. Mboki bavanga nsiensie ye nsengo biakala kintwadi ye nkisi. Nsiensie basonga vo muntu una sumuka nlongo myomyo una baka zimputa ye una zo kubila mu nsyensye.

The Rules

Mbola's food taboos, based on the similarity between the appearance of certain animals and the sores the *nkisi* causes and cures, are hereditary in the male line; that is, they bind not only the members of the clan but the patrifilial relatives who live, as the clan's clients, in the same community. These animals, marked by various kinds of "rotting," redness, or spots, have entered into a special *kinkonko* relationship, which Laman called "totemic," with the owners of the *nkisi* because they have been "buried" (*zikwa*) in it, or confided to it. *Konko* means "prohibition." The taboo on toothpicks, like the use of dust from insect bore holes (Nsemi's text, par. 10), is based on the analogy between dental cavities and other perforations. Other rules indicate the significance of some of the medicines listed above as entering into the composition of Mbola. The final mention, above, of an adze refers to "carving." The obligation to observe the rules incumbent on all members of the local community that was centered on the chief (including clan members, clients, and patrifilial children and grandchildren) meant that in daily life they enacted the metaphors constitutive of Mbola as a particular manifestation of regulatory power.

9. Those born under the protection of the *nkisi* or healed by it, and the [patrifilial] descendants of the clan that owns it, may not make the whisk nor clean their teeth with a toothpick. They may not eat leopard, *nsesi* [the dwarf antelope], or goat, nor *lwengi* and *maboka* fish, *bimbambi* beans (which resemble *makongo* beans), parrot, frog. One who eats goat will get sores; who eats the little *sidi* frog gets tooth rot and nasal infections; who eats *nsesi* will get red boils. *Maboka* [a red fish] gives red sores that turn leprous; the same for *mbambi* beans, *lwengi* fish, and the others. Not just the clan that composed [Mbola] but the whole family of the Children, Grandchildren, and Great-grandchildren, because these animals have become familiars. The adze is for fixing curses in the *nkisi,* and for relieving them. The fee: a pig, a live chicken, and "wet" palm wine [not cash equivalents], and food.

9. I kuma babutulwa wo ye babukwa wo ye bafunwa mu mvila yi wavandwa ka balendi vanga nsiensie ko ye tokuna meno mu toto ko. Ka balendi dia ngo ye nsesi ye nkombo ye lwengi [fisk] ye maboka [fisk], bimbambi [bonor], bifwanane ye makongo [bonor], nkusu, sidi, ntekudila. Kadi didi nkombo una kala mavezi. Didi sidi una bela sinza ye mputa za mbombo. Didi nsesi una baka bina bia mbwaki. Didi maboka una baka bina bia mbwaki. Bu bimeni lweka i kimbevo kia mputa za bwazi. Didi bimbambi mpe bina. Didi lwengi mpe i mpila mosi ye biobio biankaka. Ka mvila i uvendo kaka ko, kansi ye sinsi dia wonso wabutila wo ntekudilandi ye ndukudilandi ka balendi bio dia ko, kadi biazika konko. Nsengo yoyo mu koma nloko ye mu lemba nloko. Nga mfutu: ngulu ye nsusu mavunia ye bianka ye malavu nlangu ye madia.

Birthing Function of Mbola

One of the important (and expensive) functions of *nkondi* was to protect pregnant women and their newborn. Some time after the birth, the child was ritually brought out from the house by the *nganga* of the *nkisi* whose rules the mother had been observing during her pregnancy. Children protected in this fashion would be given appropriately significant names (see Chapter 6). In what follows, "the crossroads, the parting of the ways," *mpambu a nzila* (any intersection, or even a cross conveniently drawn on the ground), is often the site of ritual activity, a place of transition, of contact with strangers or the unseen. The child's protective "companion" is tied with a leaf from a palm from which palm nuts have not yet been taken; certain hawks eat palm nuts, and to dream of eating them, or that kernels are being cracked, is an omen of death.

10. *The power of the nkisi.* When a woman is pregnant, she has herself blessed at a parting of the ways and

10. *Lendo kiandi.* Vo nkento yeki, wele sakumunwa mu mpambu a nzila vwikulu nsilu. Mu vwata nsilu

puts on an amulet; this costs a
chicken and wine. When she has
given birth she may not go about
until the *nganga* comes to bring her
out. The amulet she formerly wore
is put on the child, and this
investiture also costs a chicken and
wine. They take a little calabash
and tie to it a bracelet of knotted
leaf of a palm from which palm
nuts have not been eaten; this gourd
is called "the companion"; no one
else may drink from it who was not
born to the clan, nor composed the
nkisi or been treated by it.

11. If an unqualified person uses it, the
gourd is profaned, and the child
will cry and be ill until they fetch
the *nganga* to bless it again. If it is
broken he will replace it with
another. The taboos the mother
must observe are these: she may
not eat meat that is high or maggot-
infested; if she does, the child will
be sickly. They may not sleep in a
house that has bugs on the floor,
nor eat any of the ingredients of the
nkisi.

12. The fee for bringing out the child is
three or four chickens, twice three
yards of a cloth called "shirts,"
palm wine, and a special packet of
food for the *nganga,* put in a basket
or bag. The place where it is put: it
is hung up on the wall of a dwelling, but may not be approached by
an uninitiated person.

mfutu nsusu mosi ye lavu. Bu
kabuta kalendi zyeta te ye nganga
kizi kumvaikisa. Nsilu yateka
vwata ngudi yikululu mu mwana
nkuludulu mpe nsusu mosi ye lavu.
Babongele mbinda lombwa bakengi
nsungwa ngita [=nsungwa] za
mandala, ba [palm] dikadiadilu
ngazi ko. Mbinda yoyo yibikwanga
nkangazi. Ka yilendi nwa wankaka
ko, evo kabutila wo ko evo kavanda
wo ko evo kabukwa wo ko.

11. Vo mu mpisa wana yisumukini,
buna mwana udilanga kaka ye bela
mpe, te ye bana tomba nganga yoyo
ye sakumusa mbinda yoyo diaka.
Vo zibudikidi, wana toma yankaka
yina sakumunwa. Nlongo mya
ngudi i myami: kalendi dia mbizi a
mfuku ko, kalendi dia yena ntunga
ko. Kadi vo una bio dia, wana
mwana bela ye dila beni, kadi
ngudi sumukini nlongo. Ka balendi
leka nzo yena ntunga va nsi ko,
biabio biatebwa mu nkisi kalendi
bio dia ko.

12. Mfutu mu vaikisa mwana nsusu 3
vo ya ye nzoka a nlele ubikwanga
mavwata 2, malavu nlangu ye
mpaki [=biandia] a nganga, i madia
masokulwanga mu mpidi vo nkutu.
Tueka mu fulu kikatulwanga,
umanukwanga mu baka mu nzo
yikalanga muntu, kansi kaulendi
valakana walembwa semuka ko.

Pursuing Wrongdoers

Oaths were sworn on Mbola, who would pursue any perjurer, although in fact the
victim of its wrath might not be the liar himself. It becomes apparent in the course of
the description that although a single individual develops the sores (the "rotting" which

is the mark of Mbola), Mbola's punishment bears upon the whole village, of which some other individual may have caused the trouble by violating some rule or committing an offense. The reference to "dogs" put into the *nkisi* does not necessarily imply the use of a wooden figure.

13. Oaths on the *nkisi:* only the *minkisi* can tell truth from falsehood. If someone were to swear, saying "If I did it, may Mbola rot my nose and mouth," but he did so insincerely, laughing at Mbola, his mouth and nose would rot. If he did it but does not fall ill, then others in his clan will be afflicted, because he told a lie.

13. Tweka ndilu a nkisi, muntete katwadia kedika ko vo kikilu ko, kansi miau kaka. Vo muntu vengi diambu wau bonso ena vo Mbola vobula mbombo ye nwa vo nsidi bo, kansi weti kuntatimisa vo nasevila [=sevila mu Mbola, kamba kuvengi bo ko = . . . ndefi] muna [mu Mbola], wilu vo kuvengi bo ko, yandi wele sevila ikia, wilu vo mono mpengi bo vobula mbombo ye nwa ye kola meno. Vo vengi bo, yandi vo kabelele wo ko, buna mu dikanda diandi bana wo bela, kadi luvunu katele.

Kimfuzi tells how Mbola could also regulate another kind of corporate concern, the transfer of a boy or girl as pawn in consideration of a debt between one matrilineal house and another; Mbola would punish anyone who broke the agreement. (According to his marginal note, Laman thought this agreement was a marriage.)

3. To guarantee the transfer of a boy or girl as a pawn, they pay money which is the price of the person. When it has been put on one side, the *nganga* holds a *luzimbu* shell[5] and a chicken; two others hold *mfumvu* leaves, and they ask: "Who has bought these people with money?" The *nganga* replies, "I myself am the buyer, the thing bought with money is agreed upon." He then soaks *lemba-lemba* in [palm wine] and sprinkles the mixture not in the village but at the entrance to it.

3. Mfutu vo nloko wa ngolo wasilwa ndumba vo toko mbimba [. . . kwela], buna bafutanga mbongo za ntalu a muntu, kadi muntu kasilwa mbimba. Bu zikatulwa, nganga simbidi luzimbu lwa ntela ye nsusu, mboki basidi bantu 2 mu mfumvu. Basimbidi mfumvu babikidi vo nani kwandi usumba baba mu luzimbu? Nganga ntumbu sa vo sumba kwame nsumbidi, kiasumbwa ye nzimbu kiatabika. I mwe nwiki ye lemba-lemba ye mwanga, ka va vata ko kansi ku fula dia bwala.

14. One who wants to invoke the *nkisi* by putting in or removing a "dog" pays the *nkisi's* palm wine, and a chicken for the *nganga's* work. The "dog" is placed like this: If

14. Nga ndiowo una tanga wo vo ku mbwa [=mfunia] tula vo katula, ufutuanga lavu diandi, kinganga nsusu katambulanga. Ntudulu a mbwa i yayi. Vo muntu wadiwa

someone has had something taken without payment, a person captured or something stolen, he takes *mfunya,* some remnant of what was stolen, and puts it in the *nkisi,* paying a length or two of cloth. He agrees with the *nganga* to remove the "dog" when he has received the girl or boy.[6] He takes a weaver-bird's nest and gives it to the *nganga* that he may scrape medicine of a bat, put it in the nest, and bury it at the head of the village, so that everyone may die; the same thing can be done with a bullet. They put the medicines in a consecrated gun and fire it at the entrance to the village, saying: "Strike, destroy, eat in the palm tree, eat in the *nsafu* tree, eat in the water, eat on the path," or whatever affliction.

15. That's the malice of what they do. These are the invocations: "Mbola, hunt above, hunt below, plunder and strike. Your prey is in the palm, in the *n'safu* tree. Hide a snake in a hole in the palm tree, that the tapper may die. The hole brings suffering, the curse of the palm. . . . You who built by the *mfilu* build by the *nlolo.*"[7] The one nailing in the curse says, "Do you see the witch-lights, a witch whether male or female I do not know, you find him for me. Where you see the witch-light, plunder and strike, destroy nose and mouth."

16. [Formula for] healing: "Shake your rattles. Heal inside, we heal on the

lekwa biampamba evo kenge nkole evo yibulu lekwa, buna ubonganga mfunia. Bongele bionso biyibulu evo nsuka nlele mu mbongo zi kadilu ye kwenda tula mu nkisi wowo, futidi mpe nkwangu vo nzoka. Veni mbimba kwa nganga ndevo vo bana zo katusa vo katambudi ndumba vo toko. Wele kwandi. Nga ndievo kengo, bongele zanza dia nsokuza veni kwa nganga, kidi kateba longo kia mpekwa ye tula va zanza ye zika dio ku ntu a bwala, kidi babo bafwa, kadi mpekwa mu tana bantu vo nzongo mpe i mpila mosi. Batulwanga bio mu nkati a nkele usakumunu, basikanga wo va fula dia bwala bu kakengo. Bavovanga vo tana wabeta, ku ba dila kwaku, ku nsafu dila kwaku, mu nlangu dila kwaku, mu nzila dila kwaku, ye vo konso konso bela.

15. I kimfunia kiokio ki basanga. Ntangumunu i miami, kamba Mbola ku ntandu, kamba Mbola ku banda, tana wabeta, ku ba ndilu aku, ku nsafu ndilu aku. Kamba widi mpulukusu [= nkulukusu . . . palm stam, . . . lwaza kianza] a kanza walwaza wafwa kwandi. Mpulukusu yena mpasi, yena mpanda ntente, bula ntadi wabula mabenga a ndoki, nge kwaku tungila mfilu watungila nlolo. Bwabu weti koma nloko uvovanga ena, e mweni mbinga a ndoki a nkento ndoki a bakala mono kinzeyi ko. Nge untombila yandi, e mweni mbinga tana wabeta vobuzila mbombo ye nwa.

16. Mya mbukulu: dekula minsakala wadekula minsakala miaku. Buka

outside, under the leaves, do not
shrink like *nsombe* grubs [over the
fire], do not shrink like food when
it is cooked."

mu nkati beto twabuka ku mbazi,
ku nsi makaye, makaye ko kafienge
bwafienga bwafienga nsombe ko,
kafiengi bwafienga fundi ko.

Cahier 390, Nsemi in Kingoyi

The Origin of Mbola

Stories of finding a charm or a mask in the form of a remarkable object floating in water are common in West and Central Africa. The Dan of Liberia think that when nature spirits, unhappy with their invisible, bodiless nature, want to make themselves useful, they arrange to incorporate themselves in objects. In a typical narrative that could as well be Kongo, it is said that the spirit appears in a dream to a sympathetic person to whom it can give future-telling powers, animal strength, or political influence, among other good things. "In return, the spirit dictates the manner in which it should be manifested and sustained. Its appearance can be static, in the form of a bundle of fur, antelope horns or a small snail shell filled with various ingredients. . . . At other times a spirit may ask for a mobile, living materialization and urge the chosen person to incarnate him, to perform him, with a mask" (Fischer 1978).

In this instance of Mbola, the empowering *simbi* is explicitly a former human being, but not an ancestor of the finder. After an extended sojourn in the land of the dead he has moved on to another plane of existence as an anonymous spirit who can acquire an identity and a role among the living only in the form of an *nkisi;* I have called this cosmological feature "the spiral universe" (MacGaffey 1986a, ch. 3). Although, as a *simbi,* the spirit emerges from the water, this is an aggressive *nkisi* "of the above." The specific aggressiveness appropriate to *nkondi* is incorporated, during its composition, in the form of dirt from the grave of "an exceptionally strong man." Unlike Kimfuzi, Nsemi mentions a wooden figure as part of *nkisi* Mbola. *Nsengo,* usually "hoe," is mentioned among the components, but in a context that indicates that "adze" is the correct translation.

1. Mbola has no other names, but it is called *nkondi* and it belongs in the water class. It is called Mbola because it comes from "rotting" and it "rots" living things. Its origin is as follows. Once upon a time there was a man who lived to a very great age. He died and was buried in his grave. After his burial he lived for a long time in the land of the dead and grew old there. He died once again, but found himself no closer to his relatives there in

1. Mu Mbola ka mwena nkumbu zankaka ko, kansi yandi mbatu ubikwanga nkondi, nkiangunu yandi vwilu mu kanda dia mamba. Yandi wena nkumbu yoyo Mbola mu diambu dia tuku kiandi bola, nkiangunu Mbola ubodisanga biavumuna. Mbola wena tuku kiandi bonso bwabu: Muna nsi a nkulu mwakala muntu wanuna beni. Yandi wafwa ye zikwa ku mpemba. Bu kamana zikwa ku mpemba kuna, yandi wakala ye

the land of the dead, so he thought, "What am I to do in this second death? I should become an *nkisi*." So he betook himself to a stream.

2. When he got there he met a man crossing, so he began to bob about on the surface of the water. The man's eyes opened wide, he plucked a leaf and popped it three times on his hand [in salutation]. Then he took up [the thing he saw in the water], brought it to the village, and put it in his house. When night fell, and the man went to sleep, [the ghost] revealed his name to the man in a dream, saying: "I am one who formerly lived on earth and have died the second death; take me and keep me to be your *nkisi*. My name will be Mbola, because I rotted twice. You will make me a *mpidi* basket and a *lukobe* box, that I may live inside the box, but have a statue carved that you may put me in it." So he came with his sharp knives, his adze, his hatchet and his other tools.

3. When the man awoke from his sleep he realized that he had dreamed, so he set about doing everything that he had seen in his dream. [The ghost] began to teach the man how to treat [the sick], and what songs to sing when healing or when composing [the *nkisi*]. All the songs as he was taught them in his dream, so did he sing them. And how did he first show his powers? There was a man whose mouth was

wakala ye wanuna beni kuna. Wavutuka fwa diaka kuna, kansi yandi kavutuka finina bayandi kuna mpemba ko, kansi kuna kayindula: Bwe ngina sa mu mfwa yayi ya nzole, bika yakituka kwami nkisi. Nkiangunu kayizila mu mamba.

2. Bu kayiza bwana muntu weti vioka, buna yandi wabadika diengila va mamba. Buna muntu wasangisa meso yeku-yeku ye wanamuna lukaya ye wata bimpanzingila bitatu. Mboki kananguna ye kantombula ku bula ye wankotisa mu nzo. Bwisi bu bwayila ye muntu beki tolo, buna yandi wanzaikisa nkumbu andi kwa muntu mu ndozi. Wankamba: Mono i muntu wateka kala mu ntoto ye yafwa mfwa zoole, nkiangunu umbonga ye unkeba, kidi yakala nkisi aku, kadi mono ngina kala nkumbu Mbola mu diambu dia mbola zole. Una kuntungisa mpidi ye nkobe, kidi mono yavwandanga mu ngudi a nkobe, kansi una vadisa kiteki, kidi wantula mu kiau. Mboki yandi wayiza ye bilwazu biandi nsengo ye kibi ye bitwika biankaka.

3. Muntu bu kavulumuka ku tolo ku kaba, katula ti kiongo ndozi kwandi. Buna yandi wabadika vanga bonso bu kayena mu ndozi ye wayidika bio. Mboki yandi wabadika longisila muntu bonso bu kana bukila ye nkunga mi kana yimbila mu buka vo mu vandisa. Nkunga myamyo mu keti mutela mu ndozi bu katemuni, una myo yimbila. Mboki nki watonta songa ngolo zandi? Buna muntu wakala

diseased and whose teeth were rotting and beginning to fall out. So [the healer] prepared a potion of *lemba-lemba* leaves [*lemba,* to calm] and palm wine and gave it to the sick man, who straightway got better. So the healer became a master *nganga.*

bela mu nwa ye meno mana bola ye mabadika katuka. Buna muntu wowo wazokuna mwemo wa lemba-lemba ye kinsangula ye wanwika muntu wakala bela. Yandi ntumbu vola. Nkiangunu yandi wayika ngudi a nganga.

Composition of the Nkisi

This text gives a good idea of the complexity of the material apparatus of an important *nkisi,* which in the case of Mbola includes a cargo basket, a bark box of medicines, tools, a wooden figure, a wooden *kunda* bell, and a bag with more medicines. Most of the medicines are what Laman calls "the usual." The function of the weaverbird nest was explained by Kimfuzi, in the previous text; with its criss-crossing fibers, it epitomizes the idea of "tying up" the medicines in it, and so binding those against whom the *nkisi* is activated. Composition begins with preparation of the bodies of the participants, to the accompaniment of songs describing the significance of the items used. Contact with the properly completed *nkisi* provokes trembling, a sign of the presence of spiritual force. The pile of firewood to be placed near Mbola's place of storage is one of a number of references to fire that mark the dangerous powers of this *nkisi* "of the above."

4. Its appearance is as follows: it is contained in a large *mpidi* basket and a palm bark box. In the box is a wooden bell with a medicine pack attached, wrapped in raffia, put in the box with an adze and a hatchet. Inside the basket is the statue and more bells, with weaverbird nests. There is a medicine packet on top of the box, which is covered with skin of a mongoose. There is also the bag of Mbola itself in the basket. In the bag are scrapings of these medicines: *luyala* fruit, *tondo* mushroom, *nkandikila, nzo* pepper, resin, *lusaku-saku,* skin of *mbambi,* chicken's feet, *looko* fungus, *muzaazu* cocoon, bagworm, *nkasa* poison bark, *kisimani* pod, heads of snakes, *mbidi* kernels, *sombo* palm nut, white and red clay. In the basket there is a carrying-band,

4. Nkadulu andi yena bonso bwabu: Yandi wena mu mpidi yayinene ye nkobe za . . . ba. Mu ngudi a nkobe mwena kikunda kiafumbwa ntima ye kiakangwa mpusu ye kidu-kwanga mu nkobe ye nsengo ye kibi bikalanga momo. Kiteki ye bikunda biankaka bikalanga mu ngudi a mpidi ye mazanza ma bansekoso ye mbatu ku yayulu mu nkobe vatulwa ntima ye vafu-kwanga nkanda wa mubaku. Mboki mpe salu dia yandi kibeni Mbola dikalanga mu mpidi. Va salu vena bilongo bia nteba: luyala, tondo, nkandikila, nungu za nzo, mudingi, lusaku-saku, mukanda wa mbambi, mikindu mia nsusu, looko, muzazu, kintyaba nkuni, nkasa, kisimani, ntu mia nyoka, mingidi mia mbidi, lubanga lwa sombo, mpemba, musoni. Mu mpidi mwena mukolo

because it is carried on the back the way the women of the country carry their cargo baskets. It is hung on the wall inside the house with a pile of firewood near it; the wood is piled in a corner and the basket placed on top of it.

5. When Mbola is composed, a *lusaba* shed is prepared for it as for other *minkisi*. For the beginning and the incantations, see (my description of) Mukwanga, but the songs are different. "Cross your arms on your shoulders, find the chalk" is the song they sing at the beginning when they are applying chalk [to their bodies]. When they take up *musoni* clay to make red marks, another song: "I die of shame (*nsoni*) before Makwende, the man grew strong."[8] For each ingredient there is a song. "*Lusaku-saku,* partly mad [?]; relax, your medicine is prepared, keep calm." [etc.] As they scrape each medicine they sing the song. When they pick up the raffia cloth to test whether the *nkisi* has been truly composed, as each one makes his announcement that the *nkisi* is true, trembling comes over them, they shake and the others sing the song: "Oh Mbola, the dead one without strength revived," the drum plays *ndebekete mbidimbiti.* It plays very rhythmically to aid the trembling. All those who have the gift of *mayembo* tremble. The *nganga,* with the cloth in his hand, tests the *nkisi* with his own body; if the trembling comes, the *nkisi* is good.

wanatina, kidi ku nima yinatunwanga. Yau yinatunwanga bonso bunatinanga bakento ba nsi yayi mpidi. Yandi umanukwanga mu nzo mu kibaka mbatu yala nkuni lukufi ye kibaka, kani vo ntendo kisungu ye tula wo va ntandu a nkuni ye tedimisa mpidi va yulu a nkuni.

5. Mbola bu kavandwanga, yandi ukubulwanga lusaba bonso mu minkisi myankaka. Mbadukulu andi ye mbikulu andi tala mu Mukwanga. Kansi minkunga myena diswaswani. Zinga nkondibila ku ba wo yo tombula mpemba. Nkunga wau ukidulwanga mpemba, bu bana badika vanda. Mboki bu kana nanguna musoni ye kila wo, buna nkunga wankaka: Mfwidi nsoni ku Makwende, bakala wakola. Mboki bilongo biabionsono biena kilongo nkunga. Lusaku-saku nkunku lauka. E ninga yaya wateba biaku watebila bianu. E ninga yaya Mambungu mbila mwendo. Mboki bu bana teba kionso longo i mukunga wo, kansi bu bana bonga lubongo lwa mfudila kani mukisi ku kedika wena vo ka mukisi ko, buna muntu muntu una lungidila, bu kana bika vo nkisi mu kedika wena, buna mayembo mazakumukini ye una tuntuka ye bankaka yimbila nkunga: O yaa Mbola, wafwa walembo mukindu [bwila] fula, buna ngoma yeyi luta siku ndebekete mbidimbiti. Ngoma yiluta tumbulwanga, kidi ndiena kaluta tuntuka. Mboki babonsono bena mayembo bana mana tuntuka. Nganga bu kena ye lubongo va kooko, buna kafula mukisi, fudidi na nitu ya yandi bende kani naki

kwandi mavimpi, buna mayembo
kazakumuka, buna zeyi vo naki bio
die.

Medicines for the bark box are prepared by the *nganga's* initiated wife, the *mbanda*. In Konda's description of Mbola (below), the boiling over of the pot is a divination device, but Nsemi says nothing about that. He indicates, without quite saying so, that nails were driven into Mbola to activate it.

6. Then the assistant grinds the medicines that are to be in the bark box. She takes a new clay pot, a quantity of raffia fiber, and arranges it in the pot with red clay and other medicines, and covers it with a plantain leaf. It has to boil over three times. Then they take the fibers that were in the pot when it was on the fire, and the apprentices, the master *banganga* and other *banganga* who have no apprentices, everybody male and female, tie them on [as protective bracelets, *nsunga*]. Other fibers are tied on the wooden bell, the statue, and on other boxes inside the box.

6. Mboki mumbanda una nika bilongo bina kala mu nkobe, mboki bana bonga kisa kia mona ye mpusu zazingi ye ndimba ye tedika mu kisa ye tula bilongo biankaka momo, mboki kanga kio ngongo [= lukaya luadinkonde va ntandu akinzu]. Kiau kina fuba mfuba zitatu. Mboki bana tambula mpusu kisa bu kiena va tiya ye zau zina lwata bala ba nganga ye bangudi za nganga ye bakondolo bala ba nganga bana zo lwata, buka bwa mvimba ye bakento ye babakala. Mboki zankaka zina kangu mu kikunda ye kiteki ye mu nkobe zankaka mu ngudi a nkobe.

7. Then they go to the cemetery to wherever lies buried a man who was exceptionally strong and virile. They take him and put him in Mbola, they take earth from the grave and rub it on the statue. Then they return to the grave and sacrifice a chicken and drip [the blood] on the *nkisi,* singing: "Where the chicken died, may a man die, allez! the bracelets of the master *nganga.*" After the invocation they install the spirits in the basket and the box, singing: "I took it, I put it. Eh yaya, I took it, I put it in the basket." When the *nkisi* has been installed, the apprentices and others bring out the food and drink,

7. Mboki bana kwenda ku mpemba ye vonso vadiamina muntu wakala ngolo ye kibakala kiakingi. Buna i yandi bana bonga ye sa mu Mbola, bonga kitoto vana bulu ye kusa mu kiteki, mboki vutuka ku bula ye bwila nsusu yi bana kedila mukisi ye yimbila nkunga: Ku fwidi nsusu, ku fwidi muntu, ale, wadi biyeye ku mama nganga. Mboki bu bameni vanda, buna bana soka bakisi mu mpidi ye mu nkobe ye yimbila nkunga: Nabaka, nasoka. E yaya nabaka, nasa mu mpidi, mboki nkisi bu umeni sokwa, buna bala ba nganga ye bankaka bana totula bidiu ye malavu, mboki bana vana nsompo. Mbo lusaba lubavandidi

and [the masters] are given their due. The [remains of the] shed are put at the foot of a palm which thereby becomes taboo so that no one who does not have a big *nkisi* may drink wine from it, only *banganga*.

luna tulwa va taku dia ba. Buna ba diodio dieka dia nlongo ye muntu kondolo nkisi waunene kana dio nwa ko, kansi banganga kaka.

8. Mbola has the power to denounce witches that want to eat people and also to detect and unmask thieves. By means of it, disputes are settled. If there is a quarrel and someone has taken hairs and nailed them into one *nkondi* and someone else has nailed another one, the *bankondi* will decide the matter; whoever suffers a *nkondi* affliction is the loser. If a man has taken something belonging to another and is asked about it, he may nail tokens into *nkondi* [as a declaration of innocence]; if misfortune befalls another clan then they know that one of its members stole the thing.

8. Nkiangunu yandi Mbola wena lulendo mu kambidila ndoki zizolele dia muntu ye diaka mu bakula ye kambidila mivi. Mboki mu yandi mpe mumanunwanga mpaka. Vo lweti bindama mpaka ye muntu una vemi milengi ye koma mu nkondi wankaka mpe wenzi koma mu nkondi yankaka, buna bankondi bana zenga diambu diodio ye konso kuna kwe bwila nkondi, buna yau babedidi, kani muntu yibidi kila kianga, kansi wafula wakala, buna nkoma mpuya mu nkondi vo yina kio. Bwila mu kanda diankaka, buna bazeyi vo mu kanda diodio bayiba kio.

Powers of Mbola

Not only the ailments caused by Mbola but the activating treatments of the wooden figure all concerned the upper part of the body, as befits a retributive *nkisi* "of the above," although, as we have read, Mbola emerges from the water. A number of *nkondi* figures are carved with open mouths, presumably to receive medications and offerings such as Nsemi describes. We are not told why some medicines are in a bag, others in a box; the box is left open while the "cure" is in process because otherwise the victim/patient would be trapped inside it and would not recover.

9. It has the power to seize people, locking their chests as other *zinkondi* do. If it has struck someone in the chest, then someone else must have driven in a nail. Nganga Mbola rubs *lemba-lemba* medication in a leaf of the same and ties it across the face of the statue, removes the *mpuya* (token),

9. Nkiangunu yandi wena lulendo mu kanga bantu. Kansi nkangulu andi mu ntulu bonso bubwidilanga nkondi zankaka. Kansi kabwidila muntu mu ntulu buna mpuya balubanda bankaka nkyangunu yandi bu kabwididi buna nganga Mbola una zokuna mwemo wa lemba-lemba ye bonga lukaya lwa

and then sprinkles the medication on the eyes of the *nkondi,* in its mouth, and on its chest, to calm the *nkisi* and restrain its force. He then gives the medicine to whoever came for it, but after withdrawing the *mpuya* he may not close the bark-box of Mbola until the patient is better. The one who comes to drink the medicine must be sprinkled with it on the chest and on the back; then if Mbola has stricken him he will surely recover when he has taken the medicine.

10. Mbola also has the power to remove people's teeth; indeed, many have lost teeth to Mbola. If someone has toothache, or an abscess on the gum, then Mbola has smitten him. The *nganga* will scrape the bark of *luvete,* together with *nzo*-pepper and salt, and give it to the patient; he collects dust from insect-holes in house-posts and prepares a medicine from Mbola's bag for the patient to eat, that his toothache may be cured.

11. Mbola does not have many treatments, but for conjurations see Mukwanga Yulu and for curses to recite see Mwe Kongo.[9]

lemba-lemba ye fuka lo ku luse lwa kiteki, mboki katula mpuya. Bu kameni katula mpuya mboki bulumuna mwemo [kidi kalembama ye kangisa ngolo zandi] mu meso ma nkondi ye mu nwa ye va mutima. Mboki kana kwiza tambika mwemo kwa wonso wizidi wo kansi ndiena nganga bu kameni kola mpuya kana tumba zibika nkobe ya Mbola ko, nate ye muntu una nyaka mboki kaduka yo. Ndiena wizi tambula mwemo bu kana nwika ndiena wabwilulu kwa Mbola una mubulumuna wankaka [mwemo] ku manima ye wankaka va ntulu. Mboki ti yandi Mbola wambwididi, bu kameni nwa mwemo buna i kutu ye muntu weka mavimpi.

10. Diaka yandi Mbola wena ngolo mu katula bantu meno, nkiangunu babingi bamana katulwa meno kwa Mbola. Muntu bu kena mpasi mu meno vo mputa mu mataku ma meno buna Mbola umubwididi. Kansi nganga una komba nitu a luvete ye tula nungu za nzo ye mungwa ye vana kwa ndieno wena bela koko mboki una saka mfusa mu kunzi vo mu kitungu ye teba bilongo va salu dia Mbola ye nika kidi ndiena weti bela meno kadia ye mpasi zena mu meno zamana.

11. Yandi kena mbukulu zazingi ko, kansi mu ndokolo tala Mukwanga yulu ye mu ntangumunu mu nsibulu tala mpe mu mwe Kongo.

The Rules of the Nkisi

The rules told those under the supervision of Mbola that they should avoid foods that were defective or had holes in them. The obligation of the *nganga* to be careful with fire is appropriate to an *nkisi* of the above.

12. Rules of Mbola. Do not eat manioc that has been damaged by the hoe, nor any undeveloped manioc, palm nuts, or peanuts. [If anyone has done so] the *nganga* prepares a medication to calm the field so that people may eat. *Nganga* may not lie down naked to sleep, lest the *nkondi* burn his cloth in the fire. After dark one may not illuminate the house with a firebrand.

13. When the *nganga* dies, Mbola is profaned until someone else possesses it, removes the old medicine packs, and reconsecrates it so that it recovers its strength. Profanation follows whenever anyone does something that is forbidden. Other matters are best learned from a master *nganga* who is qualified to put you on the road to fame, so that you yourself will be called a master *nganga*. When *nganga* has composed his *nkisi* he is in the business of invoking it; whenever someone comes seeking an invocation, the *nganga* goes with him, because that is his work, to make money. If he has to come a long way to perform divination he is paid an extra chicken. Invoking the *nkisi*, preparing all the medicines, burying some in the village—all the work is to help those who are sick.

12. Mina mia Mbola. Mayaka malwedi nsengo kuna kunza ko, nga madi meno ye mayaka mu mfuba vo ngazi wabwidi mu fuba kani ya nguba vo ya mayaka, buna nganga una zokuna mwemo ye lembo mu mfuba, mboki bantu bana mo dia. Nganga kana lambalala mpene ko, nga buna nkondi si kamuyoka mu nlele ku tiya. Mu nzo bwisi kamana yila ka luna kedimisa tiya ko.

13. Nganga bu kafwidi, buna Mbola sumukini nate ye muntu wankaka una vwama wo ye katula mfumbu zozo za nkulu ye vutuka wo vandulula mboki ulenda kala ngolo diaka. Nga nsumukunu zazonsono zena muntu bu kavengi diena nkanukunu, buna sumukini. Mboki mpe waluta zaya nsamu miankaka kwa ngudi a nganga, luta kala kiambu mu kaba mboki ngudi a nganga si kakutudisa mu mana ye kukumbisa nadede, mboki mwene ngeye mpe bu una bikwa ngudi a nganga. Yandi nganga bu kameni vanda yandi wena salu mu kwe lokingi ye konso konso ku bizi mu landa mu loka buna yandi ukwendanga kuna mu loka, kadi i salu kiandi kio, kidi kabaka mbongo. Kadi mu yandi mbatu mufiedolongo mbatu bankaka vo kitanzi kenzi wo loka buna utambulanga nsusu mosi mbatu. Bu keti loka nkisi buna bilongo biabionsono bitebwanga ye biankaka zika mu bwala nkiangunu salu kianganga kiena mu sadisa bena bela.

Cahier 116, Konda in Kinkenge

Pot Divination

Pot divination is often part of *nkondi* rituals. The pots for other divinatory *minkisi* such as Nsambu (Konda, 117) were painted like Mbola's. In Cuba, and apparently in South Carolina, some pots used for ritual purposes were first marked on the bottom, inside or out, with crosses (Thompson 1983, 109; Ferguson 1992, 110–16). In some divinatory procedures, supporting sticks are said to be of four different woods which would probably burn through at different speeds, permitting some control of the outcome. Konda is explicit that this Mbola has no statue.

1. Mbola is a very large *nkisi*. It is in a *mpidi* basket that is kept hung up in a corner of the house or on the outside. In it there is an axe, a hoe, and its knives, which are its weapons. Mbola has no statue, but is kept just in a basket.

2. The deeds of Mbola are powerful. When its medicines have been buried in the village, people will develop sores on all their limbs— nose, mouth, or head; that they have broken its rules is seen in these sores. When Mbola inflicts sores they are very large. *Nganga* Mbola treats them, first collecting medicines and preparing them, then setting the pot of Mbola. After driving in four pegs in a square, he fetches dry stalks for fuel and puts them under [the pot]. He paints [red and white] lines on the pot, and [the people] dance. The pot is not covered but left open.

3. When the pot has been put on the fire he pronounces the spell: "Mbola, sir, test the women, test

1. Mbola i nkisi waunene beni. Yandi wena mu mpidi. Kakebulwanga ye manukwanga va sungu kya nzo vo mbazi kamanukwanga mu keba. Mu nkisi una mwena kiubi ye nsengo ye mbeele zandi. Bina i lwazu biandi. Mbola ka yena teki ko, kansi mpidi kaka kake-bulwanga.

2. Mavanga ma Mbola mena ma ngolo. Yandi bu kazikwa mfusa mu bwala buna bantu beti mana baka mputa mu biela biabionsono mu nitu vo mu mbombo vo mu nwa vo ku ntu i kuma babana basumuna mina miandi bamona kwakwingi mu mputa zandi. Yandi Mbola bu kabungulanga mputa buna zanene beni, i kuma nganga Mbola bu kabuka buna yandi utotanga miemo miandi teka mio teba longo mboki kana tedika kinzu kia Mbola. Bu kameni koma binko biya lweka ye lweka buna i ntumbu tomba nkuni za madiadia mayuma ye tula ku nsi, mboki ntumbu kila kinzu ye kina. Mboki kakanga ngongo ko kansi kia mwasi.

3. Mboki i mwe tedimisi kio va tiya i mwe kambi nsibu nge mwene Mbola konka bakento wakonka

the men; if you find a witch, male or female, afflict him with many sores, man or woman, Lord Mbola." When the pot is on the fire the men and women dance around it, while the *ndungu*-drummer plays the Mbola rhythm, *bukwimvi, bukwimvi, bukwimvi* and they take up the song, "Eh, bring up whatever Mbola has seen."

4. The *nganga* watches to see on which side the pot spills over, which is where the witches are.[10] When he has noted it, everyone calms the patient, singing "Eh, let us calm [him]." Some take the medicinal mixture and sprinkle him with it. Witches and non-witches are begged to enter the way of the *nkisi* to heal the sick person.

5. Mbola may be called by another name, Nsansi a Mbola. It may cause boils. Its "keep off" signs may be hung on anything, an *n'safu* tree, a plantain, on paths, on money and other things. If an *n'safu,* or palm has been protected with the sign of the *nkisi* and you cross it, Mbola will attack you and do as it pleases to damage your body and kill you. These are the deeds of Mbola.

babakala ya mbuta ye yasidi dia ndoki ankento ko yatudi dia ndoki ambakala ko bungula mputa zazingi-zingi bungula bakento wabungula babakala mwene Mbola. Bu kameni kio tedika buna babana bakento ye babakala bana zungana kinzu kiokio. Mboki nsiki a ndungu una badika sika kuma dia Mbola bonso bwabu bukwimvi, bukwimvi, bukwimvi. Mboki bana nanguna nkunga e tombukila dionso dimweni Mbola.

4. Mboki nganga utalanga konso kuna vombula buna i kuna kwena bandoki. Nganga bu kameni dio dio buna babonsono bana lemba mbevo ye nkunga au mpe bana nanguna mu yimbila ebo lembano e, lembano e lembano e, lembano e. Lemba kulu, we lembano, e lembe. Buna bankaka basimbidi mwemo ye mwanga yandi mbevo. Buna bandoki ye ba nana bika bakotila nzila mu nkisi mu nyakisa mbevo yoyo.

5. Mbola mwanki mpe mbatu ubikwanga nkumbu yankaka. Ulenda bikwa Nsansi a Mbola. Yandi lenda bukula nsongo a mpela vo mafumpula. Kandu biandi bikandukwanga mu dionso dionso diambu vo mu nsafu vo mu mankondo vo mu zinzila ye mbongo ye mu biankaka. Kansi vo nsafu vo ba dina kandukwa kwa kandu bia nkisi wo buna nge muntu wamana bio labuka nkisi una kubwila ye vanga bonso bu kazolele mu teta mu nitu aku ye kuvonda. I bobo mavanga ma Mbola menina.

Mbola carries out the retributive and protective functions of other *minkondi,* but is at the same time specific in its ownership of a particular set of afflictions whose characteristics are literally embodied in the *nkisi* itself and its associated rules. The three texts invite us to fill them out or to pool details and inferences into a single account of Mbola. There is no reason not to explore such a procedure and, as I have indicated, close attention reveals how the details of the rituals support and explain one another; but it would be a mistake to assume that even in one area there was ever a single, true, and complete recipe, or a single, prescribed material apparatus.

8. LIFE AND DEATH: OBJECTHOOD OF PERSONS

The chiefs killed many of those they governed, and so they became famous.

—KINKELA NGOMA

From *nkisi* as chief to chief as *nkisi*. Unlike an ordinary headman, an invested chief was transformed (*balukidi*) into an extraordinary person with powers of life and death. During his investiture in the cemetery of the chiefs, the candidate inherited the position and powers of his predecessor. He emerged covered in red and white spots, indicating that he had become a leopard. The authenticating officials included neighboring chiefs of similar or higher rank and an *nganga* representing the benevolent *bisimbi* of the domain. Close examination of the rituals of investiture and the taboos associated with them shows that the chief, so far from being a monarch, was often the emblem, perhaps even the puppet, of an oligarchic local association of free lineages allied by marriage. Their representatives, individually related as its Children and Grandchildren to the clan that owned the title, their Fathers, controlled the chiefship in their role as the *bamayaala*, "those in charge." The ritual combination of "life," derived from "nature" spirits, and "death," derived from lineal ancestors, corresponds to the combination of lineally heterogeneous co-resident groups and dispersed descent groups in the social structure. At another level of interpretation, the rituals suggest a "philosophical" concern with the paradox of social continuity and individual transience.

The materials used in the rituals acquired symbolic value on much the same principles as those used as "medicines" in the composition of any *nkisi;* like any *nganga* the chief was bound by rules whose content complemented in action the effectiveness of the material objects. He himself was part of the total apparatus of the mobilized forces that he represented. In eastern Kongo and also in parts of Manianga, initiation to chiefship, like that to many *minkisi*, could take the form of an affliction cult, in which the candidate was summoned to the role by a disease: "The inauguration was like this. If a man is chronically ill they put him in a house for a year with his wife. He may not emerge except to relieve himself. When the year is over he is taken to Bikinda, the cemetery of former chiefs" (Bitebodi, 26; Lunungu, 172).[1]

The rituals of chiefly investiture were undeniably anchored in local politics and economics. They initiated wealthy men into what was effectively a title association whose members reinforced their oligarchic control over populations of slaves or potential slaves and who profited from the initiation fees required of new members. It is tempting, therefore, to suppose that the power of death was a ritual expression of the actual violence of nineteenth-century chiefs, who achieved renown by fighting wars, enslaving the weak, publicly executing wrongdoers, and sacrificing others in political rituals. At least in northern or forested Kongo, however, the "wars" were tests of spiritual potency that ended with the first casualty, and the content of the rituals shows that titles did not simply reflect or consecrate political and economic achievements; the power of death celebrated at investiture was only contingently related to political practice. A chief could be wealthy and warlike without being invested, and some were chosen for investiture against their will. The power of life announced in the same rituals, in the form of, for example, the capacity to make trees fruitful, is readily recognizable as "symbolic" or "imaginary"; it is methodologically unsound to accord different ontological statuses to two kinds of power intimately linked in the same ritual complex.

The problem of the nature of chiefship and the "imaginary" quality of the powers of life and death emerges clearly from a comparison of chiefs with witches and with *minkisi*. The witch, like the chief, also underwent composition (*mpandulu*) with medicines and became a kind of *nkisi* (Lutete, 221; Mampuya, 276), and some said that at night witches grew claws and teeth like a leopard's. (The composite nature of the witch is caught in the modern phrase *"il est composé,"* or *"il est double."*) A chief's power, called *kindoki,* was like that of the witch, *ndoki*, although the "witchcraft" of the witch was illegitimate. *Minkisi,* though they were objects, had a will of their own, to punish and to heal. Nsemi Isaki explains the problem:

> The *nkisi* has life; if it had not, how could it heal and help people? But the life of an *nkisi* is different from the life in human beings; one can nail its flesh (*koma mbizi*), burn it, break it, or throw it away; but it will not bleed or cry out. Yet the *banganga* think it possesses life because when it heals people it brings in a fee. Thus, whether an *nkisi* is alive with ears that hear or whether it is just a dead thing, it brings in a return. When the *nganga* chants he knows that the *nkisi* hears the words of its master as he honors and supplicates it. (Nsemi, 391)

In short, they are regarded as persons because they are treated as such and in that capacity grant favors; they work. As Chapter 5 explained, the *nkisi*-object is only the material focus of a complex of behaviors which include the *nganga*, whose initiation is simultaneously the composition and activation of the *nkisi*. *Nkisi* and *nganga* share their powers and some of their substance; the rules governing the behavior of the *nganga* obey the same principles as the "medicines" empowering the *nkisi*. The investiture of a chief was an example of the same kind of concatenation of persons, rules, and medicines. A great *nkisi* of *nkondi* type is also a chief, mediating powers of life and death and having the capacity to judge disputes, wage war, and guarantee peace. Such powers were (and are) not considered to be restricted to "persons" rather than "objects." At a certain level in Kongo thinking, it apparently makes little difference whether the container of a willful spirit be a grave, a wooden statue, or a live human body.

To see the chief as an "object" is to suggest a new perspective on the rituals of investiture. The usual assumption in anthropology is that a ritual is performed for the "benefit" of the persons in it, moving them, for example, from one status to another. With respect to Gisu circumcision, however, Jean LaFontaine has persuasively argued, "The manipulation of individuals should . . . be treated in the same way as the treatment of other symbols; that they are human beings should not blind us to this" (LaFontaine 1977, 423). She continues, "The progress of individuals through the ordered stages of a rite of passage might be regarded in much the same light as the narrative of myth, as enacting a proposition of a general social relevance." In the same way, although a MuKongo might be moved from commoner to chief by the rite of investiture, he was part of the material apparatus of a ritual which objectively represented and confirmed the truth of general principles fundamental to the constitution and continuity of social life, while at the same time the ritual was central to the political and economic processes.

This chapter conveys the general outline of chiefship rituals as we find them in the manuscripts; the rituals for several related titles in the vicinity of Lolo in northeastern Mayombe are described in detail by Lutete in the next chapter. Apparently all the rituals of investiture practiced in Mayombe were similar, no matter from which direction the groups that practiced them allegedly came. Mayombe chiefship rituals distinctively emphasize the *nkisi nsi*—literally a medication of the domain, buried in the earth (see Chapter 9). Greater differences are apparent between rituals in Mayombe and those in Manianga, no matter what the clan name, but they also appear to be a matter of variations on common themes.[2]

Unfortunately, our richly detailed texts never provide case studies that might show how competition in trade and titles worked out in practice, what took place in actual rituals, or how chiefship related to the regional political network, Lemba. There are no examples of marriage alliances, factional opposition to chiefs, criminal trials, or actual incidents of "war." In short, the politics is missing, but much can be inferred. As an "object," the chief was, like an *nkisi*, a repository of "imagined" powers; nevertheless, the chief was also an actor in "real" political events. The foreign observer seeks to separate the natural and the supernatural, though the BaKongo generally do not. They understand and experience unusual developments in the lives of individuals and groups, including wealth and unexpected death, as the effects of powers derived from the unseen world of the dead. So events express and confirm ritual, rather than the other way around.

Power of Death

Everywhere, the chief is represented as a "leopard" and a killer. Writing from Nganda, Joani Mvemba reports, "Whoever is to be invested brandishes the sword of power and having brandished it he kills a nephew and licks blood from the sword" (Lunungu, 159). Na Ndamba in Mukimbungu, after his investiture, "became one who buried people alive," *bu kamana yala buna weka nkuni a bantu* (Masamba, 278). From Diadia we hear, "If a chief was to be invested, he had to execute his nephew, the son of his own sister; if he did that, then everybody would respect him and do whatever he wanted. If anyone were disobedient the chief, who had executed his own nephew, would execute him too" (Lutangu, 212). Laman says that many of those appointed as *ntinu* refused to commit the required murder, but might submit to other tests of extraordinary capacities (LKII, 140).

Grand Hôtel de Boma — Congo

KONGO CHIEF, MAYOMBE

Grand Hotel de Boma—Congo
(Grand Hotel in Boma—Congo)
Belgian Congo (now Democratic Republic of the Congo)
Photographer unknown, ca. 1900
Publisher unknown, postmarked 1904
Postcard Collection
Eliot Elisofon Photographic Archives
National Museum of African Art

During the ritual of investiture the chief "saw" or "was licked by" the leopard, meaning that he was painted with red and white spots and identified with leopards.

The reason he wore ivory bracelets and leopard's claws and a necklace of leopard's teeth is that he might be respected as those animals are. He would be seen as frightening like the leopard and the elephant. When he put on the cap, the necklace and the bracelets, all who saw him would feel fear and respect. (Kunzi, 123)

In 1816, a tree stood outside the compound of the king of Boma, hung with the skulls of his enemies. In the vicinity of Mukimbungu, in the 1880s, local chiefs consecrated a trade pact by executing a slave whose body hung from a tree until it disintegrated. Ivory carvings from Mayombe show the chief, his *munkwisa* root in his teeth, enthroned upon the body of a slave who was bound and gagged.[3] "When a chief [with the title] Kayi Ngoma first began to rule and took charge of his market, he buried a man alive and then entered the market" (Kimbembe, 80). In 1929, in the vicinity of Kisantu (eastern Kongo), an official executioner admitted having killed six slaves at the funeral of the reigning chief's predecessor (Swartenbroeckx 1966, 171). The victims did not have to be criminals, though one who, on another occasion, broke market rules might be executed in similar fashion. It is probably irrelevant to try to distinguish between "criminal" and non-criminal victims; both established the chief's power.

A traditional anthropological comment on the violence of Central African kings is that killing, like the incest sometimes required of the ruler, marks the king's exceptional status with respect to normal society. The BaKongo indeed think that killing indicates powers that ordinary people do not have; one who could not kill as expected lacked what it takes to be chief, and one who could kill even a relative demonstrated that he would govern impartially. The concept of power is more complex than that, however; the obligatory horrendous deed is thought of as a real test, not a symbolic change of status. The witchcraft power (*kindoki*) that leaders and wealthy people must have takes the form of a sort of gland in the belly, called *kundu,* which in former times could be revealed by means of the poison ordeal, *nkasa.* The activity of the witch (*ndoki*) is to "eat people" (*dia bantu*); the more victims one eats, the more *makundu* he accumulates. This expression is not a metaphor; actual bones found around someone's house may be adduced in evidence against him. (To objections that the bones were those of a pig or other animal, the reply would be that, of course, *in daylight*, that's what they would look like.) It is true that the meal is supposed to take place in an otherworld, visible only in dreams or to diviners, who have four eyes, but it is none the less real. The chief, too, is supposed to "eat" in the visible sense that he is expected to consume conspicuously, that he should also cause his followers to eat well, and that the cost of this benefit is a certain amount of occult "eating" of nocturnal victims. In Kongo thinking, as we have seen in the analysis of tradition (Chapter 4), an ordered society is one in which "eating," both literal and metaphorical (but for whom is it a metaphor?), is properly distributed.

The Execution

In the following account from Mayombe the arbitrary exactions of the king are as evident as the fact that theatrically enacted violence celebrates his greatness and helps to keep the people terrified.[4]

> The clan which ruled over all the clans that came from Ntandu [the east] was Ma Nsundi, who oppressed them greatly. He had a rule that no one might step over the legs of the wife of the king, Ma Nsundi, nor step on her mat [both actions implying sexual intercourse]. If people did not closely follow the commands of Ntinu Ma Nsundi they were made prisoner; one who did not have 100 cloths with which to redeem himself would be executed by the royal sword.

> The king appointed one man to execute prisoners. The sword (*mbele ya makenda; kenda* to decapitate) was made with an ivory handle, well carved in the form of a woman, showing her hairstyle and her breasts; it was very sharp. This knife could not be taken outside except on the day of execution.

Bittremieux saw such a sword in Nganda Nsundi, probably in the 1930s. It was 70 centimeters long, kept in a raffia bundle along with other insignia of the chiefship, and

CHIEF ENTHRONED (IVORY)

From *Treasures from Tervuren,* pl. 10
The Royal Museum, Tervuren

handled with reverence. Originally, it had been one of four, two male and two female, of which one was damaged and two had been taken by Europeans. The "flawless" ivory carving showed a woman with her long hair dressed down her back and her hands crossed behind her; the reference of the image is to the execution, in the sacred forest, of a woman caught in adultery. If she refused to name her lover, a male dog was killed in his place (Bittremieux 1940, 119–20).

> On the appointed day, all the people of the region came to watch. From all directions they brought palm wine for the king. They laid the prisoner on his [or her] back and pegged his arms and legs to the ground. Then they sang, "Eh, Makenda, who executes people!" While they sang, *ndungu* drums, large *mbuma* drums, *ngongi* bells and wooden *mpwanda* trumpets sounded. Makenda, the man appointed to this work, danced with his sword in his hand. When he raised it to strike, he sang, "I will cut, eh, let it cut!" Uttering this threat, he furiously attacked the prisoner, severing his head. The public applauded, "E wewe!" The Children and Grandchildren of Ma Nsundi took up the head and soaked it in water until it rotted and the skin and the flesh fell away; then they hung the skull on one of the poles of the king's compound so that passing strangers might see it and know that this was the residence of a great king who executed people (Babutidi, 13).[5]

The "sword of power" (*mbeele a lulendo*), also called *kipaba,* might be modeled on Portuguese sabers (Beumers and Koloss 1992, pl. 62), although in Ngoyo in par-

Congo.
No. 30.   Exécution.

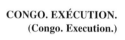

CONGO. EXÉCUTION.
(Congo. Execution.)

Loango, French Congo
(now Republic of the Congo)
Photograph by
Robert Visser, 1882–94
Publisher unknown,
published ca. 1910
Postcard Collection
Eliot Elisofon
Photographic Archives
National Museum
of African Art

ticular it might be made of wood (Bittremieux 1936, plate); in that form it was a sign rather than a weapon. According to Babutidi (Cahier 18), when the chief Makonde Mambutu was to be enthroned, he would order a sword from the smith (*ngangula*). "The *kipaba* was used as follows. If a man was sentenced by others but did not submit, they would appeal to Mambutu who, when he came, would stick his sword in the ground to open the trial. When the recalcitrant saw the *kipaba* he would immediately agree to pay his fine because the sword stuck in the public place of trial (*mbazi a nkanu*) signified that the chief had 'arisen.' The meaning of the *kipaba* is that anyone who rejected the decision of the chief would be arrested until his people ransomed him."

Power of Life

The rituals of investiture reveal the BaKongo as preoccupied with the great human paradox of the death of individuals and the perdurance of the community, and with the idea that the death of some protects the lives of others. Besides his association with leopards, the chief incorporates the powers of the *bisimbi,* localized "nature spirits." *Bisimbi* animate *minkisi,* in the sense of composite devices, and may themselves be called *minkisi* but they lead an independent existence. According to Matunta, *bisimbi* are people who died long ago. They have different names: If they are malicious, having been witches in their lifetime, they are called *nkuyu,* ghost; if generous, *nkita.* But the *basimbi* have great nobility because they have calm dispositions; they are not easily angered and they keep the *bankuyu* and *bankita* from spending too much time among the living (Cahier 284). A long essay by Kavuna of Nganda (Cahier 57) shows simultaneously the ambiguities of the concept and the grip it has on Kongo imaginations. "Why people in some areas think as they do beats me," he says; in his opinion, "it is not true that our forebears in olden times, ancestors or ghosts, were transformed into *bisimbi;* they are water spirits, *bankita, minkisi.*" He explains what *bisimbi* are by mentioning the names of well-known *minkisi,* some of which are made up in figurines, pots, or gourds, but others appear as natural phenomena, such as snakes or sparks. Much of his essay is taken up with a description of what is evidently an initiation ritual for a group of young people, intended to assure for them the benefits of regulated contact with *bisimbi.* If approached without due respect, the *bisimbi* (which Kavuna, like Lunungu, also calls *basimbi* and *nkita*) can drown the offender, but their chief business is to supply food and other good things.

What are *bisimbi*? They have other names, too. Some are called python, lightning, gourd or calabash, mortar or a sort of pot. The explanation of their names: they are water spirits (*nkisi mia mamba*). The names of some of the spirits are these: Na Kongo, Ma Nzanza, Nkondi and Londa [names of well-known *minkisi*]. They have many appearances of all kinds. Some are seen to be green, or red, black, perhaps in spotted or sparkling colors. The body in which they are appealed to (*kinitu kiambokono*) is of three or four kinds, 1) the body of a person 2) of a snake such as python or viper 3) a calabash or gourd 4) of wood or pottery. Sometimes of a spark of fire.

Truly they have great power and authority, for their power is revealed by the force they show in the water and in the gullies. They stir up very high winds and unleash tornadoes, so that the bodies of people are filled with fear and trembling. They break people's courage and render it feeble, weak, limp, petrified, hollow and fevered; they are stunned, and grovel in terror. This is how the *bisimbi* show their strength: if they see someone come to draw water from the pool where they reside, they rise to the surface and cover it with foam and turbulence, turning and twisting. So the person drawing water is scared stiff when she sees how the water boils in the pool. She may tumble into the water because she is dizzy. If she does not cry out so that those who remain in the village hear her, when next they meet her she may be dead.

Their only occupation is to draw to themselves people such as house-builders and cultivators, so that they may have produce and livestock and lots of chickens. They reveal many deeds through the signs they show. You may be astonished to see a real cock, as plain as could be, skipping about on the surface of the water; or a great long banana bunch lying on the water; or a fine pot full of food with a parrot feather in the middle of it.

The *bisimbi* live in pools, turbulent streams, and gullies. Though they control the weather, they are not "sky spirits." Lutete says that they are unusual stones found on mountaintops or in gullies where they were scattered during the rainy season by Mpulubunzi, the chief of all the *bisimbi,* identified with the southwest wind; he gives lists of them, with their names. Kavuna shows much less interest in rocks than does Lutete, but for both writers, and for BaKongo in general, *bisimbi* are endowed with creative power evident in remarkable natural phenomena, including twins and strange, twisted sticks or oddly shaped stones. Though they animate *minkisi* in general, including violent ones, *bisimbi* are primarily associated with the common interests of local communities, especially in matters of collective health and economic prosperity.

The Investing Priest

By virtue of his relationship with benevolent nature spirits, acquired at his investiture, the chief promised good hunting, abundant crops, and freedom from at least some diseases, although he did not, himself, conduct rain rituals, bless, or participate ritually in hunting or agriculture; nor was he a healer. He was supposed to be a wise arbiter who promoted harmony in his village and kept witches at bay. In nineteenth-century Mayombe, at least in Vungu, the investing official was the *nganga mbangu,* the priest of Mbenza, who was possessed by *bisimbi;* he consecrated reproduction and at least in some instances conducted rituals to make or withhold rain (Doutreloux 1967, 170; MacGaffey 1991, 53–63). *Mbangu,* another name for *nkisi* Mbenza, may refer to the lines inscribed on the candidate's body, which reappear on the sacred stones of Mbenza. The Yombe chief, like any *nganga,* is identified with his *nkisi,* the *nkisi nsi,* itself a medication of the earth that serves to domesticate the powers of *bisimbi* earth spirits. In the same way that relics of a deceased *nganga* are incorporated in the *nkisi* of his successor so as to neutralize the soul of the deceased and transfer his power (Mwe Kongo, in Nsemi, 387; and Lunkanka, in MacGaffey 1991, 137–40), the new chief is put in touch with the body of the old, with the grave of the originator of the title, or with the *nkisi nsi* (a kind of medicated grave), all together constituting an allomorphic set. At his own death his grave reveals a new *simbi* or *nkisi nsi* in the form of a rock. During the rituals, perdurance is represented by rocks or by hardwood trees such as *mbalala* or *lubota* against which the chief "leans." In Chapter 9, Lutete describes such rituals in detail.

In Kongo dia Lemba, stronghold of one of the royal factions in the seventeenth century, the investiture site (*kindakazi*) for the Nlaza clan was a large termite hill called Nzambi; the investing priest (Na Mavitu, "in charge of the entrance") controlled the rain by spreading cloths over the hill, an abode of *simbi* spirits (Kilola, 76, in MacGaffey 1986a, 82). In other districts it is evident that the *banganga* of important *minkisi* such as Bunzi, Na Kongo, Nsonde, and Ngovo, themselves representative of *bisimbi*, played an important role in investiture, although we lack a good description of it. The following account by that careful ethnographer, Lunungu of Nganda in central Manianga, is the only one from that area to describe an *nkisi* for chiefship as including a medication of the earth, but he does not use the Yombe term *nkisi nsi.* The site of investiture, the *kiyaazi,* is a fig tree:[6]

> Investiture on the leopard-skin came from *nkisi* Bweno. It includes a snail-shell, a medicine box, the fig-tree (*nsanda*) of chiefship, and the necklace of leopard's teeth. (In this fig-tree is the protective charm of the chiefship, for when it is planted they first put

medicines in the hole, then the tree.) The day they invest the chief is also the day on which they compose the *nkisi*. Many people come to see the investiture. The *nkisi* is not composed by the chief himself but by the Children. When they compose it, they go to where there is a pool. The candidate is in [a] house when the *nkisi* is composed; he emerges when it is finished. If there is no pool, the *nganga* chooses any place to dig a small hole in which he puts water; that is where the *nkisi* is composed. The reason for the pool is so that anyone who is afflicted with chronic leprosy may go there to rub mud on himself every day until he is cured.

In this *nkisi* were three parts: a snail shell, a bark box and a bundle. The shell had the work of [providing medicines] to drink and to wash with, for anyone who was smitten with leprosy. The box, to keep the grasshoppers [locusts] and the heads of snakes; the bundle, just for treating [the sick]. All three were made up with white clay, the bundle, the shell and the box. However, the shell had only white clay.[7] In the box and the bundle they put all kinds of things: snakes, or snakes' heads; locusts; and lizards, or the heads of lizards. Also there are herbs in this *nkisi;* their names are: wormwood (*ndudi-ndudi*), *lemba-lemba*, basil (both the female and the male kind), and *lubata-bata*. They are there for potions and to pour on the leprosy. Having composed the *nkisi* at the pool they return to the village and cause the chief to tread on the leopard-skin. (Lunungu, 171)

Another description from Nganda emphasizes the figure of the chief as palm wine tapster, although of course in ordinary life no chief or elder drew his own wine. Palm nuts, palm oil, and raffia cloth were among the principal exports, but the palm tree, with its combination of wine (produced from the male flower for men) and cooking oil (from the female flower in the form of palm nuts), provided a basic metaphor for the complementary productive and social relations between men and women, and thus for the abundance of life (MacGaffey 1986a, 130).

When someone had accepted the office, the Children took him and put him in the house with the corpse of the dead chief. They set him down on the wrapped bundle of the corpse and laid him out on it. While he lay on the *nyombo* they marked him with red and white clay and sang this song, "He has seen the leopard, the Spotted One, the frightful creature." Then the Children took him and carried him on their backs to his house.

After they have done this he might not go about until he had been consecrated. They tell him which is to be the day of consecration, whether *konzo* or *nsona*, for these are the days on which chiefs are consecrated.[8] On such days no work was done, for they were days of the power of the chiefs; therefore no man might take up a sharp instrument [i.e., no one might object]. The reason why they set the candidate on the *nyombo* bundle is to show that the deceased has no more power, that the one set upon him is superior in power.[9]

When all have come to the consecration of the chief, the Children bring him out and put him on a throne of five or six guns, on top of which they spread a leopardskin. The Children lower him onto this throne; he must not just sit in it, or if so he must sit with his legs properly crossed. When he is being consecrated, [with] his climbing loop on his shoulder, his knife and his palm wine tapper's trimming blade, his stick and his cap, then everything that is in our land is collected and given to him to wear or to hold, not a thing must be left out.

Thus equipped, he is consecrated with white and red clays, [marking] circles like the spots of the leopard. [They] sing songs of consecration like this: "Eh, the smith at the forge, he has been chosen, he has been sanctified. Eh, the smith, should you forget the taboo, you will see them." So singing, they finish marking his whole body, from the navel to his neck, and he clears his throat. This throat clearing is as one does who is drinking palm wine. (Matunta, 313)

The leopard, "the spotted one," with whom the candidate is identified by contact, is the mummy of his predecessor, colored in transitional red. By becoming, in the course of the ritual, "the smith at the forge," the candidate unites with the powers of the leopard those of the *bisimbi* who are smiths themselves and the source of the creative abilities of human smiths, producers of agricultural implements.[10] He is not himself a smith, although much has been written to that effect.[11]

As the investiture proceeds, oratory includes the following praise-songs:

"Clearing the throat, you the Bwende chief, you are the Pioneer who assembled a hundred clans, the Guide who shows the way among the chiefs.[12] If you were not in front there would be no leader. You are Nyumbu a Ntende, Bringer of the Palm, without you there would be no palm trees."[13] "We kneel like a goat, we kneel like a young goat. Blessings [we seek], we the Children of you the rulers; white clay we desire, not charcoal.[14] Lay aside the sword of power, do not stand it against us, we who are like a young palm tree. You created those who own palm groves. The *mpanzu* pod has exploded, every man drags the corner of his mantle" (Matunta, 313).[15]

In Manianga the candidate chief might be painted with red and white in a cave, at a rock, or at the grave of his predecessor. Particular pools and caves, abodes of *bisimbi*, are mentioned, but the spirits themselves are not named, as they are in Mayombe, and the chiefs are not identified with them or with particular rocks. There is no sense of a hierarchy of titles. Everywhere, the chief's powers included those of inflicting or curing diseases ("leprosy") that produce white patches on the skin. The reason for this selection is simply that the chief was an intermediary figure, particolored in white (the color of the invisible world) and red (the color of mediation between the worlds), who had an affinity with particolored creatures (the leopard, the *mbende* rat, the harnessed bushbuck) and particolored victims of leprosy. His "healing" of the disease was a way of stating the analogical relationship that defines him.[16]

In eastern Kongo, the chiefship described in considerable detail by the Jesuit J. Mertens differs from those we have been considering. The "crowned chief," wearer of a bonnet (*mpu*) and of a set of iron bracelets worn on the left (feminine) arm to represent the ancestral lineages, was consecrated and eventually buried by a smith, whose art is specifically related to the powers of *bisimbi*. A woman chief was consecrated along with the chief and shared in his powers, although she usually married someone else. Mertens, from observations made in 1936, records no drying of the chief's body nor any contrast between wet or dry, either between different stages of the chief's life or between chief and smith (Mertens 1942). The chief had a special relationship to leopards, whose flesh he might not eat because he too "was a leopard." Both chief and smith were invested with their powers as a therapeutic measure on occasions of collective affliction on the recommendation of a diviner, but the smith was specifically forbidden to wear chiefly insignia (MacGaffey 1986, 66–68).

Death Transcended

A chief's ritual career displays the tension between transience and permanence in diachronic fashion. He begins as an ordinary human being, associated with signs of organic growth, and ends as a rock, guaranteeing stability to his community. The terms of this transformation correspond to the two kinds of *simbi* spirit, those of the water and those of the dry land.

Everywhere, the chief's relationship with the earth, source of life and locus of death, is ambiguous; he is both united with it and separate from it. In Mayombe, he sleeps on the ground in Lulaala and is rolled on the *nkisi nsi* but afterward neither he nor those around him may throw things down. In Nganda, the chief is carried to the cemetery of the chiefs (*bikinda*); "he may not go on the ground but up in the air at all times." The new chief, as we have seen, after being laid upon the mummified body of his predecessor "to show that the deceased had no more power," is smeared with mud from the grave and marked with leopard spots; "then the Children take him and carry him on their backs to his house." In ordinary life the chief traveled in a hammock, or walked on leaves and mats spread for him (Doutreloux 1967, 171).

The verb *zingila*, "to last a long time," recurs in connection with chiefship, together with *kizingu,* "perdurance," and its apparent cognates *zinga* (a seashell) and *zinga* (to wrap) (MacGaffey 1986a, 96). Lutete wrote, "When the old ones saw how small the sea snail was (*nkodia mbu*) and yet how strong its house, they composed *nkisi* Simbu in which to hide their souls (*bilunzi*); they buried it in the forest with a small sign showing above ground, and they said, "Here, in your strong house, safeguard my life; take me with you to the sea that I may live with you, as the years come and the years return" (Cahier 233, 6).[17] In this ritual, the elder returns himself to the status of a child: "The ancestors thought the child in the womb was like a snail in his shell" (Lunungu, 175). Although in the east there is little of the emphasis on either the great age of individual chiefs or on the perdurance of chiefship that we read in Lutete's texts, the chief's physical body was everywhere subject at death to special treatments that denied the mortality of forces he temporarily embodied.

In usual Kongo practice, the chief's body was smoke-dried for several months and then impressively wrapped (*zinga*) in as many hundreds of imported cloths as the family could afford, including an outer covering of red blanket corresponding to the red cosmetic with which an ordinary body was painted. Such a corpse was called *nyombo kimbi* or *mvumbi a manzakala*, "body that has been sat with [while it was being smoked]," an expression referring to the obligation of the chief's widows to remain with it during the process (Kavuna, 65).[18] Since burial in this world was also believed to be, at the same time, investiture in the world of the dead, the grave goods and blankets accompanying the chief earned him honor in both worlds.

It is clear that at least some of the rituals presupposed the analogy that wet is to dry as transient is to durable. The chief's spiritual career began with his investiture, associating him with water, abode of *simbi* spirits and source of healing and fertility, and progressed by death and desiccation to his transformation into a dry land *simbi,* sign of everlasting life. The *nkisi* Bweno for chiefship in northern Manianga, as Lunungu has told us, "is not composed by the chief himself but by the Children. When they compose it, they go to where there is a pool. The candidate is in [a] house when the *nkisi* is composed; he emerges when it is finished. If there is no pool, the *nganga* chooses any place to dig a small hole in which he puts water; that is where the *nkisi* is composed" (Lunungu, 171).

In Mukimbungu, part of the investiture took place in a little shelter made of the fragrant leaves of the *mansisya* bush, next to a spring; after being invested the chief stamped his foot, whereupon water surged from the spring, even in the dry season (Kilola, 75). When he was moribund, the chief was strangled by the Children and Grandchildren (see below, "Na Menta"), and thereafter the wet and dry components of the chief's body were subject to discrete treatments corresponding to the difference between first and second burial in modern practice:[19]

> Invested chiefs of the Nanga clan could not die unassisted. When the chief became seriously ill, his officers put a cord around his neck and passed it through the wall; then, from the outside, they pulled on the cord until the chief died. Having done so, they could not bury him; they took him in secret to a gully and threw him in. They took green banana leaves, killed a pig or a goat, removed its entrails and tied them up with leaves. Then they announced that the chief had "strayed," or "declined," or "lain down." Afterward they put the body on a platform and smoked it for a number of dry seasons, three or four, before they held the funeral and buried it.[20] In the old days, they called burial "investiture in the other world," and so it is to this day. (Kilola, 75)

This passage, like others that mention evisceration and smoking, is not easy to understand, although the drift is clear; since the body was available for smoking, perhaps Kilola, the author, meant to say that only the entrails (the wettest part of the body) were thrown away and those of a goat substituted. Lutete in Lolo tells us that when the entrails of a goat were substituted they "represented the corpse" (*kifwani kya mvumbi*) and were treated in every way as though they were the original body. On the death of a chief in Lolo, the Children and Grandchildren went to the grave of the founder of the line to pull up *mansisya* (with a pun on *nsisya*, "soul") which they buried in a swampy place (*nyamba*). The body of the chief itself was removed at night and also put in a marsh, but his hair and nails (signs of vitality, but dry) were put in his treasure chest (*tolongo*), which became his coffin. Later, the officers went to look for the head of the late chief; if the flesh had rotted they put the (dry) skull in the chest along with the nails. The remains were mourned and wrapped in cloths, with funeral songs and lamentations, then dragged in a carriage and buried with full festivities (Lutete, 219). Whereas the chief must be "dry," it appears that *nganga* should be "wet." According to Kunzi of Mukimbungu, when a *nganga* dies he is buried at the edge of the water, so that the cool of the water may reach the body and rain may fall.

To carry the mummy to the cemetery, elaborately constructed wheeled carriages, imitating European vehicles, became fashionable in the eighteenth century; remains of such carriages could be seen in villages in the 1960s. "*Mbongi* is a kind of bier that commands great respect, more than *kipanza kia ntela* because it has two coffins, whereas *kipanza* has one coffin and the appearance of another. A frightening construction in raffia is placed on the coffin" (Lutete, 233). For an important chief or wealthy man, the family might commission a funeral chariot. One example, location unspecified, consisted of a vast platform on six small wheels, with a coffin-like small cabin in the middle, some two meters high, in which were two compartments. The corpse was placed in the upper compartment, the pottery and other grave goods in the lower. A special route to the cemetery was cut, five or six meters wide and several kilometers long (*Le Congo Illustré* 1894, 44).

A chief was buried in standing position and facing the village, so that he might send his successor good dreams. If a slave was buried with him, he was bound hand and foot and also placed in standing position. If the deceased, though wealthy, was not an invested chief, both he and the slave were laid flat (Lutete, 230).

From Chief to Object

The chief and his followers, like the *nganga* and associates of any major *nkisi,* were subject to a number of restrictions. At Nganda, the chief was addressed as follows at his investiture: "You the chief, open your ears, pay attention. If you eat standing up the *mpu* will strike. If you eat by yourself, the *mpu* will strike. If you sleep in another village, the *mpu* will strike; whatever rule you break, you will suffer for." Some of the rules were intended to control his leopardness:

> The chief may not tear at meat with his nails, for to do so is to summon the Lord of the Country (*Mfumu a nsi,* the leopard); he must cut it with a knife. He may not scratch with his nails on the ground for the same reason; leopards will attack livestock in the village. He must not eat meat that is still bloody, as leopards do. He may not eat standing up, and he may not sleep in the village of another chief. He may not carry palm wine; that is for his slaves and the Children to do. He may not open the *lukobe,* the box of medicines that is kept inside his house, lest in a little while the leopard attack the livestock. (Matunta, 314)

Among the insignia, the chief was allowed to keep in his own house only the necklace of leopard's teeth on his neck, and one tooth in the bracelet on his arm. If he were to scratch on the ground with the tooth in the bracelet and throw it away in the bush, that day a leopard would come to the village and take a pig or some other beast.

Additional rules show the extent to which the chief was a creature of the clan's relatives by marriage, its Children and Grandchildren. The power of the *nkisi* to cure leprosy provided the Children and Grandchildren with interesting means of disciplining the chief. He would contract the disease if he returned to the investiture site on his own, or if he ate the meat of goat, the harnessed bushbuck, or the striped *mbende* field-rat, and would have to pay the *banganga* to cure him by reconsecrating him. The Children kept the leopardskin itself:

> If the Children suffer an injustice at the hands of the chief or the clan of their Fathers, and are sad or angry on account of such an attempt by their Fathers, they speak as follows: "Are we not your Children? If we are not your Children, show us the place of your investiture." If the chief should argue with his Children he would contract leprosy. Until he paid a fine, the Children of the chief would hide the skin in the place where they kept it. When they put it somewhere in order to control the chiefship of their Fathers, the Fathers would have to pay them the fine of a pig, for they knew that the chiefship was in the skin. Again, if the Children brought the leopardskin into the open, that day a leopard would come and kill a pig in the village.

In effect, the restrictions could be no more than devices for controlling the chief and extracting wealth from his lineage. Some traditions required that the chief be castrated or impotent. In others, a chief was invested after a diviner recommended the ritual as a cure for a community's ailments. His function as a sort of animate *nkisi*-object is striking. Though undoubtedly some chiefs were wealthy traders and relatively powerful rulers, chiefship as such was a depersonalized power whose principles, realized in the chief, were only "contingently" (*accidentellement*) attached to his person (Doutreloux 1967, 199). Often enough, a community that felt it needed a chief for the mystical benefits that were mediated by the office had to capture some unwilling individual who would be no more than a living *nkisi* embodying in mythologized form the contradictions of Kongo society.

Na Menta

The extreme case of such objectification appears in Diafwila's account of the Nsundi chiefship in Kibunzi, which he tells in fits and starts, intermingled with other matters (Cahier 46). In the manuscript, it has been crossed out; LKM substitutes Laman's own solution to the narrative problem, in which, following Diafwila's indications, he combines the ritual events scattered through the text, eliminating repetitions. Here is my version of this solution (cf. LKII, 18–20).

Diafwila's history begins with Na Bunzi, homonymous *nganga* of *nkisi* Bunzi, which was the spirit of the domain and gave its name to the village of Kibunzi. Na Bunzi himself was not invested; he represented Mpanzu, the investing "wife clan" to Nsundi. The first chief was Na Menta, who belonged to the senior lineage of Nsundi, Kidumu a Mvula (thunderstorm).[21] It is not likely that Na Menta, if he ever lived, was in fact treated as tradition says; his story offers us a model of this chiefship.

> For the investiture of Na Menta they put him in seclusion when he was still a child. His whole clan wept and groaned, asking themselves how much would it cost and when would they see him again, when would he come back. The Children and Grandchildren made him swear [not to reveal the secrets], rubbing his mouth [in the dirt] at the crossroads and beating him every day. They would eat first, and feed him little; some days he went to bed hungry. Nobody could send him food, because he was being trained by the officials (*bamayaala*).

> When he was a grown man, he was castrated by the use of the feather of a fishing eagle (*mbemba*). Then they left him alone, but he was not yet called chief, because he was still a prisoner of the Children.

> When he was first seized they began [to plant trees] to form the fences around his compound, but only when the trees were grown would they release him to come look at his compound and have houses built there. He would not go alone but a crowd would attend him.

> When he arrived he was carefully watched. If he went to relieve himself he was supervised by the *bamayaala*; alone, he might be kidnapped by worthless persons or enemies and would have to be ransomed with a pig. It was the rule that the chief should not be alone.

> When a year had passed he summoned all the people from round about and spread the

word that the chief-elect was going to his capital (*mbanza*) to be invested. So Mpanzu collected his people to receive the fee; if the chief did not pay he could not be invested, and Mpanzu was the "wife of the country," the one who was first to invest the king and walk him on the leopardskin.

When Mpanzu had accepted the fee, on the appointed day they sounded ivory horns, drums, side-drums and bells and gathered at the *mbanza*. On the day when he obtained the title and the staff [he fought against] the enemies and the deceivers; if the chiefship did not want him, he would be unable to enter the *mbanza* and would die.[22] When the enemies saw that Na Menta had won they wept, but those of his party shouted for joy, young men and women danced and ate and drank. He entered the *mbanza* and sat on the royal mat (*nkuwu*). They placed a rod across his shoulders and instructed him, "You are to rule."[23]

Since not only is Na Menta kidnapped, but members of his own clan wail in anticipation of the cost they will bear, it appears that the Nsundi clan as a whole does not benefit from the proceedings. The clan would have included slave lineages; those who rejoiced were the free members of this and allied clans.

At last they gave him permission to take the chalk. Then he trod on the leopardskin, first gesturing with his foot, shots being fired each time. The third time he trod on the head of the leopard. [He gestures in order to "acquire the respect of the Leopard," and treads on the head of the leopard "to subdue it." "To subdue the Leopard" is to control leopards so that they do not kill livestock.—KEL]. When the chief coughs the people should sit respectfully in front of him, as much in fear as they would be in the presence of a leopard.[24] When the investiture was over he returned to his own place, now called Mbanza Kayi, the residence of an invested chief.

Na Menta's investiture resembles the composition of an *nkisi;* whereas *nkisi* Mbola was proven to have been correctly composed by an act of healing, Na Menta was tested in "battle." His violence was therefore registered as authentic, but his own mortality contradicted the power of life that he also embodied:

It was a rule in this chiefship that the invested rulers could not die of themselves. When the chief was near death, they fastened a cord around his neck, led it out through the wall of the house and strangled him. If he were to die by himself, he would take the country with him and all the people; so they killed him, that he might take some other country. At his death, the Children and Grandchildren brought funeral gifts, fired shots, and put the sign of chiefship on the ground. Men and women were not allowed to sleep together until the *bamayaala* had accepted their fees, after which it was permitted to sleep on a bed.[25] The body could not be buried immediately but had first to be dried, and the *bamayaala* had to feast on pigs and goats.

They found an expert to decorate the body, and then took it to Mbanza Nsundi.[26] It could not be carried on the shoulders but in a funeral carriage, sitting up and not lying down. In villages on the way, if young people did not hide they could be captured and sold, and their owners could not object; if they looked for what they had lost they would be told that this was [the day of] transporting the chief. Shots were fired, from the chief's compound all the way to Mbanza Nsundi. The journey could take two or three days. When they arrived the body would be buried with much honor, young men and women dancing and the elders the same, in a more stately fashion, among themselves.

Diafwila's story continues with what looks more like the history of known chiefs.

Na Mpanda took the same title, with rituals the same as Na Menta's. He was very powerful, executed people, and administered the poison oracle (*nkasa*). After his death Na Mbembo, Na Kimfuzi and Na Ntela also ruled but were not invested. Na Mbembo fought wars, imprisoned people and killed many, administered *nkasa* and sold people to Nsanda and to Boma; in his day, gunpowder, flintlocks, cloth and other goods became plentiful. Na Kimfuzi took good care of his clan. He was very rich and built an elevated house to keep his wealth in; many people came to borrow from him. He was not a member of Nsundi, though his father was; his mother was a slave, originally from Na Tuma. His friend Na Ntela of Nsundi succeeded him; Na Ntela forced many people to take the *nkasa* poison test, killed many, and was an active slave-trader. After him came Makayi Kalunga, well known as an arbiter of disputes.

Laman notes in the manuscript that Diafwila's mother knew Na Mbembo and Na Kayi Kimfuzi when they ruled, and mourned Na Mpanda when he died; also, that the coming of Europeans put an end to investiture, so that there were no true chiefs after Na Mpanda. We have no information on Diafwila's age, but if he was twenty-five in 1915, it is unlikely that his mother, who remembered mourning Na Mpanda, was born before 1850. We also read that Na Mpanda's successor, Na Mbembo, sold slaves to Boma, which suggests that though not invested he ruled at the latest in the 1860s. Na Kimfuzi's house apparently imitated those of Europeans, as did the houses of wealthy people in Boma. If Na Ntela also traded in slaves, he did so only locally; the prevalence of the poison ordeal in his day suggests a date between 1890 and 1905, when sleeping sickness was rampant and the indigenous political system was breaking down. In short, this history seems to cover about fifty years. It remains unlikely that Na Menta was a historical figure; Diafwila's account suggests that his legend provided a kind of template for the investiture of chiefs such as Na Mpanda.

Kilola of Mukimbungu describes a ritual of the Nanga clan which parallels in some ways the investiture of Na Menta. When a member of Nanga was to be invested, a woman to be his wife was sought in the two clans from which the wives of the chiefs of Nanga came, Ntambu and Nlaza. When the appointed day arrived, the *banganga* fetched the candidate and his wife. On the way to the investiture site, the Children and Grandchildren beat them with branches, wounding them severely.[27] On top of the hill called Mbanza Ngombe they made them enter a shelter, in which a bed had been prepared by the officials. "The wife went in and lay down on the bed; an official lifted her legs, the chief then lay under them and the official placed his penis in the woman's vagina. The chief than pressed in and ejaculated; the wife became pregnant, and thus the government of the country was secured [?], but the chief thereafter was impotent."[28] The paradox of an obligatorily impotent chief with many wives is solved by Kilola's further statement that the Children and Grandchildren had access to the wives, although anyone else would be killed; in this perspective, the chief was no more than an icon of the privileges of the dominant class. Another explanation suggests itself: BaKongo regularly explain physical defects in this world as powers in the otherworld; albinos are thought to be able to see better in the otherworld than they do in this, and a chief who becomes impotent after the death of a favorite wife was said to be consorting with her in the land of the dead. It may be that Na Menta and his like were deprived of mundane reproductive powers because of their role as guarantors of collective reproduction; but this is speculation.

Kilola's account is noteworthy for a unique feature, the indication that the investiture took place at a series of sites which had been the residences (*mbanza*) of previous holders of the title. The sequence began not in the candidate's village of Mpelo (which was also Kilola's own village) but in a valley, Kinzau, where he slept continently "on the ground" with his wife for four Nsona days. Then the *banganga* took him up to Mbanza Ngombe for the sexual rite described above, followed by the rite of "licking the leopard," in which the candidate was marked with red and yellow spots. The next phase, the rite of "circling the *mbende* rat," took place at Mbanza Nkoki. The striped *mbende*, linked in several chiefships with another particolored animal, the harnessed bushbuck, signifies perpetuity:

> They say that *mbende* is there [in its hole, analogous to a grave]; if one dies, another replaces it. This *mbende* is a rat which people would like to catch but are unable to. So they called it the rat of the Na Vunda chiefship and said that when it disappeared the chiefship would come to an end; the *kiyazi* had lost its power. So the Children and Grandchildren would look out for the rat when the savanna was burned [at the end of the dry season], and when they saw it they would jump for joy, sure that the clan of their fathers was assured of continuity—the *mbende* lives! (Masamba, 277)

Though *mbende* was a favorite food, it was forbidden to some chiefs on pain of leprosy, a "particolored" disease. In the last phase, the newly invested Nanga chief entered his *mbanza* of Mpelo, where "the rules of Na Ngombo and Na Nkoki" were recited, ordering that no one harass the clan's Children and Grandchildren.

Chiefship in Historical Context

"Na Mpanda took the same title, with rituals the same as Na Menta's," but Na Mpanda sounds real and Na Menta does not. We probably need to recognize some slippage between ideal and historical chiefship, though no doubt the rituals actually carried out aspired to conformity with the model and, in the minds of the participants, were no less effective for their failure to do so. This is a normal paradox of rituals and ideals all over the world; one does the best one can in the circumstances. In this concluding section I explore the question of what can be said historically about chiefs in Kongo.

Chiefs and Trade

The chiefs whose investitures and subsequent lives are described in the manuscripts clearly belonged to the period of the slave trade; they were wealthy traders in slaves and ivory who brought back from the coast such prestige goods as cannon and funeral urns. Initiated by Liverpool traders and centered on the port of Boma, the trade developed in the estuary, as opposed to the Cabinda coast, in the last quarter of the eighteenth century. In 1816, "all the great men" derived a large part of their revenue from the slave trade (Tuckey 1818, 187). The Portuguese dominated the intensifying competition.[29]

Captain Tuckey described how the representatives of the local commercial agent (the Mafouk) at Malemba on the coast boarded his ship when it arrived in 1816. Besides items of European clothing, each wore a cotton loincloth; a little apron made of the skin of a wildcat, "which is a mark of gentility, and as such is not permitted to be worn by menial attendants"; a cap of curious workmanship; many iron and copper bracelets and anklets; necklaces of elephant's tail bristles; and "all were loaded with fetiches of the most heterogeneous kinds, bits of shells, horns, wood, rags, etc." All of the party spoke English, and several of them spoke good French (Tuckey 1818, 63). The goods they sought included fancy clothes, silks, carpets, weapons, tobacco, brandy, and ceramics (Schrag 1985, 76).

Between 1821 and 1843 there was a dramatic growth in exports to Brazil, but the boom years, for Boma in particular, were those of the clandestine slave trade, from 1840 until 1863, when the external trade virtually came to an end (Schrag 1985, 54–59). At the peak, Boma exported 25,000 slaves annually. This rate of export required a society highly organized for the purpose. North of the Congo, the slaves came from eastern Mayombe and from modern Manianga; many were imported from east of Mpumbu, but others were generated from within Kongo society by an osmotic process: Slaves from the east were incorporated in Kongo communities from which other individuals were extruded. Slaves were generated internally by criminal proceedings, but also by the process of competition for ritual honors and as fines in ritual contests. Warfare, which ended with the death of one or two combatants, was another form of ordeal or magical test of spiritual virtue; the rewards to the victors included slaves (Janzen 1982, 74–75; MacGaffey 1986a, 38). Dupré believes that among the BaBembe in northern Kongo warfare was often a phase in a process of migration and resettlement; the peace treaty sanctioned a new structure of dominance in a zone of relative peace (Dupré 1985, 82).

The agents of the kings of Boma promoted the supply of slaves by deals with inland chiefs and by their ability to supply sea salt obtained from the BaSolongo on the south shore of the Congo. Kinkela in Vungu offers recollections of slaving days:

> The people of Kongo dia Lemba were our good friends, for they and our elders made a trading agreement (*luwawanu luankitila*). They brought many people here to sell, were well received, and returned home joyfully. They crossed at the ford Makanga. The BaSolongo were also our friends. They brought their artifacts to us, that sold well. They brought their dance drums and showed us their dances which, like their language, were very different from ours. Our elders told us that the BaYombe and BaSundi were our enemies, not to make war on but to kidnap. They could only obtain European goods imported at Boma by passing through our country, so our elders caught them to be our slaves. For example, if a Sundi caravan were coming, they would put out food on the road, or put grinding stones (*zinsindu*) in the village, and surround it; any Nsundi or Nyombe who bumped into them would be accused of profaning a charm. So the offender would have to be ransomed, or left as a slave. Many were captured in this way, until guns were introduced and the BaSundi armed their caravans. (Kinkela, 84)

Kongo dia Lemba, an important center of peanut cultivation in the 1880s, is located between Matadi and Mbanza Manteke; Kinkela's account shows that friendly relations obtained between Vungu and the south (the direction of "migration") and indicates the existence of another trade route, possibly the same as the one that linked Mbanza Kongo and Vungu in the fourteenth century. The BaKongo of the forest regions (as opposed to Angola) did not conduct slave raids but sold persons convicted of crimes, those who had been handed over to settle a corporate debt, and others who had simply been kidnapped or tricked into personal "debt" (Martin 1972, 117). It is noteworthy that although Kinkela writes from Vungu he describes both the BaYombe and the BaSundi as strangers (see the discussion of ethnicity in Chapter 4).

As the volume of slaves exported from Boma grew, inland chiefs increasingly preyed upon their own communities to feed the demand, and society tended toward a simple division into slave and free, into those likely to be sold and those who enriched themselves by selling others. After the cessation of the external trade, the internal trade continued; female slaves were in demand as producers of peanuts and palm oil, males as porters. Among the BaBembe at this time, small villages unable to mount armed trading expeditions on their own were dependent on larger ones for the imported prestige goods they needed (guns, cloth, salt, gunpowder) and might have had to meet the resulting debt by handing over slaves (Dupré 1985, 83).

We have seen how trade itself was organized and policed in ritual terms by the use of insignia to facilitate travel, of *minkisi* to sanction contracts, of taboos to legitimate kidnapping, and of systems of titles that linked communities along the major routes. *Nkondi* such as Mangaaka and Mabyala ma Ndembe were especially feared; they were used to open and close trade routes, to cure slaves of drunkenness, favor traders, and punish thieves (Schrag 1985; MacGaffey and Harris 1993, 42). As a cult that both facilitated regional trade and protected the rich from the envy of others, the Lemba complex in the north "played the key role of creating a ceremonial context for the economy of trade to mesh with the economy of agricultural production" (Janzen 1982, 323). Nkimba and other collective initiations of young people, such as Na Kongo, admitted only the free, established fraternal bonds between them that transcended local divisions, and taught them a private "language" that they could use in commercial relations (Bittremieux 1936; MacGaffey 1970, 249; Schrag 1985, 65).[30] The chiefs who sponsored initiations augmented their own importance and simultaneously their incomes; the rituals themselves mimicked the relations between the chiefs and the public, in that the candidates were free to exact food and other provisions from anyone and could resort to violence if they felt slighted.[31]

Chiefly titles were both a reward for wealth and a means to increase it. Most of our authors emphasize the cost of titles; in Mayombe an important constituent of the investiture fee consisted of slaves. Lutete gives few figures, but Kinkela wrote that the investors would receive "shackles of the day and of the night," that is, ten slaves of each kind; those "of the night" were handed over by occult means (*kindoki*), meaning that the corresponding number of individuals would be seen to die some time later. Doutreloux was told that these slaves were young women (Doutreloux 1967, 169–70). Besides the animals consumed at the feast, Kinkela wrote, "I have heard that one candidate was charged 30 slaves, also goats, pigs, ducks, chickens and quantities of palm wine, no telling what the cost" (Cahier 94).[32] These payments amounted to physical announcements of the kind of powers over production that the invested chief was supposed to wield. Once invested, the chief could help himself to any thing he fancied, including any woman; no one could object, because it was "a rule of the title."[33] Moreover, his death would be an occasion for further levies, either through special rules obtaining at that time or simply because social standards demanded the expenditure of huge amounts of imported gunpowder and cloth, plus ritual fees and food for feasts. Invested chiefs were buried in the royal cemetery, minor chiefs at its edge; commoners had their own cemetery, and the bodies of people of no importance might be thrown aside. The length and cost of the funeral varied accordingly.

Who benefited from all this circulation? The chief (*mfumu*) himself, no doubt, and the free members (*mfumu*) of his clan. But these people, including the chief, were under severe restrictions, imposed by the Children and Grandchildren, who were free members of other clans who were allied by marriage; they provided the *nkama* or *nkazi a mpemba* (wives of the chalk); they alone were the guardians of the insignia who were permitted to enter the sacred grove, to conduct the ceremonies endorsed by neighboring chiefs, and to supervise the ritual performance of the chief during his reign. To these chiefs, to the officiating *banganga,* to the Children and Grandchildren (the *bama-yaala,* that is, "those in charge"), and to at least some members of the owning clan, huge sums were paid, including both the products of the labor of slaves and the slaves themselves.

Marriage, Slavery, and Class

The rituals of chiefship consolidated the privileges of an oligarchy. Chiefs were members of small, regional associations of title-holders, united both by ritual and by marriage, allies in their common effort to keep the slave lineages of their respective clans under control (Rey 1969). In Angola, according to Monteiro, "A king has no power by himself, the natives simply reverencing him as being invested with the 'fetish' of chief, and he receives very little tribute from the natives of his own town; the fines and penalties levied he has also to divide with the Makotas [the elders who together administer the laws]" (Monteiro 1968 [1875], v. 1:255). It is likely that greater centralization obtained near the coast, but there is some evidence that even there privilege and wealth had to be shared to be maintained at all. In 1816 there was only one king in Boma; fifty years later there were sometimes as many as eleven, whose wealth and power was exceeded by those of untitled linguisters and brokers. The chiefs, burdened by ritual responsibilities, depended on secular figures to negotiate with Europeans (Schrag 1985, 42).

The oligarchic structure combined the distinction between slave and free with marriage politics. Matrilineal descent in Kongo (even long after the abolition of slave trading) is essentially a product of competition for control of the labor and reproductive capacity of women. Every clan included slave lineages, the offspring of female slaves, whose civil affairs, including their marriages, were managed exclusively by the free (*zimfumu*); slaves could have no extralineal allies to support their interests (Mac-Gaffey 1977a).[34] Through their chief (*mfumu*), the free members (*mfumu*) of a lineage arranged the marriages of themselves and their slaves, who could never contract marriages on their own. To the extent that a free lineage drew upon its slaves to provide mates for its own members, male and female, the two lineages were in fact engaged in symmetrical exchange, although the free lineage claimed sole authority over the arrangement and was therefore able to add to its assets the offspring of both its male and its female members.[35]

The legitimating ground of this authority was a tradition of origin that named the founder of the clan and described his emigration from Mbanza Kongo (or an equivalent) and his exploits, including the story of how he came to own the female ancestor of the slaves. The slaves, however, could produce an alternative tradition asserting that in truth they were the original free lineage. To meet this challenge, the owning lineage would have to produce allies as witnesses, whose testimony as to tradition was likely to count for less, in the nineteenth century, than their readiness to back it up with force.

> If a group has been in pawn, but another lineage redeems them, then it is said of them, *vutukulwa bavutukulwa,* "they were returned." The one who redeemed them confides the story to his juniors and so it goes on for generations, that they were "returned." If, later, the former pawns multiply and have important chiefs who become rich and celebrated, while those who redeemed them are not doing so well, their leader may challenge them: "You! you are my things, redeemed in the old days by my predecessor." The others are angry, and deny that they were ever pawns: "You are a leopard, I am a leopard," meaning, "Both of us are free men; we will take this to court!"
>
> So they send around for well-known advocates, who bring a large crowd, men and women, with *ngongi* bells, ivory horns, resonators, *tambala* drums and *ngoma* drums. They eat and drink and dance. When the debate begins, one says, "In my opinion, I was not redeemed long ago by my elders. Therefore I present two people as my gage; see if you can do better!" The other: "From the beginning I was never a pawn, here I present two people." These four are tied up and guarded by the advocates.
>
> Then they seek out the *nganga* of the Mbundu or Nkasa poison ordeal to settle the dispute. When the poison has taken effect, two of the hostages are found guilty, two are innocent. A huge fine has to be debated; the penalty will be six people and many goats and pigs. The two hostages may not redeem themselves, because they are enslaved, paid as a fee. (Mawakosi 319)[36]

Redeemed pawns were (and are) considered to be the slaves of their clansmen who redeemed them, although the transaction (historical or fictitious) was kept "secret," meaning that it could be sprung at any time as a political move, as a challenge to a trial by ordeal which was open to some degree of manipulation. An imaginary historian with adequate records might well find that neither group's pedigree bore much relation to the tangled, cognatic past which each sought to configure to its own advantage.

A free lineage secured allies by arranging exchange marriages with the free lineages of other clans; such an arrangement, repeated in subsequent generations (patrilateral cross-cousin marriage), meant that members of allied lineages stood to one another as "Children" and "Grandchildren" (*baana, batekolo*). As such, they participated in one another's rituals, in which the Children and Grandchildren of a given matrilineal house or clan, as we have seen, played a controlling part. (A person could be both a member of the chiefly clan and one of its Grandchildren.) In the Na Vunda chiefship in Mukimbungu, a stay in the cave of Na Vunda constituted a test to ensure that the candidate was not a slave; this procedure obliquely intimated that he had to have the support of patrilateral relatives (MacGaffey 1986a, 35).

> A chief joined together with his in-laws (*bazitu*) to fight their enemies; they were friends, and if one were attacked the other fought against the strangers. In those days also they would agree that if a chief collected people he intended to sell at the coast (*ku Ngoyo*), nobody would attack the caravan, because they helped one another with the guns bought at the coast. All the young men had guns in those days, and all the chiefs composed *minkisi* for war (*bisimbu*). (Lutete 233)

The relationship between free and slave was thus a class relationship, in the precise sense that the free controlled the conditions of social reproduction. Class is not a taxonomic concept; it denotes a precarious political relationship between groups, in which dominance has to be actively maintained. The constant mobility indicated in tradition testifies to this instability. In practice, the relationship between free and slave was a continuum rather than a contrast. In conjunction with marriage arrangements and the use of force, rituals (healing, divination, pursuit of justice, protection from misfortune, as well as chiefly investiture) provided important resources for those who were already powerful and wealthy, because they all required the payment of fees in kind or in cash (as we have seen in the case of *minkisi,* especially *nkondi*), and could include the imposition of fines for real or imaginary offenses. Heavy fines included slaves, and the well-to-do, accused of witchcraft, could send a slave to take the poison ordeal for them. Wealthy chiefs, wrote Kinkela, are most likely to get into quarrels, because they can afford to pay a great deal of money if anyone dies; "I know, because my chief, Na Mbangazi, was very powerful and loved fighting wars" (Cahier 94). The labor of slaves was a secondary matter, becoming important only when cash crops or porters were in demand.[37]

Na Lubuzi and His Successors

In practice, neither rituals nor pedigree guaranteed the subordination of slaves; the system was sufficiently open that some slaves, such as Na Menta's successor Kimfuzi, promoted themselves to chiefship, and some chiefs succumbed to rivals. The *nkisi nsi* (see Chapter 9) includes medicines that offer protection against envious competitors who conspire to kill the chief, make any other plot, or refuse to respond to the chief's word; investiture proclaims too stridently the violence that awaits the insubordinate. The rituals describe chiefs as aggressive, wealthy individuals, but they also, in complex ways, deny the chief any individual power at all.

Lutete's king lists (Chapter 9) sometimes run to ninety-five names, suggesting a great depth of time, but the appearance is deceptive. Closer inspection indicates that his narrative is distorted by the seductive properties of listing and numbering, devices he acquired along with literacy itself. The linear lists present some contemporaries as successors, concealing the grouping of siblings and of the elders of different lineages. They are simply the names of all the important people Lutete's informants could remember; *mfumu*, "chief," after all, means a free member of the lineage as opposed to a slave. In one or two instances a depth of only about three generations is indicated, which is not unlikely but may result from the opposite tendency, that of identifying all the chiefs with the founder of the title.

The fate of some of the chiefs in the following account of Na Lubuzi shows that their authority was vulnerable.[38] According to Lutete, the KiMongo clan crossed Nzadi at a mythical location, "The fig-tree planted by Nzondo," and came to Vungu.[39] The founding chief's name was Na Mongo, his rank KiMbenza, so the chiefs were all called Na Mongo Mbenza. The branch of the clan that came to Vungu was led by Na Lubuzi. Coming from near Vungu, they went [north] toward Mongo Lubuzi, which is beyond Lolo, looking for *nkula* [camwood, used as a cosmetic in ritual; in the seventeenth century it was a valuable commodity, taxed at 10 percent by the coastal chiefs (Fondation Dapper 1989, 248)]. Some tired of looking and stayed there; others went on to Kimpudi, where the chief was Maswa Ngoma, who governed the whole area from near Maduda to the Lwango River. He gave them a little land. After a while, Maswa Ngoma wanted to move elsewhere, so he sold the country to them for two slaves, a man and a woman. Their first chief, Makayi Mbumba, was strong in war and was also a powerful *nganga;* there is an elephant tusk on his grave. The fifth chief was also a warrior and completed the investiture (*ngyadulu*). The sixth was very powerful, but he was convicted of witchcraft and killed himself. Much the same happened to the twenty-fifth, convicted when he was quite old; he was found dead in his house with his *nkisi* round his neck.[40] The twenty-ninth also died taking the *nkasa* ordeal, and the thirty-third was killed by his sister when he refused to take it.

The thirty-seventh did better; he fought many wars, but was much liked by his people because he was good at settling disputes and he sheltered refugees. He composed the *nkisi* Simbu, making an agreement with Mpulubunzi when he did so, so that when he died, though it was in the dry season, there was a great storm and heavy rain as he went to join Mpulubunzi in the ocean. The fifty-eighth chief was a great fighter, stronger than any of the others, but he and his brother were killed in battle. The enemy captured his body and invaded the village, but were driven off. The seventy-fourth chief, Makaba, is alive now, very influential, very wealthy, and very active in government service; because he took his domain by force he is called Ntinu Makaba.

Ngambula, Nkanga Mpaka, and Carpet Government

It is difficult to bear out the grand stories of heroic chiefs by independent evidence. The closest correspondence, from the beginning of the nineteenth century to 1880, is apparent in Boma. The insignia of the Ma Mboma included metal bracelets and anklets; a necklace of ivory beads and natural coral; and a wooden baton about a foot long (which in recent times would be called *nkawa*), inlaid with copper and lead. His compound formed a succession of outer and inner courts, of which the main entrance, for defensive purposes, was only about three feet high. Young trees were planted in the outer court; an inner court contained residences of his wives. Sculptured charms in wood and stone, including two war charms, surrounded the residence; the skulls of enemies hung on a tree in the village. The king's store of European goods included several gaudy garments in red cloth and quantities of silver, glass, and crockery. His appearance contrasted with that of chiefs a little farther up river, who continued to wear animal skins and bonnets of pineapple fiber (Tuckey 1818, 140–41). By 1873, however, when Monteiro visited the (by then) nine kings of Boma, he thought they were "a miserable lot" (Monteiro 1968 [1875], v. 1:87).

Near Vivi (opposite Matadi), in 1883, "King" Masala, who had recently been royally entertained in Antwerp, turned out to be no more than the poverty-stricken head of a miserable hamlet (Liebrechts 1909, 22). Bittremieux, reporting the traditional history of Kangu (a district west of Lutete's Lolo, where the Scheut Fathers had a station), gives no intimation of grandeur. The last invested chief, he says, died in 1908; his clan's *nkisi nsi,* Nkumbuzi, was consumed in a fire in 1912.[41]

From the same station Bittremieux, telling the life story of an invested chief, Ngambula, includes the chief's recollection of a great meeting called by his predecessor, perhaps in the 1870s, to settle a dispute. The proceedings were oligarchic, in that the most conspicuous participants were members of the Lemba association, brandishing the bracelets of their dignity as they spoke. The settlement they reached included the transfer to the winning clan of a boy, Ngambula himself, who had innocently accompanied his uncle to the meeting. Ngambula was subsequently chosen as chief, despite his slave status, because no better candidate could be found. His investiture as chief included a public phase, in which he was given *mukwisa* as a sign of succession and various other objects whose significance was explained to him by the initiating *nganga mbangu.* He was enstooled under a canopy of palm leaves held up on four poles, and provided with a leopardskin, an *ngundu* bonnet, a fly whisk, and other emblems. There was also a secret phase (presumably taking place at the *nkisi nsi*) in which the candidate was said to be *banguka,* "transformed." Later, Ngambula, at the urging of his wife, undertook the expensive Lemba initiation. Eventually, his Lemba *nkisi* took pride of place over his other charms, such as Simbu and Mbudila (*minkisi* for war), and several others such as Malwangu and Mangaaka that were greatly feared and honored on the coast but seemed to have been reduced to minor importance inland (Bittremieux 1923; Janzen 1982, 83–85).[42]

The signs of wealth on old graves were no more than an abundance of gin bottles, pottery, enamelware, and an occasional flintlock or small tusk. Perhaps by then the wealth of the 1860s had already disappeared, but Babutidi, who was well aware of rapid changes in some parts of the country, says of Vungu, which he visited in the course of his fieldwork, that the people still invested chiefs and initiated boys in the traditional way (*Minsamu Miayenge* 1917). It would appear that the reality was more modest than the ideal.

Because he ruled in Mpalabala (on the mountain east of Matadi), where the British Baptists established a station in 1878, Na Nkanga Mpaka is one of the few inland chiefs in the 1880s about whom we have personal information. We know that his money came not from food production but from taxing caravans passing west from Mbanza Kongo, whence he could afford to buy his title (Nkanga Mpaka) and to confirm it by regular prestations (Weeks 1914, 47). The title drew upon the continuing role that the Kongo king played in northern Angola from the beginning of the eighteenth century as a super-*nkisi,* a source of extraordinary powers useful in regulating commerce. L. Van de Velde, who was in charge of the administrative station at Vivi (opposite Matadi) between 1882 and 1885, provides a nicely ambiguous account of Nkanga Mpaka's authority. He says the government is "feudal," and that the chiefs are the descendants of former conquerors; this view of the Kongo political system appealed to the Free State's supporters, who liked conquerors and argued that Kongo chiefs could readily be incorporated in a larger hierarchy. Van de Velde's hierarchical view of Mpalabala politics is inconsistent with the real structure of government, about which he also tells us (Sabakinu 1988, 327). Nkanga Mpaka was the head of a confederation in which each group preserved its autonomy, linked to the others only in matters of common interest. The powers of chiefs were very limited; everything to do with the public good was debated in general assemblies. There were in fact two rival clans on the Mpalabala plateau, Vuzi dya Nkuwu, who claimed right of first occupancy, and Nsaku a Ne Vunda, whose chief, Nkanga Mpaka, by allying himself with the Baptist Mission, had stolen a march on Vuzi and made himself "king." Later, his successors were officially recognized as "customary chiefs" by the government. The resulting dispute lasted into the 1960s, and may be going on still (MacGaffey 1970a, 247, 268).

A political crisis in northern Angola in the 1870s illustrates the parallel between chief and *nkisi* as forms of government. Widespread disorder at the time led certain individuals to campaign against *minkisi* as instruments of individual self-seeking, and to institute a new kind of chiefship named for its principal symbol, the mat (*nkuwu*) on which the chief was invested—hence the name "carpet government" given to the movement by the missionary who reports it. Nkuwu operated just like an *nkisi,* but in the interests of the public. When its rules were broken (in this case, rules against robbery and other crimes), the *nkisi* was profaned (*sumuka*) and its protective powers therefore annulled until restitution had been made; until then, everybody was at risk. "I have seen a whole district in tumult, and the chiefs and headmen hurrying to and fro to find and bring a law-breaker to judgment; and meanwhile, they were fearful that some rogues would take advantage of the fact that the law was dead" (Weeks 1914, 60–61). As an *nkisi*, then, Nkuwu could both cause and cure its specific affliction, social disorder. Like an *nkisi* a chief lost his power when he died, and at his funeral social disorder prevailed; no woman was safe from assault, no pig or chicken safe from seizure (Laman 1963, 91).

9. LUTETE'S CHIEFS

The chiefs Lutete Esaya describes are preoccupied with a search for long life and stability, which association with *bisimbi* through the rites of investiture seems to promise. The images of stability which pervade these rituals contrast strangely with both the wanderings and wars which make up the biography of most of the chiefs and with the violent disturbances of the times Lutete himself knew. On the one hand, the pullulation of villages formed and reformed in the midst of slavery, slave trading, war, accusations of witchcraft, and the risks of trade; on the other, eternal white rocks and the mountaintops where leopards live and chiefs store their souls. In none of Lutete's histories is there an example of the kind of stability promised by an overarching tradition that links today's uncertainties to the once and future city, Mbanza Kongo. The migrations he reports are all on the small scale, between villages he names, in an area defined by the CMA stations of Vungu, Lolo, and Yema. Like Kinkela Ngoma, his contemporary and colleague, he describes some groups as Nsundi from the east, but most of those that concern him think of themselves as immigrants from the south, on the road from Boma through Kyonzo, Nsanda, Kungu, Nsazi, Nseke a Nsinda, and Lolo.[1] Clans near Lolo traced their chiefships to Nsanda; the Nsinda grassfield was the home of the *kiyaazi* of Lutete's own clan, Mpudi a Nzinga (see below).

Lutete, unlike Lunungu, tells us nothing about his fieldwork, although he must have done a fair amount, if only to obtain his extensive king lists; in Cahier 235, he presented Laman with a bill for 210 francs for field expenses. He wrote about between twelve and twenty chiefships that he knew in his home district, northeastern Mayombe. He was clearly fascinated by the wonders around him and the possibility of the miraculous. He made lists of remarkable rocks and pools, all of them the abodes of *simbi* spirits, and described strange events associated with them. He also wrote extensively about chiefship, collecting long "chief lists," describing the magic-laden rituals of burial and investiture, recounting the feats of chiefs long gone. Much of this telling has the quality of a fairy tale and seems to belong to a remote and idealized past, but it is also evident that marvels continued to happen; he dates some of them to a year or two before he collected his data.

Lutete writes from within the ideology of chiefship; even when the chiefs are represented as tyrants, he suggests little or no criticism of them. The views of the oppressed are indicated elsewhere, in the many tales concerning the leopard, Na Ngo, and the clever little antelope, Na Nsiesie, in which the leopard is a large and fierce but stupid animal whom the antelope constantly outwits (LKIV, 114). Lutete's account, and in general all the accounts, of chiefship is comprehensible only as a declamation directed to others whose voices are not heard—slaves, women, children.

A different challenge the texts present is simply that of narrative intelligibility. Sometimes Lutete seems to be writing about chiefship in general, sometimes about particular rituals. Details of ritual are interspersed with genealogical information.

Since all of the rituals and the local histories are of similar character, I have sorted them under headings, but the reader can follow something of the original order by noting the Cahier numbers and the page numbers preceding the paragraphs in the KiKongo text. The chief lists and a few redundant passages have been omitted. This compromise resembles that of Laman's Swedish editor, although with less damage to the original text.[2]

The outline of the rituals of chiefship is fairly clear. Not every clan head (head of an exogamous clan-section domiciled in a particular territory) could afford a title, though he "ruled" (*yaala*) his village. Titles in general (*ma-bwene*) were ritual endowments, some more elaborate, weightier, and more costly than others. An aspirant could inherit one, have himself promoted to a higher title or, at greater expense, acquire a new one. The powers the new chief acquired and combined were those of life, represented by the *nkisi nsi,* and death, represented by *mbeele a lulendo,* the sword (or knife) of power. The powers sound formidable, but magic was no substitute for secular success; "If a chief had many followers and much wealth but his following and his wives died off, and his powers were not as they had been, his authority faded away and people no longer respected him" (Cahier 94).

In Mayombe, investiture sites seem to have included both remarkable rocks and sacred groves. Chiefs stored their souls in such rocks to ensure long life for themselves. The forest site was also the burying ground of the chiefs; the investiture of a new chief began there with the burial of his predecessor. The personnel required for investiture included chiefs of similar title and the Children and Grandchildren of the owning clan (the offspring of male members and the offspring of male Children). The role of the investing priest of Mbenza, the *nganga mbangu* mentioned by Doutreloux, is not clear (Doutreloux 1967, 170). On other evidence, it seems likely that the *banganga* of at least one and possibly several *minkisi mya luyaalu* (*nkondi* type), such as Nsonde, Ngovo, Na Vungu, Mwalwangu, and Mpudi a Nzinga, played a part.

There are several references here and elsewhere to persons, besides his wife, who were invested at the same time as the chief. They may be his officers, or other chiefs taking the same title. In the case of Lulendo, a special kind of *nkisi*-title that emerged in the area around Luozi (Bulu) in the 1880s, these officers were named in the same way as the medicines of an *nkisi,* to embody functions attributed to the chief (see Chapter 6).

Some Terms

Baluka: to change status, be transformed. LKII, 151 gives "to ascend the throne," but this seems to be merely a derivation from the context; see LKD, but also Bittremieux 1922–1927: baluka.

Kiyaazi (from *yaala*): place of investiture; or, a sign and source of power.

Lúbukulu: lit. "wariness"; the cylindrical bark box (*lukobe*) in which the sacred red and white clays of investiture were kept.

Lulaala: sleeping place (from *laala,* to sleep). Site in the forest where the candidate slept on the ground (avoided sexual relations). The word does not appear in LKD. It may have been related by Kongo etymology to *lulala,* a palm leaf, since according to Lutete in Cahier 231, the candidates slept on palm leaves.

Lulombe: a place aside, especially the forest grove which was both the cemetery of the chiefs and the place of investiture. In Ngoyo it was called *lombe la nkisi si* (Mulinda 1995, 153). Yans chiefs also were invested in *lulom,* the place of the tutelary nature spirit *lebui* (Thiel 1972, 70).

Lunzi, ndunzi, etc.: life chance, health, "soul," seated in the forehead (also called *lunzi;* one of four special places for ritual treatment, the others being the temples and the chest) (Bittremieux 1922–1927: s.v. lunzi). Hair and perhaps skin from this location represent the whole personality and as *kintweka* might be used to transfer power from a (dead) leopard to the chief, or from the deceased *nganga* to his successor. When the chiefs are said to bury their *lunzi* in a safe place, hair from the forehead is probably meant.

Lusunzi: a general name in Ngoyo, Mayombe, and northern Angola for *bisimbi* associated with investiture, usually in the form of remarkable rocks. According to Matunta (Cahier 296), the name indicates something that appears suddenly and splendidly (*sunzungula*); for Lutete, it comes from the related *sunzumuna,* meaning to give birth rapidly. Its associations are clearly those of beauty, fertility, and astonishment.

Luyaalu (from *yaala*): investiture, the powers it conferred, and their use in government. Guthrie says that the occurrence of the root CS100, *-biád, meaning "to rule over," only in western Bantu languages and the absence of any other CS with this meaning may signify the development of a pattern of strong paramountcy in the West at an early period (Guthrie 1970). Can also mean the chief's official praise-name.

Mbalala: a tree at whose foot the *nkisi nsi* was buried, from whose wood the chief's staff (costing nine slaves) might be carved; or, the investiture site.

Mbeele a lulendo also called *kiphaba, dikooko,* and *lusimba:* the sword or knife of power; sometimes a real knife or sword, sometimes an ornate wooden hatchet.

Mfumu: chief or free member of a clan; *mfumu ye nganga,* lit. chiefs and priests, as opposed to slaves (cf. "gentlemen").

Munkwiza (various spellings): one of the principal insignia of chiefship. Different authorities describe it as a vine (*Costus* sp.=*zingiberaceae*); as a very acid, juicy, and luxuriant plant, in which the chief's soul is believed to reside (LKII, 152); as a synonym for *mutsanga-lavu* (Bittremieux 1936, 38, 319) or *nsanga-vulu* (a plant with large, thick leaves—LKD); as a synonym for *disisa* (LKD) or *(di)sisia,* a plant with a very acid juice from which the body shrinks (Cahier 213). Lastly, *nsisia = nsala, mwela,* "soul" (Cahier 154). The plant was used in many different ways to fight against witchcraft and death. Near Maduda it was planted on the *nkisi nsi* when a chief was invested; if it did not take root, he had to be replaced (Mato, 280).

Nkisi nsi: the earth-related power source of a title; a bundle of medicines, a *simbi* stone, a medicated tree or hole in the ground. It could have an alias in the village (more accessible).

Nyàmba (also *nyámba*): a marsh or muddy place where the chief's body or his entrails were discarded. An intriguing term: In Mayombe, it could also mean an elevated place where the priests of Lemba were installed (LKD); Luniamba ("place of throwing to earth"?) is the name of the forest where the clan Me Mbenza Mbangala had their *nkisi nsi* (see below); as a verb, *nyamba* (tone unspecified) means to throw something to the ground (taboo for chiefs).

Sema, semisa: to reconsecrate after some pollution or contact with a dangerous force; to bless; to create (?). *Nsemono,* "consecration"; see below, the Makunga title of clan Mbenza.

Chiefship in the Old Days[3]

This section presents, as it were unintentionally, one of the principal ambiguities of power in Kongo thought and practice. Chiefs could be "very powerful," yet ruled over no more than one village of a few hundred persons. The text indicates, however, that a chief belonged to an association of chiefs in the neighborhood, on whom he depended for endorsement; his power was thus not simply his own. If he were not inheriting a title already owned by his clan, he could acquire a domain, or promote himself to a higher title, by appropriate payments to which his grove of trees would testify in later generations. Regular succession meant, at least in principle, that the investiture of a chief coincided with the burial of his predecessor.

11. Every chief ruled his own village, whose members respected and honored him. The chief of a very large village was very powerful; when he traveled he would be carried in a hammock, and a great crowd would accompany him. The bells of chiefship[4] and triumphant cries would sound as he approached the village to which he was going, so that all would know that an honored chief was coming.[5] In the old days there were very powerful chiefs. Their rule was not like that of government chiefs (*chefs médaillés*) today, to rule over many villages.

11. Mfumu mfumu ye diandi vata kayala ye bantu bena momo bana kumvumina ye kunsitisa [*sic*]. Mfumu yena mbanza yayinene buna wena lulendo beni, vo kazietanga lenda natwa bu kazie-tanga mu lwanda vo nsadi [kipoyi]. Buna nkangu wayingi uzietanga yandi ye zingongi bidukulu bilenda sikwa ye zinzanga, bu babadikidi wayika ku vata, kidi dionso vata dibele balenda zaya vo mfumu ya nzitusu i kuizanga. Nga mu nsi nkulu mwakala zimfumu zalulendo beni. Ngiadulu kayakala bonso mu ntangu yayi ko, bonso bueti yadila mfumu zapalata mu yala mavata mamingi.

12. In the old days, the chief was most respected who had great wealth and many slaves. When a chief was to be invested, chiefs came from distant villages to announce the rules. If the domain was not the one from which he came, he had to pay a fee in slaves, otherwise he could not rule but had to return whence he came, to his own clan and his own chiefship. But if he paid, he

12. Mfumu yabiala mu nsi nkulu lutidi zituswa beni vo wena wa mvwama ye vo wena nanga miamingi. Vo mfumu yina yala buna mfumu zina tuka mavata mena ntama bana kuiza, dia kiondo [nsiku], vo mfumu yoyo yina yala vo nsi yoyo natuka ka natuka yo, buna vo yala si kayala buna fwiti teka futa mpaku vo mvika, vi ka bua ko kalendi andi yaduswa ko, buna

could be invested, buying the land, the palm trees, the *minsafu,* the *mingyengye,* and the kola-nut trees, so that the domain became really his. He himself had to multiply all these kinds of trees so that the next generation would know that chief so-and-so had planted his trees and founded the settlement. That's how it was long ago.

fwiti vutuka yonso nsi katuka, yena kanda diandi ye kimfumu kiandi, kansi vo futidi lenda kwandi yala, buna mpe fweti sumba ntoto ye maba ye minsafu ye minkazu, buna nsi yoyo yeka yandi kibeni. Buna yandi mpe fweti buela kuna miandi nsafu ye maba ye minkazu ye mafubu ye bonso mingiengie mu songa dimbu kuna mbandu yina zimunina, vo mfumu kifwau wakuna nti miami ye wasamba lufulu lolo. I bobo bwakadila mu nsi nkulu.

Observances on the Death of a Chief [6]

Lutete does not say that the dying chief should be killed, although Bittremieux mentions this practice in passing with respect to the chief of nearby Kangu (Bittremieux and Tembo 1924, 72). As Lutete describes the proceedings, it was customary for designated Children and Grandchildren to go to the cemetery of the chiefs, there to pull up from the grave of the founding chief of the line the *sisya* plant, which by its name implies the "soul" of the dead man (it may be the same plant as *munkwisa*); it is then buried in a marsh. (In Mukimbungu, at least [Chapter 8], this plant was used in the first phase of the chief's investiture, next to a spring.) The deceased chief's "companions" (those invested with him) might not see the body and were kept off the ground, for fear of their own deaths, until the body had been raised on a platform in the first stage of his transformation into an everlasting *simbi.* In another text describing burials in general (Cahier 219), Lutete says, "In our area corpses are not smoke-dried" (*ka muyumuswanga mvumbi ko, evo yanga ko*), but they were kept on a platform to rot. "It was shameful for the heir if the body of a chief or leading man were buried in haste, because it implied that he had no money" (Cahier 219, 29).

Lutete distinguishes (not with perfect clarity) the dignities proper to different titles or ranks. The bodies of the holders of the higher titles, Nsanda, Makunga, and Vungu, were buried in a marsh, but coffins containing dry parts of their bodies (hair, nails, skull) were dragged in a funeral car to the cemetery of the chiefs, which was also the investiture site. Hair and nails, though dry, represent the body's vitality.[7] For each of these titles there was an inferior or perhaps "postulant" version, Kayi kwa Nsanda (or Makunga, Vungu), whose holder was buried less honorably; his body was not separated into wet and dry but carried on a stretcher to the cemetery and buried entire. In addition, Lutete mentions (Ki)Mbenza, whose body was not thrown in a marsh but was also entitled to a funeral car. The Children and Grandchildren conduct the ritual. (At the end of this chapter, the stories of particular chiefs include funerary details.)[8]

28. A rule of all the titles is that a chief who was not invested cannot be buried in the Lulombe with the invested chiefs, but in another place consecrated to be their cemetery.

33. If a member of a group of chiefs invested together should die, the survivors go to another village and close their ears so that they do not hear the explosions of gunpowder for their companion. As long as the corpse is on the ground, the survivors too must sit down until the day when the body is raised on firewood logs (for smoking?), when they are lifted up by the Grandchildren. Such is the custom of the day when an invested chief dies.

34. Consecration of the Lulombe. To consecrate Lulombe a Child and Grandchild go to the investiture site and take the sacred things of the *nkisi nsi: mobula* and *ngelengenze* creepers, *mbundu, munkwisa,* and a *kaka* (?). They choose a place in the forest in which to bury these things, but they leave a sign where they buried them. On an Nsona day they begin to dig the "stone," which is the name given to the grave of a chief. The reason it was given this name is that the desiccated chief became a *simbi* stone, or *nkita nsi;* a chief who lived for a very long time was called *simbi kia nsi* or *nkita nsi.* So it was with the first chief. This is the custom for blessing Lulombe. When they have someone who is to succeed [to the chiefship], the day after the burial of [his

28. Nkandu wena mu Mabwene mamonsono vo mfumu kasa baluka bwene ko, kalendi zikwa kuna lulombe ko kwaziikwa babaluka bwene, balembwa baluka bwene vuuma kyankaka kyasemwa kituulwanga bikinda biau.

33. Vo mfumu yayala mu bayadila va mosi una fwa buna basidi moyo bana kwenda vata diankaka ye bana zika matu mau bu mfuidi mpasi kabana wa dumu kia zimfula ko zeti vetulwa mfumu yau. Mvumbu bu yena va nsi yau mpe mfumu zena moyo bana vwanda va nsi nate ye lumbu kina kundukwa mvumbi mu kuni za zipingu buna bau mpe bana kundukwa mu zulu kwa batekolo. Kiokio i fu mu lumbu kifwidi mfumu yabiala.

34. Fu mu bieka Lulombe. Mu bieka Lulombe buna ntekolo ye muana bana kuenda kuna bibialulu bana bonga biasemunwa nkisi nsi Mobula ye mungelengenze ye buna zaka mpe mbundu mukuisa ye kaka dimosi buna bana sola vuma kia mfinda ikuna bana zika lekwa biobio kansi ntekolo ye mwana bana tula dimbu va bazikidi bio, buna lumbu kia nsona bana kuenda badika tima ditadi kadi ndiamu a mfumu yabikwa nkumbu tadi. E bila bavana nkumbu yoyo mu diambu kadi mfumu leta kituka simbi kia tadi vo nkita nsi, kadi mfumu ya ntama ye yazinga beni yibikwanga simbi kia nsi vo nkita nsi. Momo mena mu mfumu yantete vo fwidi kiokio. I fu mu sema Lulombe. Mu ntangu yina vo babeki muntu una vingana buna

predecessor], at night, the heir is invested at the burial place (?).[9]

35. Another custom or rule that they followed was that when a chief died everything had to be done as it had been done for the first chief. But at the cemetery another place was found for those who had not been invested. The chief's successor goes to the Bininika [?Bikinda] at the time when they begin to "dig up the stone" [to dig the grave]. At the grave of the first chief, they go to pull up *sisya;* other people go there but they avoid the grave.

This was the custom, that they chose three people to go pull up *sisya:* a Grandchild, a Child, and a member of the clan. When they went to the Lulombe the Grandchild went first, followed by the Child and the member of the clan. When they were a little way off they knelt down and proceeded on their knees until they got to the grave-site (?), where they stood together.

Here they kept silence, not saying a word. First the Grandchild took hold of the *sisya,* then the Child and then the member of the clan, and then they pulled it up together and retreated backwards, without looking behind them. When other people saw them some distance away, [someone with the role of] Na Nsuka would say, "Turn around!"[10] At the place where they

kina lumbu kina zikua dikongo mu fuku dia landa buna una vingana buene una yala vo yaduswa intumbu vingana mu mbongi.

35. Fu kiankaka evo muina usa-duluanga vo mfumu yankaka yina fwa, monso bavanga mu mfumu yantete i mana bana vanga. Kansi ku Biziami kuna sokwa vuma kiankaka vo ka babaluka ko babonsono buna ndiamu zina manasana ye ndiena wabaluka buene, mfumu yanzole yina kuenda ku Bininika [*sic*] mu ntangu bana badika zokula Tadi. Buna mu ziami kia ntete kiaziama mfumu yantete bana kuenda vuza *sisia-sisia,* basanga bobo buna bantu bankaka batekelenge kuna, kansi bana mamuka [se garer] ye ndiamu.

Buna fu i kiaki bana solua mu kue vuzi sisia batatu basolwanga 1. ntekolo 2. mwana 3. muisi kanda, buna bu bana kuenda kuna Lu-lombe ntekolo una bonga mtwala [*sic*] bosi mwana una landila ntekolo bosi muisi dikanda una landila mwana, buna bena finseke buna fukama va makungunu ye bana kuendila va makungu nate ye vana diwumbi [*sic*] buna bana telamana va mosi.

Buna bana kala napi kadi bula mbembo, buna ntete ntekolo una teka simba *sisia* buna mwana una landila ye mboki muisi kanda buna bau batatu bana dio vuzila va mosi buna bana vutukisa kinima kinima kadi tala kunima zau, buna bantu bankaka beti kubatala bu bana kala finseke, buna Nansuka una kamba lubangumuka buna mu fulu kina

turned around they put a sign, and that would be where the grave was dug. They put the *sisya* in the marsh. They dug the *sisya* on an Nsona day, and on an Nsona day also they began to dig the grave; but the Children and Grandchildren dug first, then others. This was the custom when a powerful chief died. Living chiefs could not set eyes on the body or the grave of their companion.

In some titles, the body is put in a marsh, and the hair and nails in the chief's coffin (treasure chest). Later they go to look for the body; if the head has rotted they put it in the chest with the nails. These things are mourned, and then buried with festivities. That is how it was in the old days for the Nsanda, Ki-Makunga, and DiVungu titles.

For any chief invested with one of these titles, the body may not be buried, just [his] nails or head, or else a he-goat is killed, and those things are mourned and buried with great festivities. But those who only took the Kayi version of these titles were not dragged [to the cemetery] in a carriage but on a stretcher; if the body were dragged, the village would come to an end.

39. In Lolo, when a chief with the Nsanda title dies they remove the body from the coffin and take it to bury it in a marsh. At night they replace it in the coffin with goat's entrails, and bury the coffin in [the

kibabangumukini i vana bana tula dimbu buna vana bana tula ndiamu. Buna bana tula *sisia* ku nyamba ye zika dio lumbu kia nsona kivuzwanga *sisia* ye lumbu kia nsona mpe bana badika zokula tadi, kansi batekolo ye bana bana teka timuna ntoto ibosi bankaka. Momo mena mu mfumu ya ngolo vo ifwidi wowo basanga. Mfumu zena moyo ka balendi mona Kimbi kia mfumu yau ko evo mona ndiamu.

Mboki Mabwene mankaka mvumbi yitulwanga ku nyamba zinsuki ye nzala bitulwanga mu tolongo mbosi bakwe landanga ntu a widi mfumu. Vo mvumbi yimeni bola ntu, batuulanga mu tolongo ye nzala byau bidilwanga ye mu lumbu kya nziikulu byau bivangulwanga nkembo. I bobo bwateka kala mu nsi a nkulu, kansi Bwene mpila yoyo 1) Nsanda 2) Kimakunga 3) Divungu.

Yonso mfumu una baluka Mabwene momo, mvumbi kayilendi ziikwa ko, nga zinzala kaka evo ntu evo nkombo ya mbakala yina vondwa, buna byobyo bina dilwa ye mu nziikulu bina vangulwa nkembo waunene. Kansi mu Mabwene mama vo wabaluka evo Kayi mvumbi kayilendi kokwa mu makaala ko, kansi mu kimbenza. Bila vo mvumbi yina kokwa, buna bwala busikidi.

39. Balolo. Vo bana yala buene bwa Nsanda vo mfumu una baluka Nsanda buna bu kafuidi yandi mfumu mu fuku bana katula mvumbi mu tolongo, ye bana yo kuenda zika mu nyamba, buna mu

forest cemetery] Lulombe, where
no one who has not been invested
may be buried.[11]

Upon the death of a chief who had
not been invested with Nsanda and
just took the Makayi title or a
minor initiation, they did not put
his body in a marsh but buried it
with an appropriate feast. The body
was buried in the place chosen as
the cemetery of chiefs, but a chief
of this rank could not be dragged
there in a funeral car; he was
carried on a stretcher (*kimbenza*).[12]

The bodies of those who took the
Kimbenza title could be taken for
burial in a funeral car. Those who
had the rank of Kimakunga upon
their death were buried in a marsh,
but their hair and nails were taken
to bury in Lulombe. A feast was
held for them, they were divested
of their authority, and they were
dragged with great honor in a
funeral car.[13]

dina fuku bana vingisa ndia mia
nkombo muna kimbi i mau mina
zikwa ku mfinda yina bikua
nkumbu ku Lulombe yina ndambu
buna kailendi ziama muntu
wankaka ko, evo mfumu walembwa
yala ko.

Vo mfumu yalembua baluka nsanda
wayala kayi kaka evo bundukuswa,
buna vo fuidi buna kabana tula
mvumbi andi mu nyamba ko kansi
yina zikua ye vangulwa nkungi wa
kimfumu mu nzikulu ye mvumbi
yina zikua kuna fulu kia sokwa
kiziamanga zimfumu. Bayalanga
buene bobo kabalendi kokua ko mu
makalu, kansi mvumbi yina
natunwa mu kimbenza.

Bayalanga Kimbenza mvumbi
ilenda zikua kuandi ye kokua mu
makalu. Bayalanga Kimakunga, vo
una fua mvumbi andi yina zikua ku
nyamba, zinsuki ye zinzala bina
zikwa ku Lulombe, biau bina
vangwa nkungi ye tumbula bio ye
bina kokua mu makalu mu nzitusu
beni.

The deceased chief was transformed into the *simbi* rock that symbolized perpetuity, remaining "rooted for ever." "When a great chief dies, may they say, 'A *simbi* has risen up.' May the noise of it be heard by men and women" (Cahier 232).

The *Nkisi Nsi*

The *nkisi nsi,* or "*nkisi* of the country," that is, of the chief's domain, was a medication of the earth, located in a sacred grove (Bittremieux 1946). The clan's Children and Grandchildren could go there, but not the members of the clan that owned the chiefship, except for the candidate chief himself on the day of his investiture. The grove is sometimes called Lulombe, sometimes Mbalala; the latter refers to the *mbalala* tree planted there, from which the chief's staff might be carved (LKII, 150), and at whose foot the *nkisi nsi* was buried. In other groves, the tree might be *lubota,* ironwood. Lulombe, "a place apart," is the burial place of the chiefs.

Logic indicates that each domain (*nsi*) should have its own *nkisi nsi,* but Kinkela in Vungu describes a pair of them in one domain—possibly a schism in the making:

Two *minkisi* were used to initiate chiefs, their names are Lusunzi and Mwema. Thus our country was governed in two parts, divided on account of the two *minkisi* by which the chiefs ruled. Na Mpanzu was invested at Mwema. Nsungu a Ngo and Nsala a Ngo were brothers who were invested at Lusunzi. These chiefs were invested with these *minkisi* and were very powerful, because the titles cost them plenty. Lesser chiefs from all over their area came to receive cloth bundles or animals, one or two each. If they brought palm wine, the candidates would reward them. Those who were initiated to the *nkisi,* such as Lusunzi, took the Kayi or Makunga title; the lesser chiefs were included in the title and *nkisi,* and underwent the ritual.[14]

As an *nkisi,* the *nkisi nsi* contained ingredients which functioned like *bilongo,* though Lutete does not use the term. Some of them, such as *munkwiza* and the double bell, also functioned as visible insignia. The principles governing their inclusion are the same as those for other *bilongo.* Such medications of the earth to create shrines or localized charms are certainly found all across Congo and into Zambia—and probably even more widely. For the Luba, Theuws describes the composition of a kind of *nkisi nsi* for a chief and also of a *kite,* a charm both protective and offensive, in the form of a medicated mound outside the house of an important man. As in Kongo, the medicines put in these shrines are chosen on the basis of "external resemblances, shape, color, linguistic assonances and the like. They have meaning only in the context of a total worldview" (Theuws 1992, 18, 21–23).

A unique European description of the composition of an *nkisi nsi* on the Cabinda coast comes from an unpublished manuscript by an English seaman, who remarks on the similarity between *nkisi nsi* and the great mobile *minkisi* of the region, such as Mangaaka:

When a group of natives, a band or family, settle down and form a new village, they first mark off a plot of ground for sacred purposes, and on this they plant a tree—the fetish tree. The sap of the fetish tree is always blood-red and, after planting, some of the sap is mixed with the blood of a wild fowl. The fowl is then buried and, after it has entirely decomposed, the ground, tree, and everything associated with them become sacred and receive fetish power. In the tree are placed mirrors, shells, etc., similar to those in the fetish gods, behind or in which the fetish power accumulates. These objects are affixed with clay which has been moistened in the mouth of the fetish priest. The priest erects his hut on the ground and there produces the fetish gods.[15]

The following list of components of *nkisi nsi* is from Yema (Cahier 234); they are "potent signs," both "medicines" and "insignia."

The sword of power called Lusimba is placed in the forest at the foot of a *lubota* tree, the blade upwards. The things planted or buried in the forest:
1. *Binkanda biole*—two *kinkanda* monkeys
2. *Sama dimosi dia Ngongi*—half (?) of a double bell
3. *Nzala zi 4 za Ngo ye meno mole mango*—four leopard's claws and two teeth
4. *Minkwisa miole wanika ye wanlengo*—two *munkwiza* creepers, scraped and crushed

5. *Mobula*—creeper
6. *Mungelengenze*—creeper
7. *Matadi mole mampembe*—two white stones [crystals?].

The sword or knife, one of the most common authority symbols, clearly stands for the power of death (see Chapter 8). The *kinkanda* monkey is known for its resistance to death. The *ngongi* bell is a symbol of chiefship, or rather, a sign of the chief's authoritative announcements. The chief is identified with the leopard throughout Central Africa. White stones are associated with *simbi* spirits; in this instance, crystals may be meant.

Mukuisa (*munkwiza,* etc.) is a vine (*Costus* sp.= *zingiberaceae*), a very acid, juicy, and luxurious plant. "It has an acid juice from which the body shrinks when one bites on it" (Cahier 213). Its uses are many, because it was thought to keep off witches. Chiefs' staffs and other carvings show a man biting on it; some show him sitting on a two-headed dog as he does so, clearly signifying the detection of occult evil. Dapper, describing the *nkisi* Boesi-Batta, says that the *nganga* in trance was brought back to his senses by having blown over him "a sour juice enclosed in a kind of cane." Chiefs wore it as an embodiment of their power: The chief's soul was believed to reside in it; if he pointed it at people something happened; if he dropped it, he had to go through the entire investiture ritual again. It was worn in two ways: a small piece tied to the finger, or as a girdle around the chief's loins (*luketo,* the seat of sexual energy).

> Insignia of *munkwisa* have been used for ages; they had this power, that if a chief pointed it at someone, that person would swell up and die. If the chief threw to the ground the *munkwisa* from his hips, he would be unable to lift his feet from the spot. He had to be lifted up; if not, he would die. Then they had to choose another, hand over a slave, give him the baton of a chief and make him walk on the leopard skin and the *munkwisa.* (Cahier 234)

This rule of *munkwisa* restates the chief's ambivalent relationship to the earth; he is united with it as the source of fertility, but must be kept separate from it when death threatens. *Mungelengenze* and *moobula,* climbing plants, share with *munkwisa* the significance that they live "for ever" and that they ramify, as a successful chief should, by investing client chiefs.

> *Moobula* is a vine of chiefship, greatly respected because it is the source of chiefly power, it is the soul of the chief. Once it has been planted at the crossing (?) it may not die, though the years go and the years return. On the day when chiefs are invested, two lengths of the vine are cut. One length is cut into little pieces that the candidates may wear; the other is made into a circle in the middle of which the candidates are rolled and marked with chalk. (Cahier 231)

Medicines of the Nkisi Nsi[16]

Instead of celebrating the absolute and sacred authority of the chief, some components of the *nkisi nsi* indicate that he was vulnerable to conspiracies against him. Others proclaim that he has the support of patrilateral (and affinal) allies whom his own clan should respect.

1. The insignia of chiefship. Each of them has its own explanation. Palm tree: If a man is to be invested by his fathers, the reason why they include a palm leaf is to show his clan that while their child lived with them, his fathers, he was allotted palm trees from which to draw wine and cut nuts; that he was not refused the sustenance of palm trees, but chopped wine and nuts from the tree itself. That is why they put palm beside the feet of one who is being invested.

2. They put *lemba-lemba* [*Brillantaisia alata*] so that if the chief should become very angry he may take *lemba-lemba* to "calm" his heart, so that when his heart is at peace the words that he shall speak shall come from below the navel, not from above it. For what he should say that comes from above the navel would be spoken in anger and would aggravate the affair and create problems. So the meaning of *lemba* is, "May that which the chief pronounces be well received by the chiefs and priests, may his word be acceptable to all men of goodwill, to the elders and to the youth."

3. They include *munsabi-nsabi* so that if anybody should conspire to kill the chief or make any other evil plot, then there will be those who in private conference will say, "'I know, I know' and 'I'll tell, I'll tell'; those that are plotting against us, may they desist. May the deliberations of the chief be protected, so that no sorcerer can steal your words.[17] In the council may he

1. Lekwa biabi biena diambu-diambu ye mbangudulu au. Ba. Vo muana una yadila kwa mase mandi, buna bila kiba tudilanga ba i mu songa kua bisi kanda diandi mwan'eto, bukakala kwaku disandi wabaka maba mandi katenda malavu mandi ye kwanganga ngazi zandi yandi katetua nsonde mu maba vo, utombanga malavu ye ngazi kadi ku kisaku nti aba wanate. Kiokio i bila batudilanga ba va mbela malu mandi mandiena una yala.

2. Lemba-Lemba. Bila kibatudilanga lemba-lemba bila mpasi mfumu vo una kula mbidi nganzi buna una nwa lemba-lemba mu ku nlembika ntima, mpasi ntima una lembalala mpasi makana vova mana tuka banda nkumba kameti tuka ntandu nkumba ko. Kadi mambu mamfumu mamana tuka va ntandu a nkumba nganzi itotokele ye yina vitisa mambu, buna mambu meka mampasi. Ikuma mambu mena mu lemba mena vo: mfumu makana vova mana tondwa kua zimfumu ye banganga, diambu diadi dina vovwa kua mfumu kwa babonsono a mbadiangana kuandi, momo mana vovwa kwa bavunda ye balezi.

3. Munsabinsabi. Bila kibatudilanga munsabinsabi mpasi vo bantu bankaka vo bana kubika lukanu lwambi mu zola vonda mfumu vo kubu diankaka diambi, buna bankaka kuna nenga bana vova nsabi-nsabi mangovo na ngovo [nkisi], buna bakutu kubika lukanu luambi, buna luvunzane. Nzitika [kanga] lukungu [ta ku nenga] mu mfumu, weka nsingi weka mbindi

strike his hand upon the earth [against the sorcerer] so that his stomach may swell, and by noon it is destroyed."

4. They put in *mindudi-ndudi* [wormwood] for situations in which people are gathered in secret to attack the chief by witchcraft or some other plot against him. Then in the meeting some cry "Eeeeee!" and spit and tell everything "truly" because of the bitterness in the mouth. "May he who refuses to respond to the word of the chief be blown upon by those who have Nsonde, Maluangu, Nyambi, Ngovo, and Ma Kongo ["detective" charms] so that he ceases to make trouble. May he join the *bisimbi* and descend into the sea."

5. The *moobula* creeper is put in and wound around [the chief's] loins.[18] Then they say: "May he spread out like the *moobula;* may he create Mbenza titles and Makunga titles; may he engender chiefs and priests. May he make his children chiefs. May he raise up children, may he generate honors, may the members of his clan be chiefs. May his ministers spread out, may his authority ramify like a vine. May the words that he speaks be remembered by the freemen. May his rule plunge as deep in every direction as the roots of the *moobula,* may the clan of the chiefs produce leaders, spreading their authority." That is what the creeper signifies.

weka mvandi a mbumba, kalembwa baka waku nzonzila. Kuna nenga kambandila koko va nsi kavimba vumu ka luaka ntangu mbata vumu kibuka.

4. Mundudi-ndudi. Bila kibatudilanga mu ndudi-ndudi vo bantu bana kutakana ku nenga mu vuka dia mfumu mu kindoki evo lukanu lwankaka lwambi mu bivisa mfumu. Buna kuna nenga kubana kala, buna bankaka bana vova e e e bana lobula mante ye bana vova mamo mandudi bonso bwaludila nlulukulu mu nua yandi vuka tambudila lukungu mu mfumu kavevwa kwa bansonde ye bamaluangu ye baniambi ye bangovo ye kwa bamakongo, kidi ka vuka vola mambu. Kakundana ye bisimbi kadumuka kenda muna mbu.

5. Mobula. Nsinga wowo wutulwanga ye ku nsinga wo mu luketo. Buna bavovanga mambu mama: Kakula kalamba bonso bwalambila mobula kabuta zimfumu kabuta zinganga. Katumba bana bandi kimfumu. Kabuta mbembe [ndezi abana] kabuta kunda [sikila] katumba bisi kanda kimfumu Madingizi bakula balamba bika kimfumu kiandi kalamba bonso bualambila mobula. Mambu makana vova bika mabambukulwa moyo kwa zimfumu ye banganga. Bika kimfumu kiasumama mianzi mia mpila mu mpila bonso buena mianzi miamobula, kanda dia zimfumu bika diakula zinkazi za kula za Lamba. Momo imena mu nsinga.

6. The reason the *nsanga-lavu* cane is included is so that the chief may pacify the village if quarrels should break out. If there is serious trouble, the chief takes out *nsanga-lavu* and ties a piece of it to his little finger. When he shows it on his finger the people say, "The leopard! the leopard!" and remain silent to hear what the chief has to say.

6. Munsangalavu. Bila kitudulwanga mu kidi mfumu kalembilanga bwala vo bwala buna kala nkindu-nkindu. Vo nkindu yina kala yangolo, buna Mfumu una vaikisa munsangalavu buna mfumu una bindika ndambu mu nlembo wansuka mfumu bukana monika wo mu nlembo, buna bana vova ngo, ngo, ngo, buna babo bana kala napi mu dimba ye dimba mana vova mfumu.

7. A banana shoot is included that the members of the chief's clan may know that in his fathers' village he was given banana trees for his benefit and was not denied support by his fathers; that the members of his clan, too, should not deny him support when he wishes to plant.[19]

7. Nsanga dinkondo. Bila katudul-wanga nsanga. Bisi kanda kidi bazaya vo ku kisandi wabaka mankondo ye katetwa nsonde ko bu kabunda nsanga za mankondo kua mase mandi. Mpasi bisi kanda kabana ku nteta nsonde ko buka-zolele bunda nsanga [katula va sinsa mu kunisa].

8. *Nsafu* is put in to show the people of his clan that when he was in the country of his fathers he ate *nsafu* fruits that his father and his paternal relatives had planted; that he was favored by them, and so should not be denied palms and *minsafu* and bananas or manioc when he comes to govern his clan. He should govern palms and *minsafu* and *kola* trees left by his elders.

8. Nsafu. Bila kitudulwanga nsafu mu songa bisi kanda diandi vo bu kakala ku nsi amase mandi wadia nsafu miakuna sandi ye mase mandi mambazi mwana wazolwa kwa mase mandi ikuma bukana kala nyadi mu kanda, yandi katetwa nsonde mu ba ye mu nsafu vo mu mankondo vo mu mayaka. Yandi una kala nyadi kwa maba ye minsafu ye minkazu miabika bavunda biandi.

Investiture[20]

Luyaalu means investiture, the power it confers, and government. Though there were many minor titles that amounted to little more than the local festival of this or that village, in theory the major titles formed a hierarchy. According to both Laman and Doutreloux, the highest was Vungu (which some called Mbenza; in Kinkela's usage, *mbenza* simply means "title"), followed by Makunga and Nsanda. For each of these there was also a partial or subordinate title called Kayi kwa Mbenza, Kayi kwa Ma-kunga, etc.; Kinkela even mentions "little chiefships," *bimfumu-mfumu bya bike,* prob-ably held simply by elders of the clan (Cahier 94). These subordinates were said to be *bundukuswa,* "included," but the holders could be promoted if they paid more. The great titles were those which "ramified," that is, which derived from an original ritual center to which distant chiefs traced the origin of their powers and to which others were "added." The creepers in the *nkisi nsi* speak to this idea.

In practice, since there was no mechanism for maintaining any hierarchy amid the intense competitive activity, it is not surprising that alternative rank orders were advanced. "The more groups multiplied and dispersed, the more intense and complicated became the traffic in titles" (Doutreloux 1967, 180). Lutete insists that the highest title was Mwema Lusunzi—perhaps because his own clan owned it. The songs he quotes suggest that Mwema Lusunzi subsumes Mbenza and Makunga (see below). To add to our difficulties, the names of titles were often also the names of places—*minkisi,* chiefs, clans, and settlements all being aspects of the same complex. Thus when Mabunu Makele is said to have *baluka KiVaku* and also to have *baluka Mbenza MaKele,* we are to understand that Mabunu of the Kele clan, the first woman to take a title (Mbenza) in Vaku village, assumed the name Mabunu Makele. "Clans," despite their apparently genealogical organization, took shape around a local center of power.

Since several candidates might be invested at once, *mabwene* (titles) can be regarded as memberships in a privileged association, rather than as offices. From this point of view, chiefs resemble the *banganga* of important *minkisi;* like them, they gathered whenever their particular ritual was performed, to conduct it and to share in the benefits of food, drink, and fees. There are some indications that the chief's officers were invested with him.

38. On the day of the ceremony, there may be six or eight chiefs to be invested. Very early in the morning they go the place where they are going to make *nkisi nsi.* There they dig a hole in which to bury creepers and consecrated metal objects, stones, and [objects representing] their souls. Then the paths leading to the place are well cleared.[21]

Whoever is the one being invested—or two of them, as it may be—holds the sword of power which is to be put in the ground. Other chiefs of Kayi rank hold it after the candidate. The first chief is the principal to hold the sword, or there may be two principals. When they hold the sword that is to be put in the ground, the principal puts his hand uppermost, the others after him, and together they

38. Zimfumu mu lumbu kina kiba yalanga vo bana yala basambanu vo nana, mu nsuka nabu bana kuenda ku ku bana sema nkisi ansi kuna bana zokula dibulu dibana zika minsinga ye bisengwa bia semwa ye matadi, ye bilunzi biau buna bina tulwa vana bulu buna nsambi yina toma vatwa,

wonso balukidi yandi una simba mbele lulendo bu yina zikwa vo nzole buna bau bana simba mbele Lulendo, buna mfumu zankaka ziyedi kayi, buna bana simba kunima mfumu yibalukidi, buna mfumu yantete yandi intinu wasimba mbele Lulendo evo wanzole wasimba buna bitinu biole, bu bana simba mbele yina zikua mu nsi buna ntinu bu kana nanguna koko ku zulu buna mfumu zisim-

brandish it, so that the power is "raised." Then they thrust it into the hole so that "the power stands forth." Then other chiefs stick their toes in the hole.[22] The hole signifies two things: the chief who stood the sword in the hole has the power of execution, and those who held it after him and held it in the hole have the power to bury alive prisoners, or anyone who has committed a crime such as murder or disregarding the chief's law.

40. All the chiefs roll on the ground where the *nkisi nsi* is buried to unite with the things which have become the *bisimbi* of the place and its power. The *moobula* creeper is a respected sign of chiefship; it girds the chiefs about the loins until they leave Lulaala, when the Grandchildren take it to the *mbalala* site. That is as much to say, they have gone to join the spirit in the forest and be united with the everlasting life of the *moobula,* the *ngelengenze* and the *munkwiza.*

If an invested chief should die, the heir to the bonnet, the *munkwiza,* and the Lubukulu box in which is the chalk of investiture, who is to see the *nkisi nsi* in the forest and in the village,[23] must hand over slaves and pay for the things. If he does not pay he will take office as chief and be marked with chalk, but he will not have *luyaalu* power. Only when he acquires wealth and pays slaves and fees will he get all the powers of investiture.

bidi ku nima bana sangatala moku zulu va kimosi, impila mosi vo lulendo lusangamene, bosi bu kana tedimisa mbele vana bulu mpila mosi lulendo lutelamene, buna mfumu zankaka zina tula tedimisa nlembo miau vana bulu. Buna mambu mole masonga va bulu Mfumu yitedemese mbele va bulu yandi uena lendo mu zenga muntu babana basimbi ku nima ye basimbidi va bulu bena Lendo mu zikisa ntukulu vokunisa muntu va nsi ndiena wavanga nkanu wa mpondolo wa labuka muina mfumu.

40. Mfumu zazo zivindubuluanga vana bulu dizikwanga nkisi ansi, mu bundana ye biobio bieka simbi bia nsi ye bieka lendo kia nsi. Nsinga wa mobula insinga wanzitusu wa kimfumu kadi uzingilanga yau mu luketo nate ye kina lumbu kiba katukanga va lulala, ye nsinga miomio buba vudidi mio mina kuenda filua kuna mbalala kua ntekolo. Mpila mosi bele kundana nadede ye simbi kina ku mfinda, ye kala kintuadi mu luzingulu lua moyo a mobula ye mu ngelengenze ye mukuisa.

Diambu diankaka diena vo mfumu yayala una fwa, yandi una vingana mpu ye minkuisa ye Lubukulu lwena luvemba ye mona nkisi ansi wa mfinda ye wavata. Buna fueti futa diaka muntu ye funda mu baka biobio, nga vo kana futa ko buna una bundukuswa kaka ye baka kaka luvemba, nga ka lendo kia luyalu ko. Nate mfumu yina baka kimvuama ye una futa bavika ye mafunda ibosi una mana baka lendo biabio bia luyalu.

If the nephew [who is to inherit] is young and the chief did not leave much money, the bonnet is hidden away in a bag with all the insignia until the boy grows up and becomes wealthy, then he can be invested. During his youth he first learns the business of chiefship before he is invested [?] That is how a clan's chiefship was inherited.

14. There's another thing. When the chief is being rubbed with chalk at his consecration, the chalk is first put all round his wrist and then extended up his arm to his face, so then he is invested. But if he is not invested, then the chalk only extends from his arm to his shoulder. Such a chief has only reached Kayi grade, and would have to collect more money and slaves in order to be consecrated with chalk right up to his face, to hold the sword of power and to be rolled in the hole of the *nkisi nsi*.

15. In the old days, if the chief was not rich enough to complete the ritual, he could take three or four titles, changing his official name with each initiation. The place where the chiefs supported themselves on trees was called the forest of Makwangi. When they invested chiefs they leaned against these trees. When they sat on the leopardskin in that place they remained there for four Nsona days; on the fifth they were raised in a mat and carried to the Mban-gala, a place where the *bisimbi* of chiefship were buried. There they rolled [on the ground] and held the Lusimba sword.

Vo muana nkazi inleke kaka ye mfumu kasisidi kimvuama kiakingi ko, buna mpu yina suekua mu lukatu ye yadulu biabionsono nate ye muana nkazi una kula ye kala kimvuama bosi kalenda yaduswa. Kansi bu kena nleke buna teka longuka makimfumu bu kakidi mu puma. Momo makala mu vingana kimfumu mu dikanda.

14. Diambu diadi mpe diena, mfumu bu zina kuswa luvemba mu kubayeka luvemba luna teka zungudukwa mu dikulu dia koko ibosi luvemba luna tandwa mu koko nate ye ku kini, buna mfumu yoyo balukidi. Kansi vo kabalukidi ko, buna luvemba luna tuka mu nsa[n]si a koko luna tandwa nate ye luna sukina va vembo, buna mfumu yampila yoyo kayi kabiele buna fueti yonzika mbongo zankaka ye bavika mu tomba balulua luvemba ku kini ye kuenda simba mbele lulendo ye kuenda vindumunua kwena bulu dia nkisi ansi.

15. Muna nsi nkulu vo mfumu kena kimvwama beni ko mu manisa buene lenda yala ngiala tatu vo zi ia, nkumbu mpe izisekukilanga buna ntangu ka ntangu yikana buela yala. Vuma kiena nti miasingama zimfumu nkumbu a vuma Mfinda Makuangi bu bakala yalanga zimfumu mu vuma kina bu bameni singama mu nti miomio ye bu bavuendi va nkanda ngo mu vuma kiokio buna nsona ziia 4 bana kala va Lulala ya ntanu bana nangunwa mu Lwanda ye bana natua ku na banda Mbangala kua zikwa bisimbi bia luyalu ye kuna bana vin-dumunua ye bana simbila Lusimba.

Women Chiefs; Mbenza Title, Kele Clan[24]

BaKongo usually say (see Cahier 94) that a woman could not aspire to chiefship until she had ceased to menstruate; the rule is "explained" in a tradition reported by Kinkela of Vungu, which tells how a certain woman menstruated on the day she was to be invested as chief and therefore could not go through with the ritual. Doutreloux says a woman chief, though she could not marry, might bear children (Doutreloux 1967), but this report may represent a memory of the rule prevailing in Loango in the nineteenth century that princesses might take lovers but did not marry.

The meanings and potential meanings of the equivalent phrases *sikisa kinda kya nsi* and *tetisa nkisi a nsi,* both translated from the following passage of Lutete's text as "to reconstitute the charm," lie ambiguously at the heart of Yombe chiefship ritual. *Si(i)kisa* is "to strengthen"; *tetisa* "to cause to flourish, to re-activate," is almost a synonym, but *sikisa* (short vowel) is "to (cause to) dig." As a verb, *kinda* means "to be strong, fixed, enduring," an idea associated with the trees or rocks against which chiefs "lean" to fortify themselves. From the same stem, *nkinda* is a village's protective *nkisi.* As a noun, however, *kinda* means both a *simbi* spirit and a cadaver; the plural *bikinda* is a cemetery, especially the burial place of chiefs. *Kinda kya nsi* is therefore the pit or grave in which the *nkisi* of the *nsi* (domain) is composed. It is worth recalling here that the verb *zika* or *sika,* to bury, also means "to arouse, to animate," as when tokens are nailed or "buried" in Nkondi.

In the old days if a woman wished to be invested she would pay the fees, money, and slaves, to receive the Lubukulu and the *munkwiza.* But she could not reconstitute the *nkisi nsi* in the forest nor in the village. The *mbalala* [staff] could be taken there, but she could not reconstitute the charm. For Lubukulu, *munkwiza,* and the staff one would pay six slaves and a thousand,[25] which gets you the title and rank, but you are not invested, and the white paint is not extended to your face. A chief of this kind is called "Kayi." If a Kayi of Mbenza took Makunga he was called "Kayi of Makunga."

Kuna nsi nkulu vo nkento una yala lenda vakula ye futa mbongo vo bavika lenda tambula Lubukulu ye mukuisa. Kansi kalendi tetisa nkisi ansi wa mfinda ye wabuala ko. Mbalala mpe lenda natwa kuna, kansi mu sikisa kinda kia nsi ka lendi ko. Lubukulu mukuisa mvwala lenda futa bantu ba sambanu ye funda, buna lenda bonga nkumbu yena kala buene, kansi kabaluka ko. Luvemba mpe ka luna lwakuswa ku kini ko. Mfumu yampila yoyo lenda bikwa Kayi. Kayi kwa Mbenza vo wayala Kimakunga buna una bikwa Kayi kwa Makunga.

The first female chief to take a title was anointed with Mbenza Makele but did not reach the *kimbenza* grade. She took the name Makele

Mfumu yayi yantete yankento wakuma kaka buene wakuswa Mbenza Makele kansi kabaluka kimbenza ko wabonga mpe

Mabunu. When she died, they looked for another titleholder (*mpu*), and Makele Mpanzu succeeded her. He completed the investiture, reconstituting the *nkisi nsi* in the village and in the forest; Lulombe also was consecrated, more or less as in all titles, two of them in each case. The late Makele Panzu paid nine slaves to finish the ritual.

nkumbu Makele Mabunu, yandi bu ka fwa buna batombula diaka mpu buna Makele Panzu wayala diaka. Yandi yu wamanisa ngiadulu yamvi[mba]. Watetisa nkisi ansi wabuala ye wamfinda Lulombe mpe lua semwa fisidinga mu mabuene mamonsono muna tulombe tole tole. Wedi Makele Panzu wafuta 9 dia bantu mu diambu dia kamanisa ngiadulu yayonsono.

Makunga Title, Mbenza Clan [26]

27. To begin with, if the chief is the first of his clan to take the title he should be very wealthy to acquire the *nkisi nsi*. If he is not able to pay a great deal of money he will be unable to have the *nkisi nsi;* he will be enthroned only in the public place and it will be said of him that his dignity is small. If he has not been to the *mbalala* he may not see the Lubukulu, nor look at what is inside it. When old Me Mbangala Ngoma was invested, four chiefs sat side by side, but they four were very rich and wealthy; therefore at their investiture they obtained the insignia of *nsi* and the staff.

Consecration of the shrine in the forest. At night when the chief has been painted, and the *moobula* wrapped about his loins, he may not sleep on a bed or on a mat but on the ground. They four place their feet on an anvil and on *nsanga-lavu*. To walk on these is a sign of the power of chiefship. Then at cockcrow they arise and clear a place on the very top of a hill where they are going to make the *nkisi nsi*. They first make marks

27. Muna ntete vo mfumu yantete uayala mu dikanda vo yandi imbadukulu a yalu, buna fueti kala kimvuama beni kidi kabaka nkisi ansi, vo kuna futa mbongo zazingi ko, buna kalendi mpe baka nkisi a nsi ko, buna va mbazi kaka kana yadusulua ye kambua mafiuma mena mu luyalu. Buna vo kasidi kuenda ko ku Mbalala, buna mpe kana mona Lubukulu ko kana tala mpe biena mungudi ko. Kansi wedi Membangala Ngoma bu kayala mfumu zia bayadila va kimosi, kansi bau baia bakala bisina ye kimvuama beni idiau mu ngiadulu au babaka kiyazi kia nsi ye mvuala.

Nsemono a kiyazi ku mfinda. Mu fuku mfumu bu kameni sonua ye zingwa mobula mu luketo kana leka va nkwala ko ye mpe ka va mbuka ko kansi va nsi bau baia bana tetika malu mau mu nzundu ye mu minsanga-lavu bu badieti biobio idimbu kia lulendo lua kimfumu. Buna mu nsusu yantete bana sikama ye bana sola va kiteta-teta kia mongo, vo bana sema nkisi ansi, buna bana teka sona kiyazi bana kio kanga lusaku-saku, bana

[in red and white clay] on the symbol of government (*kiyaazi*), then add to it *lusaku-saku* and *munkwiza* root. They also bury *tondi* and *semwa*.

The reasons why they include these things are:

1. *Lusaku-saku* [a kind of papyrus with fragrant leaves], that the reign may be "blessed."

2. *Munkwiza,* that the chief's rule may grow from year to year, that if it begins to die it may be revived.

3. *Tondi* [an underground mushroom], that the chief may be "acceptable" [*tondwa*] to the chiefs and priests, and that all the people may receive the words that he speaks to them.

4. *Semwa* fruits [?], that he may also be a "creator" of chiefs and that his thoughts may be joined to those of God the Creator, so that his reign, joined to the power of God, may be strong.[27]

In the rest of the ceremony for the Makunga title, the temporary roof is removed from the place where the *nkisi* is to be buried. Those who are being invested make cuts on their foreheads and cut also their nails on fingers and toes. They take skin from the brow of leopard, in which two teeth of a leopard are wrapped. Then all the chiefs take their machetes, with their clan juniors and their Children and Grandchildren, seize their knives and prepare the hole in which they will bury the *nkisi nsi.*

kanga mpe sinsi dia munkuiza, bana zika tondi bana sika mpe semua.

1. Bila kibatudilanga lusaku-saku kidi kimfumu kina sakumunua.

2. munkuiza, kidi kimfumu kina mena mvu ya mvu, vo kina tonta fua kina tedumuswa diaka, buna savila munkwisa ibuna savila kimfumu.

3. Bila kibazikilanga tondi kidi mfumu una tondua kua zimfumu ye banganga, ye bantu babo bana tonda mambu makana ku ba kamba.

4. semwa mpasi yandi mpe una kala nsemi a bimfumu mabanza mandi manabundana ye nsemi i Nzambi mpasi kimfumu kina siama bu kibundane ye ngolo za Nzambi.

Buna nyeki [?] i wena mu Buene buanka mu Kimakunga lulembe luna katukua mu vuma kina zikua nkisi ansi, buna bau bana yala bana nuata menga va mbulu zau ye zaka nsuki zambulu ye tenda nzala za moko ye za malu, bana bonga nkanda ngo wa mbulu ye meno mole mango bina kangua vana nkanda wa mbulu, buna zimfumu zina simba kuwa [tanzi] bau babo ye babipita [= bilandi biau; mwana nkazi] ye ba Na Ncuka [mwana wabuta mpangi au yankaka] ye bamfukazi mfumu bana simba mbele yibana tomina bulu dibana zika nkisi ansi.

28. When they have dug the hole they all lift up the *nkisi nsi* [and put it in the hole]; they do that because chiefship is very heavy to carry. They put the symbols (*biyazi*) on top, with stripes [in red and white?], and fill in the earth, leaving signs on the outside. After they have buried [these things] those who are being consecrated stand up near the insignia and are marked on their whole bodies, each one with white clay from ankle to face. Then the ceremony is over. Then everybody there gets *lubukulu* boxes marked with the same white clay as was marked on the *nkisi nsi* (*kiyazi*), to show respect to the symbols (*bidimbu*), because they have been consecrated and become the sign (*dimbu*) of chiefship.[28]

28. bu bameni tima bulu, buna babo bana nanguna nkisi a nsi, bana sa bobo kadi kimfumu kiena mbidi azitu mu nata kio, bana tekisa biyazi va ntandu bana viokisila ntoto muna viokusu mingulazi, bana sisa zinsongi ku mbazi, bu bameni zika bana yekua bana telama lukufi ye biyazi, kuna bana sonwa nitu yamvimba. Muntu tandu kulu luvemba tuka mu dikulu dia kanda nate ye kuna zizi, buna sukisi ngiadulu yayonsono. Buna babo kuna bana bakila tubukulu tua siwa mpezo ya kilua mu kiyazi ye bazungidila binkungu bia muna nkisi ansi kidi bamonika nzitusu mu dimbu biobio, kadi bia tumbwa, biayikidi dimbu kiamfumu.

29. In the forest they swear an oath. The senior chief says the following, while throwing down an anvil on the ground: "Eh, *mwema nzundu,* what if he were angry?" then tears off his hat and hurls it to the ground. The leaders of the ceremony proclaim: "Take your guns," whereupon all present in the forest dance war dances. When he has done that, he takes a root of *munkwiza* and says: "Eh, *mwema lusunzi,* when he threw it to the ground, bang! it was to demonstrate to the warriors; but now that they are overawed, the dead are dead!" The elders bid the chief not to be angry and bid the crowd to brandish their weapons and dance the war dance there by the *mbalala.* The drum first sounds, and they shout, "Eh, *wewe!*" Then the

29. Kuna mfinda bana dia ndefi yandi mfumu yankuluntu una samuna mama bu kana lumba nzundu va nsi E mwema nzundu [nkisi] vo kadeka [=fwema] zideka ko, una kukula budu ye banda yo va nsi bakuluntu baluyalu bana kwikisa: Nangunieno minkele kunu miabangeno, buna babo bena koko mfinda bana sanga mantulu. Bu kameni sa bobo, buna una bonga kaka [kaaka] dia munkuisa una ta bonso bwabu. E Muema lusunzi buka lumba wo va nsi ilu [sic] intumbu songa kwa bababimpita. Bwabu bitunduka, zonso zifua zifua kuandi, bakuluntu mu Kimfumu, bana boka kwa mfumu bika zenda dekieti, bankangu nanguneno minkele, buna bana dia dintulu ye bana sanga koko mbalala ngoma yina sibwa ntete, bana kumba e wewe e e.

double bell sounds, the big double-ended drums and the small ones.[29]

Landila ngongi zina sikua. Landila Bitangala bina sikua, landila bidukulu bina sikua.

30. When they have done that, the chief who has just been invested says to everybody, "Now you may dispute among yourselves, each with his own opinion, but when I deliver my staff into the hands of the chiefs, when they go to stand it where the *nkisi nsi* is, when you all see that, you are to be silent. The staff has gone to acquire its power from the *nkisi nsi,* and the chief tells you to keep quiet."

30. Buna babameni sa bobo, buna mfumu wizi yeka bwene una kamba kua babo bwabu luna vovasana muntu ye nsamu andi muntu ye nsamu andi, kansi bu ngina tambika mvwala mu moko mazimfumu, bu bana zo kuenda tedimisa zo vana vena nkisi ansi buna beno babo bu luna mona bobo, buna luna kala napi. Mvwala yele baka lendo kiandi kua nkisi ansi, buna mfumu una vova beno babo ipi.

Signs and Rules

Like the components of other *minkisi,* the signs, rituals, and medicines of chiefship, potent in themselves, imposed rules constraining the conduct of the chief and his followers. The external insignia of a chief include his bonnet, *mpu* or *budu;* his sword or knife "of power," *mbeele a lulendo;* his staff, *mvwala;* the double bell, *ngongi,* used to announce his coming; and several vines or creepers, of which the most frequently mentioned is *mukuisa (munkwiza,* etc.). *Mukuisa* was one of a number of objects that could be called *kiyaazi* (pl. *bi-*), "insignia."

Rules Concerning Mukuisa[30]

30a. It was the rule that when a successor chief died, his *kiyazi* was buried with him in his coffin. But the *kiyazi* of the first chief in the series was permanently conserved, because when the chief acquires his cap (*budu*) the blessing would come from the *kiyazi* of the original chief.

30a. Mwina wena vo mfumu yalandila yala vo fuidi buna ye yazi kiandi kina tulwa muna kimbi. Kansi kina kia mfumu yantete kikebuanga mvu ya mvu, kadi vo mfumu una vumbula budu buna lusakumunu luna tuka muna yazi kia mfumu yantete.

From the place where the *mukwisa* fell to the ground the chief must himself be picked up and carried home without touching the ground. Arriving at his own place, he must

Mu fulu kina kisotokene mukuisa mfumu fueti nangunwa nate ye ku nsi andi mu zulu kaka kana kuendila bu kalueki ku nsi andi una vutuka semisa mukuisa wankaka

consecrate[31] another *mukwisa,*
which will cost a slave, and be
carried into the forest to the place
of investiture where is the *nkisi nsi,*
to be restored to sanctity. He must
stay in the house, as before, nine
Nsona days [nine weeks]. On the
first day, when the invested chief
returns from the Mbalala, if several
are invested together and have been
marked with white and red clays,
everybody in the village will shout
together, "The Leopard, the
Leopard! Oh, oh!" Thereupon all
the chiefs go into the house, where
they must not sleep on a mat or on
a bed but on palm leaves. There
they remain until an Nsona day
when they emerge and the leopardskin is brought out; the whole
village is outside. When they have
sat on the leopardskin everybody
hails them with a loud shout, "The
Leopard, the Leopard! Oh, oh, oh!"
This is repeated for nine Nsona
days and on the tenth they leave the
Lulaala. In this state they are said
to be in Lulaala, the "sleeping
house."

kansi buna una futa mvika mpe una
natwa diaka kuna luyalu kuena
nkisi ansi wena ku mfinda una
vutuka biekwa nlongo, ye una
sonwa diaka ye una kala mu nzo
vwa dia zinsona bonso muna
mbadukulu. Kadi mu lumbu
kiantete vo mfumu una yala bu
kameni tuka ku Mbalala, vo
babingi bayadidi va kimosi buna bu
bameni sonwa ndimba ye mpezo
buna babo va buala bana bokila mu
kumbu kimosi Ngo, Ngo, O, O.
Buna babo zimfumu bana kota mu
nzo ye mpe ka balendi leka va
nkwala ko evo va mbuka ko, kansi
va mandala kaka, buna nate ye
lumbu kia nsona kaka balenda
vaika ku mbazi buna nkanda ngo
una vaikusua ye bantu babo mu
buala bana kala va mbazi bu
bameni vuanda va nkanda ngo buna
babo bana kubakumba kumbu
kiakinene beni, Ngo, Ngo, o, o, o,
nate ye bana mana 9 dia nsona ye
kumi i bosi bana katuka va Lulala.
Nkadulu yoyo ibikuanga bena va
Lulala.

Rules of the Staff [32]

30b. If the chief stands up to travel and
the staff is brought out, the
members of his clan must go
indoors. When he is on the road
with his Grandchildren, clan
members follow after.

A member of the clan may not hold
the staff. One who holds it must be
invested.

If the chief goes to the market,
everybody must be quiet and sit on
the ground to hear what the chief

30b. Vo mfumu una telama mu kuenda
nzila, bisi kanda diandi mvuala bu
yina vaika buna kota mu nzo nate
ye mfumu una tuama ye bana ku
fula ye batekolo buna bisi kanda
bana landa va nima.

Muisi kanda kalendi simba ko
mvuala kamana yo simba buna
fueti yala kaka.

Vo mfumu una kuenda ku zandu,
buna babo bana kala napi ye bana
vwanda va ntoto, ye bana dimba

has to say. When he has made his announcement he pulls up his staff and the market may begin.

If the chief is going to confer a title, when he arrives in the village where the investiture is to be held he stands his staff upright in the middle of the village until the ceremony is over.

If when people are fighting the chief takes his staff to the scene; the combatants on both sides, hearing that the chief has come with his staff, must leave off their fighting.

The staff is to stand by the pillar of the chief's house at all times.

mana vumuka mfumu, bu kameni vumuka buna una vuza mvwala, buna bosi balenda sumba.

Vo mfumu una kuenda mu yeka kimfumu, buna mu vata dina dibana yala, mfumu bu ka lweki muna, buna una tedimisa mvwala va kati dia bwala, nate ye bana sukisa ngiadulu yayonsono.

Vo bantu bankaka beti nuana mvita vo mfumu una bonga mvwala ye nata yo ku mvita, beti nuana mvita bu bawilu vo mfumu yena ye mvwala uizidi buna ndambu ye ndambu bana yambula mvita.

Mvwala yina telama va kunzi ntangu zazo mu nzo ya kimfumu.

Forbidden Animals[33]

At his investiture, the chief was marked or painted with spots, like the leopard, or with red and white stripes, as "protection" (*kila,* to paint lines; *kidukwa,* to be protected). In this particolored state, he was also a mediator between the worlds of day and night. He controlled *bwazi,* "leprosy," a disease which was not in fact leprosy but gave the sufferer blotched skin. Since the chief "is" but also is not a spotted beast, he had to be separated from spotted animals, which include the wildcats and certain striped animals upon which the leopard preys. Striped and spotted animals were signs of authority because they mediated between the visible and invisible worlds, being neither one color nor the other but a bit of both. Both the bushbuck and *bwazi* were said to be "red," the color of dangerous mediation (Bittremieux 1936, 151).

21. The forbidden animals are spotted. An invested chief may not eat them nor, formerly, could his whole clan, lest they contract leprosy: leopard, bushbuck, wildcat, serval, civet, and the marsh-dwelling antelope. The reason why those animals are proscribed is that they resemble the body [of the chief]. The bushbuck that was forbidden at the *mbalala* may not see the *simbi* buried in the earth; the buck that saw the *simbi* died suddenly. A member of the

21. Bulu biena nlongo biena matona matona. Mfumu yayala kalendi dia bio ko ye mu kanda dia mvimba kuna nsi nkulu kabalendi dia bulu biobio ko, nga buna bana kala buazi. Ngo, nkabi, nsingi nzuzi masisa, nzoba, mvudi nyamba. E bila bata bulu biobio nsiku mu diambu dia kadi i kifwani kia nitu andi. Nkabi wasikulwa vindu kuna mbalala vo: kalendi mona simbi kia zikwa mu nsi antoto ko. Nkabi kua mona simbi kina buna ka fua

clan may not see the *mbalala* site.
A Child or a Grandchild may, and
the Children look after it. Members
of clan may never see the *nkisi nsi*
that is in the village.

32. If the chief should be angry and
throw down his anvil as a challenge
to another chief, then the war must
be fought. The same if he throws
munsangu-lavu to the ground; they
must fight. If the chief throws down
these symbols in anger and the war
is not fought, his belly would swell
up and he would die. Or if he
should bang his fist on the ground
they would also have to fight. This
is an important rule of this *nkisi*.

Members of the clan that has
consecrated this chiefship may not
eat the harnessed bushbuck lest
they contract leprosy. If so, the
consecrated chief must go to the
shrine and say: "You, *nkisi nsi,* hold
the authority and the power
established by the ancestors and the
old ones of the earth, which cannot
be uprooted; the chiefship is
destroyed but, if you restore it, it
will be restored, to give victory in
war." (P.S.: While the chief speaks
he may drive his staff into the
ground, having fixed tokens to the
point.)[34]

"May the sign of the leopard be
seen in the forefront of the battle;
do you, Leopard, keep the souls of
all chiefs and ministers who
confide them here to you. Be the
witch male or female, whether he
come in the shape of an animal, a

mviku, vuma kia mbalala kilendi
mona muisi makanda ko, mwana vo
bana balenda mona kio, ye bana
mpe bakebanga. Nkisi ansi
wukalanga ku buala bisi kanda
kabalendi mona wo ko mvu ya at
mvu.

32. Vo mfumu una lumba nzundu va
nsi mu nganzi ye mfumu yankaka,
vo bafueti nuana mvita, buna
bafueti nuana kaka. Ibobo vo una
lumba munsangu-lavu va nsi, buna
mvita yina nuanua kaka. Vo mfumu
una lumba yazi biobio va nsi mu
nganzi ye mvita ka yina nuanua ko,
buna mfumu una vimba vumu ye
fwa. Evo nkome [*knytnave*] kuandi
kamana yo lumba va nsi mvita yina
nuanua kaka. Wowo i nlongo
waunene mu yazi kiokio.

Nkabi kabana yo dia ko mvu ya
mvu mu kanda dibayedi buene
bobo, vo bana dia nkabi, buna bana
kala bwazi. Buna mfumu yi biekele
una kuenda simba yazi ye una vova
mambu mama, Ngeye nkisi ansi
una simba kimfumu ye lulendo
kisenene bakulua nza ye banunu
ipangi [?] kakilendi vuzwa ko kia
vuzuka kimfumu kivuzukidi, kansi
bu una sikila i buna mpe kimfumu
si kiasikila, vana ndungunu mu
zimvita. (P.S. Vo mfumu una vova
una somika mvwala va nsi ye vana
nsongi a mvwala sika tedimisanga
mfunya.)

"Bika dimbu kia ngo kia monika ku
ntwala mvita, bika ngeye ngo
wasunga [keba] muela mfumu zazo
ye madingizi mamo bana kuiza
swaka lunzi biau kwaku. Ndokia
nkento ndokia mbakala mu bulu
kakuizila mu nuni mu sioto, bula

bird, a frog, crush his head! Cruel Leopard! who gnaws the heads of *ndwangi, nsuma,* and *nkabi* antelopes, rend the witch's body, plunge claws and teeth into his chest. May the *nkabi* antelope pass by here, and may he die, for he has trodden on the head of Mbenza Me Mbangala.

"When the power of this *nkisi* was first shown in ancient times, the *nkabi* that crossed the hill died. Since then, in this generation, the antelope(s) that appeared there have been revealed [to hunters] and have died. The Children and Grandchildren have eaten them; those that are alive to this day have seen this." When the chief has given power to the *nkisi nsi,* they sing a song, that the chief may heed the laws that they have heard.

ntu Mankeme [ngo] Makuenze [ngo] wakuenza [dia] ntu mia-baduangi ye bansuma ye bankabi, yandi beni ndoki uyunguka bonzuta [byten om kropp = bweta mu ngolo] mu ntulu tongidika nzala ye madinu mu ntulu. Nkabi kaviokila vava kafwa kwadi, kadi buna uizi diata ntu a Mbenza Me Mbangala.

"Buna Lendo kia yazi kiokio kia monika Ntete mu nsi nkulu ntama beni nkabi yaviokila vambata mongo una yafwa. Landila mu mbandu yayi nkabi yaviokila vana yasolulwa yafwa, kansi bana ye batekolo badia zo momo mamonika kwa bena moyo nate ye bwabu." Buna mfumu bukameni vana lendo kwa nkisi ansi buna bana yimbila nkunga wau mpasi mfumu kana toma sungama mina mibauilu.

The Chief and the Earth[35]

The rites of investiture linked the chief with the permanence of the earth and the life-giving powers of the spirits in it. He was rolled on the ground over the *nkisi nsi;* he was required to sleep on the ground in the Lulaala; the place and sign of investiture might be a *simbi* stone, a cave, or the cemetery of his predecessors. Once thus linked to the earth as a mediator between life and death, he might not see the rivers that mark the boundary between them. He might not drop the *mukuisa* from around his loins; if he threw it down, or his chiefly bonnet, war had to break out or he himself would swell up and die. Even women might not throw firewood heavily to the ground.[36] The *simbi* stone that anchored his chiefship and gave him the power of life was death to other chiefs and to stray antelopes; the anvil, another *simbi* sign, also declared war when the chief threw it down. After his death, the soul of the invested chief ascended to the sky, leaving behind a stone as his monument, his *simbi.* These connections with the earth correspond to the clays in an ordinary *nkisi,* incorporating the power of the dead by contiguity.

Mbenza and Makunga, identified in the following song, were apparently regarded as the highest titles, and were perhaps the same. In Cahier 234 ("Women Chiefs," above) Makunga seems to rank higher. Mbenza is also the name of an *nkisi* to whose cult the begetters of children were initiated, and is also used as a term for *minkisi* in general.

Song:
Eh, straighten up,
Obey the rules; Mwema
    Nzundu, Father Mbenza.
The sacred anvil,
Father Na Mbenza,
Obey his commandments.

Obey his laws, eh.
Father Na Mbenza.
Obey the taboos of the *nkisi,*
Root of *munkwiza* oh, oh,
    Father Mbenza Makunga, eh!
Obey the rules of investiture,
Father Mbenza Makunga!

Nkunga:
E lusunga, sung'e [toma tala
    mina].
Luiza sungamana.
Mwema nzundu [nkisi]
Tata Nambenz'e.
E Mwema nzundu
E lusunga, sung'e;
Lwena sungama mina miandi e,
    Tata Nambenz'e.

E lusunga, sung'e,
Lwena sungamana nlongo mwema,
    Nsinsi dia minkuisa. O O O
E tata Mbenza Makunga.
E lunsunga, sung'e,
Lwena sungamana mina miandi
    mia yalu,
Tata Mbenza Makung'e.

34. This song is much sung at Mbalala, since it is greatly respected. After the musical instruments have played for some time, the chiefs take their places. When they have been frighteningly painted with red clay, the people, seeing them, shout "Leopard! Leopard!"

When the forest ritual is finished they set all the chiefs in litters, every man with his staff, while large and small drums accompany the march. When they arrive in the village they sit on leopardskins while everybody else sits on the ground and looks at the chiefs, shouting "*ngo, ngo, ngo . . .*"

That is the investiture and the power for this title. People say that *nkisi nsi* exists but they cannot tell what kind of thing it is. But we know that whether [it takes the

34. Nkunga wowo uyimbulwanga beni beni kuna Mbalala, kadi nkunga wanzitusu, buna sikwa biabio bina sikwa beni beni, buna zimfumu ziyele bele vuanda kiau vuma, buna bameni kimbula sona ndimba, buna banka bu bakubatala buna beti vova kua yau Ngo, Ngo, Ngo.

Bu bamanisa salu ku mfinda bana tula mfumu zaza mu maluanda, buna tangala ye dukulu bina kuiza sikua nzila yamvimba, buna ye Mvuala andi muntu ye Mvuala andi bana kala mu lwanda. Bu bana lwaka ku bwala bana vwanda va nkanda mia ngo, buna babo bankaka bana vuanda va nsi buna babo bana tala zimfumu bana vova Ngo, ngo, ngo, ngo, ngo.

Yoyo ingiadulu ye lendo mu buene bobo, bantu bavovanga vo nkisi ansi wena, kansi kabalendi songa wo nkumbu ko, vo nki alekwa, kansi tuzeyi bwabu, vo ngongi, vo

form of] a double bell, a creeper, or a stone, at times [the chiefs] travel with the *bisimbi,* keep company with them, and hide their souls there.

munsanga-lavu vo mbele, vo tadi, buna ntangu zanka bana zieta mu bisimbi ye sueka mioyo miau muna ye kundana ye bisimbi.

In modern Ngoyo, the *fumu mpezo,* who is the priest of the *nkisi nsi* and guardian of the sanctuary, Lulombe, must avoid the political chief, the *fumu nkaazi.* He is forbidden to fall to the ground, lest he destroy the fertility of the soil, and to see either the sea or white men. Formerly the political chief "covered" him (*fuka,* hence the title Mafouk) in dealings with Europeans. Mulinda notes that the king, the Ma Ngoyo, combined both functions at the level of the state (Mulinda 1995).

Further north, in the Republic of Congo, *minkisi mya nsi* are remembered as part of the religious topography of the former kingdom of Loango. They are distinguished from ordinary *minkisi* by their clear identification with dominant clans and their territories; thought of as water spirits, they may be enshrined in caves, ravines, or groves. Unlike ordinary *minkisi* they are both localized and endowed with distinct personalities and biographies. Sometimes they are represented by a statue (*nkhosi*) and served by an *nthomi.* They also function as tutelary divinities for the healers of the neo-traditional religious movement Mvulusi ("Savior"), who regularly denounced all ordinary *minkisi* and their *banganga* as agents of the Devil (Hagenbucher-Sacripanti n.d.). This ideological structure recapitulates the public/private opposition found in the prophet movements of Lower Congo (Zaire), where also the prophets are at least latently associated with nature spirits.

The Rules of Mwema Lusunzi, Chief Lubuzi, Clan KiMongo[37]

The laws of the title are these:

1. If a woman puts down firewood, she may not drop it heavily lest the chief's belly swell up.

2. No one may throw down a stone or an anvil. If the chief's wife is bathing, no man may set foot in the water or see her naked, on pain of death.

3. The chief's foot may not be trodden upon.[38]

4. It is a taboo of Lusunzi that the chief may not eat goat.[39]

1. vo nkento una tula zinkuni va ntoto kana lumba zo ko, vo una lumba zo vindu buna mfumu una vimba vumu.

2. muntu nkutu kana lumba nzundu vo tadi. Nkento wankama vo wena ku nlangu bakala kalenda tula malu mandi mu nlangu ko vo mona nkento mpene ko, buna fueti zengi.

3. Mfumu kalendi diatwa va ntandu tambi ko.

4. kalendi dia nkombo ko. Yandi wayala nkombo nlongo muema Lusunzi.

5. When the chief eats he must first rub chalk on his ears.

5. Bu kana dia fueti teka kusa luvemba mu matu.

6. When the chief travels in a hammock the Grandchildren and slaves [of the clan] carry him; whenever he arrives in a village, the head of the village must precede the hammock.

6. vo mfumu una natua mu luanda batekolo ye bavika bana kunata ye dionso vata kana luaka mfumu a vata una vana ntululu aluanda.

The Territorial Spirits

All over Kongo, invested chiefship is associated with *simbi* spirits, the work of the smith, and with remarkable rocks and caves. The chief himself is not a smith, but in the east a smith is the investing priest (Mertens 1942, 311; MacGaffey 1986a, 66). *Bisimbi* (also called *bankita*) are spirits of those who have "died the second death" in the land of the dead, have acquired greater permanence than named ancestors, and have come to be associated with particular locations, especially with remarkable rocks and pools at which all kinds of marvels occur. They make themselves known and useful to the living by animating *minkisi,* by providing treasures from the earth, and (when chiefs were invested) conferring on the chief the power of life. Like all other powers, they could capriciously cause trouble, especially to those who ignored them or broke their rules.

For Lutete, the *bisimbi* that served as *biyaazi* of various chiefs were usually specific, named rocks of remarkable appearance. Similar but smaller stones, found "sculptures," played an important part in the rituals of *nkisi* Mbenza (MacGaffey 1991). Chiefs arranged long life for themselves not only through the rites of investiture but, we are told, by confiding their souls to such rocks; others are said to have used sea shells for this purpose.

Lutete describes the three *simbi* stones of the clan Mpudi a Nzinga: (M)Pangu Lusunzi, his wife, and his treasure chest. Pangu Lusunzi is a rock planted in the earth, as though someone had buried it there, standing up. "It has a white child with two eyes, that looks upwards and cannot sleep." Pangu Lusunzi transformed himself miraculously (*wakivanga wakisunzu*) and so obtained chiefship for himself, of which he was proud. His pride is unmistakably virile, incompatible with female functions: "[I]t was observed long ago that if a pregnant woman saw him, her pregnancy would depart, so pregnant women avoid the place to this day."

Once upon a time, (M)Pulubunzi, who lives in the deep of the ocean but travels in the rain to scatter *bisimbi* in the form of the red and white stones which one discovers in gulleys and pools, came across Pangu Lusunzi in the Nsinda grassfield. She saw Pangu Lusunzi standing there and asked him why he did so. He said, "Thus I made myself, not to lie down." She said, "Lie down!" Pangu Lusunzi said, "I refuse." After that they wrestled; Pulubunzi was stronger and defeated Pangu Lusunzi, who broke in half about the middle. Upon this there came a heavy rain, a storm that lasted two days, with great peals of thunder. People passing by saw the stump of Pangu Lusunzi, cut off as though by a saw, and stood it up again.

The wife of Pangu Lusunzi is Ngwa Mayene ("Mother Breasts"), a female *simbi* in the form of a remarkable stone which has a breast just like that of a human being. The treasure chest of Pangu Lusunzi is a stone with four corners, as smooth as a real chest. These are the three *bisimbi* of the Mpudi clan, the pride of the Children and Grandchildren. "And I myself" (concludes Lutete), a Child of Mpudi a Nzinga, "who surrounded (*zingalakana*) all the clans," came from the place where Pangu Lusunzi miraculously appeared; "he made me, hair and nails, the invincible one who fought with Pulubunzi." Other people who don't have a remarkable *simbi* stone are despised.[40]

On the coast Mpulu Bunzi, regarded as feminine, was identified with the west wind, bringer of rain. The story of her encounter with Pangu Lusunzi should be set beside that of her encounter with the rainbow serpent Mbumba Luangu, recorded by Bittremieux and analyzed by De Heusch (Bittremieux 1936, 247–65; De Heusch 1982). Mpulu Bunzi, allied with Nzuzi, the thunder, defeats Mbumba Luangu to bring on the rainy season. The erotic content of the story is appropriate to the creative power of the *simbi,* represented by Lutete as male and as the pride of the patrifilial Children and Grandchildren, the guardians of the Mpudi *kiyaazi.* Elsewhere he describes Mpulu Bunzi's wife Ngwa Mayene as having four breasts, two in front and two behind— presumably a different stone. "Hair and nails" are the parts that grow; the expression means the whole, vital person.

In Nsinga, the Simbi *Is Pungi*[41]

Pungi, like the better-known Mbenza, was a begetter's cult as well as an *nkisi nsi.* *Luseemo,* which (like *lusunzi*) means "something very splendid" (LKD), could refer not only to the white *simbi* stone but to the ritual in which the begetter of children is "blessed," *semokene* (from *sema*). "Blessing" means to protect the subject from the potentially dangerous consequences of close contact with a spiritual force; membership in the *nkisi* was open only to men (MacGaffey 1991, 53–63).

35. (M)Pungi. It is a kind of *luseemo,* a white *simbi* stone in the forest at a spring. The people of Nsinga country do not have *nkisi* Mbenza as their *simbi,* but Pungi instead. If a man fathers a child, all those who have been blessed go there, pushing him in front. When they arrive, they surround the stone and he licks it. The first time, they all shout, "Eh, he has been blessed!" This happens three times.

35. Pungi. I mpila lusemo vo simbi kia mpembe i tadi ku mfinda ku nto a nlangu. Bantu mu nsi yina ya Nsinga ka babakidi simbi kia Mbenza nkisi ko, kansi Pungi i simbi kiau. Vo muntu meni buta mwana, buna babo basemuka bana kuenda kuna. Buna balwaka kuna, buna bana kuntuamisa ku ntwala. Bu bana luaka kuna buna babo bana zungidila simbi, buna yandi una semuka una venda muna tadi mu penda yantete bu kavendele buna babo bana kumba E semo-kene, e, e, buna una venda penda

yanzole bana kumba diaka e
semokene, e, e, buna una buela
kumba nkumba yantatu bana vova
Meni semuka, e, e, e.

36. Part of his strength comes from Mangundazi, who is the oldest of the *bisimbi*. Pungi has a rule that a man who has been blessed may not throw a stone to the ground in anger, nor threaten anyone with a harmful object, lest his belly swell up. Therefore the elders knew that Pungi is the younger brother of Mangundazi—Mangundazi the elder had a deputy in the village.[42]

36. Kansi ndambu a ngolo zandi zatuka kua Mangundazi. Mangundazi i nkuluntu a bisimbi, kadi Pungi uena muina mpe vo muntu wasemuka una lumba tadi va nsi mu nganzi vo lekua kafuemene vo una vialakana mu nsilulu buna vumu kina vimba. Ikuma bazeyi bakulu vo Pungi i mpangi ya nleke kwa Mangundazi, Mangundazi nkuluntu wabaka tomi ku buala.

The Chief Prolongs His Life (Cahier 232)

In the stories of great chiefs the poetic quality of Kongo reflections on death and perdurance is especially striking. True or not, the particularities of individual narratives invest the ritual details with human immediacy. Nkodo Masu is the principal mountain south of Maduda.

36a. When a chief's hair began to turn grey, he would go climb the hill, Nkodo Masu, all the way to the top. He took a stone, spat on it, and threw it into the hollow in which leopards give birth.[43] It is as though he were hiding his life there [the leopards will defend it against witches].

36a. Vo mfumu wabadika mena mvu, buna wayenda maka mongo wa Nkodo Masu nate kabinduka, kabonga kani tadi lobudila dio Mati i mweka losa dio kuna nkindibidi kuena nluka ubutilanga bango. Bu kasidi bobo i mpila mosi ikuna kele sueka moyo andi kuna.

Makayi kwa Nsundi was the first chief who went to give his life to that *simbi*. He took the white stone on which he had spat and said, "Let us join our lives together, *simbi* planted in the earth; may my life grow with yours, that I may rise up. I have come to you, I have escaped being eaten by a female or by a male *simbi*;[44] may I become something that grows and spreads forever, magically protected. When

Makayi kwa Nsundi yandi i mfumu yantete wayenda vana luzingu lwandi kwa simbi kiakina buna mu tadi diodio dia mpembe ka lobudila mante kavova bika twa bundana yaku mu luzingu simbi kia nsi kia mena ibuna bika moyo ami wamena yaku, yadumuka. Ngizidi kwa ngeye mono kidiua [*sic*] kua simbi kia nkento mono kidiua kua simbi kia bakala ya yika kimenamena kiamena mpangu ye nlongo,

a great chief dies, may they say, a *simbi* has risen up. May the noise of it be heard by men and women." So saying, he arranged his stone on the rock, licked it three times, and rested his back against the rock, that is, he entrusted his life to the *simbi*. This chief lived a very long time.

When he was sick to death, he lay for a long time in his bed, until he said, "Go find the three stones in the *simbi* Lusunzi, but do not touch the stone that leans against the rock, for my life is in it." They went to fetch the three stones and put them in the hearth (?).[45] His life immediately came to an end. Then a sign was heard in the heavens, and another in the forest. Almost every year they pick up a wild animal that has died because it is very slippery on the hill where the stone is; an animal that trod there would fall down. Downstream, on a flat stone, suddenly he died forever.[46]

kufuidi mfumu yanene bika basa vo simbi kidumukini. Kumu kiwakana kua babakala ye bakento, buna wasingika tadi diadi muna ntadi ye wavenda yo mpenda tatu ye wayekila nim'andi muna ntadi mpila mosi wayenda yekula moyo andi kua simbi kina. Buna mfumu yayi wanuna beni beni.

Bu kakala mu yela kua mfuilu wazingila beni va ntanda, nate ye kakamba vo luenda landa matadi matatu kuna Lusunzi, kansi dina diasingama ntadi ka lusimbi ko, kadi moyo ami wena muna. Buna bayenda landa matadi matatu bayiza mo tula ku fukwa moyo andi intumbu tabuka. Buna dimbu kiawakana mu zulu dimbu mpe kiawakana kuna mfinda. Bosi fisidi mvu ka mvu nga ku simbi kina banangunanga bulu kia mfinda kiafwa mu diambu dia kuna mbata kua sukina ntadi kuena mbidi a ndelo bulu kamana diata kuna intumbu viatuka nali ye kuna ndimba nlangu va tadi dia nsen-zebele nawa fuidi kia Makilu.

The Fate of Lusunzi in Ngoyo

Catholic missionaries systematically destroyed the shrines of *minkisi nsi* in Ngoyo. In the Musée de l'Homme in Paris there is an iron object called Lukalala, a twisted rod with a flat disk at each end, each of which has a cross on it and rattles around it. It is said to have been used in the cult of Lusunzi, a female spirit of the waters, of fish, and of lightning. Accompanying it is the letter of a Christian, Domingo do Nsangu, aged 78, addressed to a Kongo priest, Father Lourenço Mambuko, asking for the return of objects given to Father Tastevin by an *nganga* called Konko.[47]

Consequently, Father, as I said to you yesterday, I thought all night about the objects which Father Constant Tastevin removed from the forest, and I said to myself that one should speak to him so that he does not take them to Europe; to call Konko and return them to him to be put back where they were. Otherwise it could happen that the King of Cabinda (Ngoyo), once chosen, could not be crowned before having taken oath and received the holy water at that place, where the bronze [*sic*] object was. After that ceremony, he has to complete that of Lemba, otherwise the king may not be crowned; if that is omitted, the consequences could be harmful.

Moreover, these are sacred objects left by the ancestors, and if they are abandoned, it is because the king is not crowned. What's more, they are not fetishes, but sacred objects of the pagan saint, Lusunzi. . . .

Because I am the last son of the former chief of the town still remaining in this, Christ's world, and an old man, several people came to speak to me about this matter, that I should give it some care. . . . They are pagan objects, they have their owner, and one cannot take them like this, because they are pagan saints and not things of sorcery. This I know. Konko is afraid, and that is why he confessed against his will.

A note by Tastevin says the king of Ngoyo (Cabinda) was obliged to be purified at the temple of Lusunzi (a sacred grove near the River Tombe-tombe) and crowned at that of the spirit Kanga. The last invested king of Ngoyo died in 1830. Lusunzi, as the name of *nkisi nsi,* was known all over Mayombe and in northern Angola, but was not found in Manianga (Bittremieux 1946).

Some Famous Chiefs

As I argue in the next chapter, "the land of the dead" is a site of both theory and memory, which work as aspects of knowledge that we can distinguish only analytically; stories, true or not, situate individual chiefs in a past which, for historians, may include details of "what happened," or what perhaps typically happened, but also, for the BaKongo, attest to the truth of the basic principles and forces that govern life today. "Ritual," linking the chief with the powers of the dead, is simultaneously the "myth" of the deeds of his ancestors, the two aspects together enacting, as LaFontaine puts it, propositions of general social relevance (Chapter 8).

Maswa Ngoma, Clan Mpudi (Cahier 235)

17. Maswa Ngoma, Me Ngonda Mbungu, and Mambuku Mbaka took the Bwene title and were invested on the same day. Maswa Ngoma paid nine people, as did the others, nine each. So they were able to compose the *nkisi nsi* in the forest and in the village. In the forest it included a chief's bell, a knife blade, a bracelet without joint, and an elephant tusk. Inside the bell were put leopard's claws and skin from the leopard's brow.[48] Part of the bell remained outside and was marked with stripes like the

17. Maswa Ngoma Mengonda Mbungu Mambuku Mbaka, bababa bayala Buene ye bayala lumbu kimosi. Maswa Ngoma wafuta vwa dia bantu Mengonda vwa dia bantu Mambuku vwa dia bantu. Ikuma basemisa nkisi ansi wamfinda ye wavata wamfinda ingongi ye nsengele mbele ye nlunga waka-mbua kiku, ye mpungi a nzau Mu ngudi a ngongi muatulwa nzala za ngo ye nkanda wambulu wango Buku kia ngongi kina sala ku mbazi kiau kina sonwa mingulazi mingulazi bonso buena nkayi.

bushbuck. These things were buried at the foot of a huge ironwood tree that stands to this day, and is known as the *simbi kya nsi.*

Biobio biazikwa va nsina lubota lwalunene luena nate ye buabu. Lwau lwayika simbi kia nsi.

In this ritual it is evident that a group of equals are invested together, as with certain important *minkisi.* The knife blade lacking a handle, *nsengele mbele,* signifies unity; its loss, discord.[49] The "bracelet without joint" presumably has similar value.

17a. *Moobula* is in [the *nkisi nsi*] and *mungele-ngenze* too, still today. They say that this is the life of the chiefship, which will be as extensive as the creepers. As long as the *munkwiza* lasts, so will the authority of the chief. The name of their title when they were invested was Mwema Lusunzi; it exceeded Mbenza, Makunga, and Nsanda in power and strength, because it originated in Mpangu Lusunzi, which is a rock with four corners in the grassfield called Nsinda. The old chiefs who ruled the Kipudi clan were invested with Mwema Lusunzi; the chief being invested at that place was painted all over his body, and stood on the head of Mpangu Lusunzi until the painting was finished.

The drum of Lusunzi is buried at the *mbalala* in the forest, entirely buried, standing up, under the earth. It is a sign that the invested chief will die when the drum emerges by itself and is heard in the village; then the chief is dead. Another prohibition is that when a chief consecrated to Mwema Lusunzi dies, he may not be buried in the country he ruled over, but in another country. His entrails, however, are removed and buried where he ruled. The body is taken

17a. Mobula uena vana ye mungelengenze wena vana nate ye bwabu. Batanga vo kiokio izingu kia kimfumu buna lambila moyo a mobula ye mungelengenze ibuna buna lambila kimfumu, ye buna lambila moyo a sisi diamukuisa bobo buna lambila kimfumu. Baba bayala nkumbu a Buene Mwema Lusunzi bwavioka lulendo ye ngolo wavioka Kimbenza ye kimakunga ye Nsanda kadi tuku dia buene buabu bwa mwema Lusunzi bwa tuka muna Pangu Lusunzi, itadi diena mbula mi ia diena mu Nseke a Nsinda. Bakulu bayala ntama mu kanda dia Kipudi vana babalukila Muema Lusunzi. Buna mfumu wayala ivuma kina kasonunua nitu yamvimba watelama vana mbata ntu a Pangu Lusunzi nate kamana sonwa.

Ndungu a Lusunzi ya zikwa ku Mbalala ku mfinda, yayonsono yina zikua ku nsi a ntoto yantela, dimbu kiena vo mfumu yayala una fwa ndungu yivaika ku mbazi yau kibeni ye yina wakana ku buala buna mfumu yifwa. Nsiku wankaka vo mfumu wabaluka mwema Lusunzi una fwa nitu andi ka ilendi zikwa mu nsi yikayadila ko, kansi mu nsi yankaka, kansi bana katula mindia ye zika mio mu nsi yikayadila, mvumbi mpe yina natwa fuku ye fuku nate ye mu nsi

in dark of night to the country where it is to be buried. Maswa Ngoma was buried in Tiaba country, his entrails in Nseke a Nienge. Investiture with Mwema Lusunzi costs twelve slaves; Kayi is six, and Nsuka only costs two. Those who have these ranks are just buried in their own domains.

yikana zikwa. Bwene bwa Muema Lusunzi mu baluka bo futa 12 dia bantu vo va kayi buna bantu basambanu vo Kinsuka [Kinsweka] buna bantu bole kaka una futa, bena ngiadulu zazi bana ziama kaka mu nsi zibayadila. Maswa Ngoma waziama mu nsi ya Tiaba [?] ndia miandi miazikua mu Nseke a Nienge.

Later in this notebook Lutete reports that Maswa Ngoma, having stored his soul in a small, spiral shell, lived to be very old. Before his death he promised that when he died he would remain one day in the grave, then on the second a sign would be heard at the water and in the heavens; a great storm of thunder and rain would follow, in which he would make his way to the sea. And so it was. On the second day, the storm raged and the signs were loud in the heavens; on the third day, when they looked at his grave they saw that it had cracked open. "This *nkisi* is there to this day."

The Dangers of Nsinda

19. From the time of the ancestors no chief bearing another title might pass the field of Nsinda, where Mpangu Lusunzi is, on pain of death. A certain chief who came from Vungu and whose name was Na Yalala, wanting to return to his own country [near the Congo], took the route across the Kimbauka plateau. He did not know there was a protection against stranger chiefs walking there, so he crossed the shrine and the streams there. When he emerged on to the forbidden field, his arms and legs began to swell up; by the time he had crossed it his belly was distended. They put him in a litter, but he died shortly after. This happened not long since; only two years have passed.[50]

19. Muna ndambu ya nseke Nsinda muena yandi beni Pangu Lusunzi tuka bakulu ntama beni kamu lendi vioka mfumu yayala bwene bwankaka ko, nga una fwa. Mfumu yatuka ku Vungu nkumbu andi Nayalala waviokila nzila yankaka bu ka zola vutu kuna nsi andi, buna waviokila muna nzanza Kimbauka. Kazaya ko vo kinda kiena muna kiadiatanga mfumu yala buene bwankaka ko, bu kazumbuka kinda kina ye nlangu mina bu e kavaika mu nseke a nkondo, buna malu ye moko biabadika vimba, bu kamanisa nseke vumu kinene mewana, buna bantula munleto, ka ntama ko wafwa . . . momo makala kantama beni ko, mvu miole kaka miameni vioka.

Nkosi Tona

The texts show again and again the ambiguities of power and its relationship to international trade in the nineteenth century. Though Nkosi Tona was a great chief on whose name oaths were sworn by his successors, the group he ruled over was too small and at first too poor to bury him appropriately. Large, ornate terra-cotta "urns" (*mabondo, minkudu*) and other grave furniture (*mintadi*), such as were eventually placed on his grave, began to be made in the vicinity of Boma during the boom years of the slave trade, as commodities for conspicuous consumption which visitors to the coastal depots took home with them (see Chapter 4). The story of Na Mongo Pungi shows the importance of the ivory trade, and that of Me Mbuku Mbangala literally attaches magical importance to indigo cloth, which was imported in large quantities and was also often incorporated in *minkisi*. The investiture of Mbenza Me Mbangala shows how wealth in slaves could be converted into chiefship.

37. On the grave of Nkosi Tona are remarkable red terra-cottas that came from Ngoyo long ago. When Nkosi Tona died the body remained for a long time. His kinsmen were too few. [Only when] the young men had grown up and the girls were married could they celebrate the funeral and bury the body with great honor in his forest of Mbamba. The chiefs who came after him, when they swore an oath would say, "By Nkosi Tona in Mbamba!" If the chief swore such an oath, war could not be put off but had to be fought.

37. Va ziama Nkosi Tona vena nkudu miangitukulu mia mbwaki mia-tukanga ku Ngoyo ntama beni. Kosi Tona bu kafua, mvumbi yazingila beni bana babuta busi biandi bakala babake nate bayunduka bakala bandumba nate bakuela, bakembila mvumbi andi bosi yadiamusu mu nzitusu beni mu mfinda andi mu Mbamba zi Mfumu za landa va nim'andi vo bana dia ndefi ye vova [n]Kosi Tona mu Mbamba. Vo mfumu una dia ndefi yoyo buna mvita ka yilendi simakana ko nate ye nwanwa kaka.

38. When Nkosi Tona was alive he went to store his soul in Pangu Lusunzi, to hide his life in the box, Pangu Lusunzi [a large coffin-shaped *simbi* stone]. He stored his soul in Mangwa Mayene.[51]

38. Kosi Tona bu kakala moyo wayenda yehula moyo andi kua Pangu Lusunzi ye wayenda sueka moyo andi mu nkele Pangu Lusunzi ye wayenda kula Bunzi kiandi muna Mangwa Mayene.

Na Mongo Mvangi[52]

3. When Na Mongo Mvangi was invested with KiMongo he finished the title and the whole ritual; they created the *nkisi nsi* in the forest that he might receive the Lubukulu box. In this title (*bwene*), Mwema Lusunzi, there is a root of *mun-kwisa* in which was placed the soul of the candidate and those of [his

3. Na Mongo Mvangi bu kayala Kimongo yandi wamanisa Buene ye ngiadulu uamvimba basema nkisi nsi ku mfinda katambula lubukulu. Mu Buene buabu Mwema Lusunzi i sinsi dia mukwisa. Vana kati dia mukwisa vatulwa lunzi bia yandi una yala ye Kapiti ye Mfuka ye Nansuka ye yau bana yeka

officials] Kapiti, Mfuka, and Na Nsuka. When they took this rank, they wrapped their souls with leopard's claws and the hair from its brow and then buried the *munkwiza* root. Having dug the hole they recited [a formula] twelve times. They marked themselves with the chalk of chiefship and repeated [the formula] sixteen times. They tried to lift up Mwema Lusunzi but were unable to; this was to show that the chiefship is a great burden.

Then these praises are recited: "As Mwema Lusunzi flourishes, so may the chief flourish. Where the *simbi* is planted, there also chiefship is planted. The chief is *simbi,* the chief is leopard." When the chief jumps, everybody says, "The *simbi kia nsi* has jumped; may a sign be heard in the heavens when the time comes.[53] Where the chief speaks, the lion and the leopard are speaking.[54] What is said is pleasing to the assembled dignitaries."

buene, bana vuika lunzi biau mu nzala za ngo ye mika mia ngo mena va mbulu. Bu bana zika sinsi dia mukuisa bu bameni zokula bulu babo bana tanga, ntanga kumi ye zole buna una kusa kimfumu una zimunina tanga makumasambanu ma ntanga. Bosi bana nanguna muema Lusunzi buna babo beka lembua meni mu nanguna. Basanga mpila yoyo i mu diambu dia kimfumu kiena mbidi a zitu mu yala kio,

buna mvila zazi zina tangumuna vana. Bonso buna sansila Mwema Lusunzi ibuna bana sasila [sic] kimfumu. Bwa menina simbi i buna buna menina kimfumu, mfumu i simbi, mfumu i ngo, kuna dumuka mfumu babo bana ta simbi kia nsi kidumukini, bika dimbu kiawakana mu zulu, ntangu bu yina lunga. Kueti vova mfumu kueti vova nkosi ye ngo. Makana vova mana zolwa kwa zimfumu ye banganga.

Na Mongo Pungi and the Last of the Elephants [55]

7. Na Mongo Pungi also went once to Ngoyo. There were elephants once, here in Lubuzi, but this chief bought a great many guns and killed numbers of them. There used to be lots of them, but they were zealous in killing them. So the custom was in the old days, if a chief had killed elephants, at his death elephant tusks and bones were put on his grave. Many chiefs' graves have tusks to this day.[56]

7. Na Mongo Pungi mpe wayenda ngienda mosi ku Ngoyo. Zinzau zateka kala muamu Lubuzi, kansi mfumu yayi mpe wasumba nkele miamingi wavondisa zinzau zazingi. Nga nzau zateka kala mu ndambu yayi zazingi, kansi basa kimfuzi mu vonda zo. Ikuma fu kiakala yau mu nsi nkulu vo mfumu una vondisa nzau buna vo fwidi buna mpungi ye bivisi biatulwa va ntandu a ndiamu. Ndiamu za zimfumu zazingi zena zimpungi nate ye buabu.

Me Mbuku Mbangala[57]

Ma Mbuku Mbangala was the first of five chiefs to take the Mbuku title; their ritual was that of Mwema Lusunzi (*bayalanga Buene Mwema Lusunzi*). In this account, the dominant theme is that of the perdurance of the chiefship, represented by *simbi* trees and a spotted *simbi* stone. The formula, "That which was planted amid taboos . . . ," refers to *bisimbi*. Elsewhere, Lutete explains that Me Mbuku Mbangala composed an *nkisi* called Kinkoko kya Mbongo ("Pool of Wealth") which had two functions, long life and wealth. When he composed the *nkisi* he buried in it a rag saved from a length of indigo ("black") cloth, six yards, which he acquired when he sold a slave. The rag went into the bottom of a pool called Simbu and became a huge bundle of cloth that lasted forever, until his death. The pool became black, so that no one could see what was under the surface. As Nganga Kinkoko, Mbuku Mbangala ordained that though the years come and the years return, women could not drain the water for fish, nor a man cast a net in it. After his death the pool divided into two parts (Cahier 225).

11. Me Nkondo Mpungi and Ma Mbuku Mbangala bought the land from the Nsaku clan. Ma Mbuku Mbangala paid two people and Me Nkondo Mpungi one, so Ma Mbuku Mbangala was the leader. He was also the first to be invested with the title, at the investiture site called the Court of Bwene.[58]

11. Menkondo [M]Pungi ye Ma Mbuku Mbangala basumba nsi yina kwa bisi Kinsaku. Me Mbuku Mbangala wafuta bantu bole ye Menkondo Pungi wafuta muntu mosi ikuma Membuku Mbangala yandi inkuluntu ansi. Yandi mpe wateka yala Buene ye va vuma kia luyalu kiena nkumbu Mbazi a buene kuna kua yadila widi Membuku Mbangala.

12. They set up two trees there, the first a *mungongo,* to signify that the chief's life might not be "disturbed," for he had enshrined a local spirit.[59] Secondly, a *mungodila* [vine?] to "strengthen" the chief. That is the explanation of the trees, which are there to this day and are called *bisimbi.*

The late Me Mbuku Mbangala was a very great and strong chief who had many powers and many *minkisi.* When he was invested with his rank of "Mbuku" and took hold of the sword of power with which to execute people, he went to be

12. Nti miole basema mika singama wantete mungongo, wutanguna mfumu kabudika moyo ngongo, kadi simbi kia nsi katanguni, wanzole mungodila nkwikila mfumu diambu bankadila dio yoyo imbangudulu mu nti miomio nti mina miena nate, ye buabu nti mina miabikua bisimbi.

Wedi Me Mbuku Mbangala wakala mfumu yayinene ye yangolo beni wakala simbu biabingi ye nkisi miamingi. Mu luyalu kabaluka kimbuku kasimba Lusimba mu zengisa bantu kakuenda vindumunua kuna bulu dia nkisi a nsi.

rolled in the hole of the *nkisi nsi.* Among the magical capacities that he acquired, he pronounced an edict that at the time of his death he should remain firm in the land and not rise up. [And here is the oath:] "That which was planted amid taboos and sacredness, which was planted in the earth and as a *simbi,* will be a sign forever."

Mu bisimbu kavanda kasila Piku vo mu lumbu mu ntangu ya mfuilu andi una sikila mu nsi andi ka dumuni ko. Kimena-mena kia mena mpangu ye nlongo, kia mena ye nsi, ye simbi kina kala dimbu kia mvu ya mvu.

13. When he died they dug a very deep grave and found at the bottom a great big stone. They brought it up and took it out of the forest, rolling it to the Nkondo field, as a memorial to remind the clan of Ma Mbuku Mbangala.

13. Buna bu kafwa bu batima ndiamu bu yasinuka beni buna kuna nsi bamona tadi diadinene beni buna batombula dio buna bavaikisa dio kumfinda ye banengumina ye bavaikisa dio mu nseke a nkondo ye disongwanga bisi kanda mu bambukila Mambuku Mbangala moyo.

In his lifetime he said, "In my grave there is a *simbi;* when it is in the field a leopard will come to claw at it, and the likeness of his spots will remain on it." So the stone is called the *simbi* of Ma Mbuku Mbangala.

Bukakala moyo yandi wavova mu ndiamu ami muna simbi ye bu kina kala mu nseke ngo yina kuiza fukila vana ye kifwani kia matona mandi kina sala vana. Buna tadi dina dibikuanga simbi kia Mambuku Mbangala.

Me Mbangala Ngoma and His Successors[60]

The name of the *nkisi nsi,* Luniamba, suggests both *nyamba,* a marsh, and *nyamba,* to throw down, both of which are linked to the rituals of chiefship; see "Some Terms: *Nyàmba*" at the beginning of this chapter. It is likely that both references, and perhaps others, were present in the minds of ritual experts.

Mbenza Me Mbangala and their *nkisi nsi* in the forest, called Luniamba.

Mbenza me Mbangala ye nkisi au ansi ku mfinda wena nkumbu Luniamba

2. In this chiefship the chiefs were especially strong in fighting other clans. When they fought, their people were very warlike and the chiefs themselves led at the forefront of the battle; on that account their soldiers were well disciplined and burned the villages

2. Mu kimfumu kiaki mfumu zaluta mu ngolo, mu nwanisa makanda mankaka bu banwanisa mvita buna bantu bau bakala kikesa, yau kibeni zimfumu batwama ku ntuala mvita, mu diodio makesa mau matumamana beni ye mu diodio mpe bayokisa mavata mabantu bankaka.

of other groups. The Mbangala people are of the Mbenza clan, but because of their strength in war and their success in whatever quarrels they were engaged in, the name of their clan was changed long ago to Mbenza Me Mbangala.[61]

3. For that reason the first to be invested took the name Me Mbangala Ngoma. He was a very powerful ruler. When his investiture was over he had acquired the tufted bonnet, the *nkisi nsi,* the staff of chiefship, iron bells, the *lubukulu* box, the skins of two kinds of wildcat;[62] also he sat upon a leopardskin, for which he paid 10 slaves by daylight and 20 by night, so his dignity was famous.[63] The staff of chiefship may not be seen or held by members of the clan; one who holds it will be chief. The Children and Grandchildren may hold it. The *nkisi nsi,* too, may not be held or seen by those in the clan, only the Children and Grandchildren. The man who carved the staff and made it frightful received a slave as payment.

4. Me Mbangala Ngoma was a very wealthy chief who used to go to Ngoyo [to trade in slaves]. His wives were not allowed to encounter a man in the forest; they wore a bell when they were in the forest, and any man who heard it would immediately hide. If a wife of the chief met a man and mentioned the matter, the man would be killed. That was the power that he received at his investiture.

Bisi Mbangala ibisi Kimbenza kwau, kansi mu dialmbu dia ngolo zingi mu nuana mvita ye bangisa mambu makidi mama ke meka manamanene, buna mu nsi nkulu ntama beni bavilulwa nkumbu a mvila Mbenza Me Mbangala.

3. Ikuma mfumu yantete bukayala, buna wabonga nkumbu Me Mbangala Ngoma. Yandi Me Mbangala Ngoma wayala mu ngolo beni, ye bukayala wamanisa ngiadulu andi, wabaka mpu ya mbondo ye nkisi a nsi ye mvuala yakimfumu, bimpambu, lubukulu, nkanda nsingi, nkanda wayi, ye kavwanda mpe va nkanda ngo, mu diodio kafuta bavika kumi bamwini ye bavika 20 bafuku. Ikuma buene buandi bua tunda beni. Mvuala yakimfumu kayilendi mona muisi kanda ko evo simba yo ko, vo mvuala a kimfumu yina simbwa kwa muisi kanda, buna ndiena simbidi yo una yala. Bana ye batekolo balenda simba. Nkisi ansi kaulendi simbua mpe ko ye vo monua kua bena mu kanda ko, kansi bana ye batekolo. Muntu wavala mvuala uatambula ye watoma yo kimbula watambula muntu i mfutu.

4. Kadi me Mbangala Ngoma wakala mfumu ya mvuama beni, yandi wakala kuendanga mpe ku Ngoyo, bakento bandi kabalendi buabana bakala mu mfinda ko, wonso nkento una kuenda ku mfinda ye kimpambu dionso bakala bu ka wilu kimpambu buna intumbu suama, kadi vo nkento andi una buanwa kua bakala, buna vo nkento wizi ta nsamu, buna dina bakala dina zengwa. Kiokio lendo katambula mu ngiandulu andi.

When he sat in judgment and addressed the people, they would respond: "Lord, it is the mouth of the lion, not the mouth of the leopard," because they compared his vigor with the strength of the lion. To elicit their response he did not shout, but waved his buffalo-hair whisk at the crowd, which would immediately shout back.[64]

He died when a buffalo killed him. Women saw the buffalo and brought the news to the village. When they had gone, the buffalo hid itself near the path and stood on a rock. The late chief did not know that the buffalo was near where they loosed the dogs. When the buffalo found itself surrounded it advanced on the chief and knocked him down, but he leapt up, holding the buffalo by the horns. He called to his son to come kill the animal while he had hold of it. The son ran up, but when he shot the buffalo one bullet hit the chief in the head. Another hit the buffalo in the ribs. The buffalo and the chief both died. When they saw that, all the members of the clan swore a prohibition and said that from generation to generation in this land which Me Mbangala Ngoma had ruled, no buffalo such as had destroyed him should die. This law stands, and to this day they do not kill buffalo in these parts.

5. Where he was buried they put two magnificent and greatly esteemed terra-cottas that cost four slaves in Ngoyo. Members of the clan of the late Me Mbangala Ngoma can

Bu kazonza mambu bu kakumbisa buna bankangu bana vutula bonso buabu Nnua Nkosi, kadi ka nnua Ngo ko mwene, mu diambu dia ngolo ye kikesa buna bamfuanikisa ngolo za nkosi. Ye mu kumbisa mpe kalendi kumbisila mu nnuako, kansi buka songa kaka mfunga mpakasa kuena bankangu, buna bankangu intumbu tambudila.

Kansi mfwilu andi mpakasa yamvonda. Bakento bamona mpakasa, bayiza samuna nsamu ku buala. Bubayenda, buna mpakasa uasuama lukufi ye nzila uele telama kuandi va ntandu atadi. Yandi uedi Me Mbangala Ngoma kazaya ko vo mpakasa yena yandi lukufi lu bakotisa mbua, mpakasa bukakala vulumuka imuizu kuena mfumu ye wa mbuisa mfumu, kansi buna wedi mfumu wavumbuka nsualu muna mpoka za mpakasa ika buna wabokila muan'andi twiza vonda mpakasa kadi yandi nsimbidi buna muan'andi wayenda nsualu, se buka veta mpakasa nsadi yanka yele mu ntu a mfumu nsadi yankaka yele mu lubanzi lua mpakasa mpakasa fuidi mfumu fuidi. Buna bu bamona bobo bisi dikanda babo bakokuluka kandu ye bata vo, ye kuna nsangu ye kuna nsangudila muamu nsi yasidi yala Me Mbangala Ngoma muedi kuiza kwandi mpakasa bonso kavetulua kalendi fwa ko kandu tetele nate ye mu mbandu yayi balembakananga vonda mpakasa mu ndambu yayi.

5. Va kaziama vatulua nkudu miole miangitukulu beni ye mianzitusu beni beni, bavika ba ia miafwa ntalu ku Ngoyo. Bisi kanda dia wedi Me Mbangala Ngoma

never see the grave in which he was buried. After his death, Nsekoso Pwati succeeded him; he too was very powerful and fought many wars. During his reign he caused to be forged a chief's bell that was more admired than that of any chief in the region, since it was a remarkable size, maybe two meters long.[65]

The 22nd chief of this line, Ntipi Soka, was very strong. [He was succeeded by] Mayema Ndinda, Na Mwanda Mbuku, and Na Ngumba Mbuku. Nzadi Mambwana, Ngombo Mambwana, and Kyamu kya Mambwana [Nos. 31–33] were women, but very strong in war. Mayedo Singi [35], Ndimba Nganga [37], Wungungu [39], Mbembele Lukanda [7], Me Nsanga Mbumba [9], Mbilu Masanga [15], Lembo Maka [18], and Ma Mbuku Mbumba [20] were strong rulers whose fame traveled widely to other countries.[66]

6. The place where Me Mbangala Ngoma died was given the name "The stone of Me Mbangala Ngoma." The place where he was buried may never be seen by a member of the clan. Only Children and Grandchildren may see it.

kabalendi mona ndiamu yikaziamu ko mvu ya mvu. Me Mbangala Ngoma bu kafua buna Nsekoso Puati wavingana kimfumu ye wayala mpe mu ngolo beni uanuanisa mpe zimvita zazingi. Mu ntangu yikayala wafudisa ngongi yanzitusu yavioka za mfumu zazo mu ndambu ansi yayina kadi yena meta mosi ye ndambu fisidi nga meta zole yena yena yangitukulu beni.

Ntipi soka [mfumu] uakala nkua ngolo beni i mfumu ya mu 22. Mayema Ndinda Na muanda Mbuku Nangumba Mbuku. Nzadi Mambuana Ngombo mbuana kiamu kia Mambuana mfumu zozo zitatu zabakento, kansi bakala ngolo beni mu nuanisa mvita Mayido Singi Ndimba Nganga Wungungu Mbembele Lukanda Mensanga Mbumba Mbilu Masanga Lembo Niaka Mambuku Mbumba. Mfumu zazi za yala mu ngolo beni. Ngolo zau zayenda kumu muamuingi mu nsi zankaka.

6. Vuma kia fwila Wedi Me Mbangala Ngoma kia vewa nkumbu tadi dia Me Mbangala Ngoma. Vuma kika zikwa kakilenda mona muisi kanda ko kuele mvu ku vutukidi mvu. Bana kaka ye batekolo balenda mona kuna.

Concluding Comment

In Chapter 8, I quoted Jean LaFontaine's suggestion that the progress of individuals through a rite of passage might be regarded as the enactment of a proposition of social relevance. The "proposition" basic to the rituals of investiture is the paradox of the death of individuals and the perdurance of the community. The invested chief begins his career amid wet, vegetable marks of growth and change; by hiding his soul with the *bisimbi* he conventionally lives to a great age, and at his death he merges with them among everlasting rocks. During his life his problematic relation to the earth is indicated by taboos against touching it or throwing things down on it. The physical movements of the rituals are accompanied by declarations that are "illocutionary acts" rather than factual statements (Tambiah 1968, drawing upon Austin). As such they are to be evaluated not as true or false but aesthetically: Were they done well, or well said, in the right way and the right context? When performed "well," they are effective, creative: they make chiefship happen, they make *minkisi* experientially real. We read that on the second day after the death of Maswa Ngoma, who had stored his soul in a shell and so lived to an advanced age, a sign was heard in the heavens, a great storm raging as the chief made his way to the sea; this story is "true" whether the storm occurred or not, and even though Maswa Ngoma may never have existed. "On the third day, when they looked at his grave they saw that it had cracked open. This *nkisi* is there to this day." Such statements (verbal, gestural, or merely "imagined") are explanatory comments on events, and thus "theoretical." By their sheer resonance and creative power they confer upon the texts a literary or poetic quality to which I have alluded more than once; this quality is neither the casual product of fancy nor simply the splendid echo of a magical past.

The nature of the theoretical component in Kongo political culture is taken up in the next chapter, which also situates Lutete's stories of combative chiefs in forgotten villages as local traces of an equatorial tradition continental in scale and millennial in history. The political structure of Kongo society, in which the patrifilial Children and Grandchildren of a matrilineal clan regulate its affairs, was observable in impoverished form in the 1970s, contradicting the simple image of matrilineal hierarchy set down in colonial ethnography. Echoes of past grandeur were there, too, in stories of great chiefly domains transcending the gritty labors of peasant life. The real lives of Ba-Kongo then, as they had been in the experience and the memory of Lutete and his colleagues, were not splendid, nor can we discern any time in the past when drought, war, enslavement, and disease did not pose constant threats.

10. REFLECTIONS AND EXTENSIONS

*The complex dialectic of interest and theory in each social
formation engenders its own tolerable falsehoods.*

—KWAME ANTHONY APPIAH

*Si la mémoire est une source imparfaite pour l'historien, ce sont
précisément ces imperfections et ces défaillances qui légitiment
la transformation de la mémoire en objet d'histoire.*

—ROBERT FRANK

The primary data at hand are texts in KiKongo, describing rituals. The descriptions are partly based on observation but mostly on memories of chiefship as it used to be, in the minds of the authors and their informants in the 1910s. The language in which memories are reported is rich and subtle, full of polyvalent references to the perceived qualities of plants, animals, and objects, giving a concrete sensuousness to political relations. The rituals themselves deploy the same devices in a reversed and complementary way; to a considerable extent, the material insignia and procedures of investiture, like the ingredients and rules of *minkisi,* reveal their meaning when they are recognized as words. Behind the rituals that mobilize chiefs and *minkisi* we feel the presence of fundamental existential concerns with life and death, mapped on a cosmology itself described in the familiar terms of male and female, village and forest, land and water, night and day. This cosmology constructs experiences of power which are therefore, as the philosophers say, "theory-laden."[1] It consists of "propositions" arranged in a hierarchy of descending generality, and consequently of decreasing scope and authority. The hierarchy is apparent in Kongo traditions, which begin with a universal origin, describe the basic principles of social organization, and eventually incorporate or explain the success or failure of this or that chief, the origin of this or that manifestation of power (Janzen and MacGaffey 1974, 88). The story as it unfolds organizes the world with respect to space, time, and power.

The historical importance of such a cosmology (or indeed any cosmology), with its particular array of spiritual forces representing potential causes of unusual events, is that it provides both the cognitive framework and the motivation for social action. The expression of cosmological assumptions, and the deployment of means to respond to them, are found in ritual. Rituals, including dances, *minkisi,* and chiefly titles (which, as we have seen, were specialized *minkisi*), readily diffuse from one area to another in Central Africa, and apparently have done so since time immemorial.[2]

Similar rituals of chiefly investiture are found here and there among the BaKongo and their neighbors, though with none of the regularity that would permit us to say without embarrassment "the BaKongo do this," or "the BaPende do that." The boundaries of these quasi-ethnic, quasi-linguistic identities owe such definition as they have to colonial ethnography and administrative action; the units of comparison cannot be "Kongo" and "Pende" but themes and practices irregularly distributed among Pende, Kongo, Suku, Yanzi, Tio, and others, all of whom share a similar cosmology and therefore dedicate their rituals to similar ends. All share the ideas that power is derived from the land of the dead "across the water"; that chiefs, as guardians of public order, are necessarily killers; that they are the nominees or representatives of descent groups; that the interests of local groups in collective well-being are tended by the priests of localized nature spirits or geniuses; that chiefs, as killers, are very much like witches, except that the latter are deemed to act solely in their personal, anti-social interests; and that healers and diviners, though in principle they mediate the powers of the dead to address individual problems, may also be witches, secretly.

Nor is this tradition limited to southwestern Congo. Describing the cultural unity of the Central African rain forests, Vansina writes, "Around 1850 the peoples of central Africa from Duala [southern Cameroon] to the Kunene river [southernmost Angola] and from the Atlantic to the Great Lakes shared a common view of the universe and a common political ideology. This included assumptions about roles, statuses, symbols, values and indeed the very notion of legitimate authority. . . . Obviously, in each case the common political ideology was expressed in slightly different views, reflecting the impact of different historical processes on different peoples. But the common core persisted" (Vansina 1989, 341).[3] He goes on to link this political constellation to a common tradition that must date back to the dispersal of the Western Bantu languages between 2,000 B.C. and about A.D. 500, and whose diffusion and adaptation he traces.

Cultural standards form a nested hierarchy such that those of less salience for the tradition as a whole ("profane") are more open to modification than those of higher order (relatively "sacred"). Tradition is neither static nor monolithic but "a moving continuity," a cybernetic hierarchy of conceptual and institutional commitments. "Continuity concerns basic choices, which, once made, are never again put in question," whether it be the central role in misfortune attributed to witches or the adoption of agriculture. "These fundamental acquisitions then act as a touchstone for proposed innovations." The course of history, then, is "the unfolding of the consequences of ancestral decisions or their concrete adaptation in the face of new circumstances. . . . [A] tradition chooses its own future; the basic choices are followed by subsidiary choices, which close certain options for the future and leave other options open" (Vansina 1991, 258–59).

The cultural unity of the rain forests, in both Central and West Africa, can be demonstrated not only internally but externally; neighboring cultural traditions or "civilizations" (for example, in Sahelian West Africa or in the Nile Valley) are grounded in very different cosmologies, ritual practices, and political institutions. The contrasts correspond roughly to linguistic distributions. A recognizable cultural unity characterizes the speakers of Western and some but not all Eastern Bantu languages. It is also found in the forested regions of coastal West Africa among Kwa-speaking peoples such as the Yoruba who speak languages related to Bantu in the larger Niger-Congo family.[4] Although linked to language, this tradition is not a linguistic phenomenon but is related to the history of the forests and the social organization of its inhabitants; it is not found among speakers of languages from other branches of Niger-Congo who live north of the forests, such as the Adamawa-Eastern division of Niger-Congo or Central Sudanic.

A cultural tradition is neither a continuously communicated body of lore nor a set of mental habits but an ongoing social practice which relies on, produces, and modifies the knowledge it needs (Barth 1987). A. Pickering, in his studies of scientific innovation, advances a useful model for the process by which a tradition is modified or developed; he calls it "the mangle of practice." Innovation, or cultural extension, is directed neither by pre-existent cultural standards, as the objectivists hold, nor by contingent social interests, as the relativists have it, but by the way in which an existing apparatus (techniques, procedures), an existing theory (witchcraft, *simbi* spirits, attributions of value to persons and objects), and a concept of the problem constrain the work of an innovator (political leader, diviner, farmer). "The mangle of practice" is the dialectic between resistance (when the desired goal is not reached) and accommodations to it in the course of the innovative search. A successful innovation is a satisfactory but potentially unstable association of procedure, theory, and goal, in the form of new knowledge. Pickering emphasizes that his perspective is thoroughly historical, not determinist; cultural standards and social interests are present, but are themselves subject to being re-shaped by the mangle (Pickering 1994).

The Land of the Dead: Journeys and Models

Chiefly traditions on the grand scale are anchored in history, since the "migrations" of which they speak follow paths that correspond to the major nineteenth-century trade routes, along which the movement of commerce was facilitated by ritual, political, and marital alliances. The migration stories can be mined for information about what nineteenth-century chiefs were like, but this process itself throws into relief the features of the stories which cannot be taken literally; the landscape traversed is a cosmographic and not simply a geographical one. Moreover, their internal logic, as well as their function, is inherently unhistorical, as Europe has understood history since the nineteenth century (Frank 1992). They are doubly exclusive, in that their function is to define the identity of groups in competition with one another and (within each group) to insist on the authority of the free over the slave members.

"The past" in tradition (*kinkulu*), unlike popular recollections of what, say, the missionary Westlind did in 1885, is not the same country as the historian's past. After Belgian Congo introduced "customary courts," traditions were treated as though they were meant to be verifiable records of past events, but to the elders who recite (and construct) them, they are products of revelation rather than of memory or research. Ethnographers collected traditions as potentially historical data, but a tradition recorded and printed out of its political context is as "cold" as an *nkisi* in a vitrine, and as difficult to interpret.[5]

Stories of the origin of *minkisi*, like those concerning the origin of chiefship, describe events on two scales. Some describe the original revelation of an *nkisi* to its first *nganga.* Others report, with historical verisimilitude, the place from which, like a chiefly title, the *nkisi* was derived, and to which the candidate *nganga* might repair for initiation. Both kinds of story describe contact with the dead; the supposed original contact is re-enacted in the consecration of a new *nganga* or chief. We readily class the initiatory trips of the *banganga* as "symbolic" or "metaphorical," though the land of the dead is real to believers, who may even search for it on a map. Nsemi, in his long essay on *minkisi,* comes close to recognizing the metaphorical nature of the land of the dead, and yet fails to do so in an interesting way: The *banganga,* he says, can descend beneath the sea and compose *minkisi* there for a period of a month or two. When they return they are all covered with red clay (*ndimba*), "although they themselves do not really cross over the water, *their minkisi alone do it"* (Cahier 391).

At the end of Chapter 4, I suggested that all places of traditional origin, including Mbanza Kongo, were cemeteries, local versions of the land of the dead, from which chiefly and magical powers were derived in the rites of investiture. I also held that the Nzadi ("large river") crossed by the migrants was a cosmological boundary between the visible and invisible worlds. This same boundary could be identified with the Congo, with the effect that, in the nineteenth century, Kongo chiefs, invested with the power of life, were forbidden to set eyes on it; nor might they encounter white men, considered to be visitors from the land of the dead. This taboo is perfectly consistent with the idea that at his initiation the chief contacted the dead; thereafter, the rule against contact in daylight itself emphasized his continued occult (nocturnal) role. The geographical reality of the Congo River (or of the Atlantic Ocean) does not preclude its cosmographic function.

Though we are inclined to accept the land of the dead without question as common sense, as a sort of "heaven," a place to store used souls, perhaps with comforting psychological value, quite a few African peoples manage to do without one. Why is there a land of the dead? Its principal characteristics are that it is ambiguously distant and that it is a source of enlightenment.

Metaphors and Mirrors

BaKongo speak of the land of the dead as analogous to the land of the living, that is, as similar to it in many respects though contrasted in others. The dead live in villages, they cook, cultivate, and have parties. On the other hand, in some ways, the land of the dead inverts the land of the living in a sort of mirror image; the dead are awake when we are asleep, their skin is white not black. The exact similarities and differences are a matter of debate; do the dead have children? do they become white on arrival, or only after a passage of time?

The land of the dead is elsewhere, but its specific location is situational; it is across or under the water, but any water will do—the Atlantic, the Congo River, or a local stream. Journeys to and fro insert space, establishing distance and thus difference; but the land of the dead, like "the Congo," is near at hand as well as far away; "the land of the dead is quite close to the village or away on the [grassfields], so that the invisible ones are able to mix with the living in their work" (LKIII, 15). Sometimes it is said to be in the forest, where the wild animals are the livestock of the dead; while hunting, one may experience a shift of vision and find himself in the village of the dead, whose chief wants to know why his cattle are being slaughtered. Funerals are a dangerous time because then the passage to the otherworld is open and the dead hang about. The land of the dead is also elsewhere in time; at night the dead occupy the houses of the living and cook on their fireplaces. In short, the relation between the worlds is in tension, sometimes near, sometimes far; now you see it, now you don't.[6]

Luc de Heusch comes close to the line of argument I am pursuing in an essay called "The King Comes from Elsewhere" in which he says, "The symbolic space with which we shall be concerned here is a world of elsewhere wherein a certain type of power is rooted" (De Heusch 1991). He notes that Rwanda kingship is based on a time-space formed by a central river separating the kingdom into two symbolically marked areas (116). Various Central African kings, drunken and otherwise, come from across the river. The Lunda chiefs among the Yaka, like Kongo chiefs, brought with them from their place of origin the sacred kaolin with which they are marked at their investiture and whose name, Mpemba, is also that of the land of the dead (Devisch 1988). Mpemba is also the name of the lake, the Upemba depression, from which the Luba traditionally came; Luba kings re-enact this journey when in the course of their initiation they repair to a lake where their candidacy is tested by "white" spirits (Petit 1995). The king, possessed by these spirits, is responsible for the prosperity of his realm, although he also derives violent powers from his patrilineal ancestors (Petit 1996, 357).

The ambiguous relationship between the worlds is analogous to that in all metaphor between literal meaning and its correspondence with an experience that the metaphor illuminates. A metaphor begins by surprising us with new insights, but gradually merges with ordinary language; at the limit the tension between the two parts of the analogy, the sense that a metaphor is present at all, tends to disappear. The quality of "tension" in metaphor, the way it both fits ordinary experience and yet stands apart from it ("now you see it, now you don't"), means that the use of it is not a simple, static structure of illustrative analogy but a hesitant process of inquiry, aided by memory and imagination.[7]

Comments on the land of the dead, or the realm of the dead which is nighttime, usually include statements about "seeing." Mpemba means "white" and refers to the white clay with which chiefs and *banganga* are marked with circles around the eyes so that they may see the invisible. BaKongo say, "The dead see more clearly than we do"; with them there are no obscurities, truth is evident, deception is revealed, and witches are not allowed into the village.[8] That is why the living can obtain power and knowledge from the dead by appropriate rituals but the dead do not need power or advice from us. Diviners used, and still use, mirroring devices in order to acquire knowledge from the otherworld. In times past they used the reflecting surface of a natural pool or of water in a pit dug for the purpose. In the nineteenth century, glass mirrors came into use, including those attached to *minkisi* as "eyes." Mirrors reflect not just the physical world but its essence and are thus a source of knowledge about it. To see something in a mirror is to see something which is not there, which is elsewhere; "a field of sight suggests always a beyond or beneath which is not seen" (Ong 1977, 122). Part of the personhood attributed to *minkisi* comes from the fact that one "sees" oneself in them, one is both observed and observer; it does not matter that in practice many *nkisi-*mirrors were obscured by sacrificial blood and other materials.

The metaphorical relationship between the worlds creates a conceptual space in which BaKongo inscribe models of their society. By enabling the living "to see more clearly," the dead provide them with a theory of their experiences. The Kongo anthropologist G. Buakasa, in his detailed ethnography of witchcraft (*kindoki*), speaks of it as existing at three levels: 1) an event, such as an illness, 2) an authoritative, explanatory scenario presented by the diviner (*nganga*) in the form of a discourse, and 3) a social situation full of conflicting interests (Buakasa 1973, 284–88). Buakasa describes the explanatory scenario as a "theoretical construction" of the event, drawing upon "a pre-existent system" which is thought of as "hidden" and thus not accessible to everyone. At its most general, this hidden system "explains" why life is not always ordinary. The explanation requires contributions of memory and imagination that the ritual participant's mind supplies, as it does for the incompletely seen objects that, in a museum context, aggressively displayed, become "African art" (Vogel 1997, 72).

I showed in Chapters 5 and 6 that *minkisi* are not portraits of spirits but statements of the relation between social and physical problems and the forces invoked to deal with them; elaborate ones are also, concretely, checklists of the rituals of invocation, including the procedures and the taboos to be observed. Chiefship investiture can be read in the same way. Chapters 8 and 9 showed how the candidate chief and his entourage were required to express in their behavior complex statements concerning the paradox of individual mortality and social continuity, and the dialectic of law and violence in social life. The most obvious example of the way in which a chief is deployed as a ritual object is the smoke-drying of his body, but the evidence is that he was already an "object" before his death. In Lutete's account, the ritual presents the chief as a mediator between the living and the dead, charged with protecting his people from social disorder. The chief's power of life, represented by his plantations of useful trees, is derived from the earth and the tutelary *simbi*. Because the earth is also a locus of death, the chief's relationship to it is ambivalent and loaded with taboos. The rituals as reported to us are also a dramatization of the relations between clans and between free persons and slaves. They incorporate a model of chiefship which is both sociological and philosophical, linking the political structure to the dimensions of time and space in the life of the community.[9] They are not so much magical efforts to bring about prosperity as, like the myths, reflections on the nature of things, or at least on how things ought to be.

Theory, Myth, and Ritual

It may seem overly generous or merely metaphorical to speak of Kongo "theory." R. Horton prudently says, "It is certainly wise to insist that, in using the concept of 'theory' in the translation and interpretation of alien thought, we exercise great care" (Horton 1993, 132). Horton's own, well-known view (the "Similarity Thesis") is that African traditional thought is like science in being a system for the explanation, prediction, and control of space-time events (Horton 1993). He says that this conclusion results simply from taking the statements of traditional thought at face value. As we have seen, *nkisi* Mbola, for example, purports to explain, predict, and control rotting of parts of the body; as a theory it may be defective, but its intention is "scientific."

Support for Horton's point of view comes from philosophers of science, who have shown that in practical reality science frequently fails to live up to its own preferred image of itself as a rigorously analytical procedure. On the other hand, critics have written a library of objections to Horton's thesis. They say, among other things, that elements of folklore lack the rigor and testability expected of theory; their content is vague and variable and they are not subject to sustained debate among experts. Ideas about how to explain, predict, and control are universal, but that does not make us all scientists. Horton himself has reviewed and replied to his critics; it is not necessary to go over the ground again, but it may be suggested that his case would be much stronger if he had compared traditional African thought not with natural science but with social science.[10] Experts in both fields give at least lip service to the idea that their procedures and findings are subject to testing. Both are ambiguously authoritative; both the social scientist and the diviner are invoked competitively by the parties to judicial and political disputes. The public is often scornful of particular branches or practitioners of the discipline, but still buys the product in considerable quantities, in spite of the lack of clear evidence that it has any definite value.

Horton himself raises an objection to his thesis to which he confesses that he has no good answer. It is this: The thesis asserts that religious doctrine, saying for example that spirits cause disease, must be taken literally, but that scholars cannot take literally religious narrative, that is, myth. It is not right, however, to apply evidential criteria inconsistently (366). Much depends here on what one understands by "literal." Stories of migration do not correspond "literally" to geographical reality, nor are many of the incidents embedded in them credible as historical events, but they offer cognitive models closely resembling those of social science. In Chapter 4 I suggested that traditions telling, for example, how the chief and his followers crossed the river in nine canoes should be read as models of the contrast between social disorder and an ideal order of right government, right marriage, and right eating. Another folk narrative anticipates the theory of the anthropologist Meillassoux about how elders manage to control their cadets (MacGaffey 1986a, 27). Some stories, such as that concerning *nkisi* Ndundu (Chapter 3, translation exercise #3), can be read either as an account of an origin of the *nkisi* in the remote past (the journey of the *nganga* to the land of the dead) or as a script for the *nganga's* initiation (secluded in a special enclosure) in real time. Such narratives are not simply fantastical, and probably should not even be called religious; the objection to the thesis may not be as strong as it appears to be.[11]

In a sustained critique of the idea that tradition provides models for social action, P. Boyer points out that the idea of a "cultural model" presupposes a kind of text containing information and conceals the fact that "tradition" (such as *kinkulu*) is an interactive event (Boyer 1990). It is only authentic when it is spoken ex cathedra, as it were, by a qualified person (for example, a headman authorized by his maternal ancestors) on an appropriate occasion (a dispute between lineages). Tradition is defined by its occurrence as an event, not by its content. Boyer goes on to criticize the common anthropological assumption that observed events are held together by underlying worldviews, collective representations, and cultural models. Where are these located, and why should we assume that in the recitation of them all members of the audience hear the same thing? The different social statuses, and thus the different competencies of members of the audience, are displayed in the interactive event which is the recitation of tradition; it is essential to the idea of tradition that there be "those who know, those who don't, and those who know who knows what" (Boyer 1990, 20).

These features of tradition do not, in fact, disqualify the idea of a cultural model; they draw attention to its political character. Boyer has allowed himself to accept a folk assertion about truth which is itself a political move. Contest is built into traditions and rituals, in the way, for example, that chiefs and their powers are defined *in opposition to* witches and magicians. As normative models, traditions are invoked in an effort to impose order; we should notice by whom and for whom they provide prediction, explanation, and control. Their function may be to obscure reality rather than explain it (Buakasa 1973, 290), but we need not therefore deny the cognitive component in the models. The active question for the BaKongo is, Whose *kinkulu* is true?, but nobody questions *kinkulu* itself nor the powers that it legitimates. In addition to the cognitive component we have to respect the *motivational* component precisely because the models are at least latently political.

A curious inversion of Horton's thesis can be found in Lévi-Strauss's view of myth as a product of the intellect, whereas ritual is a response to "anxiety." Myth consists of words; ritual, of gestures and the manipulation of objects. This polarity is what has to be explained, although Lévi-Strauss recognizes that there are intermediate forms between myth and ritual (Lévi-Strauss 1981, 669). Myth is eminently scientific, he says, in that it creates order by imposing divisions and contrapositions on experience. It is interested in the discrete; the resulting structures are scientific because they are already present in nature. The essence of ritual, on the other hand, is a desperate attempt to re-establish the continuity of lived experience; it multiplies fine distinctions to the point that it almost negates division and contrast entirely, restoring continuity, as for example by endlessly repeating the same formula (Lévi-Strauss 1981, 672–75).

Lévi-Strauss goes on to cite Dumézil's demonstration that in archaic Roman religion we find, on the one hand, a small number of major divinities, arranged in a structure of grandly distinct oppositions to one another; on the other, a multitude of barely distinguishable minor divinities assigned to various phases of ritual. He notes that the same hierarchy of divinities occurs in African religions which he does not name, but the example of Kongo *minkisi* is clearly appropriate (as also would be the *orishas* of the Yoruba and the *bocio* of the Fon). He explains this organization into higher and lower divinities as the result of the struggle between myth and ritual. "A bastardization of thought, brought about by the constraints of life," ritual encourages the illusion that it is possible to return from the discontinuous to the continuous (Lévi-Strauss 1981, 674–75).

Whether or not such relations between myth and ritual reflect the struggles of the mind, they clearly have a political dimension. Kongo myths have the function of establishing contrasts between each exogamous, landowning clan-section and its competitors and between the free, who can tell such stories, and the enslaved, who by definition are disqualified from doing so. Important *minkisi,* those most closely related to chiefship and the exercise of power, are accompanied by stories of origin and references to controlling distinctions between masculine and feminine, the above and the below, punishment and healing, war and childbirth. In practice, all these are invidious distinctions, normative claims held against one party by another, and resisted accordingly. In the struggles of everyday life and the multitudinous practices of trivial *minkisi* whose performance is accompanied by a minimum of words, these values confusedly merge and emerge, so that the motivated distinctions and contrapositions of the Kongo political mind are constantly denied, as they are in historical reality.

Historical Reflections

Traditions of the chiefs and their rituals are rooted to some degree in history and practice, but we have already seen that it is difficult to tell where practice ends and imagination begins. G. Dupré, who reports the following story widespread among the BaBembe in north Kongo, treats it as the biography of a historical individual, born about 1815, who as the outstanding magically endowed leader (*nkanyi*) among the BaBembe brought peace and regional integration to the country in the turbulent years 1860–1870. The historical evidence, however, is that no such pacification took place until the French occupation in 1908.

> Mwa Bukulu in Nkila, on the Mouyondzi plateau (which is said to be the original settlement in that region) belonged to the clan Mimbundi. His father was Mimandu, the clan of the first occupants. Mimbundi arrived later, from the same direction as Mimandu, and took over the chiefship because they were more numerous. When Mwa Bukulu was born, he was taken in charge by Ntsakala Kongo, of his father's clan, who bathed the infant in water drawn that same morning, wrapped him in a cloth, and made a raft for him out of three banana trunks. Then he took him to the pool called "the Sun and the Moon," and put him on the raft to spend the night on the surface of the water. The following morning, the father accompanied Ntsakala Kongo to the pond, where they found the infant, his body covered with spots of black, white, and red.[12] When he grew up, Mwa Bukulu married and fathered a child, but he also developed breasts like a woman and could nurse a child, healing it by so doing. He could cause or stop the rain, for the benefit of both agriculture and warfare (flintlock muskets do not work in the rain). His nephew Mbanga Ntsika kidnapped unsuspecting travelers; Mwa Bukulu, though not himself a war leader, protected Mbanga from reprisals by bringing on a drought, threatening the enemy with famine. He became famous as a healer and peacemaker. After his death the cloth-wrapped effigy (*muziri* [*muzidi*]) containing his bones became a powerful rain-shrine in Nkila, the religious center of the BaBembe to this day. (Dupré 1985, 121–33)

There may well have been such a person as Mwa Bukulu, but the names of the places and of the clans may be the only factually historical elements in the story; every other element belongs in the stereotypical picture of the invested chief who passes the test of spiritual approval at the *simbi* pool or cave under the supervision of the *simbi* priest from the affinal or partner clan. The first incident of the story is cognate with Babutidi's account (Chapter 4) of Ma Nsundi and Ma Luangu. The myths and rituals of chiefship, though they vary from place to place and no doubt from performance to performance, all presuppose a certain cosmology, which they enact and confirm. This cosmology is a "theory" of real life, tidier and more intelligible than actual experience. In historical truth, it changes as the society changes, and in so changing reveals its hierarchical structure, in that lower-level elements disappear or change first. A world-view is not a single, take-it-or-leave-it proposition but a hierarchy of propositions with varying degrees of salience.[13] In the seventeenth century a hierarchy of *bisimbi,* each with its *kitomi,* corresponded to a hierarchy of political domains. In nineteenth-century Mayombe there were great spirits such as Lusunzi (in various local incarnations) but also lesser ones incorporated in ordinary *minkisi* or simply present here and there in streams and rocks. In the late twentieth century the idea of *bisimbi* persists, but with no sense of hierarchy; the idea is there, but its content is impoverished. New *minkisi* emerged and died out during the nineteenth century, as no doubt they had before; in the late twentieth they are still very much present in Kongo life, but only as furtive charms and medicines for individuals; none are carried about in litters like great chiefs. Chiefs have disappeared altogether, except as a memory partially attached to presidents and politicians. The basic ideas still reign, among professors as well as peasants: that power in this world is obtained by occult negotiations in the other, and that it can be am-bivalently used for private or public good.

The various stories of the origin of chiefships and of *minkisi* form a metonymic chain, linking the experiences of the present to a remote "past" which is simply a statement of the most general conditions of human existence. Rituals of investiture, divination, and invocation, by applying that knowledge metaphorically, shape subjec-tive experience as an experience of power. Chief and *nganga* are invested with their particular powers by being placed in contact with the body of the predecessor, the grave of the founder, the place of origin, Mbanza Kongo. Myths of origin are templates for investitures in which body parts (bones, hair, nails) of officeholders from the begin-ning to the present are (supposedly) incorporated in the cemetery of the chiefs, the "basket of the ancestors," reliquaries, the *nkisi*-object. At the low end of the hierarchy we find mundane events (an illness, an "accident") which carry meaning only because some ritual process, some qualified expert able to see hidden causes, situates them in the scheme of things. Metaphor as usually described by rhetoricians assumes that metaphor moves from the known to the unknown; to the peoples of this region, how-ever, both worlds are real, both belong to the same order of reality (De Boeck 1994, 467). The relationship is even reversed: "witchcraft" is known, but the facts of human motivation and action are unknown until the diviner completes his task and his analysis is accepted.

The question of how to distinguish "fact" from "model" is central to the use of oral tradition as historical data. What counts in tradition, however, is its form and its authoritative recitation in a forensic context; the content is highly variable and primar-ily of "literary" value. Memorably dramatic episodes, couched in evocative language, become quasi-independent modules that drift from one context to another. The stories of the dancing hero who cleverly avoids a pit trap, the animal divided into four pieces in a situation of conflict, the woman who wanted to be chief but menstruated at the wrong moment, the hero whose destiny was guided by a magical rubber ball, the young men whose rebellion failed when they had to admit they did not know the secrets of the elders, and the rainbow serpent appear here and there from the Atlantic coast to Zambia but are not uniformly known to any population.[14]

What history can be read from these stories? Dupré reads the story of Mwa Bukulu as the record of a profound social transformation. Yoder, following the methodological example of J. C. Miller and others, treats the story of the woman who menstruates at the wrong time and therefore cannot be chief as a "cliché" to be taken, not literally as an account of a historical event, but as a historically credible representation of a class of events which amounted to a shift in Kanyok society from matriliny to patriliny (Yoder 1992, 43). Considerable doubt must be cast on this interpretation by the fact that the matrilineal BaKongo—*some* BaKongo—tell the same story (it was told to me in Mbanza Manteke in 1965, and it is also the opening event in one of the dynastic myths of Ngoyo). Yoder believes that the supposed structural shift is confirmed by the fact that the chief's closest officers among the Kanyok are matrilateral relatives—a survival from earlier matriliny? By that reasoning, the BaKongo, whose chiefs and headmen are supervised by patrifilial Children and Grandchildren, were once patrilineal—highly unlikely. In short, we are as yet far from discovering a method for dealing with this kind of data, although the distribution of the stories may have historical implications.

Tradition and the Kongo Kingdom

The earliest date that can be inferred from traditions recorded in the Cahiers is about 1840; this eighty-year span matches the one I was able to infer from traditions I heard in the 1960s. The political-economic system partly revealed in the Cahiers probably began to come into existence in the late seventeenth century, reaching its full development north of the Congo only in the nineteenth. What preceded it? How much about the remoter past can be inferred from the nineteenth-century material?

In various parts of Central Africa, even where no strongly centralized political unit with its own professional historians exists, it has been possible to recover historical indications going back as far as about A.D. 1000. The Kongo Kingdom, which may have come into existence in the thirteenth century and lasted, at least in name, until the end of the nineteenth, has preserved nothing much of its origin besides the legend of Mutinu Wene, supposed founder of the kingdom, despite relatively abundant documentation for the late fifteenth century onward.

It seems obvious, however, that even the story of Mutinu Wene is another myth in cosmographic setting that explains the origins of ordered society: the ambitious young man who kills his father's sister (thus breaking his relationship to the clan of his father, normally his patron) and crosses the river in canoes with his many followers, among whom he divides the new territory. It is potentially of historical interest that the migration should have gone from north to south, which was no doubt the route of the original Bantu-speaking inhabitants, and that the story should mention Vungu in particular. Yet even this story may be no more than an item from the common stock of Central African folktales; similar stories with different characters occur in Soyo and in the Niari valley. The tale of Mutinu Wene is first reported only in 1624, at a time when the kings were asserting claims to absolute authority, which a tradition of a violent conqueror seemed to legitimate. This version of the kingship was opposed by another, which emphasized the consent of the governed (Thornton 1983, 117–18). These opposed views of the nature of ideal government are current in Kongo today and may well have been complementary elements of an ideology of government from ancient times.[15] Apart from the story of Mutinu Wene, there is no evidence of the origin of the kingdom in conquest. A simple failure of visitors to record whatever traditions were told in Mbanza Kongo in the sixteenth century is less likely as an explanation for the silence than the fact that Afonso I Mvemba Nzinga (1506–1543) in effect re-founded the kingdom with Christianity as its legitimating cult, thus perhaps rendering earlier traditions irrelevant (Hilton 1985, 62).

Besides the (recent?) tradition of conquest, the conjunction of descent (represented by the royal cemetery) and locality (represented by a *simbi* priest) is one of the few features of modern investitures also identifiable in the old Kingdom. In the fifteenth century, the investing priest was the Mani Vunda, who had a special relationship to significant stones.[16] The only indication of violence attributed to the office (and tenuous, at that) is that the king who was baptized in 1491 won a battle against "rebellious subjects" apparently as part of the ritual, not of baptism, as understood by the Portuguese, but of investiture with new powers, as understood by the BaKongo. In the mid-sixteenth century Andrew Battell reported, "In Cases Criminall they proceed but slenderly, for they doe very hardly and seldome condemne any man to death."

In the seventeenth century the role and the rituals are described in more detail; the royal regalia conferred by Na Vunda included an iron chain, indicating a *simbi* function. In the provinces the investing priest, the *kitomi,* "god of the earth," was associated with rocks, water, and special trees (thus, a *simbi* priest). On the other hand, his role included several features which in the nineteenth century were attributed to the chief.[17] The *kitomi* was not allowed to marry, although he had female companions (Thornton 1983, 59). "In some provinces, where superstition is at its height, it is believed that the *kitomi,* because of the excellence of his character, may never die a natural death; otherwise, everyone would die and the country would be destroyed. To prevent such a calamity, when the *kitomi* becomes ill and his illness appears to be fatal, the chosen successor takes a big stick or a cord and sends the invalid immediately to the other world, and thus by violent death exorcises the dire prediction" (Cavazzi de Montecuccolo 1965, v. 1:92). Thus the role of the *kitomi,* "in some provinces," included features attributed, in some of our manuscripts, to the nineteenth-century chief. There are no indications that the king himself or any provincial governor was treated in this way. There is no record in the sixteenth century that anybody was smoke-dried although, according to Hilton, by the end of the seventeenth century the Angolan BaKongo had developed the practice of taking the dried bodies of nobles to Mbanza Kongo (known at the time as "Mpemba") to be buried in one of the royal cemeteries; the burial itself required the participation of a Catholic priest (Hilton 1985, 216). In the 1850s, the king's body also was dried before burial. In short, only some of the same elements we find later can be identified in the kingship, and they are combined in different ways at different times.

A number of features of the Kongo kingdom in the sixteenth century also occurred among the BaKuba at about the same time. Proto-Kuba arriving from the north brought with them the Mongo pattern of chiefly insignia, including the leopardskin, the stock of chalk for investiture, and the legitimating role of localized nature spirits (*ngesh*). The priest of the nature spirits, who played a necessary role in investiture, was the head of a clan supposedly descended from the conquered autochthonous population; he was the guardian of certain royal charms and made offerings on behalf of the chiefdom to its tutelary *ngesh* at a river or lake (Vansina 1978, ch. 11).

At the end of the seventeenth century, while the BaKuba (Bushoong) were developing a new, centralized, and splendid kingship, partly as a result of Kongo influence associated with expanding western trade, the old Kongo Kingdom was replaced by a different, decentralized political system associated with new patterns in trade and a new social structure (Broadhead 1979; Vansina 1992). Perhaps we should see the important caesura as occurring in 1715 when Pedro IV reconstituted the kingdom with institutions which, according to Thornton, differed little from those described by nineteenth- and twentieth-century ethnographers (Thornton 1983, 117).[18] Instead of being grouped in domains governed and taxed by officials appointed by the king, from about 1700 onward local communities of kin-related individuals were incorporated in chiefships of varying size—some very small—each dominated by a particular matrilineal clan to which the chief belonged. In some areas away from the nodes of the trade network, it would be more accurate to speak of government by consortia of local clan-sections. In this new system, the old capital, Mbanza Kongo, as an important chiefship among others, dominated the part of northern Angola intersected by the principal routes between Mpumbu and the Angolan coast, including Luanda.

It is tempting to think of the transformation of the kingdom as the removal of a hierarchical superstructure imposed on an older, simpler, kin-based organization which survived. It may well be, however, that what is usually regarded as the salient feature of Kongo social structure, matrilineal descent, is itself relatively recent, or rather, a recent modification of a very old form of organization widespread in Central Africa. Throughout the rain forest, social structure is fundamentally bilateral, although in some groups along the southern edge it moved in a matrilineal direction (that is, matrilineal nodes emerged as relatively substantial, corporate elements in the bilateral network), to constitute the so-called "matrilineal belt," extending from the Atlantic to the Indian Ocean.[19] This shift probably took place in large part as a result of the slave trade and the demographic changes it induced; slavery had been the economic base of the Kongo capital from the beginning, but the Atlantic trade encouraged the formation of groups descended in the female line (Thornton 1980; Thornton 1983, 17–23). From very early times, the basic unit of production and competition in the rain forest was the bilateral "House," a local group resident in its own village or village section and led by a big man, an ambitious leader (Vansina 1991, 75). Political and economic competition focused on control of women as both laborers and producers of future labor. In the simplest situation, a group could only acquire women as wives by ceding women to other groups in exchange, or acknowledging a debt to be repaid in the next generation (patrilateral cross-cousin marriage). No doubt it was possible to acquire extra members by force or fraud, but in the absence of a means of monopolizing force no group could permanently outdo others by hoarding women. It is not necessary for this kind of exchange that the parties be organized as descent groups at all.

Well documented though the early history of Kongo is, it has not been possible to verify (nor categorically to deny) the existence of matrilineal descent before the seventeenth century. The specific effects, not of slavery (which already existed) but of commercial demand on both coasts, induced demographic and structural changes that included the expansion of matrilineal elements. From the sixteenth century onward, the demand for slaves on the coast generated a steady movement of captives from the interior. At the coast the European slavers preferred men, destined for work on American plantations, but because women were the source of "wealth in people" (*mbongo bantu*), inland groups receiving slaves preferred to retain women.[20] It became possible to acquire women without having to give other women in exchange; both the male and the female children of enslaved women were themselves slaves, but only the females were potential sources of future wealth. Within the bilateral framework, woman-holding corporations expanded; the presumptively perpetual character of matrilineal descent groups as corporations simply means that they claimed authority over their estates in women from generation to generation.[21]

Chief and Priest

The development of matrilineal features in social structure can be attributed in some considerable measure to the common effects of the Atlantic trade in certain areas of Central Africa, but the ideas and rituals of chiefship cannot be reduced to this factor even though chiefs were the primary organizers and beneficiaries of the trade. Chiefship was in some degree both a form of centralized authority and a ritual complex. The amount of real power supporting the chief's authority varied with his personal ability and with the secular resources available; the chief's authority, established by ritual, was at least partly independent of his real power. Ritual elements could be invented or diffused, at different times and from different directions. Conceptual oppositions, between the powers of life and death and between the legitimate and illegitimate use of such powers, constituted the ideological tradition that for thousands of years guided the peoples of the rain forests in their southerly dispersal (Vansina 1991). For them, as Vansina says, "The quintessence of leadership was the leopard" (74), but the legitimate power to kill was always in perpetual tension with the illegitimate death-dealing of witches and the elusive mysteries of fertility and prosperity (MacGaffey 1972; Mac-Gaffey 1986b, 180–87). Such a tradition should be regarded not as a set of mistaken notions but as a kind of social science, a working theory of human experience. The land of the dead, from which all exceptional powers are supposed to come, provides a stock of vital metaphors made immediate and real by the fact that they are simultaneous with experience itself. There is no reason to assume that these metaphors are worked out to the same extent or with the same results in all times and places where the tradition is domiciled (Barth 1987, 80).

As a kind of collective *nkisi*, a Kongo chief exerted imaginary as well as real powers (the distinction is mine) on behalf of himself, the local oligarchy which nominated and installed him, and perhaps also of his ordinary followers. How much "real" power any particular chief wielded evidently depended on his or her personal qualities and resources as well as on those of the supporting community and its economic and political environment. As the central object in the continuous performance of his office, he also, by his insignia and the taboos binding upon himself and others, actively expressed "reflections" on life and death, the transient and the permanent in social experience. The contrast between youth, wetness, and organic vitality, on the one hand, and age, dryness, and perdurability on the other, may be universal, but the expression of such ideas in treatments of the body of the chief is not. In Manianga, in adjacent areas south of the Congo, and in northwestern Angola, the body of a deceased chief was smoke-dried, as we have seen, "to give it the perdurance of stones." Lutete, in northeastern Mayombe, denies the use of a fire for the purpose, but the body was nonetheless dried, and "transformed" into a *simbi* stone at burial. In Mukimbungu, the dying chief was strangled, and it was announced, not that he had died, but that he had "declined" (see Chapter 8). Among the eastern BaKongo, when the chief was near death, two men placed his spear across his throat and killed him by kneeling on it. A finger joint and clippings of hair and nails were removed to place in the ancestral basket, *lukobi lu bakulu*. The body was not smoke-dried but it was exposed, leaning against a rock, for as long as a year and was eventually buried in secret, at night (Van Wing 1959, 119). ("Leaning" against rocks or trees occurs in rites of investiture; it is apparently meant to associate the chief with their perdurance.)

The distribution of particular ritual forms of chiefship in southwestern Congo hints at histories of diffusion, some recent and some very old, of which they are residues. Comprehensible within, and to some extent legitimated by, common assumptions, the various local traditions in ritual practice have a high degree of compatibility with one another and can be read as allomorphic, or as "saying the same thing" in different ways (Ceyssens 1984, 86). In Mayombe the details of *minkisi* give clear indications of a "cultural current" along the coast, from Gabon to northern Angola, mediated no doubt by BaVili (Loango) traders. Other routes of cultural diffusion run through Mayombe to and from the east. The name "Nsundi" comes from a northern province of the old kingdom located around the Manyanga market. The Nsundi trade network probably extended to Loango on the coast from very early times; its eastern extension went well beyond Manyanga and Mpumbu to the Kwilu River (Martin 1972; Vansina 1974). Across this distance, the terms for markets, market days, and currencies originate in the west (Vansina 1991, 162). Angolan Kongo, commercially integrated by routes that ran from Mpumbu and the Kwilu to Mbanza Kongo and the Angolan coast, showed a degree of difference in commercial organization, social structure (not adequately studied), and ritual features. In the north a chief's central place is likely to be called *nganda* (probably of eastern origin), whereas in Kongo south of the Congo *mbanza* is more usual. In the north, a village is *bwala;* in the south, *vata.* The term *nkita* for nature spirit is generally northern; it recurs farther east, among the Tio and into the lower Kasai, as *nkira.* The village charm *nkinda* has a similar distribution. From west to east, intriguing variations are reported on the relation between the violent chief and the benevolent forces, represented by the priest, of the nature spirit of his domain.

Yanzi

Among the BaYanzi of the lower Kwilu, the rituals of chiefship reflect the same ambiguous distribution of authority as in Kongo. The chief's domain, *mpu,* is a territory owned by the lineage which allegedly was the first to occupy it; the inhabitants include the owners' patrifilial Children and Grandchildren, as well as its slaves, clients, and in-marrying women. The tutelary spirit of such a domain is the Lebwi (various spellings), its priest the Nga Lebwi. Lebwi is manifested in whirlwinds, twins, and other abnormalities of nature, which are themselves *lebwi.* Like *bisimbi,* such spirits live in forests, watercourses, or large rocks; the ground near these habitations is called *Lulom lebwi* (cognate with KiK. *Lulombe,* investiture site). They are responsible for communal hunting luck, prosperity, and fertility, they regulate sexuality and reproduction, and are said to be the origin of all *minkisi.* Lebwi brings its servant information and instruction in dreams; it has a shrine in the forest and an alias in the village in the form of a bark box under the bed of the priest.

The power of Nga Lebwi is contrasted with that of the chief, who is identified with the leopard and may not be invested until a leopard has been killed, indicating that his deceased predecessors accept his candidacy. The dead leopard is believed to be, in fact, his now twice-deceased predecessor; at his own death his nails will be cut and his teeth broken to render him less dangerous in his leopard phase. Chiefs and members of the owning lineage are buried in their own cemetery, but any living member of the chief's clan who approaches will be smitten with leprosy; the Grandchildren conduct the burial. Whereas the dead Kongo chief might be divided into "wet" and "dry" portions, buried separately, Yans practice accords an exclusively dry burial to the chief and a wet one to Nga Lebwi. The chief's body is put with much cloth in a large basket and dried over a fire for nine days; during this time it does not rot, thanks to certain mushrooms placed under the body. It would be a serious matter if the body were to rot, because any liquid that drained from it would render the earth sterile. The chief might not be buried if there were rain. Nga Lebwi, on the other hand, is buried in a swamp (De Plaen 1974).

After the requisite death of a leopard, the chief-designate goes into seclusion for a period of up to four months. Although we do not hear what happens during this time, there is no indication that he is invested with powers of life; on the contrary, they are reserved to the priests of Lebwi. Whereas the chief's charm, which is his link with his ancestors, contains earth from the cemetery, that of Nga Lebwi comes from the forest shrine. At his investiture the chief gives white chalk to the Nga Lebwi, who at his own investiture gives red chalk to the chief. Nga Lebwi must have nothing to do with litigation. The chief takes care to dissociate himself from the use of fetishes as a means to private profit, although he may make use of an Nkosi as an instrument of retributive justice (Swartenbroeckx 1969, 208–209).

It is said that in the past a Yans chief at his investiture strengthened the royal bracelet by using his witchcraft power to kill several people; he might also sacrifice a slave, pouring his blood on the bracelet. We recognize here the killing "by day and by night" that Kongo chiefs supposedly performed on the like occasion. The bracelet, however, came from the Lunda, in the east, probably in the late eighteenth century. Although there is no report that the priest, Nga Lebwi, was not allowed to die naturally, in other respects he resembles the *kitomi* or earth-priest of seventeenth-century Kongo and nineteenth-century Loango.[22]

Yaka-Lunda

In his discussion of chiefship among the BaYaka, a group to the east of the Ba-Kongo and lingistically very close to them, Devisch notes a division of traditions between the chiefs, said to be descendants of Lunda immigrants from still farther east, and the autochthonous people (Devisch 1988).[23] The Yaka chief's domestic life is said to display Kongo (that is, pre-Lunda) traditions, but "as a political title-holder he exhibits Lunda traditions" (266). The rulership insignia said to date from the immigration, perhaps in the eighteenth century, include a sword, white clay, a leopard pelt, two small anvils, and a copper arm-ring. All of these and more elements of Lunda-Yaka chiefly ritual appear in Kongo, all the way to the coast; they are therefore not specifically Lunda, and must antedate the Lunda migration. In none of the Laman manuscripts is there any mention of a new fire ceremony on the occasion of an investiture, but such a ceremony occurred in Loango in the nineteenth century, and in the seventeenth it was performed by the *kitomi* for the new duke of Nsundi (de Montesarchio 1976, 213). The two "anvils" (iron spikes) which warn the ruler of the approach of witches also occur in seventeenth-century Kongo, and were still in use in eastern Kongo in the 1930s (Mertens 1942); elsewhere they were replaced by the spikes driven into Nkondi. The elaborate, hierarchical Yaka cosmography of chiefly origins and authority has no counterpart in Kongo, where as we have seen there is no social division between "autochthons" and "invaders."

Yaka rites of chiefly investiture reverse the role assignments found among the BaKongo. Tsakala, the investing priest among the patrilineal [?]Yaka, represents the chief's maternal line, whereas among the matrilineal Kongo he was likely to represent the Fathers; in both cases he is associated with the reproductive potency of the land. In other respects, the investitures are similar. The Yaka candidate for office (*n-yaadi,* cf. KiKongo *mbyaazi*) "sleeps on the ground"; the vine *n'ngubanguba* is wound around the initiates in the enclosure, its many nodules signifying the expectation "that the chief may beget many subordinates." The sexuality merely implied in Kongo rituals at this point is made explicit in erotic dances. Formerly the candidate was required to sacrifice a nephew; nowadays a black goat will do, evoking "the killing with the sword of rulership" (279). The success of the investiture was tested by a collective hunt, and the planting of trees expressed the relationship of the office to the ancestors [what ancestors?]. The Yaka investiture, like that described by Matunta (in Chapter 9), transfers to the nation the basic metaphor of the palm tree (267). The chief's bodily transitoriness is "concealed through a mystifying cult" (261), but whereas in Kongo, according to Diafwila, the cord of strangulation is passed through a hole in the back wall of his house, among the Yaka the chief's insignia take this route. Among eastern (Kasai) Pende, the chief's body itself is taken for burial in the same way (Strother 1993, 162). The back of the house is everywhere associated with women's activities and with death, represented by the household garbage pit.[24]

The Aluund (Lunda) of the upper Kwango, whose political structure is much more developed than anything found in Kongo in the nineteenth century, make explicit, as it were, many associations which remain latent in Kongo thought (that is, the symbolic "grammar" implies that they could be made, but evidence is lacking that they are in fact made). Direct correspondences include the following. The paramount chief, the Nzav, combines the functions of political head, *mwiin mangaand,* with that of "lord of the soil" (*mwiin mavw*), responsible for fertility and prosperity (De Boeck 1994). These functions are thought of as masculine and feminine, respectively, and Nzav is also thought of as both the father of his people and "the ultimate maternal uncle." Elders, and still more so the Nzav, are thought to be like trees, firmly rooted in the earth; by his increasing immobility, a senior man is also rooted in the ancestral past, and exemplifies "the ideologically important 'unchanging continuity' of the societal order, against the transformations of society as it is lived in everyday life." Elaborate rituals to seclude, control, and protect the body of the Nzav, who is not allowed to show disease or old age, make it into an object, an unchanging entity, secluded, orificeless, and institutional, situated outside ordinary human and social exchange, as De Boeck puts it. The royal bracelet is believed to prevent the Nzav from engendering; "he sleeps on the ground," on a bed without legs. Mediating between male and female, he becomes god on earth, *nzaamb paansh,* a title identical with that of the king of Kongo in the fifteenth century.

Within an area of considerable linguistic and cultural homogeneity, we find it impossible to identify distinct clusters of ritual practices that could be listed as separate political systems. The data, imperfect though they are, indicate, or perhaps "hint at," a kind of layering of items diffused at different historical periods. For example, the Lunda *lukanu* bracelet, with the sacrifices offered to it, seems to have reached the Lower Kwilu in the nineteenth century. Other items which the Lunda may have brought with them from the east were already present as a result of some much earlier movement which need not be thought of, however, as a migration. The "basket of the ancestors" is found in slightly variant forms among Kongo and Teke-speaking peoples within reach of the Niari valley and Mpumbu, its diffusion associated, it would seem, with trade developments in Loango in the eighteenth century. Such innovations were readily absorbed into the ritual practices of the communities they reached because they were compatible with much older and more fundamental principles diffused throughout the area perhaps 2,000 years ago. In eastern Congo, the separation of powers between earth spirits and dynastic spirits is characteristic of both Lunda and Luba polities. Luba royal initiation by contact with nature spirits and *mpemba* is specifically close to Kongo practice, and the ambiguous reference in such initiations to an original sacred foundation, the "Luba empire," parallels the reference to Mbanza Kongo in Kongo tradition (Petit 1996; Roberts and Roberts 1996, ch. 5).

Ambiguities of Violence

The rituals of investiture identify the Kongo chief with the leopard, and some of them required him to perform public acts of exceptional violence: to kill his nephew, to hand over ten or more slaves to the investors, to sponsor dramatic public executions, and so on. How much of this violence in fact occurred? Why is it specified in some rituals but not all? All of it seems quite likely, except that the same text that speaks of slaves handed over "by day" mentions twice as many handed over "by night." There are eyewitness testimonies to enemy skulls displayed outside compounds, slaves murdered to seal agreements, and wrongdoers buried alive in the marketplace; it is a commonplace of the texts that chiefs "oppress and kill and make war upon other clans." Sculpted staffs and soapstone figures unambiguously celebrate the brutal capabilities of chiefs. How much of this violence was part of the history of the times rather than of the essence of chiefship? What is the relation between model and "fact"? During the First World War, when the Cahiers were being written, BaKongo were appalled to hear of the continuing slaughter in Europe; their own wars, being essentially divinatory ordeals or trials by combat, ended after the first casualties:

As soon as one or two people had died, they would halt and sound the *ngongi* so that the chiefs could negotiate, saying, "Put up your weapons!" Everyone returned to the village. When they were ready they beat the great *nkoko* drum; the chiefs sounded *ngongi* at all the entrances, and the war was over. Those responsible for the deaths accepted responsibility (*Yoso nda mfwidi bantu si batambula masumbu*) and paid the victor "thousands" (*mafunda,* cloth bundles or the equivalent) and slaves; if two men died, they paid two people and two thousand. In their wars few died. (Mato, 280; cf. Dupré 1985, 82–84)

This is not "war" in the usual meaning of the word but witchcraft continued by other means. The goal was neither the destruction of the enemy nor a high body count. Individual killers were neither glorified nor obliged to undergo purification. The troops were tested individually by a war *nkisi* before the battle, not for courage but for vulnerability; they were disqualified if they touched the legs of the *nganga's* wife as they passed under them in a symbolic birth. The protocol is consistent, however, with the fact that the warring "clans" were localized, voluntary associations dominated by particular matrilineages; they were neighbors, intermarried to some degree, and did not identify themselves as perpetual enemies.

In his introduction to a collection of essays on violence, David Riches remarks that the act of violence is always one of contested legitimacy, thus a sign of the presence of political competition (Riches 1986, 9). The essential personnel in the act of violence are the performer, the victim, and "the witness," that is, the audience whose judgment is sought with regard to the legitimacy of the event. Violence, whether "real," as in stabbing, or "imaginary," as by sorcery, is both highly visible and highly comprehensible; its performance requires little more than the resources of the human body (Riches 1986, 11). The properties of violence, unique among social acts, "make it highly appropriate both for practical (instrumental) and for symbolic (expressive) purposes: as a means of transforming the social environment (instrumental purpose) and dramatizing the importance of key social ideas (expressive purpose), violence can be highly efficacious." These two functions of violence correspond to the actual use of violence, as in war and kidnapping, and to its dramatization in chiefly myth and ritual. Clearly the two are not independent, but neither does the one follow from the other. Moreover, the specific content, certainly of ritual violence, and to a considerable extent also of practical violence, is culturally embedded; that is, it conforms to a particular tradition.

The "West" or the "modern" tends to be seen in the eyes of its native inhabitants as quintessentially civilized in part because they represent it as a domain of reasonable discourse from which violence is excluded; war is waged in *other* parts of the world, murderers are hidden away in jails. Violence is thus exceptional, deviant, the fault of others, although in the 1990s it became more difficult to sustain this comforting image. Fredrik Barth mentions the peculiar disparity in our culture between ethical principles supporting justice and security, and "the known existence of crime, perversity, and war." The codifiers of our theory of man live on the polite side of this dichotomy, while persons who pass across it are "subject to elaborate rites of brutalization or rehabilitation," in jail or the electric chair. In other societies, this privileged innocence is not possible. The New Guinea village Barth is writing about is "a world where attacker and victim were known to each other as social persons"; guests at festivals were known individually as the agents of specific acts of violence against their neighbors (Barth 1975, 144–45).

In her discussion of the Piaroa of Venezuela, Overing reports that they believe that all deaths are murders effected and also avenged by sorcery, although Piaroa life is free of physical violence and, from an observer's point of view, very peaceful (Overing 1986). BaKongo, too, think of themselves as constantly subject to violent attack, although (in the twentieth century at least) they have had a reputation for "pacifism," and physical violence among them is mostly the work of the police. I once asked a man what had happened to his first wife; with resignation, not anger, he replied, "Oh, her parents ate her on our wedding night." Such "eating," provoked in this instance by the quasi-legitimate dissatisfaction of the parents over the amount of marriage money they had received, happens "at night," invisibly, but it is real, not metaphorical, in the minds of those who speak of it. The occult power that makes such violence possible is *kindoki,* which all elders have in some degree and which is also a necessary attribute of chiefs and *banganga.* The ambiguities of the capacity for violence—an evil in private hands, beneficial when exercised by the guardians of public order; a terrifying and ever-present reality which is nevertheless invisible—complicate any attempt to interpret the models and realities of chiefship in the nineteenth century, or of dictatorship in the twentieth.[25]

Given the wide distribution of the idea that "the chief is a leopard," we can say that authority itself, at whatever level, was and is understood in Central and West Africa as necessary public violence. In Benin, "the right to kill is *the* defining characteristic of kingship" (Ben-Amos 1976, 246). The violence of chiefs is culturally much more complex than the familiar functionalist idea that a sovereign should monopolize the power of life and death, or that he is obliged to defend the polity against invaders. That the chief at his investiture kills his nephew may state by implication that he will rule impartially, or that he has ceased to be an ordinary human being defined by social bonds, but it also implies a very particular view of human life and its availability as raw material for "symbolism." Among the eastern Luba, every new chief was anointed on his forehead with blood from a man sacrificed for the purpose. The chief put his foot on the skull and drank the victim's blood mixed with beer; unless he could do this he was no true chief (Lucas 1966, 90). The Nyim of the Bushoong (Kuba) was believed able to transform himself into a leopard and among the BaTetela the assimilation of the lineage chief to the leopard was so strong that he abstained from eating its flesh, for "the leopard does not eat the leopard" (De Heusch 1985, 98). Such a lineage chief was said "to destroy men as the leopard destroys goats" (De Heusch 1954, 1019). The Kanongesha of the Ndembu in modern Zambia sat on lion- and leopardskins and wore a bracelet made of human genitalia which was soaked in sacrificial blood at each installation. He was a sorcerer who could cause barrenness in both land and people should he touch his bracelet to the ground (Turner 1957, 318–21).

Not only chiefs but also elders draw upon the violence of the dead. Many who write about religion in Central Africa dwell sentimentally upon the benevolence of ancestors, but the evidence to the contrary is overwhelming. Lunungu wrote concerning the dead that they excel in malice (*kimfunya*), because they envy the living (Cahier 158). The Yanzi distinguish between "good and "bad" ancestors, but regard them all as more or less "bad" and honor them more out of fear than out of respect or friendship

(Thiel 1972, 104). Father Hulstaert, in correspondence with Placide Tempels, wrote: "Here [among the Mongo] they say that the dead work with the intention of diminishing life in the living, that they try to lead the living into their world, that they work not for good but for ill. When a living man invokes the spirit of his deceased father, it is always for the sake of harming other living persons; the living does not invoke them to protect or strengthen himself directly. The protection is negative; it is obtained by diminishing the life-force of the aggressor" (Bontinck 1985, 71).

Identification of authority with violence did not mean that in fact chiefs always ruled by force; from northern Mayombe we learn that a chief may be invested when it is seen that his deeds are remarkable, but only if he looks after people well and provides for strangers. "Though he looks like a chief, but does not do good, he cannot be given chiefship" (Mvubu, 343). *Kindoki,* the idiom of power, is also, by its ambiguity, a medium of negotiation, providing sanctions against chiefs as well as in support of them. It is in such negotiation, and not in electoral procedures, that a specifically African conception of democratic accountability may be found (Comaroff and Comaroff 1997, 141).

The relation of violence to other values is quite complex. The Kanongesha of the Ndembu, for example, was a ritual figure unable to control his nominal subordinates. Discussing the role of the Tetela lineage head, De Heusch notes that although the ritual characterizes chiefship as violent, in fact the candidate chief must be generous with his gifts if he is to be allowed, once in his lifetime, to wear the leopardskin; the circulation of goods, linked to the circulation of women as wives and mothers, expresses the perpetuation of life itself. At the festival in which the chief became a leopard, his wives as well as the members of his lineage were also allowed to wear the leopardskin (De Heusch 1954, 1021–22). Among the Shona in Zimbabwe, where the chief is a "lion," David Lan notes that although, by their very nature, the spirits of dead chiefs are conquerors, warriors, and killers, "it is through their violence that the fertility of the earth is made available to their descendants" (Lan 1985, 152).

The Tetela lineage head, like most Kongo chiefs, achieved his position by obligatory generosity, and De Heusch can only explain his identification with the leopard by drawing upon psychoanalysis. René Girard has included African examples of violence related to royalty in his *Violence and the Sacred* (Girard 1977). Girard ranges widely in search of illustrative examples, which he believes generate a theory of the nature of "primitive religion." Necessary elements of this theory include the sacrifice of a surrogate victim and the oedipal association in royal rituals of the king's obligatory incest with his symbolic death. According to Girard, the king assures the well-being of his people by taking their sins upon himself. Examples of this complex are said to exist in eastern Africa, "between Egypt and Swaziland," but appear to be lacking in the west. In none of the rituals of Kongo chiefship, for example, can the chief be regarded as a scapegoat; blood is not poured upon him, nor is royal incest practiced. Despite the insistence of Frazer, Girard, De Heusch, and others, there is no objectively verifiable, unitary phenomenon to be called "divine kingship." Even within the areas of the Bantu languages, clear contrasts as well as parallels appear between, for example, the rituals of violence in southwestern Congo and those of the interlacustrine kings (Rwanda, Buganda).

In a sustained discussion of the ideology of violence in Buganda, Ben Ray demonstrates (contrary to long-established ideas on the subject) that the Kabaka, the king, was not divine, though he possessed the sacredness that goes with central authority (Ray 1991). Because he was the central principle of order in the realm, the forces of anarchy were believed to be let loose at his death, but this was neither a cosmological statement nor just a figure of speech, since violent political conflict broke out among rival chiefs and princes. The king's body was eviscerated and dried over fires during the five-month mourning period (111), but this drying was a preservative measure as the ceremonies of the interregnum unrolled; there is no indication that it contrasted with wetness attributed to the new king. Killings were ordered throughout the king's reign, to express his right and obligation to kill on behalf of public order. The more the king killed, the more respect and vitality he seemed to possess (178); some of the many victims were criminals, but as many were men and women seized at random and sometimes horribly tortured. If the violence was deemed to have got out of hand, the king might be killed, but regicide was a political rather than a ritual act (181). At his death he was said only to have "gone away." The person of a deceased king was represented, as in a number of eastern kingdoms, by a spirit medium through whom he maintained contact with the living king (123). Despite the presence here as in the west of the ideology of the leopard, in the lacustrine region of East Africa we are dealing with a very different political system and with a very different idea of the chief's function (Beidelman 1966; Carlson 1993).

Power in Modern Times

In his discussion of an elusive axiom widely known to BaLuba, *Le pouvoir se mange entier*, "Power is eaten whole," J. Fabian comments that in the Luba as in Bantu languages generally, "to eat" is often used to denote access to power. The elephant is a chief among animals because it eats more than others. "These are images which depict access to power as ingestion/incorporation rather than occupying a position or territory, or imposing order." Power is understood as a personal property, but is "tied to concrete embodiments, persons, and material symbols, rather than to abstract structures such as offices, organizations, and territories" (Fabian 1990, 24–25). The metaphor of eating dominates the political culture of sub-Saharan Africa in the late twentieth century, but the linguistic association between "wealth" and "eating" is centuries old (Rowlands and Warnier 1988; Schatzberg 1993). It is a premise of "the politics of the belly" that people admired for their success achieve it by eating the substance of others, using means which, in lesser men, would be criminal. Presidents and politicians are expected to demonstrate a capacity for larceny, "corruption," and violence, as well as princely largesse toward their followers. At every political level, however, "eating" is polysemous: it means not only to feed oneself, not at all easy in an economy of poverty that is wracked by "structural adjustment," but also "to accumulate, exploit, attack, conquer or kill by witchcraft" (Bayart 1993, 269). In Nigeria in the 1980s popular opinion held that "almost everyone uses rituals to get money. It usually involves killing a small child"; similar beliefs circulate in Ghana (Matory 1994, 218; Meyer 1995).[26]

Social scientific recognition of this complex has been inhibited by the conventional treatment of "religion" and "politics" as separate substances, and by the "anthropologization" of indigenous belief, treating it as though it were characteristic only of "traditional," rural populations circumscribed by ethnic boundaries (Geschiere 1997). As I mentioned in Chapter 4, the liberal ethnocentrism of foreign commentators also inclines them to pass by in silence beliefs which they cannot personally endorse. Faced with the incredulity of strangers, educated Africans, however, do not hesitate to invoke "African realities not apparent to the Cartesian rationality of the North" (Gruénais 1995, 165).

President Mobutu Sese Seko appealed to traditional values that were explicitly in opposition to "Cartesian rationality" in 1966 when he deliberately entrapped four well-known politicians into a plot against him and then publicly executed them. After that, everybody knew that the easygoing politics and musical-chairs governmental changes that had prevailed in what was then the Democratic Republic of Congo were no more. In the face of worldwide protests, Mobutu argued at the time that he was expected to conduct himself with the decisive violence characteristic of "a Bantu chief." There is no reason to think that Mobutu had any true understanding of the chiefly tradition, but the tradition itself is pervasive (Josephson 1992, 249–54). In 1980, popular opinion explained the arrival of Ba'hai missionaries in northeastern Congo (Zaire) by the "fact" that in order to pay for the expensive new airport in Kisangani the President had had to admit a new group of traders in souls whose nocturnal activities would bring in foreign exchange. On the other hand, the executions did not earn the President widespread admiration. My neighbors in 1966 were stunned —aesthetically imagined violence is easier to live with than the real thing.

The chief as killer in defense of the public good readily slips into the mode of the chief as sorcerer and cannibal. Opposition to Mobutu in the 1990s included scandalous and often pornographic stories, widely circulated in the press as well as by word of mouth, which accused him of strengthening his person and his regime by witchcraft and by occult techniques obtained from all over the world. It was believed that he was obliged to hand over the souls of citizens to pay for these secrets, as witches do and chiefs did. After it became known that he was being treated for cancer, a vaccination campaign failed because of the rumor that its real purpose was to collect children's blood to send to Switzerland for the president's treatment. In popular opinion, the death of a prominent politician is never "natural," but always the result of some kind of sorcery (Sabakinu 1988b, 182). When the opposition parties denounced "the harmful influence of the marabouts and other occult, destructive practices that govern us" they were not using metaphor.

In 1991–1992, when there appeared to be a chance of constitutional reform and an end to dictatorship, ambitious politicians joined prayer groups in which they confessed to having been witches, to having eaten people, participated in blood sacrifices, and so forth; their claim was that as *reformed* witches they were particularly competent to deal with the iniquities of the regime in power. Leading figures of the Mobutu regime explained how the dictator kept himself in power by such devices as his picture on the banknotes, which supposedly enabled him to keep an eye on everybody; others blamed another occult force, the CIA. Some of these disaffected politicians have published accounts of the sorcery in which they say they engaged on behalf of the regime (Schatzberg 1997). This understanding of politics is not irrational or simply traditional; Congolese public life, "a world in which fact and fiction are interchangeable" (De Boeck 1996, 92), is a field of occult forces in which nothing is ever what it seems and no one can say what "really" happened, though the hurts are real. Whatever the judgment one makes about rationality, the fact is that Congolese at every social and political level act in response to political events on the basis of a sense of causality which social science does not take sufficiently seriously.

Across the Congo in Brazzaville the National Conference of 1991 was discussed by the participants in language appropriate to the kind of meeting that is called to relieve a family of the destructive effects of witchcraft in their midst (Gruénais 1995, 171). To speak of sorcery and fetishism in the context of the politics of democratization may smack of exoticism, but it is difficult to conceive of a politician in Congo [or Zaire] not basing his position in part on magico-religious forces (Gruénais 1995, 165). In any event, in both the Republic of Congo and the Democratic Republic of Congo (then Zaire), these confessions and reconciliations came to nothing. Although everyone can express himself freely at such meetings, it is tacitly agreed that there will be no consequences. The accused elders and politicians admit their fault without giving away the secrets of their relations with the invisible, and the outcome of the palaver is to reestablish the hierarchy of power. According to the philosopher Eboussi Boulaga, commenting on these conferences, the archetypal rituals of the palaver, the fête, the game, healing, and the initiation rite underlie the proceedings; through them, and through the language of the imagination, the norms and values of political culture are expressed and confirmed (Robinson 1994, 60).

When Laurent Kabila's miscellaneous army displaced Mobutu in 1997, some of its units conceived their task as that of rounding up witches to purify the country of corruption. Kabila employed a different idiom to convey essentially the same analysis when he refused to have anything to do with even the opposition to Mobutu, on the ground that, despite their long record of determined struggle, they were all contaminated by Zaire.

Coda

We have moved in this chapter from the apparent exotica of divination, chiefly investiture, and underwater journeys in pursuit of magical power to the more familiar topics of African despotism, "the peace process," and the prospects for democracy. At the end of *Paths in the Rainforests* Vansina declares the death of the ancient and powerful Central African cultural tradition, because its institutions were more or less violently destroyed between about 1880 and 1920 and the cognitive core, he says, went into "an irreversible crisis" (Vansina 1991, 247). The continued vitality of traditional concepts of power in the political life of modern nations suggests that the announcement may have been premature. Under the deceitful label of "customary law," indigenous institutions were seriously distorted but not entirely abolished; domestic relations and access to land remained under local control in a zone of limited autonomy which continued to shape the cognitive orientations and personal consciousness of individuals.

"Witchcraft" (that is, *kindoki*) is not primitive thought "surviving" in modern times and "adapting" to the stresses of modernity, but is itself a mode of modernity, a theory and practice of power in societies of the twentieth century whose history and civilization are not reducible to or even readily translatable into the languages of others.[27] At a sufficient level of abstraction, it is true, *kindoki* can be seen as little different from other theories of power that dwell on its moral ambiguity, but abstraction denatures the thing itself; to know *kindoki* is to recognize its implication in specific economic, social, and political institutions evolved by a tradition which, in Congo, has so far outlasted the enormous forces arrayed against it since Esaya Lutete's day.[28] In denying the usefulness of a distinction between religion and politics (and especially of the disciplinary vocabularies and preconceptions that go with them) I am also denying the usefulness of contrasting the "traditional" (religious) with the "modern" (political), while not in the least denying that things change. But no insistence on the creditable "dynamism" of African societies can relieve serious commentary of the challenges and disturbing excitement entailed in coming to terms with their traditions.

APPENDIX: A LIST OF LAMAN'S CONTRIBUTORS

Biographical notes compiled with the assistance of Jacques Bahelele, June 1995. Pastor Bahelele, a very old man in 1995, had long been the best-known SMF pastor, respected also for his vernacular publications on Kongo lore. Other information comes from missionary publications, including *Minsamu Miayenge.* The list shows the writer's name, the numbers assigned by Laman to the Cahiers he or she wrote, and the mission station to which he belonged. Quotations are identified in the text by the author's name, followed by the number of the Cahier.

Name	Cahier	Station
Babembe (?)	001–004	Kolo

Name	Cahier	Station
Babokidi Davidi	005	Kinkenge

Village Kungu, near Kinkenge. Taught in many villages. Wrote hymn #365 in *Nkunga mia Kintwadi,* much sung even today. A believer until his death.

Name	Cahier	Station
Babutidi Timotio	006–023	Kinkenge (Kisenga)

Born in the village of Kisonga [*sic*], close to Kinkenge, in about 1893. The first MuKongo to teach French, having studied at the Colonie Scolaire in Boma with the intention of assisting Dr. Laman on his research travels. Went with Laman to French Congo in 1916, when he was 26. Wrote hymn #732 in *Kintwadi.*

Name	Cahier	Station
Basukisa Samuel	024	Kinkenge

Village Ntadi-Nkondi, near Kinkenge. With Mrs Børisson wrote hymns #335 and 442 in *Minkunga Miayenge,* much sung in our churches. Died in the faith.

Name	Cahier	Station
Baya Filimoni	025	Kinkenge

Also from Ntadi-Nkondi. A teacher, he fell into the prophet movement (*kingunza*) and was sent away to Upper Zaire. Died not long after returning to his village in 1959.

Name	Cahier	Station
Bitebodi Andela	026	Madzia (Mansimu)

Completed training as a pastor in 1942.

Name	Cahier	Station
Demvo Thomas	027–044	Kingoyi

Village Kindamba-Madungu, near Kingoyi. He was very tall and robust. He was a teacher at Kingoyi, especially for women in training to be teachers; he taught Bahelele's wife in 1911. He became ill and was sent for treatment to Brazzaville, where he died.

Diafwila   045–053   Kibunzi
Village Kibunzi, where he was one of the first teachers. His son the pastor Samuel
Nsimba died in an airplane accident in 1948.

Kavuna Simon   054–065   Nganda
Born probably in 1878 in the village of Kibonda, on the Congo River near Bulu (Luozi). As a boy, he worked briefly for a Swedish official in Bulu, then as a house servant
for the SMF in Nganda and elsewhere. According to his own account in *Minsamu
Miayenge* (1901, 1904), he went to school in Mukimbungu. He married in 1909, but
his wife died two years later. After studies at the Kingoyi Seminary he was sent as a
pioneer evangelist to Kolo, among the BaBembe in French Congo; Kolo had been
conquered by the French only in 1911. On his return he became pastor of Nganda; after
that station closed in 1914, he remained there to look after twelve missionary graves.
In 1914 he wrote an article in *Minsamu Miayenge* urging his compatriots to respect the
KiKongo language, which he taught many people to read. In 1916–1917 he returned
to Kolo to carry out research for Laman. When he died he was buried next to the
missionaries in Nganda. He had only one eye.

Kiananwa Abeli   066–073   Kibunzi
Born about 1878, in Kisengele, not far from Kibunzi. Stationed at Diadia from 1892,
he helped to found the station at Kinkenge in 1897. He was the first and subsequently
the most frequent Kongo contributor of homilies and reports to *Minsamu Miayenge*. In
1908 he demanded that the Kongo teachers of the SMF be allowed to meet annually by
themselves, rather than under missionary supervision as had been the practice. Very
well known and esteemed in all the Protestant mission churches, noted for his opposition to alcohol, dancing, jewelry, and nudity. An accomplished singer and composer
of hymns, he served the Church for at least fifty-five years.

Kibangu Yelemia   074   Kingoyi
Born about 1893 in Mpete, near Kingoyi, on the frontier. He entered the Kingoyi Seminary in 1912, where he became the doyen of the Kongo teachers because he knew French
well and had earned an official diploma in French Congo. He was well informed on many
subjects. In 1928 he went to Sweden with Edward Karlman, where he lived for a year
and learned Swedish. After his return he continued to teach at Kingoyi until his retire-
ment. Bahelele called him Manianga's first philosopher, because conversation with him
was always rewarding. A good photograph of him appears opposite p. 64 in J. Hedlund's
Svart på Vitt (Stockholm: SMF, 1972); also in *Mavanga ma Nzambi,* opposite p. 83.

Kilola Esai   075–078   Mukimbungu
Village Mpelo, near Songololo, included in the Mukimbungu mission district. A
much-loved and respected catechist.

Kimbembe André   079–082   Madzia

Kimfuzi André   083   Kibunzi
Village Mpelo, near Kibunzi. A very well-known man whose clan gave the land for the
Kibunzi mission. As a boy of twelve, he succumbed to the missionary's bribe of a knife
and entered school, although his family warned him of the dangers of learning witch-

craft there. Baptized in 1895, he studied to be a teacher in 1898 with Laman, with whom he traveled the following year to see about founding a station at Nganda. Assigned to teach at Nsweka, Mukimbungu district, in 1908. When he died, a monument was built on his grave to show how much he was respected. His photograph appears in *Mavanga ma Nzambi.*

Kinkela Ngoma	084–094	Vungu

Kionga Aseli	095–114	Kingoyi

Born about 1898, in Madungu, near Kingoyi. He came to the mission quite young and was educated there. He is mentioned by Laman as his most helpful informant in the study of tone in KiKongo. Became a respected primary school teacher, but at the end of his life he left the church and married two wives; he died unrepentant.

Konda Jean	115–122	Kinkenge

Village Nkindu, close to Kinkenge; this was also the village of Mbumba Filip, the well-known prophet.

Kunzi Yelemia	123–137	Mukimbungu

Village Mukimbungu, where he went to school. A daughter was born to him in 1904. In 1906 he was in charge of the school for boys, but after 1910 he was named chief of the administrative *chefferie* of Mukimbungu, which he governed strongly.

Kwamba Elia	138–151	Kingoyi (Numbu)

Village Kindamba, close to Kingoyi, where he was the first convert. Traveled with Laman in 1915. He committed adultery several times but was reinstated and is remembered as a good teacher and faithful member of the church.

Lemba Joseph	152	Mbanza Ngungu

Loko	153	Manianga

Lunungu Moise	154–191	Nganda

Village Kimayenge, near Nganda. A very knowledgeable and well-known man. He was sent as a missionary to Indo in French Congo, where his memory is respected. On his return to Zaire he went to Matadi as editor of the bulletin *Minsamu Miayenge.* He died in Matadi.

Lusa Meso	192–196	?

Lusala Yoane	197–201	Nganda

Village unknown, but he lived near Nganda. He was short but stocky. A respected teacher.

Lutambi Samuel	202–203	Madimba

Village Madimba, where he died.

Lutangu Aloni M.	204–215	Diadia (Kimpunga)

Village Diadia. Good teacher and pastor, author of hymn #327 in *Kintwadi,* much sung to this day. Killed by a buffalo. (In his Cahiers he invariably writes his name "A. M. Lutangu.")

Lutete Esaya   216–237   Lolo
Born near Lolo, went to school at the CMA station in Vungu in 1899. Taught in Lolo
in 1904 and was probably responsible for the success of that station, reported the
mission in 1916. He subsequently worked at Vungu. Frequent contributor to *Minsamu
Miayenge*. The most prolific of Laman's contributors.

Lwamba Josefi   238–240   Lolo
Formerly a drunkard and ne'er-do-well, he served the CMA well until his death in
1924 (Kuvuna 1984, 24).

Mabaku Pauli   241   Kinkenge
Village Kungu-Yeliko. Teacher, hard worker.

Mabwila   242–244   ?

Mafula Loti   245–248   Mbanza Manteke
A slave bought by the American Baptist Foreign Missionary Society mission in Mbanza Manteke, where he became a teacher and where his tombstone could be seen in
1965.

Makasi Esaya   249   Manianga

Makundu Tito   250–266   Mukimbungu
Born within a year or two of 1870 in Madimba, very close to Mukimbungu. He had
only one eye. He and David Malangidila were Laman's principal assistants in translating the Bible and writing the KiKongo grammar (LKG). In 1898 he was teaching at
Nsweka. He had an encyclopedic knowledge of KiKongo and knew a great many
proverbs and stories. In the course of his long life he served as informant to a number
of ethnographers. After having been a Christian for some time he lapsed from the faith,
marrying two wives and taking to dancing and drink, but he reformed in 1895 after a
warning dream and an attack of the disease *lubanzi*.

Malanda Isaki   267   Kinkenge
Village Mazinga in Kinkenge district. A teacher, he was later chosen to be a pastor, in
which role he worked hard for many years until he retired.

Malumba Benyamin   268–275   Musana
Village Mbiongo. Went to Musana from Mukimbungu as a nurse, having learned nurs-
ing at Kingoyi in 1927. Died in 1935.

Mampuya K. P.   276–277   Musana

Mampuya and Lunungu   338

Masamba Matende Mose   278   Mukimbungu
Died in his village, Matende.

Mato Davidi   279–280   Maduda
Many stories told of his heroic leadership (Kuvuna 1984, 106–109; his photograph, p.
41).

Matunta Philémoni   281–317   Musana
Village Mbiongo, like Malumba. He went from Mukimbungu station to Musana with the missionary Westlind. A knowledgeable teacher, he wrote many homilies in *Minsamu Miayenge*. In 1910 he was a leader among the teachers who were protesting against aspects of their treatment within the mission church. In 1919 he was assigned to Madzia.

Mawakosi Samuel   318–320   Mukimbungu
Village Nsweka, on the bank of the Kwilu (Mukimbungu). Effective teacher, although his life was full of misfortunes. As a boy he was seized by the Free State's mercenaries as a hostage for the payment of an alleged debt. Suffering from a chronic sore and rejected by a girl to whom he proposed, he joined the SMF as a carpenter. Baptized in 1897. His wife Malia Zampungi, whom he married in 1901, died with her child in 1908; they were buried by Kilola at Nsweka. A few days later, his house and all his belongings were destroyed in a grass fire.

Mawuku Filemoni   322   Madzia

Mayoka Yakobi   323   Nganda
Village Londe, at some distance from Nganda. After teaching for a while, he became a telephone operator at the Songololo railway station. Having earned a lot of money, he returned to his village and became a successful trader; "I remember him coming one day to my village to sell cloth and other things," writes Bahelele. He died in 1942. His son Basolwa Kapita is a well-known Manianga writer, author of a history of the prophet Mbumba Filip and his followers.

Mayuku Abraham   324   Nganda
Village Kingila, not far from Nganda. Teacher.

Mbaku Simon   325   Kinkenge
Village Lukozi-Kimbambi, close to Kinkenge. Remained a believer to his death.

Mbazi   326   Nganda

Mfwandulu   327   ?

Mindoki Ngideoni   328–337   Nganda
Village Luhombo, not far from Nganda, perhaps three hours on foot. A tall, thin man; married Masika Elizabeth, some of whose many children are still alive. Became a pastor in the Nganda district.

Mpengani Luka   339–341   ?Kolo
Village Mbiongo, like Matunta. Sent from Mukimbungu as a missionary to Kolo, with Kavuna. Graduate of the Kingoyi Seminary, spoke very good French. He was teaching at Mukimbungu in 1925.

Mvubu Tomasi   342–344   Kiobo, Maduda

Ndibu Kapita Joseph   345–365   Kingoyi
Village Mpangala. He was *ngang'a nkisi,* but gave up both that and one of his wives

and was baptized in 1912, relatively late in life. In 1926 he was about 50, noted as a speaker and for his loyalty to the mission. Because his name happened to be Kapita he was appointed village headman (*kapita*) between about 1908 and 1918, when he went to seminary, becoming pastor of the parish of Tembisa. He wrote his own autobiography in Cahier 345, describing among other things his experiences as a father of twins (Janzen and MacGaffey 1974, 57–60; Janzen 1982, 87–89).

| Ndongala | 367–368 | Mbanza Ngungu |

Ndundu Aaron   369   Nganda
Village Kimwema, not far from Nganda. Educated at Nganda, where he later taught. An albino, as his name indicates.

Ngiendolo Daniel   370   Nganda
Village Nsundi, but was taken to Mbanza Ngoyo. As a boy, he entered the mission at Nganda, later spent two years in the seminary at Kingoyi. Respected catechist.

Ngiuvudi Paul   410–411   Musana
Originally called Nyuvudi. Village Niangi, near the Zaire in Mukimbungu district. He was taken by the missionary Westlind to the village of Ntombo-Manianga in Musana district. The missionary put pressure on him to marry a local woman by whom he had many children, some still alive to this day. His wife died and he married again. He was much loved as the pastor of Musana, but was caught up in the prophet movement and exiled to Upper Zaire. He returned to Musana, died when very old, and was buried near the church.

| Ngoma Petelo | 371–372 | Mboka; Yema Yanga |

| Ngoma Yosua | 373–381 | Musana |

Nkuzu Esaya   382–383   Mukimbungu
Village Niangi. A short man, a very good teacher, much respected in Bulu and other Manianga villages. He died in 1982.

| Nkwangu Lazalo | 384 | Diadia |

Nsakala Elisa   385   Nganda (Luwala)
Village Luwala, but was taken to Londe [Nganda district, or Matadi?]. At first she was a mission teacher, but after her son became a Catholic priest she converted to Catholicism.

| Nsembani Samuel | 386 | Mbanza Nsanga |

Nsemi Isaki   387–400   Kingoyi
Born about 1888 in Bwende, not far from Kingoyi. After teaching for a while he was chosen to be pastor in Kingoyi district. A much respected and well-loved member of the church, an exceptional preacher. His two grandsons are Protestant pastors.

Ntungu Esaya   401–408   Kasi
Village Nkwanga. Became an adherent of the prophet movement, died in Upper Congo.

Ntwalani Mesaki   409   Kasi (Kilwangu)
A teacher, he joined the prophet movement and died in exile in Oshwe, Upper Congo.

Nzimba   412   ?

Wamba N. Enoki   413–428   Mukimbungu (Bulu)
Born in Bulu, but taken to Kisinga. Spent three years in seminary, became a respected
Bible teacher and pastor, known as "the theologian." He was also secretary to the
meetings of the SMF teachers. Wrote a number of hymns. His wife was barren, so he
had no children. His mother was thrown alive into the Zaire as a witch, with a stone
around her neck.

Zoyo Zakalia   429   Kinkenge
Village Betelemi (Bethlehem), about 1.5 kilometers from Kinkenge. One of the teach-
ers who learned French in the Kingoyi Seminary and began to teach it there in 1925.
His son, very old, lives in Luozi.

NOTES

1. Introduction

1. The image of traditional thought as unchallenged and unchanging is in part adopted from African folk, among whom whatever is deemed true has by definition been so since ancestral times (Mudimbe and Appiah 1993).

2. The anthropological literature on this subject is large and growing (Frank 1995; Jewsiewicki 1995; Meyer 1995; Gore and Nevadomsky 1997; Meyer 1997).

3. For an extended discussion of similar developments in Cameroon, see Geschiere and Fisiy (1994). For detailed comment on the role of "traditional religion" in contemporary Nigerian politics, see Matory (1994).

4. Plural society, in its political aspect, has been called "mixed government" by Richard Sklar (1993). The conflict of legitimacies is not limited to areas in which centralized traditional polities are found, nor to periods of outright hostilities.

5. My remarks above about "witchcraft" and political culture do not assume that either is the same throughout Africa.

6. Photography is a case in point. Once the railway from Matadi to Kinshasa was opened in 1898, photographers could bypass the already clothed and converted population of Lower Congo. Photographs of European activities near the coast are abundant, as are those of naked natives in the interior, but the area with which this study is concerned is relatively undocumented, except for the work of Swedish missionaries such as Laman and Hamar.

2. Texts and Contexts

1. For accounts of "the factory system," see Schrag (1985); Friedman (1991).

2. For currencies and values at the coast, see Schrag (1985); Martin (1987).

3. The preceding paragraphs are based on contributions to *Le Congo Illustré*, 1892–1895, with additional details from LKI, ch. 12, which affords a great many more, and which is itself partly based on Cahier 54, by Kavuna. See also Janzen (1982, 30–36).

4. As an English trader Phillips was not favorably disposed toward the Free State, which despite its name and charter was turning into a Belgian monopoly. Nevertheless his assessment is correct. See also Axelson (1970).

5. In 1883, Stanley received a note from the officer in charge of Lutete, a station on the left-bank transport route: "Les habitants de Balabumba sont des c—. J'ai brûlé leur village; rayez de la carte." Stanley took disciplinary action (Liebrechts 1909, 41).

6. Compare the chain gang in Matadi as described by Conrad (1995, 33).

7. The wage paid for the entire trip from Matadi to Mpumbu, lasting at least a month, was seven strips of twelve handkerchiefs each. The overall transport cost was

one pound sterling per load, or thirty-five pounds per ton. "Fiery, ardent spirits" were prepared especially for the African trade (Ward 1890, 84).

8. Archives Africaines (Brussels), R. F. (1379) carnet F. Van de Velde, n.d.

9. And still, in 1965, dumps of broken crockery. Samarin quantifies porterage in detail. One answer to Samarin's question why BaKongo were not recruited for other occupations than portering was that porters were in very short supply and only BaKongo could survive. They carried minimal food or bargained for it along the way; non-Kongos were at a considerable disadvantage in this process. Moreover, porters were normally replaced at Lukunga, the halfway point, so that they could rest, eat, or go home. Here again non-Kongos would have been handicapped. In short, the transport was sustained by the Kongo community as a whole, not just by the porters. See also Conrad's description of the route as he saw it in 1890 (1995, 39, 150–60).

10. On the competition not only between Catholic missions and the State but among themselves, see Kratz (1970).

11. Historical details concerning the Alliance's stations are taken from its annual reports and from missionary letters in *The Alliance Weekly*. Information about individual Kongo teachers comes sometimes from the same sources but more often from their own contributions to the Protestant bulletin, *Minsamu Miayenge*.

12. The initial consonant is a bilabial fricative, between English "b" and "v." Some historians write "Bungu."

13. The question of Ntinu Lukeni and what one is to make of the story is reviewed by Bontinck (1972). See Chapter 10.

14. "Un peut partout, le Père [Vandendyck, in 1912] cherchait à affaiblir la position des protestants" (Kratz 1970, 73).

15. Post-colonial critiques of Redemptorist and SMF practice, both by insiders, are found in Axelson (1970, Part III); Kratz (1970, ch. 8). These writers are exemplary in their inclusion of named Kongo evangelists.

16. It is probably significant of the same unrest that the Catholic missionaries in this area found it increasingly difficult from 1915 onward to enforce their ban on dances they considered obscene (Kratz 1970, 155).

17. The idea of human flesh sealed in a container itself conforms to that of an *nkisi;* see Chapter 5.

18. Kongo cosmology, taken for granted when rituals are performed or traditions recited, has the value of what David Carr calls "pre-theoretical awareness" (1986, 18).

19. On this incident, which took place in November 1893, see also Axelson (1970, 260). An administrative report written in 1931 adds that when the authorities retook the village they held a certain Bonza (a slave whom they had appointed kapita) responsible for the incident, but he fled. Unable to capture him, they seized "hostages," of whom two "ont été jugés et pendues en example." The people were terrified by these measures. When Bonza, accompanied by the Swedes, told his side of the story to the authorities, naming two individuals as the real instigators of the revolt, his medal of office was returned to him and the villages were reorganized into the "chefferie artificielle" of Kingila.

20. Since independence, similar beliefs have been attached to graduate study abroad.

21. Ramona Austin interviewed a number of chiefs in Mayombe in the 1980s, but the nature of their chiefships and rituals remains to be established.

22. The trade in slaves is fundamental to Kongo history from the seventeenth to the nineteenth century, but the idea of the chief as killer is much more widespread and evidently centuries older. Chiefs are "leopards" throughout the rain forest. See Chapter 10.

23. A chief of importance might be called *ntinu,* "king," but many individuals known in European accounts as "kings" were no more than leaders of a few hamlets. *Nkuluntu* = headman, elder.

24. Van Wing, admitting that chiefs, though supposedly opposed to all fetishes, were often "féticheurs de profession," treats the fact as a deviation from traditional values. Thus an artificial distance in time is introduced to explain the nonconformity of practice to theory (1959, 152).

25. Since colonial times, *banganga* have been under a cloud; they are supposed to represent superstition and paganism, so no *nganga* now admits to being one, preferring instead such labels as "herbalist." In the 1980s, the term "ancestral healer" became fashionable.

26. Magistrates face the problem that though they and the witnesses who come before them believe that witchcraft is a real threat and a social scourge, the law itself does not recognize it. Judges find other titles under which to condemn persons believed to be witches.

27. Yoruba witch covens are modeled on women's market associations and designated by the same term (Apter 1993, 118).

28. *Kundu diambongo kahanda. Handa* (*vanda*) is the verb "to compose an *nkisi.*" *Kundu* is supposedly an internal sac of witchcraft substance or power, comparable to the pack of animating medicines in an *nkisi.* People in the village, as victims, correspond to game animals in the inverted world of the forest.

29. For a modern account of these beliefs, presented as facts, see Bockie (1993); also MacGaffey (1994).

30. This section includes extracts from my "Ethnography and the Closing of the Frontier in Lower Congo, 1885–1921" (1986b), which contains more information about frontier conditions and gives specific references to *Minsamu Miayenge,* from which much of that information was drawn.

31. The principal ethnographies written by foreigners include, in Mayombe, those of Bittremieux and Doutreloux; in Manianga, Janzen; south of the Congo, MacGaffey; in the east, Van Wing. To these we must add the work of the Kongo anthropologist Buakasa among the Bandibu; and, in French Congo, Dupré's work on the BaBembe and BaNzabi and P.-P. Rey on the BaKunyi.

32. See the Appendix, whose contents have been pieced together from fragments with the notable assistance of the late Pastor Bahelele.

33. Kavuna, describing the rituals of *nkisi* Na Kongo for protecting babies, says that he himself was protected in this way.

34. A translation of this second text can be found in LKI, page 95.

35. Kiananwa died ca. 1952, after 55 years of service to the Church. Filed teeth were a fashion, nothing to do with fighting.

36. I am deeply indebted to Dr. Sigbert Axelson for a copy of LKM, which he found lying about in the mission at Mindouli. The text is now available on microfilm from the Center for Research Libraries, 6050 Kenwood Avenue, Chicago, IL 60637.

3. Translation, Exoticism, Banality

1. In this book I have generally omitted these diacritical marks. In the manuscripts, the initial /n/, /m/ may be omitted, as in *sisia* for *nsisya.*

2. A. Jacobson-Widding, for example, has studied the description of the *nkisi* Mbumba in the third volume (1979, 239) and comes to erroneous conclusions because she is not aware that she is dealing with an amalgam of two different texts, from Cahier 16 and Cahier 97 by Babutidi of Kinkenge and Kionga of Kingoyi, respectively.

3. "Although it is true that books have been published in what are called Acoli and Alur languages, the written forms and the language spoken by missionary-trained Acoli and Alur do not represent what is spoken in the villages" (Okot p'Bitek 1971, 4–5). I have been arguing this point with John Thornton for some years. Whereas I agree with Bentley's comment, Thornton points out that seventeenth-century KiKongo documents "were composed and checked by native speakers of KiKongo, not Europeans trying to write in a foreign language" (Thornton 1992, 210n.). I found in the 1960s, however, that long-time mission servants and pastors tended to speak their native KiKongo with Swedish or English accents, using the relatively linear forms of European discourse; on occasion, other BaKongo parodied their speech.

4. For an overview of linguistic policy, evangelism, and colonial control in Belgian Congo, see Fabian (1983).

5. For a parallel discussion of similar problems, see Fabian (1992).

6. Janzen's own glosses on *koma* (1982, 248) are, "to strike, augment, obligate, assemble or constrain." The verb *banda,* "to nail, strike," can carry the same senses as *koma.*

7. By strict local criteria, the traditions as written down by Lutete and others are not *kinkulu,* whether their content is "true" or not. *Kinkulu,* as an indigenous genre, is an authoritative account of a group's origins, recited in a political context by a man who is qualified by descent, training, or revelation to do so. In principle, it cannot be written down, though in recent decades the literate have been doing so (MacGaffey 1970, 208).

8. "We speak to communicate. But also to conceal, to leave unspoken" (Steiner 1975, 46).

9. The French translation of Olfert Dapper's original compilation in Dutch is unreliable, but the Fondation Dapper's republication of it includes corrigenda by A. Van Dantzig.

10. The fact was pointed out to me by Dr. Matuka Yeno Mansoni.

11. Kiananwa, in Kibunzi (Cahier 69). The translation makes use of Laman's notes, in Swedish. Cf. Laman 1957, page 125. The last exchange is a proverb, "If two people do something in the same way they had the same teacher." The reference to ironworking implies that the instruction included elements of *kindoki.*

12. For a splendid cap of parrot feathers for *nganga* Mabyaala, see MacGaffey and Harris (1993, 38).

13. "Whatever treatise on the art of translation we look at, the same dichotomy is stated: as between 'letter' and 'spirit', 'word' and 'sense'" (Steiner 1975, 262).

14. The word "occult" makes a useful bridge. Although it is often used to refer to the "supernatural," it means simply that which is hidden from view or known only to

the initiated, to experts. A MuKongo would quite rightly regard Washington, D.C., as a hotbed of *kindoki.*

15. In the Pike Street Market, Seattle, in July 1995, I was happy to see that an imitation *nkisi nkondi* for sale in a curio shop was in fact labeled "Nkisi Nkondi, $300."

4. Tradition and Trade

1. The most sustained effort was Laman's. His chapters on tradition (LKI, ch. 2–4) are patchworks of paragraphs and phrases taken from here and there in the Cahiers.

2. *Kanda* denotes a group of any kind, as in *kanda dya bandombe,* "black people." In traditions, *kanda* can mean either "clan" or the cumbersome "clan-section," but in most contexts is conveniently translated "clan." Lwamba is clear that the section, unlike the clan, is exogamous and has [in principle] a unified genealogy (Cahier 239).

3. *Mpumbu* means "east," but can also be the Kongo name of Malebo Pool and the great market at what is now Kinshasa.

4. Lutala is cognate with Mutala, mentioned above by Lunungu. These names refer to a place of investiture, in which the candidate chief "looks at" (*tala*) the things which are the source of the power of chiefship.

5. I have no information about Kinkela Ngoma except that he taught at the CMA station in Vungu.

6. *Nkanda* or *lukanda* normally means an iron ring such as encircles a barrel, but here it seems to mean a throwing knife. For another attempt to translate this passage, see LKI, 25. Lutete mentions *lukanda* as one of the constituents of *nkisi nsi,* buried in the forest when the chief took the Nsanda title (Cahier 235). An ancient "war of the throwing knives" occurs in Kuba tradition (Vansina 1978, 37).

7. This is the first mention of Nanga, a well-known clan name. The text goes on to say that in the beginning there were no clans, but that when they came into existence they took the names of the first heroes.

8. The full name of the clan, Nanga Na Kongo, implies that Nanga's patron was the king in Kongo. Na is a term of respect whose variants include Ne, Mwe, Ma.

9. The list is the same, with the inclusion of Mbenza, Nanga, and Makaba, as that which Doutreloux (1967, 31) says is standard in Mayombe, except that it substitutes Mamboma [from (M)Boma] for Matsundi [Nsundi]. No correspondence exists between these names and any that existed in Mbanza Kongo in the sixteenth and seventeenth centuries.

10. In the earliest days of the Free State, Vivi, opposite Matadi, was H. M. Stanley's headquarters.

11. *Kaba,* to divide, to apportion; *dikabu,* a section. The same verb occurs with nine clans (or multiples) in Kuba stories about the "original" crossing (Vansina 1978, 43).

12. The chief, his clan or clan-section, his village, and often his *nkisi* (charm) were called by the same name.

13. *Nkondo a Nanga,* the baobab of Nanga, that is, the hollow baobab from which came forth a woman with four breasts, "and that's why the clan is divided into four lineages."

14. Isangila is on the Congo, east of Seke-Banza. It was an important node in the trade network. See Map 1.

15. Every MuKongo belongs to a matrilineal clan, but is also (unless he is a slave) affiliated in the status of *mwana,* "Child," to his father's clan, his "Fathers" (*mase*).

16. *Mfingulu ya diikana,* the "eat me" insult, is a woman's ultimate weapon in village quarrels.

17. Bittremieux notes that such predecessors are not mentioned in Yombe traditions (Bittremieux and Tembo 1924, 71n.).

18. The orthographic conventions of the manuscript do not permit us to be sure, but "Nkumba" here is presumably *nkummba* (short vowel), "navel." See below, *Nkummba a Wungudi.*

19. In Nsundi tradition from Nganda Nsundi in northern Mayombe, Mwembe is explicitly the "original" place whence the mythical nine clans set out (Bittremieux 1940, 51).

20. *Noka,* to rain. The configuration of a central authority and four subordinates is a cliché of Kongo political thought (MacGaffey 1970, 237).

21. *Tona,* to see. The name generates a praise-name —this one or another—to explain its alleged significance. The significance in turn is explained by an allegedly historical incident. Mazinga is the name of the chiefdom.

22. The difficulty of translating this passage comes from the fact that the verb *buta,* "to engender," describes both fathering and mothering.

23. The ahistorical status of Ma Lwangu is further defined by Babutidi's report that white people do not make *minkisi* because, when they separated from Africans, Ma Lwangu forbade it, whereas he enjoined the BaSundi to do so to protect themselves against being eaten by witches (Cahier 22). Note that according to one school of thought concerning the historical value of tradition (discussed in Chapter 10), the story of the succession to chiefship should be interpreted as recording a shift from matrilineal to patrilineal descent, though in Kongo no such shift occurred.

24. Biebuyck (1985, v. 1:57–60, 81–90) shows the complete incoherence of the classificatory efforts of art historians in southwestern Congo. He says Boone's book shows the incredible tangle of migration; in fact it simply adds together the welter of guesses about ethnicity offered by different visitors over the years. A European going around asking people what sub-tribe they belong to may hear any one of a number of answers, because the BaKongo are not well versed in nineteenth-century anthropology.

25. For a trenchant critique of ethnicity and ethnic labels to the east between the upper Kasai and Lubilash rivers, see Ceyssens (1984, 33–59).

26. The legitimacy of sub-tribal names is challenged in a recent study of the techniques, styles, and terminology of Kongo pottery, which is said to display astonishing unity (Pinçon and Ngoïe-Ngalla 1990).

27. Five and seven occur rarely in traditions. Two, in the form of a balanced opposition, is common in ritual contexts, and one is apparently regarded with some unease. Ten is important in calculations, but is not used ritually.

28. It remains to be explained why such an appeal to a source of authority should be cast in the form of "migration." See Chapter 10.

29. The name Na Mbinda in the manuscript should probably be Ne Mpinda. Ne Mpinda at Boma owned an *nkisi* dedicated to river trade, derived from the famous Mpinda shrine on the Solongo side. From 1775 until well into the nineteenth century, Solongo salt was the principal commodity which Boma exchanged for Nsundi slaves

(Schrag 1985, 60). The cemetery of the kings of Boma was situated on Kinsala Island, the place of their original settlement.

30. Bittremieux comes to essentially the same conclusion with respect to "the BaSundi." He denies the existence of any essential Nsundi group and points out that groups were constituted on a variety of bases—alliance, political subordination, recognition of the same territorial spirit, etc. (1940, 51).

31. One elder, sitting with me within earshot of the Congo River to the north, and seeing my puzzlement in this regard, said, "Not *this* Nzadi, the other" (gesturing toward the South, where there is in fact no river).

32. Migrations do occur, of course, but the migrations of "conquerors" had a particular appeal in the age of imperialism (Vansina 1974; Leach 1990). Until about 1960, the pre-colonial "history" of Africa was mostly a matter of migrations by conquering "Hamites." Later, the racial element was left out, but maps illustrating African history were still laced with arrows. Since then, Africans have more or less settled down.

33. Anthropologists are familiar with the similar belief of Trobriand Islanders in the South Pacific that the spirits of the dead go to Tuma, an inhabited island often visited by living Trobrianders.

34. *Muziki* is a code name for the python. The Kanyok tell a similar story: One who entered the sacred forest of the *bakisi* could not escape until a sacrifice of a white goat or chicken had been made (Yoder 1992, 27). In Ngoyo, the symbol of the transmission of royal power was a block of chalk guarded in a temple.

5. Complexity, Astonishment, and Power

1. Guthrie, referring to CS 1072 *-kítì and CS 1073 *-kítì or *-kícì, with somewhat different distributions, suggests that they derive from a common root with the original meaning of "fetish," later extended to include "spirit" (Guthrie 1970). This will not do; "fetish" is a relatively recent European term which is not a translation of any African term or concept but a label for the problem of understanding certain aspects of African cultures (Pietz 1987).

2. For most of the *minkisi* mentioned or described in the Cahiers, no corresponding object can be found anywhere. Most of the hundreds now in museums are anonymous, and the accession literature relating to them is deplorably superficial. Others probably numbering in the thousands were destroyed as the BaKongo converted to Christianity. Further details concerning the *minkisi* discussed here, including the accession numbers of such as are in the Ethnographic Museum, Stockholm, and a list of more than 300 named and documented *minkisi*, may be found in MacGaffey 1991.

3. These oppositions are general in Central Africa (Willis 1981; Ceyssens 1984; Beidelman 1986).

4. A cock's tailfeathers (called *mimbemba* in one source) were especially favored; cf. *mbemba*, vulture. As in Europe, the cock is seen as dismissing the spirits of the night.

5. *Mbùmba* is a multivocal term which has been subject to misinterpretation. In its most general sense, it means simply an *nkisi;* thus, "*m'vandi a mbumba,* a sorcerer"—LKD. Many *mbùmba* incorporate the word in their proper names; for example,

Mbumba Cindongo, described in 1697 as an *nkisi* to control epidemics and in 1915 as a cure for boils. In both eastern Kongo and Mayombe, versions of Mbumba are violent *minkisi* of the *nkondi* type; for example, Mbumba Luangu, into which nails were driven and which controlled the rain. Because Mbumba Luangu is the name of the rainbow serpent, De Heusch mistakenly takes all mentions of *mbumba* as referring to it. Hilton introduces what she calls the "mbumba dimension" in Kongo religion, meaning everything to do with water spirits and fertility; her usage is based on the word *mbombo,* which in the seventeenth century as in the twentieth meant "fertility," but which she incorrectly reads as a variant of *mbùmba.* In advance of further confusion, we might note that *bùmba* (low tone) is a medicine bundle, but *mbúmba* (high tone) means "pottery making"; and that *mbùmba* can also mean a cat, a secret, or a sour stomach (Bittremieux 1936, 173; Bontinck 1970, 81; De Heusch 1989; Hilton 1985, 13; Van Wing 1959, 391).

6. Kilola's list is heterogeneous. "In our country the elders classified *minkisi* in five types, 1) of the above; 2) *nkisi miandùngu,* those [composed with] drums [or perhaps "in a special basket," *n'dúngu*]; 3) of the house; 4) of the water; 5) for controlling the rain" (Cahier 77).

7. Complementing her "mbumba dimension," Hilton writes of the "nkadi a mpemba dimension," a bizarre collection of everything else in Kongo religion, including nonexistent "sky spirits." The dead live on or under the earth (or in "America," etc.), not in the sky (Hilton 1985).

8. Kalabari spirit sculptures are regarded in the same way as localizations of a spirit force which is thereby subjected to a degree of control (Horton 1965, 8).

9. Interesting similarities with the composition of *minkisi*—shining elements, knots, spitting on the charm, grave-dirt, etc.—appear in Southern "voodoo balls" (Owen 1969, 171ff.).

10. In Gabon, the Fang and BaKwele believe that the umbilicus is the main point of entry for witches and that it can be protected by something white or shiny; moreover, cowry shells are thought of by the BaKwele as eyes (Siroto 1979, 281, 287). The ventral medicine pack on an *nkisi* in the British Museum (1905 5-25 2) consists of the head of some small rodent, presented teeth first. This highly unusual effect, like the molar, illustrates the endless variety of metaphors in *minkisi.*

11. For example, the Hammar collection in the Swedish Ethnographic Museum, No. 1906.39, esp. items 13–126.

12. *Nkisi* ingredients in Kongo and the contents of *prendas* or *ngangas* composed in the Kongo-related Cuban practices called Palo Monte or Reglas de Congo are strikingly similar (Cabrera 1971; Cabrera 1986 [1979]).

13. *Sakumuna:* this and some other words, usually translated "to bless" in modern times, carry the sense "confirm and strengthen."

14. For a longer list of the usual medicines see Nsemi, Cahier 391, translated in Janzen and MacGaffey 1974, 36; for a modern list and its meanings, see Janzen 1978, 184. "Some things are invested with particular powers by virtue of their names. . . . these things work more like incantations than like objects with properties; they are a sort of objectified words (*mots réalisés*)" (Mauss 1990, 460).

15. *Minkisi* called Ngovo appear widely. The one described is from Kiobo (Swedish Ethnographic Museum 19.1.764; MacGaffey 1991, 110).

16. The only known example of Lunkanka, the one that Matunta describes, is in the Stockholm collection (1954.1.2338). See MacGaffey 1991, 124–41.

17. This idea of "appearance" is the origin of the category *fétiches d'élégance* that appears in some publications on *minkisi* of the Royal Museum, Tervuren.

18. Body hair and head hair have contrasted values. Hair from the crotch and the armpits might be put in so that the *nkisi* might be strong like a person; in this context it was called *luswamu,* something "hidden" (Diafwila, 47).

19. Examples of these auxiliary objects are shown in MacGaffey and Harris (1993). A *kunda* in the British Museum (1905 11-11.59) is doubly double, having four bells all carved from the same piece of wood.

20. *Meeso ma ndubikila.* A more literal translation might be "the eyes that are alert (for danger)," but Laman adds *ndwenga,* "intelligence," as his own gloss.

21. The classical Greek term for the statue of a god was *agalmá,* from *agamái,* "I am astonished."—Diskin Clay, personal communication.

22. The phrase used, *i sunzungulu,* attracts a special entry in LKD: "an expression indicating something that arrives rapidly and complete; which is magnificent, majestic, beautiful."

23. For another translation of this text, see Laman (1963, 187).

24. Laman (1963, 188–89) translates this curse, appending to it another from some other source.

25. Goats and especially pigs are "capital goods," in that to sacrifice them indicates that the issue is one of human life or death. Goats (*nkombo*) may be thought to represent a human being because they can stand on two feet and they can kneel. *Nkombo* also means "fault." Sheep do not appear in the texts as sacrificial animals. Although I use the word "sacrifice" from time to time, the usage is loose; Kongo is not a "sacrificing society" in the sense defined by Nancy Jay. The ritual killing of animals contains no element of either communion or expiation; it is a gift to an *nkisi* or it mimes intended violence (Jay 1992).

26. A striking feature of the inventory is that few of its items are repeated in other districts. A list of *minkisi* collected by Catholic missionaries in Kangu, some 50 kilometers west of Lolo, identified and briefly annotated in KiKongo by A. Tembo, a mission servant and collaborator of Bittremieux, shows no more than a dozen also identifiable at Lolo. (All the *minkisi* on Tembo's list are in the Royal Museum of Central Africa, Tervuren; Tembo's original text has recently been discovered by Hein Van Hee.).

27. Texts for Londa and Na Kongo for areas other than Lolo have been translated and published (MacGaffey 1991).

6. *Nkondi: Minkisi* to Kill People Swiftly

1. In the texts, *nkondi* is found in different noun classes with the plural prefixes *ba-*(personal), *mi-* (functional), and *zi-* (class 9, 10, appropriate to some kinds of objects, those "whose names have been formed as a rule from primitive words which by their meaning indicate the most characteristic qualities of the object [in this case, from *konda,* to hunt]") (LKG, 75). Asked to comment on these prefixes, Kimpianga kia Mahaniah said, "*zinkondi* is grammatically correct, but *minkondi* feels better." The prefix is usually omitted, but it reappears before a qualifying adjective: *nkondi zantilumuka, nkondi miamfyedila.* Some *nkondi* have no other proper name than Nkondi. Others carry a specific name (eg., Mavungu, Na Mpindi, Nkondi a Mungundu). In mod-

ern Christian Manianga, *kinkondi,* to seek out *ngang'a nkondi* to have him track and punish a thief, is regarded as a form of witchcraft (Janzen and MacGaffey 1974, 45).

2. In modern Manianga the term *nkondi* is scarcely remembered, having been replaced by the eastern term *mpungu.* Mpungu is said to be appealed to mostly by thieves and other wrongdoers who wish to protect themselves from pursuit.—Kimpianga kia Mahaniah, personal communication.

3. A map of dialect areas appears as the frontispiece to Laman 1936; the "western" region corresponds to the eastern edge of the modern district of Mayombe (that is, the speech of Lutete and Kinkela). The "northeastern" region is close to Brazzaville in the modern Republic of Congo.

4. Figures with a small number of nails are found among the BaSongye in eastern Congo, and in parts of Nigeria, but they appear to have an entirely different significance.

5. *Nzundu* originally meant both "hammer" and "anvil." Dapper's description of *nkisi* Kikokoo in Loango, a statue in black wood, clearly indicates that it was believed to control storms and pursue witches. He reports an incident in which certain Portuguese stole the *nkisi,* broke it, and sought to repair it by driving a nail into it; whereupon Kikokoo, furious, wrecked a Portuguese ship (Fondation Dapper 1989, 262).

6. Texts for several *nkondi* appear, with translations and pictures, in MacGaffey 1991. "*" indicates *nkisi* statues well known in the art world, for which no text is known to exist.

7. Nkisi miamionso vo biteke biena zimbau mibikuanga nkumbu Nkosi, mu d.d. mibuidilanga muntu mu ntulu ye milenda dukisa buala mu fintanguntangu (Lutete, 229). Guthrie finds CS 1101 *-kóci, "chief," mainly in eastern and southern Bantu (but also in Luba) and argues from the difference in distribution that a common origin with CS 1102 *-kóci, "lion," is unlikely.

8. Minkisi miazinkosi vo mu kanda dia bantu mu fuilanga yela kwa luka menga vo sisuka. Ngolo zau mu vonda bantu nswalu (Lutete, 216).

9. *Nkosi* could be derived from *kosa,* to crush, which is what pneumonia seems to do to one's chest. Pneumonia is one of the diseases included in the ailment *lubanzi,* characteristically inflicted by Nkondi; L. Van de Velde (1886, 372) mentions that diseases of the lungs were common in the dry season. Among the Punu (northern Kongo) of Gabon, *kosi,* said to be derived from *kwoda,* "to resemble" [?], is the name given to the class of retributive charms, corresponding to *nkondi.*—Alisa LaGamma, personal communication.

10. Lwamba of Lolo, Cahier 239; Laman Collection No. 19.1359, also shown in Laman 1963, fig. 13. In this instance the *nkomono* ("nailing," that is, invocation) of the *nkisi* is effected by taking kaolin from it to a crossroads and saying, "Nkondi Nsanda, whoever stole the thing, cover his body with sores."

11. The carving of animals is rarely lifelike. Dogs can be mistaken for leopards because they may be spotted to indicate their intermediary function between the visible and the invisible. According to Lutangu (Cahier 312), leopards are not represented as *minkisi* because they are associated with chiefship. Leopard's teeth and claws were sometimes included in *minkisi,* however.

12. African dogs do not usually bark; hunters attach wooden bells or rattles to them to know where they are. *Dibu* is also the name of "a tree that puts witches to flight" (Cahier 231, 8).

13. *Yulu* is cognate with *zulu,* "above." For another selection from this text, see Chapter 3 under "Translation Exercises."

14. The significance of these procedures is discussed below.

15. In Mayombe, Nzazi, the lightning, is said to be a dog.

16. Various names applied to the hardware driven into a wooden figure: *mpuya, kisengo* (iron), *mbau* (wedge), *nsonso* (nail; originally, a wooden peg), *baaku* (knife), *mbeezi* (knife). There is nothing special about these words, with the exception of *mpuya,* which specifically refers to the process of *koma nloko.* Often the iron used consisted of worn-out knives or hoe blades; other hardware includes European nails and screws. There are a number of testimonies to the use of wooden wedges, and some examples are found in museums.

17. This *nkisi,* collected in Mayombe by Bittremieux, was exhibited in Frankfurt am Main in 1986; by then it had acquired a collection of skulls and bones hung over its uplifted right arm. A drawing of the *nkisi* on the poster for the exhibition exaggerated this grisly but adventitious feature for dramatic effect (Thiel et al. 1986).

18. The *nkisi* is Ma Kongo, mentioned in the seventeenth century. The fruit is *nsafu,* a kernel of which is placed in the *nkisi,* whose container in this instance is a clay pot. In addition, there seems to be a special connection between *nkondi* and the *n'safu* tree (*Canarium schweinfurthii*), from whose wood the figure is usually made, despite its apparent unsuitability, being resinous (Lehuard 1980, 116). Exploding gunpowder, besides arousing the *nkisi* (and the client, as I have seen for myself), includes a reference to thunder, *ndumu a mvula,* which was the name given to gunpowder when it was first imported. Some *nkondi* carry powder flasks such as hunters use (for example Rotterdam 28500, Museum voor Volkenkunde, Rotterdam, MvVR29500).

19. Matuka Yeno Mansoni helped me struggle with this passage. See Chapter 3, "Translation Exercises."

20. Body fluids in general have opposed values, as both blessing and cursing.

21. The author says that Nkondi ya Mfyedila is called by this name to distinguish it from other kinds of *nkisi* that attack people, inflicting illness. Despite the nailing it received, he specifically contrasts this kind of *nkondi* with *nkondi ya nkoma,* "nailing *nkondi.*"

22. In some pot rituals, the wood of the *luveete* tree is specified—possibly with a pun on *veta,* to hunt. For Me Kongo Nsambu, sticks of *mwindu, nsanda, nlolo,* and *mfilu* are prescribed (Cahier 8).

23. The sign of the cross is a "cosmogram," a microcosmic mark drawn on the ground to indicate that the individual in question stands at a crossroads between unseen causes and visible effects. It is not a residue of Christian influence. The analogy between witches and rats is reproduced in miniature rat traps attached to *minkisi.*

24. Nsemi, Cahier 387; Nkuzu, Cahier 382. Example of the baton of Na Kongo, ill. MacGaffey (1991, 78).

25. Ngangula yombo wadiata nkuhu meni semwa. Matunta, Cahier 299, Cahier 313. See Laman (1957, 10–13, 148–49).

26. Dupré comments on the integrative functions of experts circulating between villages (1985, 79).

27. *Mpeto,* related to *veta,* "to hunt," can also mean "a trap." See the discussion of hunting, above. *Maniangu,* "prohibition," should not be confused with Manianga, the district.

28. Correspondence, Ridyard and Shawcross, in accession files for Nkondi Man-gaaka, Manchester Museum, Manchester, England.

29. Of two famous examples of Kozo, the caniform *nkisi* from Cabinda, shown in W. Rubin (1984, v. 1:66, 67), one is covered with tokens, the other shows hardly any.

30. The complete text can be found in MacGaffey (1991); extracts and pictures are in MacGaffey and Harris (1993, 80–86).

31. The figure is specially carved to show its genitals. Male *minkisi,* if they have genitals at all, are exceedingly well endowed (for example, British Museum 1954 AF23 1632, or Museo Pigorini 84204); this feature has nothing to do with fertility. In use, the figure would "hide its shame" with a cloth which the *nganga* could whip aside to heighten the drama of the proceedings. The figure, though human, need not be sexed if sexual organs are not part of the metaphorical statement. Of those examined by Lehuard, 75 percent were asexual (1980, 127). Exposing the genitals is the worst of insults, a woman's ultimate resort in village quarrels. The genital endowment of some *nkondi* may record the practice of the *nganga,* stripping himself naked when uttering a curse or provoking his *nkisi* (see text in this chapter by Demvo, Cahier 30).

7. Composition and Powers of an Nkondi Called Mbola

1. In double-column text, square brackets in the KiKongo indicate a marginal comment in KiKongo or Swedish by Laman in the manuscripts, except that occasion-ally I insert [*sic*], [illeg.] or [?] to indicate my own doubts. Square brackets in the English always mark interpolations of my own.

2. Bittremieux says the principal part of Mbola was a crock (Bittremieux 1922–27: s.v. Mbola).

3. The passage literally refers to the enclosure itself by a term, *ngudi a nkama,* which often indicates "a great chief." LKD, 707 says it is "a euphemism for Mbola."

4. The song sung at the preparation of Mbola is a complex pun, in which "the girl I met on Nkandu day" (that is, at the market) refers to the medicines being prepared (*zandu* means both market and a packet of medicines; the medicines are being pre-pared on a mat of palm leaves). *Nkandu* also means "prohibition." Songs sung to accompany the composition of *minkisi* often include erotic jokes.

5. This small, spiral shell was formerly a unit of currency.

6. See Kimfuzi's par. 3, above.

7. Untrustworthy translation. *Mfilu* and *nlolo* are two small savanna trees that are said to grow near each other and are always mentioned together; they have black and red fruits respectively. Their leaves were sometimes placed under a bridal bed to en-courage reproduction, for which red and black are the appropriate colors (Cahier 330).

8. Makwende, a praise-name of the leopard, is applied to Mbola, as to other *minkondi,* because they too are hunters and may contain, as in this case, leopard ele-ments.

9. Cahiers 387 and 388 describe these *minkisi.* Formulae of invocation were readily transferred from one *nkisi* to another.

10. "And the word of the Lord came unto me a second time, saying, 'What seest thou?' And I said, 'I see a seething pot; and the face thereof is toward the north.' Then the Lord said unto me, 'Out of the north an evil shall break forth upon all the inhabi-

tants of the land'."—Jeremiah 1: 13–14. Recent translations prefer "from" rather than "toward" the north.

8. Life and Death

1. *Bikinda,* from *kindama,* to be upside down. The cemetery of the chiefs.

2. In the east the principal writers are Diafwila in Kibunzi, Kilola and Kunzi in Mukimbungu (on the south bank), Lunungu and Matunta in Nganda.

3. Royal Museum, Tervuren, RG 38571, 43708.

4. Babutidi, 13. For a description of a similar execution in northern Angola, see Weeks (1914, 62).

5. In 1725, the Superior Council of Louisiana, which used violence to support what little authority it had, needed to engage a regular executioner. The only candidate of the necessary strength and disposition was one Louis Congo, who had arrived from Africa only four years before. He was able to demand a high price for his services: his freedom, that of his wife, a plot of land, and a personal ration of wines and spirits. For breaking on the wheel or burning alive he charged 40 pounds; for flogging, 10 pounds (Hall 1995, 131).

6. In the seventeenth century it was usual to plant a fig tree when a new village was founded.

7. The shell, or sometimes a bark box (*lukobe*), containing the white clay used to mark the chief on ritual occasions, was called *ndembo;* Luba chiefs kept a bowl of chalk for the same purpose (Petit 1995). For other lists of ingredients of *nkisi nsi,* see the next chapter.

8. Konzo and Nsona, two of the four days of the Kongo week (MacGaffey 1986a, 44). The others are Kenge and Nkandu.

9. A similar procedure might be followed in the investiture of the successor to a deceased *nganga* (Dupré 1985, 242).

10. In a Kuba sub-group, Biyeng, the chief similarly acquires both "sorcery" powers (*bukum*) and those of "vital force" (*magnon*) (Josephson 1992, ch. 6).

11. In a review of associations between ironworking and leadership in Central Africa, De Maret uses words like "association" and "connection" far too loosely (De Maret 1985). In Rwanda and other parts of eastern Africa, the king may well have been thought of as a smith, but the image of *le roi forgeron* was not mentioned with respect to Kongo until the mid-seventeenth century; it probably came from Angola. It was used in succession debates in the eighteenth century to stress his role as benevolent arbiter, in opposition to the tradition of violence (Thornton 1993, 189–95). The idea of the king as smith confuses the role of the king with that of the *simbi* priest (MacGaffey 1986a, 67–68).

12. On the king in Mbanza Kongo: "I have been present on more than one occasion when his majesty has had a tickling in the throat and has coughed and spluttered to free the passage. All present clapped their hands most vigorously" (Weeks 1914, 40).

13. "Palm shoots" are offspring, the next generation of the people, not literally the trees. Mahaniah's comment on the phrase *nyumbu a ntende* was, *Mfinda yikondolo ntende kayena zingu ko,* "a forest without palm shoots cannot last," that is, a village

without a younger generation will die out. Because, in a later passage, the expression (used in the plural) seems to refer to those who are dependent on these rituals, LKD glosses it as "the BaBwende."

14. Accused persons who were exonerated were marked with white; the guilty, with black.

15. The mantle, *lubongo lu nsundi,* a large sheet of raffia cloth, worn over one shoulder. Part of the regalia of some chiefs, who as an act of braggadocio drag one corner on the ground. The gesture is reported from the seventeenth century, and I have witnessed it myself (see also Mertens 1942, 79).

16. This association among chiefship, leprosy, and the harnessed bushbuck (*Tragelaphus scriptus*) recurs among the Mbundu in Angola (Miller 1976, 69).

17. Simbu is the name of a war-*nkisi,* often composed by chiefs, but here *kisimbu,* from *simba,* "to hold," is an amulet.

18. Reports on smoke-drying in Manianga include Manker (1932); Widman (1967); Reikat (1990). Fu-kiau, writing from northeastern Manianga, says specifically that the purposes of drying the body were to celebrate and honor it and to give it "the perdurance of stones," *kum'vana zingu kia tadi* (Fu-Kiau kia Bunseki 1967).

19. The account of funeral practices in LKII, ch. 5 is a hodgepodge of snippets from here and there, paraphrased and combined with personal observations by Laman or the editor.

20. *Sivu bibakengi makolo,* lit. "seasons for which they tied knots," presumably referring to a tally.

21. The English text (Laman 1957, 140) confusingly says, "the last king," but the manuscript clearly says "the first."

22. Upon taking control of the province of Nsundi in 1652, the new "duke" had first to survive a mock battle; victory gave him rights over lands and waters (Thornton 1983, 58).

23. The detail about the rod (*Mboki bana kunsingika nkau va vembo*) comes from Kiananwa's Cahier 70.

24. "The Leopard" here is *bango,* the personal plural prefix indicating "leopards as a class."

25. "To sleep on the ground" is to abstain from sex; to sleep, literally, on the ground is to risk the disease *nsi,* from offending *nkisi nsi,* the *nkisi* of the chiefship. The supervisory role of the *bamayaala* is very similar at a modern funeral (MacGaffey 1970, 150–69).

26. The craftsman might make an image of the deceased to be put on the grave; more likely he constructed a *nyombo,* a sort of mummy coverd with large numbers of blankets (Laman 1957, pl. 1. and pp. 89–90). It appears that the chiefs living in Kibunzi were taken to an Mbanza Nsundi, probably a former village now a royal cemetery; the investiture may also have taken place there. The text does not suggest that any paramount was involved or any other officials than Mpanzu, the priests of Bunzi, Nsonde, and Mwandazi, and the *bamayaala,* Children and Grandchildren of Nsundi.

27. Among the Eastern Pende also, the candidate may be whipped with branches.—Zoë Strother, personal communication.

28. Cahier 75. This is the usual position for sexual intercourse. The passage gave Laman trouble; he placed question marks, and made notes in KiKongo and Swedish. Though only partly legible, the notes include the phrase *zika lusala lwa mbemba,* "thrust in a vulture feather," which links this text directly with Diafwila's description

of Na Menta. The paraphrase of Kilola's text in Laman (1957, 142) omits the sexual details. The infertility of invested chiefs, brought on by various means, is a recurrent theme in southwestern Congo.

29. For changes in trade and politics on the coast in the nineteenth century, see Martin (1972, ch. 7–8). For an overview of nineteenth-century trade routes and practices in the Congo estuary, see Broadhead (1971).

30. Bittremieux says that anybody could be admitted with the permission of the chief of the *nsi*, but he also makes it clear that a sharp social distinction existed between those who had been initiated and the "dogs" who had not (1936, 202).

31. The *mukanda* initiation camps of the BaPende, sponsored by chiefs, also mimicked the predatory relations between the chiefs and the public.—Zoë Strother, personal communication.

32. Cf. Doutreloux (1967, 169–170, 190). The night people became a source of occult power for those who received them, exactly as an *nkisi* derived force from a victim imprisoned in it, and a witch accumulated witchcraft powers (*makundu*). Cats and dogs were also handed over. Apparently cats were valued because they killed rodents that ate food stores; anybody who killed one incurred a heavy fine (Cahier 173). *Wàyi*, cat, not to be confused with *wáayi*, slave. Kilola, giving a similar list, says there must be nine of everything (Cahier 75).

33. Among the eastern Pende today, a chief at his investiture may seize any woman to be his ritual wife.—Zoë Strother, personal communication.

34. An administrative report on Kibunzi in 1936, long after the "abolition" of slavery, shows that the proportion of slave to free women in some clans was as high as two to one.

35. Ceyssens analyzes in detail the marriage strategies of elders in a very similar situation in Katanga: "Tout en respectant, de principe, le mot d'ordre séculaire de l'exogamie, le chef kongodinga se fait 'donneur de femme', recourt pratiquement à l'endogamie centripète, en assimilant des esclaves et en annexant des clients. Cette politique de récupération, qui permet de consolider le groupe local, s'impose d'autant plus que la matrilinéalité prédomine fondamentalement dans notre unité d'analyse" (Ceyssens 1984, 369).

36. For an account of similar proceedings under Belgian rule in the 1950s, see Janzen and MacGaffey (1974, no. 27).

37. The common anthropological picture of African slavery dwells on processes of assimilation whereby strangers become kin (Miers and Kopytoff 1977); it neglects the complementary processes by which slaves are internally generated. Slavery is intrinsic to matrilineal descent in Kongo, not an incidental or additional feature. On the economic risks of war to the war leader (*mfumu muzingu*) see Dupré (1985, 83).

38. Cahier 235, p. 5 ff., paraphrased. For more on Maswa Ngoma, see Chapter 9.

39. Nzondo was a primordial half-man whose crossing of Nzadi was accompanied by miracles symbolic of sexual fertility (Bittremieux 1920). Several places on the Congo River are said to be the site of this crossing.

40. Concerning the Tio: "It was said that when any single person in the *ndzo* was believed to have killed too many others in the *ndzo* he could be forced to commit suicide by hanging or the *ndzo* members would do away with him and fake it as suicide" (Vansina 1973, 33).

41. The medicine chest associated with it is in the Royal Museum, Tervuren (RG

22459). The note accompanying it, evidently written by a young convert of the Catholic mission at Kangu, says that it was used by the kingmakers to enthrone the chiefs of Kangu, that it owned all other fetishes in the domain, and that it guaranteed plenty of meat and prevented sickness. Anyone who violated the rules of Nkumbuzi, by working on an Nsona day for example, would be killed (information from Hein Van Hee).

42. The *nganga* of Mbudila was a woman, who tested warriors for battle by passing them between her legs. The apparatus of Simbu, or Nkinda Nsimbu, included a large cooking pot of medicines, described by Bittremieux as the "mother fetish"; a large snake that slept under the bed of *nganga* Mbudila would wake in time of danger and crawl into this pot. There was also a wooden figurine whose medicinal belly-pack included hair from every inhabitant of the village. In the mirror surmounting the pack the *nganga* could inspect the souls of men bound for war; if she saw blood in the mirror, the man could not go, but those whom she passed would not die, though they might be wounded. The figure could be laid on its face so that the hearts of the enemy would likewise "lie down." The *nganga* could also use the *nkisi* to defend the village against leopards. Both the pot and the figurine were sprinkled with the blood of a pitch-black he-goat. The Simbu that Bittremieux describes, now in the Royal Museum, Tervuren, is a female figure; he does not indicate the sex of the *nganga,* who was perhaps also female. Other elements of the *nkisi* included a raffia bundle of medicines with a *kunda* bell attached to the outside, and a small pot for boiling water on a fire of *luveete* wood to detect witches. Bittremieux's description is very similar to that of Babutidi in Cahier 14, but more detailed; it may well have come from Ngambula himself (Bittremieux 1922–1927, 603–607; Bittremieux 1923). An *nkisi* Simbu could also be an *nkisi nsi*. Its origin can be traced to the Punu in Gabon, where myth celebrates Simbu as a female conqueror, founder of a lineage and tutelary spirit of the conquered territory.— A. LaGamma, personal communication.

9. Lutete's Chiefs

1. See Map 2. The road appears on maps of the period, but no longer exists. Between 1896 and 1912 the Redemptorist Fathers established stations at the first three of these places from their base at Matadi (Kratz 1970).

2. Much of Lutete's writing on chiefship occurs paraphrased in Laman (1957, 150–153).

3. *Ngiadulu muna nsi a nkulu,* Cahier 216. The numbers attached to paragraphs indicate the page in Lutete's manuscript.

4. *Ngongi,* the double, clapperless bell.

5. Delcommune's description of Jouco-Pava (Nsuka Pava), wealthy and powerful minister of trade for the nine kings of Boma, is similar, though Jouco-Pava, who was not invested as a chief himself, went on foot (Delcommune 1922, 52).

6. Cahier 231. "In Pende thought, the inauguration of the chief correctly begins with the death of the preceding chief. If you ask how they select and inaugurate a new chief, they will immediately begin to tell you how they bury his predecessor."—Zoë Strother, personal communication.

7. Elsewhere (Cahier 219, 33) Lutete says that if a chief dies far from home his body is buried there; in his home village his people kill a goat, put its entrails in a coffin, and eventually drag them in a car, as though they were the remains of the chief.

8. For a summary of available information on smoke-drying, *niombo,* and the associated musical instruments, with numerous photos, see Reikat (1990).

9. *Mbongi* can mean a men's house, a mortuary, or a special kind of coffin. See Chapter 9.

10. Na Nsuka is one of the chief's officers (Doutreloux 1967, 191–95). His title cost only two slaves (Lutete 234, 25).

11. *Tolongo:* "grande caisse ordinairement finement décorée dans laquelle un chef cache ses trésors et dans laquelle il sera inhumé."—LKD.

12. Laman 1957, 90 describes the construction of *kimbenza* as a kind of coffin; Lutete, in Cahier 219, describes it as a stretcher of two poles carried by four men. At the "coming-out" of a chief of the highest rank among the Eastern Pende, he should be carried on a figurated wooden coffin called *mbenza.*—Zoë Strother, personal communication.

13. Cahier 234. *Tumbula:* "enlever la puissance à un chef"; reverse of *tumba,* "to consecrate."—LKD. In a parallel ritual in Nganda, the new chief was laid upon the wrapped corpse of his predecessor "to show that the deceased had no more power" (Cahier 313).

14. "Nkisi mimyole myayaadilanga zimbenza, nkumbu za minkisi i zazi: Lusunzi ye Mwema. I kuma nsi eto yayaadulwanga mu ndambu zoole kansi yavaswa mu ndambu zoole mu kuma kya nkisi myomyo myayaadilanga mfumu zozo. Nampanzu wayaadila ku Mwema. Nsungu a Ngo ye Nsal'a Ngo bakala zimpangi babaluka ku Lusunzi. Mfumu zazi zabalukila mu minkisi myami, i zau zakala mfumu za ngolo" (Kinkela, 94, 37).

15. Notes, apparently by Arthur Clare (1898), among the accession papers for *nkisi* Mangaka in the Manchester Museum. See discussion by Hagenbucher-Sacripanti (1973, 31).

16. Cahier 236, Kimbidi chiefship, Nsundi clan.

17. *Nsabi,* "I know," from *zaya,* to know. *Ngovo,* from *vova,* to speak, was the name of an *nkisi* and was also a title equivalent to "foreign minister" in both Loango and Boma. *Mvandi a mbumba,* sorcerer, one who composes *mbumba,* a bundle of medicines (here, with sinister intent).

18. Doutreloux says the *mobula* is a sort of cross-belt of woven fibers (1967, 168).

19. The "banana" is *nkondo,* plantain, not the sweet banana, *tiba.* The latter renews itself indefinitely, and is therefore likened to the matrilineage, whereas the plantain, which has to be replanted every few generations, is like *kitaata,* the relation to father's and father's father's clans.

20. Lutete's text here should be compared with Doutreloux's account of investiture, which mentions many of the same locales, titles, and clans (Doutreloux 1967, 167–96).

21. Cahier 232.

22. *Nlembo* could be "fingers."

23. *Nkisi nsi wavata.* Major *minkisi* sometimes had a representative or shrine in the village (*vata*), less sacred and more accessible than the primary version in the forest.

24. Cahier 234.

25. Literally "a thousand," this word designated a bundle of cloth of standard value.

26. Cahier 236, Kimbidi chiefship, Nsundi clan. The medicines listed are additional to those Lutete has already mentioned.

27. *Semwa,* pass. of *sema.* This paragraph reflects Christian influence. It can be argued that creation ex nihilo is foreign to Kongo thought. The matter was controversial in Laman's day and remains so. See MacGaffey (1991, 54).

28. *Nsongi* is a "pointer"; *dimbu* is the ordinary word for a sign. It is known that caves and rocks were painted red and white during chiefly investitures.

29. *Mwema* is as it were the title of a *kiyaazi,* a specific entity functioning as a source of power; here, an anvil, *nzundu,* and Lusunzi, a *simbi* stone. *Lusunzi,* from *sunzuka,* means "remarkable, splendid"; it was probably applied to all *simbi* stones used as *biyaazi.* The anvil is related to the creative power of *bisimbi.* The *bababimpita* are "those painted as warriors, with black lines."

30. Cahier 231. In northern Mayombe, "If they chose someone to be invested as chief, they took *munkwisa* and planted it over the basket of the old ones (*kobi bakulu,* the *nkisi* of chiefs); if it flourished, they knew that he could be chief. If not, they would assume that the candidate's conduct was evil, that he was greedy and could not be chief. They would choose another successor" (Cahier 280).

31. *Semisa,* causative form of *sema,* to bless, confirm, restore to purity.

32. Cahier 236. Chiefship of Mbenza Me Mbangala.

33. Cahier 235. Chiefship of Maswa Ngoma.

34. *Mfunya,* tokens attached to an *nkisi* to guide its operations. The spikes usually driven into a wooden *nkondi* might also be driven into the ground (see Chapter 6). Bittremieux collected an ornate staff with a sharp metal point, and a similar one is in the Museum voor Volkenkunde, Leiden (1934, pl. 9).

35. Cahier 236. Chiefship of Mbenza Me Mbangala.

36. In Kanyok myth, the hero Cish Mukul orders that firewood must be set down gently (Yoder 1992, 37).

37. Cahier 235. Na Lubuzi and his successors have already been mentioned in Chapter 8, above.

38. This rule is apparently explained by Babutidi's account of a chiefship ritual in Mayombe, in which the investing chief, Na Mbenza, trod on the candidate's foot while marking him with the sacred white clay (Cahier 18). It would not do for anyone else to seem to repeat the gesture.

39. *Dia nkombo,* lit. "to eat goat," refers to seeking refuge by an act of submission to another chief, equivalent to *lokila kunda.* The phrase also means "to admit a fault."

40. Another paraphrase of this part of Cahier 233 is Laman (1963, 37).

41. Cahier 232.

42. *Ma-ngu-ndazi,* a person of great honor (LKD). *Mangundazi a mangundazi* = king of kings (Cahier 225, 31).

43. *Kindibida,* to dig, hollow out.

44. The construction here is in the negative mood, expressing surprise that something did not happen. LKG, 281.

45. *Fukwa,* a pile of hot ashes in the hearth; *bisimbi* and *simbi* stones are associated with water and should be kept separate from fire, which connotes violence and death.

46. *Tadi dya nsenzebele,* "the flat stone," recurs inscrutably in tradition. Near Mukimbungu, the Na Vunda chiefs were invested on such a stone. "There they spread the leopardskin and the mat, and put the iron chest upon it. The place remains exceedingly sacred to this day; no member of the Kivunda clan may walk on it, but only the Children and Grandchildren" (Masamba, 277).

47. Extracts, translated from the Portuguese. Accession number of the object, 34.28.2.

48. The skin of the brow, whether of leopard or of a deceased officeholder, was incorporated in the successor's medicine kit; it was called *kintweka.* Cf. *lunzi,* Chapter 9.

49. The BaYaka associate such a knife especially with women (Devisch 1993, 216 and pl. 11).

50. That is, about 1913. Swelling of the body was (and is) regarded as a typical sign of the displeasure of an *nkisi* whose taboos have been violated.

51. Cahier 236. Mangwa Mayene, "Old Mother Breasts," was a rock, regarded as a *simbi,* with four "breasts," two in front and two behind. Cahier 234, 26.

52. Cahier 235. Clan KiMongo was a branch of Mbenza led by Na Lubuzi (see Chapter 8) which lived at "Mbanza Nsundi"—which one? The Lubuzi River runs by Maduda and Tshela to join the Chiloango.

53. This expression refers to the thunder that is heard when such a chief dies and becomes a *simbi.*

54. G. Buakasa: lion and leopard are proverbially associated throughout Kongo, as in blessings: "May he have the force of the lion and the leopard to triumph over all enemies."

55. Cahier 235, KiMongo clan; Pungi is the second chief on Lutete's list, after Na Mongo Mvangi.

56. By 1850, the only ivory arriving at the coast came in caravans from the interior, so perhaps we can date Na Mongo Pungi's career to the 1840s (Broadhead 1971, 160).

57. Cahier 232.

58. *Mbazi* is the usual word for a public place, the space in which some public function, in this case chiefly investiture, takes place. Land was conveyed only as a transaction in the prestige sphere, that is, against other prestige goods such as camwood or, here, slaves. The transaction was not so much a purchase as an acknowledgment of client status, of a subordinate position with respect to another chiefship.

59. The tree planted is chosen for its name, which becomes an attribute of the chiefship; in this case, *mungongo* invokes *ngongo,* "perturbation," to signify "May witches be perturbed." In ordinary *minkisi,* Calabar bean, *ngongo,* has a similar function. *Mungodila* evokes *ngolo,* strength.

60. Cahier 236. Clan Mbenza me Mbangala, location not indicated. Luniamba is not mentioned again; it may be derived from *nyamba,* to throw down (see Chapter 8). Presumably Me Mbuku Mbangala belonged to this group (see above). "The rules of the staff," "Forbidden animals," and "The chief and the earth" (above) all refer to this chiefship.

61. *mbangala* = club, from Portuguese *bengala,* walking stick.

62. *nsingi* = a wildcat, *mbala;* name also refers to a witch. *wayi* = another wildcat; name also refers to a witch. Both witches and wildcats (which are particolored) mediate between the seen and the unseen.

63. "All Tio believed that when the king was introduced he had to kill twelve people by witchcraft to find the strength to rule" (Vansina 1973, 172).

64. *Kumbisa bantu,* to cause the people to shout; the rhetorical technique of the elicited response. See Chapter 3, translation exercise number 1.

65. There is an *ngongi* of something like this size in the Ethnographic Museum, Berlin, #33940.

66. The numbers of the several chiefs are taken from a list of 49 provided by Lutete.

10. Reflections and Extensions

1. Kongo cosmology and the evidence for it are laid out in *Religion and Society,* ch. 2–4 (MacGaffey 1986a).

2. Apart from stories of ritual transfers over short distances, the Cahiers afford no evidence of trade in ritual properties. It is intriguing to note, however, that at Lolo *nkisi* Lau, for hunting, bore a name cognate with that of the Luba culture hero, the hunter Mbidi Kiluwe, and that the ritual of this *nkisi* repeats a theme of travel down the spine, "God's highway," that is central to the Luba myth. Coincidence? Recent transfer? Ancient heritage?

3. My conclusions in this matter, at least with respect to the area of Western Bantu, are similar to those of Vansina, although they were arrived at from an entirely different perspective and by a different method (MacGaffey 1972; MacGaffey 1979). Broader questions of anthropological method are at issue here. In a provocative critique of prevailing comparative practices, M. Strathern finds that the apparently numerous social systems of Melanesia should be considered as versions of one another, ramifications of a single set of social arrangements to be studied, if the data were available, as diverse outgrowths of a single historical process analogous to that which formed European societies (Strathern 1988, 340–43).

4. In Nigeria, the leopard is the animal counterpart of the Oba of Benin, who takes human life. For the Yoruba, *Aye* is the tangible world of the living and *Orun* the invisible realm of spiritual forces such as gods, ancestors, and spirits. "Such a cosmic conception is often visualized as either a spherical gourd, whose upper and lower hemispheres fit tightly together, or as a divination tray. . . . The intersecting lines inscribed on the surface by a diviner at the outset of divination symbolize metaphoric crossroads . . . the point of intersection between the cosmic realms" (Drewal and Pemberton 1989, 14).

5. In recent decades, elders have learned to incorporate in their traditions genealogical and geographical elements to meet European expectations, and historical materials gleaned from Catholic missionary publications.

6. This account of the land of the dead is based not only on the manuscripts but also on field experience.

7. See Beidelman's stimulating discussion (1993) of social imagination.

8. Among the Baule of Ivory Coast, whose cosmology is similar, the otherworld is called "the village of truth," in opposition to this world of deceptive appearances (Ravenhill 1994, 25).

9. For similar functions of the myths and rituals of *orisha* among the Yoruba, see Matory (1994).

10. Masolo reviews the philosophical debate about science, models, and rationality in Africa, including the question whether Horton (and others) are comparing appropriate discourses (Masolo 1994, ch. 6).

11. "Events of common experience and actions undertaken in common are constituted when we gather together sequences of events or sub-actions by projecting onto

them a structure comprising a beginning, middle and end. . . . Experience of action is embodied in and constituted by the story that is told about it" (Carr 1986, 149).

12. *Nsakala* is a rattle such as women use to lull children. *Bukúlu,* "ancient times"; *búkulu,* "therapy." The banana, which rots easily but springs up to bear fruit again in nine months, embodies a conventional life/death metaphor repeated in the name of the pool. The spots, comparable to "the mark of the leopard," certify approval of the candidate on the part of the *bisimbi* who live in the pool. The story is one of the rare Kongo examples of a tradition in which the chief is descended from immigrants, while his "father," the investing priest, represents the autochthons.

13. Vansina displays Kuba cosmology as a sequence of propositions arranged in order of logical priority (Vansina 1958). With certain modifications this scheme would probably hold anywhere from southern Cameroon to Zambia.

14. The rainbow serpent, Mbumba Luangu, appears in Bittremieux's account of Kinkimba. De Heusch makes much of it in his structuralist analysis of Central African myths (Bittremieux 1936; De Heusch 1982). It is mentioned only once in the manuscripts (Cahier 296), but is well established in coastal areas from Ngoyo to Gabon.

15. The TuKongo and other peoples of the upper Kasai contrast chiefs "of the above" (predatory, accumulative) with those "of the below" (peaceable, redistributive) (Ceyssens 1984, 111). The contrast is that between "life" and "death," or between the two major classes of *minkisi.*

16. Contra Thornton, there are no indications of major *ideological* differences between the urban and rural sectors of the kingdom although, to be sure, rural communities frequently contested the central authority and its demands (Thornton 1983, 57).

17. The guardian of the *nkisi nsi* on the Loango coast is also called *nthomi,* or was until recently (Hagenbucher-Sacripanti 1973).

18. Hilton indicates changes in kinship terminology and social organization taking place among the Angolan political elite in the seventeenth and eighteenth centuries which I find difficult to evaluate but which deserve further investigation (Hilton 1985, ch. 8).

19. Mary Douglas anticipates much of my argument in a discussion of "pawnship," in which term she includes all forms of qualified citizenship. On the other hand, Douglas does not mention the slave trade and its possible demographic and structural effects (Douglas 1964; MacGaffey 1970; Van Velsen 1964; Mitchell 1956).

20. With respect to African slavery in general, this motivation is much disputed (Robertson and Klein 1983).

21. This interpretation is the opposite of that advanced by Hilton, who assumes that matrilineal descent always existed and that the emergence of what she calls patrilineal categories was a function of increased centralization in the kingdom combined with Christian baptismal practice (Hilton 1985, 88–90).

22. There are scattered and brief references to similar practices elsewhere in the Congo basin. In Zimbabwe, among the northern Shona, according to David Lan, "The fullest demonstration of how age and the authority of the lineage are associated with dryness occurs at the burial of a chief. The body is not buried immediately but is laid out on a platform either in a hut or in an enclosed grave, with pots placed beneath to collect the body fluids as they emerge. Only when all the wetness of life has drained away and nothing but hard, dry bones remain may the head of the royal lineage be placed in the earth with his ancestors." His spirit becomes a *mhondoro,* lion (Lan 1985, 93).

23. The seventeenth-century expansion of the Lunda from what is now southeastern Congo is partly attributable to wealth derived from the Angolan trade in slaves and ivory.

24. King MboMboosh of the Bushong was also strangled by a rope pulled through the back of the house (Vansina 1978, 68).

25. The BaKongo have been noted in modern times for the absence of violence among them. By contrast, in Northern Ghana, where I have spent some time, violence is never far below the surface.

26. Linguistic evidence shows that the association between "eating" and "wealth" is ancient in Central Africa.

27. Zoë Strother's account of her fieldwork, "Suspected of Sorcery," describes Pende chiefship today with the kind of eyewitness realism that the Kongo texts lack; it also vividly illustrates the contemporary role of witchcraft in the interpretation of events and the negotiation of relationships (Strother 1996).

28. The most thorough exploration of this theme in contemporary Africa is that of Peter Geschiere in Cameroon (Geschiere 1997), but see also Anderson and Johnson, 1995, on the persistence and political effectiveness in Nilotic societies of a very different tradition. For the mobilization of ritual and kinship values ("villagization") in stressful urban conditions in the Congo, see Devisch 1996.

REFERENCE LIST

Anderson, D. M., and D. H. Johnson, eds. 1995. *Revealing Prophets: Prophecy in Eastern African History.* London: James Currey.

Apter, A. 1993. "Atinga Revisited: Yoruba Witchcraft and the Cocoa Economy, 1950–1951." In *Modernity and its Malcontents,* ed. J. Comaroff and J. Comaroff. Chicago: University of Chicago Press.

Ardener, E. 1989. *The Voice of Prophecy and Other Essays.* New York: Basil Blackwell.

Axelson, S. 1970. *Culture Confrontation in the Lower Congo.* Falkøping, Sweden: Gummesons.

Barth, F. 1975. *Ritual and Knowledge among the Baktaman of New Guinea.* New Haven: Yale University Press.

———. 1987. *Cosmologies in the Making.* New York: Cambridge University Press.

Bastin, M.-L. 1994. *Sculpture Angolaise.* Lisbon: Museo Nacional de Etnologia.

Bateson, G. 1972. *Steps to an Ecology of Mind.* New York: Ballantine.

Bayat, J.-F. 1993. *The State in Africa: The Politics of the Belly.* London: Longman.

Beidelman, T. O. 1966. "Swazi Royal Ritual." *Africa* 36 (4): 373–405.

———. 1986. *Moral Imagination in Kaguru.* Bloomington: Indiana University Press.

Ben-Amos, P. 1976. "Men and Animals in Benin Art." *Man* 11: 243–52.

Bentley, W. H. 1889. *Life on the Congo.* London: Religious Tract Society.

Berger, I. 1997. "Contested Boundaries: African Studies Approaching the Millennium." *African Studies Review* 40 (2): 1–14.

Beumers, E., and H.-J. Koloss, eds. 1992. *Kings of Africa.* Maastricht: Foundation Kings of Africa.

Biebuyck, D. 1985. *The Arts of Zaire.* Berkeley: University of California Press.

Bittremieux, L. 1920. "Mayombsche Reisboek." *Congo* 2 (2): 247–59.

———. 1922–27. *Mayombsche Idioticon.* Ghent: Erasmus.

———. 1923. "Van een ouden blinden hoofdman." *Congo* 2 (4): 531–52.

———. 1934. *Mayombsche Namen.* Leuven: Drukkerij Paters der H. H. Harten.

———. 1936. *La société secrète des Bakhimba au Mayombe.* Brussels: Institut Royal Colonial Belge.

———. 1940. "Nganda Tsundi: volk en vernomden." *Kongo-Overzee* 6: 49–65, 113–34.

———. 1946. "De 'goden' van Kakongo en Ngoyo." *Kongo-Overzee* 10 (12–13): 1–10.

Bittremieux, L., and A. Tembo. 1924. "De geschiedenis van Kangu." *Congo* 1924 (1): 71–79.

Blier, S. P. 1993. "Truth and Seeing: Magic, Custom and Fetish in Art History." In *Africa and the Disciplines,* ed. R. H. Bates, V. Y. Mudimbe, and J. O'Barr. New York: Harper. 139–66.

Bockie, S. 1993. *Death and the Invisible Powers.* Bloomington: Indiana University Press.

Bontinck, F. 1970. *Diaire congolaise (1690–1701) de Fra Luca de Caltanisetta.* Louvain: Nauwelaerts.

Bontinck, F., ed. 1972. *Histoire du royaume du Congo.* Etudes d'histoire africaine. Louvain: Nauwelaerts.

———. 1985. *Aux origines de la philosophie bantoue: la correspondance Tempels-Hulstaert (1944–48).* Kinshasa: Faculté de Théologie Catholique.

Boone, O. 1973. *Carte ethnique de la République du Zaire, quart sud-ouest.* Tervuren: MRAC.

Boyer, P. 1990. *Tradition as Truth and Communication.* Cambridge: Cambridge University Press.

Broadhead, S. 1971. "Trade and Politics on the Congo Coast, 1770–1870." Ph.D. diss., Boston University.

Broadhead, S. H. 1979. "Beyond Decline: The Kingdom of the Kongo in the Eighteenth and Nineteenth Centuries." *International Journal of African Historical Studies* 12: 615–50.

Buakasa, G. 1973. *L'impensé du discours.* Kinshasa: Presses Universitaires du Zaire.

Cabrera, L. 1971. *El Monte.* Miami: Rema Press.

———. 1986 [1979]. *Reglas de Congo.* Miami: Ediciones Universal.

Carlson, R. G. 1993. "Hierarchy and the Haya Divine Kingship: A Structural and Symbolic Reinterpretation of Frazer's Thesis." *American Ethnologist* 20 (2): 312–35.

Carr, D. 1986. *Time, Narrative, and History.* Bloomington: Indiana University Press.

Cavazzi de Montecuccolo, J. A. 1965. *Descriçao histórica dos trés reinos do Congo, Matamba e Angola.* Lisbon: Junta de Investigaçoes do Ultramar.

Ceyssens, J. H. C. 1984. "Pouvoir et parenté chez les Kongo-Dinga du Zaire." Ph.D. diss., Catholic University of Nijmegen.

Comaroff, J. L., and J. Comaroff. 1997. "Postcolonial Politics and Discourses of Democracy of Southern Africa: An Anthropological Reflection on African Political Modernities." *Journal of Anthropological Research* 53 (2): 123–46.

Conrad, J. 1995. *Heart of Darkness.* London: Penguin.

Cornet, J. 1975. *Art from Zaire: 100 Masterworks from the National Collection.* New York: The African-American Institute.

Crick, M. 1976. *Explorations in Language and Meaning.* New York: John Wiley.

De Boeck, F. 1994. "Of Trees and Kings: Politics and Metaphor among the Aluund of Southwestern Zaire." *American Ethnologist* 21 (3): 451–73.

———. 1996. "Postcolonialism, Power and Identity: Local and Global Perspectives from Zaire." In *Postcolonial Identities in Africa,* ed. R. Werbner and T. Ranger. London: Zed.

De Heusch, L. 1954. "Autorité et prestige dans la société tetela." *Zaire* 10: 1011–27.

———. 1971. *Pourquoi l'épouser?* Paris: Gallimard.

———. 1982. *The Drunken King.* Bloomington: Indiana University Press.

———. 1985. *Sacrifice.* Bloomington: Indiana University Press.

———. 1989. "Kongo in Haiti: A New Approach to Religious Syncretism." *Man* 24: 290–303.

———. 1991. "The King Comes from Elsewhere." In *Body and Space,* ed. A. Jacobson-Widding. Uppsala: Almqvist & Wiksell International. 109–117.

De Maret, P. 1985. "The Smith's Myth and the Origin of Leadership in Central Africa." In *African Ironworking, Ancient and Traditional,* ed. R. Haaland and P. Shinnie. Bergen: Norwegian University Press.

De Plaen, G. 1974. *Les Structures d'autorité des Bayanzi.* Paris: Editions Universitaires.

De Saussure, F. 1966. *Course in General Linguistics.* London: Peter Owen.

Delcommune, A. 1922. *Vingt années de vie africaine, 1874–1893.* Brussels: Ferdinand Larcier.

Dennett, R. 1906. *At the Back of the Black Man's Mind.* London: Macmillan.

Desroche, H., and P. Raymaekers. 1976. "Départ d'un prophète, arrivée d'une église." *Archives de Sciences des Religions* 42: 117–62.

Devisch, R. 1988. "From Equal to Better: Investing the Chief among the Northern Yaka of Zaire." *Africa* 58: 261–89.

———. 1993. *Weaving the Threads of Life.* Chicago: University of Chicago Press.

———. 1996. "'Pillaging Jesus': Healing Churches and the Villagisation of Kinshasa." *Africa* 66 (4): 555–86.

Dimomfu, L. 1984. *L'art de guérir chez les Kongo du Zaire: discours magique ou science médicale?* Brussels: CEDAF.

Douglas, M. 1964. "Matriliny and Pawnship in Central Africa." *Africa* 34: 301–313.

Doutreloux, A. 1967. *L'Ombre des fétiches.* Louvain: Nauwelaerts.

Drewal, H. J., and J. Pemberton III. 1989. "The Yoruba World." In *Yoruba: Nine Centuries of African Art and Thought,* ed. A. Wardwell. New York: Center for African Art.

Dupré, G. 1982. *Un Ordre et sa destruction.* Paris: ORSTOM.

———. 1985. *Les Naissances d'une société.* Paris: ORSTOM.

Dupré, M.-L. 1975. "Le système de forces *nkisi* chez les Kongo d'après le troisième volume de K. Laman." *Africa* 45 (1): 12–28.

Evans-Pritchard, E. E. 1937. *Witchcraft, Oracles and Magic among the Azande.* London: Oxford University Press.

Fabian, J. 1983. "Missions and the Colonization of African Languages." *Canadian Journal of African Studies* 17 (2): 165–87.

———. 1990. *Power and Performance.* Madison: University of Wisconsin Press.

———. 1992. "Keep Listening: Ethnography and Reading." In *The Ethnography of Reading,* ed. J. Boyarin. Berkeley: University of California Press.

Ferguson, L. 1992. *Uncommon Ground.* Washington, D.C.: Smithsonian Institution.

Fields, K. 1982. "Political Contingencies of Witchcraft in Central Africa: Culture and the State in Marxist Theory." *Canadian Journal of African Studies* 16 (3): 567–93.

Fischer, E. 1978. "Dan Forest Spirits: Masks in Dan Villages." *African Arts* 11 (2): 16–23.

Fondation Dapper, ed. 1989. *Objets Interdits.* Paris: Fondation Dapper.

Frank, B. 1995. "Permitted and Prohibited Wealth: Commodity-Possessing Spirits, Economic Morals, and the Goddess Mami Wata in West Africa." *Ethnology* 34: 331–46.

Frank, R. 1992. "La mémoire et l'histoire." *Cahiers de l'IHTP* 21 (November): 65–72.

Friedman, K. E. 1991. *Catastrophe and Creation.* Chur, Switzerland: Harwood.

Fu-Kiau kia Bunseki, A. 1967. "La momification Kongo." [In KiKongo]. MS.

Fuglestad, F. 1992. "The Trevor-Roper Trap or the Imperialism of History: An Essay." *History in Africa* 19: 309–26.

Geschiere, P. 1997. *The Modernity of Witchcraft.* Charlottesville: University Press of Virginia.

Geschiere, P., and C. Fisiy. 1994. "Domesticating Personal Violence: Witchcraft, Courts and Confessions in Cameroon." *Africa* 64 (3): 323–41.

Girard, R. 1977. *Violence and the Sacred.* Baltimore: Johns Hopkins University Press.

Gore, C., and J. Nevadomsky. 1997. "Practice and Agency in Mammy Wata Worship in Southern Nigeria." *African Arts* 30 (Spring): 60–69.

Gruénais, M. E., Mouanda Mbambi, and J. Tonda. 1995. "Messies, fétiches et lutte de pouvoirs entre les 'grands hommes' du Congo démocratique." *Cahiers d'études africaines* no. 137, 163–93.

Guthrie, M. 1970. *Comparative Bantu.* London: Gregg Press.

Hagenbucher-Sacripanti, F. 1973. *Les Fondements spirituels du pouvoir au royaume de Loango.* Paris: ORSTOM.

———. n.d. *Santé et rédemption par les génies au Congo.* Paris: Publisud.

Hall, G. M. 1995. *Africans in Colonial Louisiana.* Baton Rouge: Louisiana State University Press.

Hallen, B. 1995. "Some Observations about Philosophy, Postmodernism and Art in Contemporary African Studies." *African Studies Review* 38 (1): 69–80.

Hallen, B., and J. O. Sodipo. 1986. *Knowledge, Belief and Witchcraft: Analytical Experiments in African Philosophy.* London: Ethnographica.

Harbeson, J. W. 1997. "Area Studies and the Disciplines: A Rejoinder." *Issue* 25 (1): 29–31.

Hilton, A. 1985. *The Kingdom of Kongo.* New York: Oxford University Press.

Horton, R. 1965. *Kalabari Sculpture.* Department of Antiquities, Federal Republic of Nigeria.

———. 1993. *Patterns of Thought in Africa and the West.* New York: Cambridge University Press.

Jacobson-Widding, A. 1979. *Red-White-Black as a Mode of Thought.* Uppsala: Almqvist & Wiksell International.

Jacques, T. C. 1997. "Is There an African Philosophy? The Politics of a Question." *SAPINA* 10 (2): 53–89.

Janzen, J. M. 1972. "Laman's Kongo Ethnography." *Africa* 45: 12–28.

———. 1978. *The Quest for Therapy in Lower Zaire.* Berkeley: University of California Press.

———. 1982. *Lemba, 1650–1930.* New York: Garland.

———. 1985. "The Consequences of Literacy in African Religion: The Kongo Case." In *Theoretical Explorations in African Religion,* ed. W. Van Binsbergen and M. Schoffeleers. London: Routledge & Kegan Paul.

Janzen, J. M., and W. MacGaffey. 1974. *An Anthology of Kongo Religion.* Lawrence: University of Kansas Press.

Jay, N. 1992. *Throughout Your Generations Forever: Sacrifice, Religion, and Paternity.* Chicago: University of Chicago Press.

Jeannest, C. 1883. *Quatre années au Congo.* Paris: Charpentier.

Jewsiewicki, B. 1983. "Rural Society and the Belgian Colonial Economy." In *History of Central Africa,* ed. D. Birmingham and P. Martin. London: Longmans. 95–125.

———. 1995. *Chéri Samba: The Hybridity of Art.* Westmount, Québec: Esther A. Dagan.

Johnston, H. H. 1884. *The River Congo.* London: Sampson, Low.

Josephson, B. R. 1992. "The Leopard and the Pangolin: Power in the Biyenge Chiefdom." Ph.D. diss., University of Virginia.

Kasfir, S. 1984. "Masks from the Towns of the Dead: The Igbo-Idoma Borderland." In *Igbo*

Arts: Community and Cosmos, ed. H. M. Cole and C. C. Aniakor. Los Angeles: Museum of Cultural History, University of California.

Kaspin, D. 1996. "A Chewa Cosmology of the Body." *American Ethnologist* 23 (3): 561–78.

Kavuna, S. 1995 [1915]. "Northern Kongo Ancestor Figures." *African Arts* 28 (2): 48–53.

Kratz, M. 1970. *La mission des Rédemptoristes belges au Bas-Congo: la période des semailles (1899–1920).* Brussels: Académie royale des Sciences d'Outre-Mer.

Kuper, A. 1979. "Regional Comparison in Africanist Anthropology." *African Affairs* 78 (310): 103–113.

Kuvuna ku Konde Mwela. 1984. *Kinkulu kia Dibundu (CMA history).* Boma, Zaire: Communauté Evangélique de l'Alliance au Zaire.

LaFontaine, J. 1977. "The Power of Rights." *Man* 12: 421–37.

Laman, K. E. 1912. *Grammar of the Kongo Language.* New York: Christian Alliance.

———. 1936. *Dictionnaire Kikongo-Français.* Brussels: Institut Royal Colonial Belge (republished in 1964 by Gregg Press).

———. 1953. *The Kongo I.* Uppsala.

———. 1957. *The Kongo II.* Uppsala.

———. 1963. *The Kongo III.* Uppsala.

———. 1968. *The Kongo IV.* Uppsala.

Lan, D. 1985. *Guns and Rain.* London: James Currey.

Lapsley, S. N. 1893. *Life and Letters of Samuel Norvell Lapsley.* Richmond, Va.: privately printed.

Leach, E. R. 1990. "Aryan Invasions over Four Millennia." In *Culture through Time: Anthropological Approaches,* ed. E. Ohnuki-Tierney. Stanford: Stanford University Press. 227–45.

Lehuard, R. 1980. *Fétiches à clous du Bas-Zaire.* Arnouville: Arts d'Afrique Noire.

———. 1989. *Art Bakongo: les centres du style.* Arnouville: Arts d'Afrique Noire.

Lévi-Strauss, C. 1962. *The Savage Mind.* Chicago: University of Chicago Press.

———. 1981. *The Naked Man.* New York: Harper and Row.

Liebrechts, C. 1909. *Congo: Léopoldville, Bolobo, Equateur.* Brussels: Lebègue.

Lucas, S. A. 1966. "L'Etat traditionnel luba." *Problèmes sociaux congolais* 74: 83–97.

Luhrmann, T. 1986. "Witchcraft, morality and magic in contemporary London." *International Journal of Moral and Social Sciences* 1: 77–94.

MacGaffey, W. 1968. "Kongo and the King of the Americans." *Journal of Modern African Studies* 6 (2): 171–81.

———. 1969. "The Beloved City: Commentary on a Kimbanguist Text." *Journal of Religion in Africa* 2: 129–47.

———. 1970. *Custom and Government in the Lower Congo.* Los Angeles: University of California Press.

———. 1972. "Comparative Analysis of Central African Religions." *Africa* 56: 263–79.

———. 1977a. "Economic and Social Dimensions of Kongo Slavery." In *Slavery in Africa,* ed. S. Meirs and I. Kopytoff. Madison: University of Wisconsin Press.

———. 1977b. "Cultural Roots of Kongo Prophetism." *History of Religion* 17 (2): 177–93.

———. 1978. "African History, Anthropology, and the Rationality of Natives." *History in Africa* 5: 101–120.

———. 1979. "African Religions: Types and Generalizations." In *Explorations in African*

Systems of Thought, ed. I. Karp and C. Bird. Washington, D.C.: Smithsonian Institution Press.

———. 1981. "Ideology and Belief." *African Studies Review* 24 (2/3): 227–74.

———. 1982. "The Policy of National Integration in Zaire." *Journal of Modern African Studies* 20 (1): 87–105.

———. 1983. *Modern Kongo Prophets.* Bloomington: Indiana University Press.

———. 1986a. *Religion and Society in Central Africa.* Chicago: University of Chicago Press.

———. 1986b. "Ethnography and the Closing of the Frontier in Lower Congo, 1885–1921." *Africa* 56 (3): 263–79.

———. 1987. "Lulendo: The Recovery of a Kongo Nkisi." *Ethnos* 52: 339–49.

———. 1988. "Complexity, Astonishment and Power." *Journal of Southern Bantu Studies* 14: 188–203.

———. 1990. "Religion, Class and Social Pluralism in Zaire." *Canadian Journal of African Studies* 24 (2): 249–64.

———. 1991. *Art and Healing of the BaKongo Commented by Themselves.* Stockholm: Folkens Museum.

———. 1994. Review of *Death and the Invisible Powers,* by Simon Bockie. *African Studies Review* 37 (3): 124–25.

MacGaffey, W., and M. D. Harris. 1993. *Astonishment and Power.* Washington, D.C.: Smithsonian Institution Press.

Malinowski, B. 1923. "The Problem of Meaning in Primitive Languages." In *The Meaning of Meaning: A Study of the Influence of Language upon Thought and of the Science of Symbolism,* ed. C. K. Ogden and I. A. Richards. New York: Harcourt, Brace & Company, Inc.

Manker, E. 1932. "Niombo: Die Totenbestattung der Babwende." *Zeitschrift fur Ethnologie* 2: 159–72.

Martin, P. 1972. *The External Trade of the Loango Coast.* Oxford: Clarendon.

Martin, P. M. 1970. "The Trade of Loango in the Seventeenth and Eighteenth Centuries." In *Pre-colonial African Trade,* ed. R. Gray and D. Birmingham. London: Oxford University Press.

———. 1987. "Power, Cloth and Currency on the Loango Coast." *Muntu* 7 (2): 135–47.

Masolo, D. A. 1994. *African Philosophy in Search of an Identity.* Bloomington: Indiana University Press.

Matory, J. R. 1994. *Sex and the Empire That Is No More.* Minneapolis: University of Minnesota Press.

Mauss, M. 1990. *The Gift.* New York: Norton.

Mbembe, A. 1988. *Afriques Indociles.* Paris: Karthala.

McLeod, M. D. 1976. "Verbal Elements in West African Art." *Quaderni PORO* (1976): 85–102.

Mead, G. H. 1934. *Mind, Self, and Society.* Chicago: University of Chicago Press.

Mertens, J. 1942. *Les chefs couronnés.* Brussels: Institut Royal Colonial Belge.

Meyer, B. 1995. "'Delivered from the Powers of Darkness': Confessions of Satanic Riches in Christian Ghana." *Africa* 65 (2): 2236–55.

———. 1997. *Commodities and the Power of Prayer: Pentecostalist Attitudes towards Con-*

sumption in Contemporary Ghana. Working Paper: Globalization and the Construction of Communal Identities. Amsterdam: WOTRO.

Miers, S., and I. Kopytoff, eds. 1977. *Slavery in Africa.* Madison: University of Wisconsin Press.

Miller, J. C. 1976. *Kings and Kinsmen.* Oxford: Clarendon.

Mitchell, C. 1956. *The Yao Village.* Manchester: Manchester University Press.

Mitchell, W. J. T. 1986. *Iconology.* Chicago: University of Chicago Press.

Mkandawire, T. 1997. "The Social Sciences in Africa." *African Studies Review* (40): 2.

Monnier, L. 1971. *Ethnie et intégration régionale au Congo: le Kongo Central.* Paris: EDICEF.

Monteiro, J. J. 1968 [1875]. *Angola and the River Congo.* 2 vols. London: Frank Cass.

Montejo, E. 1968. *The Autobiography of a Runaway Slave.* New York: Pantheon.

da Montesarchio, G. 1976. *La prefettura apostòlica del Congo alla metà del XVII sècolo.* Milan: Giuffrè.

Morphy, H. 1994. "The Interpretation of Ritual: Reflections from Film on Anthropological Practice." *Man* 29 (1): 117–46.

Mudimbe, V. Y. 1993. "From 'Primitive Art' to 'Memoriae Loci.'" *Human Studies* 16: 101–110.

———. 1994. *The Idea of Africa.* Bloomington: Indiana University Press.

Mudimbe, V. Y., and K. A. Appiah. 1993. "The Impact of African Studies on Philosophy." In *Africa and the Disciplines,* ed. R. H. Bates, V. Y. Mudimbe, and J. O'Barr. Chicago: University of Chicago Press.

Mulinda, H. B. 1985. "Le nkisi dans la tradition du Bas-Zaire." In *Fétiches: objets enchantés, mots réalisés,* ed. A. De Surgy. Paris: Ecole Pratique des Hautes Etudes.

———. 1995. "Masks as Proverbial Language: Woyo, Zaire." In *Objects: Signs of Africa,* ed. L. De Heusch. Tervuren: Musée Royal de l'Afrique Centrale.

Myers, F. R. 1995. "Representing Culture: The Production of Discourse(s) for Aboriginal Acrylic Paintings." In *The Traffic in Culture,* ed. G. E. Marcus and F. R. Myers. Berkeley: University of California Press.

Okot p'Bitek. 1971. *Religion of the Central Luo.* Nairobi: East African Literature Bureau.

Olivier de Sardan, J.-P. 1992. " Occultism and the Ethnographic 'I'." *Critique of Anthropology* 12 (1): 5–25.

Ong, W. 1977. *Interfaces of the Word.* Ithaca: Cornell University Press.

Overing, J. 1986. "Images of Cannibalism, Death, and Domination in a 'Non-Violent' Society." In *The Anthropology of Violence,* ed. D. Riches. New York: Basil Blackwell.

———. 1987. "Translation as a Creative Process." In *Comparative Anthropology,* ed. L. Holy. Oxford: Blackwell.

Owen, M. A. 1969. *Voodoo Tales.* New York: Negro Universities Press.

Owomoyela, O. 1994. "With Friends Like These. . . . A Critique of Pervasive Anti-Africanisms in Current African Studies Epistemology and Methodology." *African Studies Review* 37 (3): 77–102.

———. 1997. "African Philosophy: The Conditions of its Possibility." *SAPINA* 10 (2): 119–43.

Petit, P. 1995. "The Sacred Kaolin and the Bowl-Bearers: Luba of Shaba." In *Objects: Signs of Africa,* ed. L. De Heusch. Tervuren: Musée Royal de l'Afrique Centrale.

————. 1996. "'Les charmes du roi sont les esprits des morts': les fondements religieux de la royauté sacrée chez les Luba du Zaire." *Africa* 66 (3): 349–66.

Phillips, R. C. 1887. "The Social System of the Lower Congo." *Journal of the Manchester Geographical Society* 3: 154–69.

Pickering, A. 1994. "Objectivity and the Mangle of Practice." In *Rethinking Objectivity*, ed. A. Megill. Durham, N.C.: Duke University Press.

Pietz, W. 1987. "The Problem of the Fetish, II: The Origin of the Fetish." *Res* 13: 23–45.

Pinçon, B., and D. Ngoïe-Ngalla. 1990. "L'unité culturelle Kongo à la fin du XIXe siècle. L'apport des études céramologiques." *Cahiers d'Etudes Africaines* XXX (2): 157–78.

Pipes, D. 1997. *Conspiracy: The Power of the Paranoid Style in History*. New York: Free Press.

Proyart. 1776. *Histoire de Loango, Kakongo, et Autres Royaumes d'Afrique*. Paris.

Ravenhill, P. 1994. *The Self and the Other: Personhood and Images among the Baule, Côte d'Ivoire*. Los Angeles: Fowler Museum of Cultural History, University of California.

Ray, B. C. 1991. *Myth, Ritual, and Kingship in Buganda*. New York: Oxford University Press.

Reikat, A. 1990. *Niombo: Begraebnisrituale in Zentralafrika*. Cologne: Rautenstrauch-Joest-Museum.

Rey, P.-P. 1969. "Articulation des modes de dépendance et des modes de production dans deux sociétés lignagères." *Cahier d'études africaines* 9: 415–40.

Richards, A. 1939. *Land, Labour and Diet in Northern Rhodesia*. London: Oxford University Press.

Riches, D. 1986. "The Phenomenon of Violence." In *The Anthropology of Violence*, ed. D. Riches. New York: Basil Blackwell.

Roberts, M. N., and A. F. Roberts, eds. 1996. *Memory: Luba Art and the Making of History*. New York: Museum for African Art.

Robertson, C. C., and M. A. Klein, eds. 1983. *Women and Slavery in Africa*. Madison: University of Wisconsin Press.

Robinson, P. T. 1994. "Democratization: Understanding the Relationship between Regime Change and the Culture of Politics." *African Studies Review* 37 (1): 39–67.

Rorty, R. 1979. *Philosophy and the Mirror of Nature*. Princeton: Princeton University Press.

Rubin, W., ed. 1984. *Primitivism in 20th Century Art: Affinity of the Tribal and the Modern*. 2 vols. New York: Museum of Modern Art.

Rowlands, M., and J.-P. Warnier. 1988. "Sorcery, Power and the Modern State in Cameroon." *Man* 23: 118–32.

Sabakinu. 1988a. "La région de Matadi dans les années 1880." In *Le centenaire de l'Etat Indépendant du Congo*, ed. J. Stengers. Brussels: Académie Royale des Sciences d'Outre-Mer. 323–49.

————. 1988b. "Le radio trottoir dans l'exercice du pouvoir politique au Zaire." In *Dialoguer avec le léopard?* ed. B. Jewsiewicki and H. Moniot. Paris: Harmattan. 179–94.

Sahlins, M. 1976. *Culture and Practical Reason*. Chicago: University of Chicago Press.

Samarin, W. J. 1985. "The State's Bakongo Burden Bearers." In *The Workers of African Trade*, ed. C. Coquéry-Vidrovitch and P. Lovejoy. Beverly Hills: Sage Publications. 269–92.

Schatzberg, M. 1993. "Power, Legitimacy and 'Democratisation' in Africa." *Africa* 63 (4): 445–61.

Schatzberg, M. G. 1997. "Alternate Causalities and Theories of Politics: Explaining Political Life in the Congo (Zaire)." Unpublished paper.

Schrag, N. 1985. "Mboma and the Lower Zaire: A Socio-economic Study of a Kongo Trading Community, 1785–1885." Ph.D. diss., Indiana University.

Siroto, L. 1979. "Witchcraft Belief in the Explanation of Traditional African Iconography." In *The Visual Arts: Plastic and Graphic,* ed. J. M. Cordwell. The Hague: Mouton.

Sklar, R. L. 1993. "The African Frontier for Political Science." In *Africa and the Disciplines,* ed. R. H. Bates, V. Y. Mudimbe, and J. O'Barr. Chicago: University of Chicago Press.

Söderberg, B. 1985. *Karl Edvard Laman.* Stockholm: Svenska Missionsförbundet.

Stanley, H. M. 1879. *Through Darkest Africa.* 2 vols. New York: Harper.

Steiner, G. 1975. *Beyond Babel.* New York: Oxford University Press.

Strathern, M. 1988. *The Gender of the Gift.* Berkeley: University of California Press.

Strother, Z. 1993. "Eastern Pende Constructions of Secrecy." In *Secrecy: African Art that Conceals and Reveals,* ed. M. H. Nooter. New York: Museum for African Art.

Strother, Z. S. 1996. "Suspected of Sorcery." In *In Pursuit of History: Fieldwork in Africa,* ed. C. K. Adenaike and J. Vansina. Portsmouth, N.H.: Heinemann.

Swartenbroeckx, R. P. 1966. "L'esclavage chez les Yansi." *Bulletin de la Société Royale Belge d'Anthropologie et de Préhistoire* 77: 145–204.

———. 1969. "La magie chez les Yansi du Congo." *Bulletin de la Société Royale Belge d'Anthropologie et de Préhistoire* 80: 187–226.

Tambiah, S. J. 1968. "The Magical Power of Words." *Man* 3: 175–208.

Theuws, J. 1992. *Space, Travel and Ritual among the Luba.* Ghent: Africa Gandensia.

Thiel, J. F. 1972. *La Situation religieuse des Mbiem.* Bandundu, Zaire: Centre d'Etudes Ethnologiques Bandundu.

Thiel, J. F., ed. 1986. *Was sind Fetische?* Frankfurt am Main: Museum für Völkerkunde.

Thompson, R. F. 1983. *Flash of the Spirit.* New York: Random House.

Thompson, R. F., and J. Cornet. 1981. *The Four Moments of the Sun.* Washington, D.C.: National Gallery of Art.

Thornton, J. 1980. "The Slave Trade in Eighteenth-Century Angola: Effects on Demographic Structures." *Canadian Journal of African Studies* 14: 117–271.

———. 1983. *The Kingdom of Kongo.* Madison: University of Wisconsin Press.

———. 1992. *Africa and Africans in the Making of the Atlantic World, 1400–1680.* New York: Cambridge University Press.

———. 1993. "'I am a subject of the King of Congo': African Political Ideology and the Haitian Revolution." *Journal of World History* 4 (2): 181–214.

Tuckey, J. K. 1818. *Narration of an Expedition to Explore the River Zaire.* London: Murray.

Turner, V. W. 1957. *Schism and Continuity.* Manchester: Manchester University Press.

Van de Velde, L. 1886. "La région du Bas-Congo et du Kwilou-Niadi." *Bulletin de la Société Royale Belge de Géographie* 10: 347–412.

Van Velsen, J. 1964. *The Politics of Kinship; A Study in Social Manipulation among the Lakeside Tonga of Malawi.* Manchester: Manchester University Press.

Van Wing, J. 1959. *Etudes Bakongo.* Brussels: Desclée de Brouwer.

Vansina, J. 1958. "Les croyances religieuses des Kuba." *Zaire* 12 (7): 725–58.

———. 1961. *De la tradition orale.* Tervuren, Belgium: MRAC.

———. 1965. *Les Anciens royaumes de la savane.* Léopoldville: Institut de Recherches Economiques et Sociaux.

———. 1973. *The Tio Kingdom.* London: Oxford University Press.

———. 1974. "Probing the Past of the Lower Kwilu Peoples." *Paideuma* 19 (20): 332–64.

———. 1978. *The Children of Woot.* Madison: University of Wisconsin Press.

———. 1985. *Oral Tradition as History.* Madison: University of Wisconsin Press.

———. 1989. "Deep-down Time: Political Tradition in Central Africa." *History in Africa* 16: 341–62.

———. 1991. *Paths in the Rainforests.* Madison: University of Wisconsin Press.

———. 1992. "The Kongo Kingdom and its Neighbours." In *Africa from the Sixteenth to the Eighteenth Century,* ed. B. A. Ogot. Paris: UNESCO. 546–87.

Vincent, J. 1990. *Anthropology and Politics.* Tucson: University of Arizona Press.

Vogel, S. 1997. "Baule: African Art through Western Eyes." *African Arts* 30 (4): 64–77.

Ward, H. 1890. *Five Years with the Congo Cannibals.* New York: Robert Bonner.

Weeks, J. H. 1914. *Among the Primitive Bakongo.* London: Seeley Service.

Widman, R. 1967. *The Niombo Cult among the Bwende.* Stockholm: Etnografiska Museet.

Willis, R. 1981. *A State in the Making.* Bloomington: Indiana University Press.

Wilson, B., ed. 1970. *Rationality.* New York: Harper.

Wiredu, K. 1992. "Formulating Modern Thought in African Languages: Some Theoretical Considerations." In *The Surreptitious Speech: Présence Africaine and the Politics of Otherness, 1947–1987,* ed. V. Y. Mudimbe. Chicago: University of Chicago Press. 301–332.

Yoder, J. C. 1992. *The Kanyok of Zaire.* Cambridge: Cambridge University Press.

INDEX AND GLOSSARY

WYATT MacGAFFEY,
formerly John R. Coleman Professor of Social Sciences at Haverford College, has published extensively on African social structure, history, art, religion, and politics. His books
include *Custom and Government in the Lower Congo* (1970), *Religion and Society in
Central Africa* (1986), and *Astonishment and Power* (1993; with Michael D. Harris). In
1994 he was awarded a Fellowship by the John Simon Guggenheim Foundation.

DATE DUE